Statistics and Data Visualisation with Python

This book is intended to serve as a bridge in statistics for graduates and business practitioners interested in using their skills in the area of data science and analytics as well as statistical analysis in general. On the one hand, the book is intended to be a refresher for readers who have taken some courses in statistics, but who have not necessarily used it in their day-to-day work. On the other hand, the material can be suitable for readers interested in the subject as a first encounter with statistical work in Python. *Statistics and Data Visualisation with Python* aims to build statistical knowledge from the ground up by enabling the reader to understand the ideas behind inferential statistics and begin to formulate hypotheses that form the foundations for the applications and algorithms in statistical analysis, business analytics, machine learning, and applied machine learning. This book begins with the basics of programming in Python and data analysis, to help construct a solid basis in statistical methods and hypothesis testing, which are useful in many modern applications.

Chapman & Hall/CRC

The Python Series

About the Series

Python has been ranked as the most popular programming language, and it is widely used in education and industry. This book series will offer a wide range of books on Python for students and professionals. Titles in the series will help users learn the language at an introductory and advanced level, and explore its many applications in data science, AI, and machine learning. Series titles can also be supplemented with Jupyter notebooks.

Image Processing and Acquisition using Python, Second Edition
Ravishankar Chityala, Sridevi Pudipeddi

Python Packages
Tomas Beuzen and Tiffany-Anne Timbers

Statistics and Data Visualisation with Python
Jesús Rogel-Salazar

For more information about this series please visit: https://www.crcpress.com/Chapman--HallCRC/book-series/PYTH

Statistics and Data Visualisation with Python

Jesús Rogel-Salazar

CRC Press
Taylor & Francis Group
Boca Raton London New York

CRC Press is an imprint of the
Taylor & Francis Group, an **informa** business

A CHAPMAN & HALL BOOK

First edition published 2023
by CRC Press
6000 Broken Sound Parkway NW, Suite 300, Boca Raton, FL 33487-2742

and by CRC Press
4 Park Square, Milton Park, Abingdon, Oxon, OX14 4RN

CRC Press is an imprint of Taylor & Francis Group, LLC

© 2023 Taylor & Francis Group, LLC

Library of Congress Cataloging-in-Publication Data

Names: Rogel-Salazar, Jesus, author.
Title: Statistics and data visualisation with Python / Dr. Jesús
  Rogel-Salazar.
Description: First edition. | Boca Raton, FL : CRC Press, 2023. | Series:
  Chapman & Hall/CRC Press the python series | Includes bibliographical
  references and index. | Identifiers: LCCN 2022026521 (print) | LCCN 2022026522 (ebook) | ISBN
  9780367749361 (hbk) | ISBN 9780367744519 (pbk) | ISBN 9781003160359
  (ebk)
Subjects: LCSH: Mathematical statistics--Data processing. | Python
  (Computer program language) | Information visualization.
Classification: LCC QA276.45.P98 R64 2023 (print) | LCC QA276.45.P98
  (ebook) | DDC 519.50285/5133--dc23/eng20221026
LC record available at https://lccn.loc.gov/2022026521
LC ebook record available at https://lccn.loc.gov/2022026522

ISBN: 978-0-367-74936-1 (hbk)
ISBN: 978-0-367-74451-9 (pbk)
ISBN: 978-1-003-16035-9 (ebk)

DOI: 10.1201/9781003160359

Typeset in URWPalladioL-Roman
by KnowledgeWorks Global Ltd.

Publisher's note: This book has been prepared from camera-ready copy provided by the author.

To Luceli, Rosario and Gabriela

Thanks and lots of love!

Contents

List of Figures

List of Tables

Preface

"THIS IS THE LAST TIME" are the words I remember thinking after finishing the corrections of *Advanced Data Science and Analytics with Python*[1]. However, I do know myself and here we are again. Actually, this is exactly what happens after finishing running a half-marathon: After the race I think I would not sign up for another one, and then a few weeks later I am training again. The same has happened with this book. Although I thought I was not going to write another one, the niggling feeling was there and the end result is in your hands.

[1] Rogel-Salazar, J. (2020). *Advanced Data Science and Analytics with Python*. Chapman & Hall/CRC Data Mining and Knowledge Discovery Series. CRC Press

The motivation for the book has been the conversations with colleagues and students about the need to have a statistical bridge for graduates and business practitioners interested in using their skills in the area of data science and analytics. The book is also intended to be a refresher for readers that have taken some courses in statistics, but who have not necessarily used it in their day-to-day work. Having said that, the material covered can be suitable for readers interested in the subject as a first encounter with statistical work in Python.

The book is good as a refresher on statistics, but also a bridge for graduates and business practitioners.

Statistics and Data Visualisation with Python aims to build statistical knowledge from the ground up enabling us to understand the ideas behind inferential statistics and formulate hypotheses that can serve as the basis for the applications and algorithms in business analytics, machine learning and applied machine learning. The book starts with the basics of programming in Python and data analysis to construct a solid background in statistical methods and hypothesis testing useful in a variety of modern applications.

Statistical concepts underpin applications in data science and machine learning.

As with my previous books, Python is the chosen language to implement computations. Unlike other books in statistics, where step-by-step manual calculations are shown, we concentrate on the use of programming to obtain statistical quantities of interest. To that end, we make use of a number of modules and packages that Pythonistas have created. We assume that you have access to a computer with Python 3.x installed and you are encouraged to use a Jupyter notebook. For reference, the versions of some of the packages used in the book are as follows:

We use Python 3 in this book.

Python - 3.8.x	pandas - 1.3.x
NumPy - 1.21.x	SciPy - 1.7.x
StatsModels - 0.13.x	Matplotlib - 3.5.x
Seaborn - 0.11.x	Plotly Express - 5.6.x
Bokeh - 2.4.x	pandas Bokeh - 0.5

Versions of Python modules used in this book.

As before, I am using the Anaconda Python distribution[2] provided by Continuum Analytics. Remember that there are other ways of obtaining Python as well as other versions of

[2] Anaconda (2016, November). Anaconda Software Distribution. Computer Software. V. 2-2.4.0. https://www.anaconda.com

the software: For instance, directly from the Python Software Foundation, as well as distributions from Enthought Canopy, or from package managers such as Homebrew.

We show computer code by enclosing it in a box as follows:

```
> 1 + 1   % Example of computer code


  2
```

We use a diple (>) to denote the command line terminal prompt shown in the Python shell. Keeping to the look and feel of the previous books, we use margin notes, such as the one that appears to the right of this paragraph, to highlight certain areas or commands, as well as to provide some useful comments and remarks.

The book starts with an introduction to what statistics is and how it has evolved over the years from the administrative activities around a city and its population, to the powerful tool on which a lot of us come to rely on a day-to-day basis. The first chapter serves as a preamble to the rest of the book and this can be read independently of the rest of the book.

Since we will be using Python throughout the book, in Chapter 2 we present a programming primer that provides the basics of Python from assigning variables and managing collections like lists, tuples and dictionaries to building programming logic using loops and conditionals. In Chapter 3 we build from the basics of Python to start using some powerful modules that let us delve into statistical

Python Software Foundation
https://www.python.org

Enthought Canopy https://www.enthought.com/products/epd/

Homebrew http://brew.sh

Chapter 1 serves as a preamble to the rest to the book.

Chapter 2 is a Python primer and 3 introduces some useful Python modules like NumPy, SciPy and pandas.

analysis in an easy way. The chapter introduces NumPy, SciPy and pandas to manipulate data and start extracting information from it. If you are familiar with Python you can safely skip these two chapters and jump straight into Chapter 4.

I recommend you read Chapters 4 to 6 sequentially. The reason for this is that later chapters build on the content from previous ones. In Chapter 4 we discuss different measures that are important in descriptive statistics and provide the footing to consider datasets as a whole. In Chapter 5 we talk about random variables and probability, opening up the discussion to different probability distributions that let us start thinking of hypothesis testing. This is the subject of Chapter 6, where we look various statistical tests, both parametric and non-parametric.

Chapter 4 covers descriptive statistics, Chapter 5 discusses probability distributions and Chapter 6 hypothesis testing.

If you are interested in jumping to a particular section of the book, use the diagram shown in Figure 1 where you can follow the flow chart depending on the characteristics of the data you have. Note that each test has some assumptions behind it; use the information in the rest of the book to support your analysis. Bear in mind that there is an element of randomness and uncertainty in any given data, and I hope that the discussions do not leave you singing random Pavarotti songs like good old Rex the Runt's friend Vince. The chapters mentioned above shall let us handle that randomness and uncertainty in a systematic way.

Consult Figure 1 to quickly decide the type of test you may need.

♪ Ta-raa-raa-raa ♩ Raa-raa-raa ♫
♪ RAA-RAA ♫

Remember that statistics is a discipline that studies methods of collecting, analysing and presenting data. With the latter

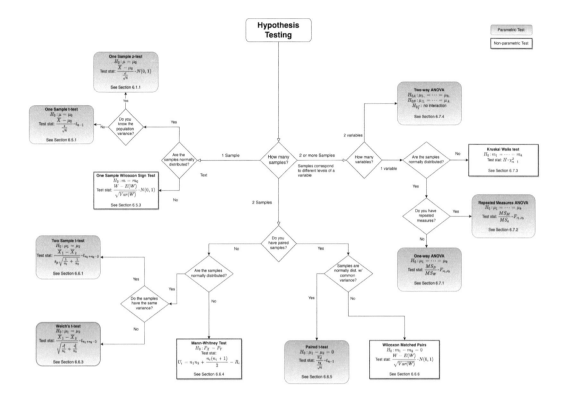

Figure 1: Do you know what type of data you have? Use this flow chart to guide you about the tests you may want to use.

in mind, the last two chapters of the book are dedicated to the discussion of data visualisation from perception of visual aspects, to best practices in Chapter 7 and examples on how to create common statistical visualisations with Python in Chapter 8.

Chapters 7 and 8 cover different aspects of data visualisation.

I sincerely hope that the contents of the book are useful to many of you. Good statistical thinking is a great tool to have in many walks of life and it is true to say that the current availability of data makes it even more important to have a good grasp of the concepts and ideas that underpin a sound statistical analysis, with great visuals to support our arguments. Stay in touch and who knows I may be saying "maybe one more" after having uttered yet again "this is the last time"!

London, UK   *Dr Jesús Rogel-Salazar*
                                                June 2022

About the Author

Dr Jesús Rogel-Salazar is a lead data scientist working for companies such as Tympa Health Technologies, AKQA, IBM Data Science Studio, Dow Jones, Barclays, to name a few. He is a visiting researcher at the Department of Physics at Imperial College London, UK and a member of the School of Physics, Astronomy and Mathematics at the University of Hertfordshire, UK. He obtained his doctorate in Physics at Imperial College London for work on quantum atom optics and ultra-cold matter.

He has held a position as Associate Professor in mathematics, as well as a consultant and data scientist in a variety of industries including science, finance, marketing, people analytics and health, among others. He is the author of *Data Science and Analytics with Python* and *Advanced Data Science and Analytics with Python*, as well as *Essential MATLAB® and Octave*, published by CRC Press. His interests include mathematical modelling, data science and optimisation in a wide range of applications including optics, quantum mechanics, data journalism, finance and health tech.

Other Books by the Same Author

- *Data Science and Analytics with Python*
  CRC Press, 2018, ISBN 978-1-138-04317-6 (hardback)
  978-1-4987-4209-2 (paperback)

  Data Science and Analytics with Python is designed for
  practitioners in data science and data analytics in both
  academic and business environments. The aim is to
  present the reader with the main concepts used in data
  science using tools developed in Python. The book
  discusses what data science and analytics are, from the
  point of view of the process and results obtained.

- *Advanced Data Science and Analytics with Python*
  CRC Press, 2020, ISBN 978-0-429-44661-0 (hardback)
  978-1-138-31506-8 (paperback)

  Advanced Data Science and Analytics with Python enables
  data scientists to continue developing their skills and
  apply them in business as well as academic settings. The
  subjects discussed in this book are complementary and a
  follow-up to the topics discussed in *Data Science and
  Analytics with Python*. The aim is to cover important
  advanced areas in data science using tools developed in

Python such as SciKit-learn, pandas, NumPy, Beautiful
Soup, NLTK, NetworkX and others. The model
development is supported by the use of frameworks such
as Keras, TensorFlow and Core ML, as well as Swift for
the development of iOS and MacOS applications.

- ***Essential MATLAB® and Octave***
  CRC Press, 2014, ISBN 978-1-138-41311-5 (hardback)
  978-1-4822-3463-3 (paperback)

  Widely used by scientists and engineers, well-established
  MATLAB® and open-source Octave provide excellent
  capabilities for data analysis, visualisation, and more.
  By means of straightforward explanations and examples
  from different areas in mathematics, engineering, finance,
  and physics, the book explains how MATLAB and Octave
  are powerful tools applicable to a variety of problems.

1

Data, Stats and Stories – An Introduction

Data is everywhere around us and we use it to our advantage: From wearing clothes appropriate for the weather outside, to finding our way to a new location with the aid of GPS and deciding what to buy in our weekly shopping. Furthermore, not only are we consumers of data but each and every one of us is a data creator. It has never been easier to create and generate data. Consider your daily use of technology such as your humble smartphone or tablet: How many emails do you read or write? How many pictures do you take? How many websites do you visit? And many other similar questions. Each of these interactions generates a bunch of data points.

There are even accounts about the amount of data that is being generated. For example, in 2013 SINTEF[1] reported that the 90% of the world's data had been created in the previous two years. And the pace will keep up and even accelerate given the number of new devices, sensors and ways to share data.

[1] SINTEF (2013). Big Data, for better or worse: 90% of world's data generated over last two years. www.sciencedaily.com/releases/2013/05/130522085217.htm. Accessed: 2021-01-01

In this chapter we will look at how the current availability
of data has given rise to the need for more and better data
analysis techniques. We will see how these techniques
are underpinned by strong foundations in statistics. We
will also cover some of the historical developments that
have made statistics a sought-after skill and will provide a
framework to tackle data-driven enquiry. Let us get started.

Here's what to expect in this
chapter.

1.1   *From Small to Big Data*

BIG THINGS START FROM SMALL ones. Think of the vastness
of a desert, and consider the smallness of each grain of sand.
Or look at a single star and expand your view to the large
number of them in a galaxy, and then to the number of
galaxies, most of them seeded with their own black holes.
The same applies to data: Each data point on its own may
not be all that powerful, but when combined with others the
possibilities open up.

We will come back to these black
holes, bear with me.

The interest in data may range from looking at historical
trends that in turn may hold some clues as to what may
happen in the future and even tell us what we should do.
These are the different levels required for a robust analytics
environment. Or put in different terms:

There are different levels of
analytics, take a look.

- Descriptive analytics - use data in aggregation to look at
  the past and answer questions such as "what happened?"

- Predictive analytics - use statistical models and
  forecasting techniques to answer questions such as "what
  will happen?"

- Prescriptive analytics - Use optimisation and simulation techniques to look at possible outcomes and answer questions such as "what will happen if...? and what should we do?"

Name	Value	Bytes	Magnitude
Byte (B)	1	1	1
Kilobyte (KB)	$1,024^1$	1,024	10^3
Megabyte (MB)	$1,024^2$	1,048,576	10^6
Gigabyte (GB)	$1,024^3$	1,073,741,824	10^9
Terabyte (TB)	$1,024^4$	1,099,511,627,776	10^{12}
Petabyte (PB)	$1,024^5$	1,125,899,906,842,624	10^{15}
Exabyte (EB)	$1,024^6$	1,152,921,504,606,846,976	10^{18}
Zettabyte (ZB)	$1,024^7$	1,180,591,620,717,411,303,424	10^{21}
Yottabyte (YB)	$1,024^8$	1,208,925,819,614,629,174,706,176	10^{24}

Table 1.1: Common orders of magnitude for data

The use of relevant data is central to each of these types of analytics. As such, the volume of data together with their variability and richness can power up various applications. These days, services underpinned by machine learning have become all the rage, and every successful company out there is actually a data company in one way or another. *The Economist* reported in 2017 that the data created and copied every year will reach 180 zettabytes in 2025. Sending that information via an average broadband connection, was calculated by *The Economist* to take 450 million years[2].

Just for reference, one single exabyte corresponds to 1,048,576 terabytes (TB). You can refer to Table 1.1 to look at the relationship between different common measures for data. You may want to know that it would take 728,177

That is 180×10^{21} or 180 followed by 21 zeros.

[2] Loupart, F. (2017). Data is giving rise to a new economy. *The Economist* - www.economist.com/briefing/2017/05/06/data-is-giving-rise-to-a-new-economy. Accessed: 2021-01-02

floppy disks or 1,498 CD-ROM discs to store just 1 TB worth of information. 1024 TB is one petabyte (PB) and this would take over 745 million floppy disks or 1.5 million CD-ROM discs.

These references may only be meaningful to people of a certain age... ahem... If not, look it up!

Numbers like these sound fanciful, but consider that there are examples of companies resorting to the use shipping containers pulled by trucks to transfer data. Given the different geographical locations where relevant data is generated and captured, it is not unusual to hear about physical transfer of data. A simple example is provided by the capture of the first image ever obtained of a black hole in 2019. With the use of eight radio telescopes located around the globe, scientists where able to record an image of a black hole by improving upon a technique that allows for the imaging of far-away objects known as Very Long Baseline Interferometry, or VLBI[3]. Each telescope would capture 350 TB of data per day for one week. In this way, from each grain of sand, a great desert is created.

Including the "Gran Telescopio Milimétrico Alfonso Serrano" at INAOE, an institution where I spent some time as a young optics researcher.

[3] The Event Horizon Telescope Collaboration (2019). First M87 Event Horizon Telescope Results. I. The Shadow of the Supermassive Black Hole. *ApJL 875*(L1), 1–17

The telescopes are not physically connected and the data is not networked. However, they synchronise the data with atomic clocks to time their observations in a precise manner. The data was stored on high-performance helium-filled hard drives and flown to highly specialised supercomputers — known as correlators — at the Max Planck Institute for Radio Astronomy and MIT Haystack Observatory to be combined. They were then painstakingly converted into an image using novel computational tools developed by the collaboration. All that for a single, magnificent image that let's us gaze into the abyss.

All five petabytes of observations.

They used Python by the way! You can look at the image here: `https://www.eso.org/public/news/eso1907/`.

The availability of data in such quantities is sometimes described using the umbrella term "Big Data". I am not a huge fan of the term, after all *big* is a comparative adjective — i.e. "big" compared to what and according to whom? Despite my dislike for the term, you are likely to have come across it. Big data is used to describe large volumes of data which we would not be able to process using a single machine or traditional methods.

Big compared to what and according to whom?

In the definition provided above you may be able to see why I have a problem with this term. After all, if I am a corner shop owner with a spreadsheet large enough for my decades-old computer I already have big data; whereas this spreadsheet is peanuts for a server farm from a big corporation like Google or Amazon. Sometimes people refer to the 4 *V*'s of big data for a more precise definition. We have already mentioned one of them, but let us take a look at all of them:

- Volume – The sheer volume of data that is generated and captured. It is the most visible characteristic of big data.

Volume – the size of the datasets at hand.

- Velocity – Not only do we need large quantities of data, but they also need to be made available at speed. High velocity requires suitable processing techniques not available with traditional methods.

Velocity – the speed at which data is generated.

- Variety – The data that is collected not only needs to come from different sources, but also encompasses different formats and show differences and variability. After all, if you just capture information from StarTrek followers, you will think that there is no richness in Sci-Fi.

Variety – Different sources and data types.

- Veracity – This refers to the quality of the data collected. This indicates the level of trustworthiness in the datasets you have. Think of it – if you have a large quantity of noise, all you have is a high pile of rubbish, not *big data* by any means.

  Veracity – Quality and trustworthiness of the data.

I would like to add a couple of more V's to the mix. All for good measure. I mentioned **visibility** earlier on, and that is a very important V in big data. If the data that we have captured is sequestered in silos or simply not made available for analysis, once again we have a large storage facility and nothing else.

No, visibility is not one of the traditional V's but it is one to keep an eye on :)

The other V I would like to talk about is that of **value**. At the risk of falling for the cliché of talking about data being the new oil, there is no question that data — well curated, maintained and secured data — holds value. And to follow the overused oil analogy, it must be said that for it to achieve its potential, it must be distilled. There are very few products that use crude oil in its raw form. The same is true when using data.

The final V is that of value. Data that does not hold value is a cost.

We can look at a proxy for the value of data by looking at the market capitalisation of some of the largest companies. By the end of 2020, according to *Statista*[4], 7 out of the 10 most valuable companies in the world are technology companies that rely on the use of data, including Microsoft, Apple and Alphabet. Two are multinational conglomerates or corporations whose component firms surely use data.

[4] Statista (2020). The 100 largest companies in the world by market capitalization in 2020. www.statista.com/statistics/263264/top-companies-in-the-world-by-market-capitalization. Accessed: 2021-01-03

The other company in the top 10, funny enough, is an oil company. See the ranking in Table 1.2.

Table 1.2: Ranking of companies by market capitalisation in billions of U.S. dollars in 2020

Rank	Name
1	Saudi Arabian Oil Company (Saudi Aramco) (Saudi Arabia)
2	Microsoft (United States)
3	Apple (United States)
4	Amazon (United States)
5	Alphabet (United States)
6	Facebook (United States)
7	Alibaba (China)
8	Tencent Holdings (China)
9	Berkshire Hathaway (United States)
10	Johnson & Johnson (United States)

According to Gartner[5], more and more companies will be valued on their information portfolios and the data they have. Companies are using data to improve their businesses from operations to services, increase revenue, predict behaviour, etc. Using the different forms of analytics we mentioned earlier on, companies are able to look at what has happened in the recent past, and be able to predict what will happen and drive changes given different scenarios. This is an area that will continue developing and change is required. For example, current Generally Accepted Accounting Principles (GAAP) standards do not allow for intangible assets such as data to be capitalised.

In any event, companies and businesses in general are in an environment where customers expect them to provide

[5] Gartner (2017). Gartner Says within Five Years, Organizations Will Be Valued on Their Information Portfolios. www.gartner.com/en/newsroom/press-releases/2017-02-08-gartner-says-within-five-years-organizations-will-be-valued-on-their-information-portfolios. Accessed: 2021-01-04

services that are personalised, and cater to their wants and
needs with every transaction or interaction. This requires a
panoramic view informed by the richness of data including
the customer journey and user experience, sales, product
usage, etc. Measuring the value of our data can be a hard
task. James E. Short and Steve Todd tackle[6] the problem
with a few different approaches including monetisation of
the raw data itself by analysing its value for their customer;
the usage value that the data holds, in other words, how
frequently the data is accessed, the transaction rate or
application workload; the expected value of the data by
looking at the cash flow or income they generate or
comparing to existing, tracked datasets.

[6] Short, J. E. and S. Todd (2017).
What's your data worth? MIT
Sloan Management Review,
sloanreview.mit.edu/article/whats-
your-data-worth/. Accessed:
2021-01-08

Independently of the valuation of the data that businesses
may be able to undertake, there is no doubt that better data
enable better decisions; which in turn leads to better
outcomes. For instance, in 2014 the McKinsey Global
Institute reported[7] on the use of customer analytics across
different sectors concluding that data-driven organisations
are better equipped and can improve profits and growth.
Companies that leverage their customer data are 23 times
more likely to acquire customers, 6 times as likely to retain
their customers, and 19 times as likely to be profitable as a
result.

[7] McKinsey & Co. (2014). Using
customer analytics to boost
corporate performance.

All the benefits we have mentioned above are part of the
appeal in developing internal data science teams and
analytics squads that are able to harness the power of data.
There is no doubt that this is a way forward, but it is
important not to be distracted by dazzling artificial

Strong foundations in statistics can
help your A.I. journey!

intelligence promises. That is not to say that A.I. or its cousin, machine learning, are not useful. However, in many cases we forget that strong foundations in data analysis and statistics underpin a lot of the successful stories out there.

For all the great outcomes provided by the use of data, privacy and ethics are important ingredients to include. There are some excellent resources you can look at such as the work of Annika Richterich[8], or look at the cautionary tales edited by Bill Franks[9]. This is a vast area outside the scope of this book. However, it is paramount to remember that behind each data point there may be a corporation, an individual, a user whose information is being analysed. Bear in mind their privacy and consider the ethical implications of the decisions that are being made with the help of this data.

[8] Richterich, A. (2018). *The Big Data Agenda: Data Ethics and Critical Data Studies.* Critical, Digital and Social Media Studies. University of Westminster Press
[9] Franks, B. (2020). *97 Things About Ethics Everyone in Data Science Should Know.* O'Reilly Media

In previous works[10] I have argued about the rise of the role of data science and analytics in modern business settings. You will find my referring to data science jackalopes to counter the need for magic unicorns that are able to cover the data workflow and produce results in no time, while still having a fabulous mane. Data science, as a team sport played by a team of data science jackalopes, may indeed use some deep learning or support vector machines, they may invent something new or adapt an existing approach. What I have found though, is that if you can answer a question simply by aggregating, slicing and dicing — counting really — well-curated data and do so rigorously, then it is OK and you are definitely in the right track.

[10] Rogel-Salazar, J. (2017). *Data Science and Analytics with Python.* Chapman & Hall/CRC Data Mining and Knowledge Discovery Series. CRC Press; and Rogel-Salazar, J. (2020). *Advanced Data Science and Analytics with Python.* Chapman & Hall/CRC Data Mining and Knowledge Discovery Series. CRC Press

Think of it from your experience. Consider the following example. You have just attended a fine social event with colleagues and are thinking of going back home. The weather in London is its usual self and it is pouring down with cold rain and you have managed to miss the last tube home. You decide to use one of those ride-hail apps on your mobile. It does not matter how many clever algorithms – from neural to social network analysis – they have used, if the cab is not there in the x minutes they claimed it would take, the entire proposition has failed and you will think twice before using the service again.

I bet you can transpose this to a more sunny setting. Remember that any resemblance to actual events is purely coincidental :)

I am sure you have experienced this at some point.

Part of the success (or failure) in the example above is down to having a good user experience (UX) in designing the product and presenting correct and useful information. That information needs to rely on accurate data and its robust analysis. Perhaps a weighted average is a good measure for the time presented to the user and may be quicker to calculate than using a more computationally expensive method that takes longer to update. Understanding uncertainty, probable outcomes, and interpreting the results rests on a solid foundation of statistical concepts. This is the main motivation behind this book.

This is the motivation behind this book.

1.2   Numbers, Facts and Stats

THINKING ABOUT STATISTICS AS THE art of learning from data, provides us with a powerful perspective. Statistical knowledge helps us tackle tasks that deal with data in general: From collection, to analysis and even presentation of results. Not only is statistics an important component of the scientific process, but also of many everyday subjects from weather to insurance, health and sport. A good statistical foundation will help us understand a problem better and lead us to sound conclusions, as well as spotting areas that require further analysis.

Statistics enables the creation of new knowledge.

Consider how many decisions, even opinions, are based on data as evidence. It stands to reason that having a good grasp of statistics can help us assess the quality of an analysis presented to us; perhaps even carry out the analysis ourselves. Statistics is therefore more than just numbers and facts such as 9 *out of* 10 *dental professionals prefer this toothpaste*, or *the possibility of successfully navigating an asteroid field being approximately* 3, 720 *to* 1. The real power of statistics is to understand how they came up with those figures: How many dentists and hygienists were asked? What were they consulted on and what other toothpaste brands were presented to them? As for our protocol android, how recent is the data consulted? Is that the figure for freighters only? And what are the chances of a collision given that 5 of the main characters in the story are on board?

Having a good grasp of statistics can help a lot.

Although that is the colloquial usage.

I am sure C3-PO will be able to answer these and more.

As a matter of fact, a good statistical analysis will also take into account uncertainties and errors in the results presented. You will hear about conclusions being statistically significant (or not) and care is taken to ensure that the analysis is based on reliable data, that the data in question is analysed appropriately and that the conclusions are reasonable based on the analysis done. The current

A good statistical analysis takes into account uncertainties and errors.

scientific and business environments have more and better data to be analysed and given the benefits that statistics brings to the table, no wonder there has been a surge in the need for people with statistical skills. If on top of that you consider that quite a few of the tools used in statistics are a good foundation for applications of machine learning and artificial intelligence, then the requirement is even more compelling.

Some even call it statistical learning.

You may think that statistics is a recent human endeavour, particularly when looking at the prevalence of mathematics and even computational prowess that is emphasised these days. However, statistics has had a long journey. Our capabilities for storing and analysing data have been evolving gradually and areas such as data collection started much earlier than the computer revolution. One of the earliest examples of data collection is the Ishango Bone[11] dated 18, 000 BCE and discovered in 1960 in present-day Uganda. The bone has some non-random markings thought to have been used for counting[12].

[11] de Heinzelin, J. (1962, Jun). Ishango. *Scientific American* (206:6), 105–116

[12] Pletser, V. (2012). Does the Ishango Bone Indicate Knowledge of the Base 12? An Interpretation of a Prehistoric Discovery, the First Mathematical Tool of Humankind. *arXiv math.HO 1204.1019*

Other tools and devices have been used to keep track of information or for performing calculations. For example, the abacus provided ancient cultures with a calculating device that is used to this day. Simply look at the soroban competitions in Japan. As for early examples of abaci, perhaps the Salamis Tablet[13] is one of the oldest counting boards, certainly a precursor. Discovered in 1846 in the Greek island of Salamis dating back to 300 BEC and used by the Babylonians.

算盤,そろばん - Calculating tray.

[13] Heffelfinger, T. and G. Flom (2004). Abacus: Mystery of the Bead. http://totton.idirect.com. Accessed: 2021-02-03

Different forms of counting have been developed by very different people at different times in various different places. For example, the Incas and other cultures in the Andes in South America would use knots on a string, known as a *quipu* or *khipu*[14] to record and communicate information. Pre-dating the height of the Incan Empire as far back as 2500 BCE, quipus would be able to record dates, statistics, accounts, and even represent, in abstract form, key episodes from traditional folk stories and poetry. The Mayans[15] in Mexico and Central America (Classic Period – 250-900 CE) developed a positional vigesimal numeral system requiring a zero as a place-holder. Its use in astronomy and calendar calculations was aided by their number system. A remarkable achievement!

With the registering of information, it becomes possible to keep records of all sorts: Goods, taxes, assets, laws, etc. One of the earliest examples of the practice comes from Ancient Egypt where specialised bookkeepers would maintain records of goods in papyrus as early as 4000 BCE. Papyrus was not only used for administrative accounting, but also for recording literature and even music[16]. In more recent times, paper-like material has been used by other cultures for record-keeping. For instance, the use of *amate* in pre-Hispanic civilisations such as the Aztecs. An example of economic records is shown in Section 2 of the Codex Mendoza[17] listing 39 provinces containing more than 400 towns that were required to pay tribute. The codex has been held at the Bodleian Library at the University of Oxford since 1659.

[14] Buckmaster, D. (1974). The Incan Quipu and the Jacobsen hypothesis. *Journal of Accounting Research* 12(1), 178–181

[15] Díaz Díaz, R. (2006). Apuntes sobre la aritmética maya. *Educere* 10(35), 621–627

[16] Lichtheim, M. (2019). *Ancient Egyptian Literature*. University of California Press

From *āmatl* in Nahuatl.

[17] Hassig, R. (2013). El tributo en la economía prehispánica. *Arqueología Mexicana* 21(124), 32–39

An impressive achievement of ancient data storage is epitomised by the Library of Alexandria (300 BCE - 48 CE) with half a million scrolls covering a large proportion of knowledge acquired by that time. We all know what happened when the Romans invaded ... and it is indeed the Romans who we shall thank for the origin of the word *statistics*. Let's take a look.

The Romans have a lot to answer for.

1.3   A Sampled History of Statistics

THE WORD STATISTICS IS DERIVED from the Latin *statisticum collegium* or "council of state" which could be understood to be an account of the state of affairs. This is also where the Italian word *statista* (politician/statesman) originates and where the relationship with the word *state* becomes clear. The word *statistics* was used to encapsulate the information resulting from the administrative activity of a state, in particular economic data and its population.

Statistics was an account of the activities of a state.

In the eighteenth-century, in the book by Gottfried Achenwall[18] entitled *Staatsverfassung der heutigen vornehmsten europäischen Reiche und Völker im Grundrisse*, the term *statistik* was first used to mean the comprehensive description of the sociopolitical and economic characteristics of a state. In the process, Achenwall provided a word for this description in various other languages. By the following decades, the term was broaden to include the collection and analysis of wider types of data and started being used in conjunction with probability to end up becoming what we now know as statistical inference. The rest is history.

[18] van der Zande, J. (2010). Statistik and history in the German enlightenment. *Journal of the History of Ideas* 71(3), 411–432

We will talk about statistical inference later on.

Today, the term has a much wider meaning including not only the colloquial use of the word to mean *facts and figures* but also the branch of mathematics dealing with the collection, analysis, interpretation and representation of data and the different types of methods and algorithms that enable us to analyse data. Many have been the contributions and contributors to the science of statistics and here I would like to mention but a few.

People talk about statistics to mean *facts and figures*, but the term is broader than that.

Some fundamental concepts, such as the mean of two numbers or the mode, were well-known to the ancient Greeks. Extensions to obtaining the mean (or average) of more than two numbers was used in the late sixteenth century to estimate astronomical locations. In 1750s Thomas Simpson showed in his work on the theory of errors that the arithmetic mean was better than a single observation.

What was not known by the ancient Greeks!!

The median is another important basic measure that we all learn at school. It was first described by Edward Wright, a cartographer and mathematician, to determine location for navigation with the help of a compass. Another important application of the median includes the work of Roger Joseph Boskovich, astronomer and physicist, who used it as a way to minimise the sum of absolute deviations. This is effectively a regression model[19] based on the $L1$-norm or Manhattan distance. The actual word *median* was coined by Francis Galton in 1881.

Some of these measures are discussed in Section 4.2.

[19] Rogel-Salazar, J. (2017). *Data Science and Analytics with Python*. Chapman & Hall/CRC Data Mining and Knowledge Discovery Series. CRC Press

Now that we have mentioned regression, it is pertinent to talk about least squares. Apart from Boskovich's efforts mentioned earlier, Adrien-Marie Legendre's work in the area is perhaps better known. In 1805 Legendre made contributions on least squares in the context of astronomical calculations[20]. Some say that least squares is to statistics what calculus is to mathematics. It is a standard approach that many of us would have been introduced to in many courses of probability and statistics.

[20] Samueli, J.-J. (2010). Legendre et la méthode des moindres carrés. Bibnum journals.openedition.org/bibnum/580. Accessed: 2021-02-14

And talking about probability, it started as a way to understand games of chance among mathematicians such as Pierre de Fermat and Blaise Pascal in the mid-1600s. Some of the elements of early probability had been proposed a century earlier by Girolamo Cardano although not published at the time. Jacob Bernoulli applied the techniques to understand how, from given outcomes of a game of chance, it was possible to understand the properties of the game itself, starting us up going down the road towards inferential statistics. Abraham de Moivre considered the properties of samples from Bernoulli's binomial distribution as the sample size increased to very large numbers ending up with a discrete version of the normal distribution.

The history of probability is much broader than the few things mentioned here. Studying the outcomes of games of chance and gambling is definitely the start.

I promise we will talk about inference shortly.

Data was also used to quantify other phenomena. For instance, in 1662 John Graunt estimated the population of London using records on the number of funerals per year, death rate and the average size family. Pierre Simon, Marquis de Laplace used a similar method for the French population in 1802. Among the many contributions that Laplace made to the wider field of mathematics and physics, he also played an important role in the establishment of the normal distribution generalising the work of Moivre.

Statistics starts to be used in a variety of problems.

In 1774, Laplace proposed an error curve[21] — now called imaginatively the Laplace distribution — noting that an error in a measurement can be expressed as an exponential function of the absolute value of its magnitude. In 1880 his formulation of the Central Limit theorem confirmed the assumptions that Carl Friedrich Gauss used for his derivation of the normal distribution — also known as the Gaussian distribution— to model errors in astronomical observations. In many applications, it is often the case that we treat the error of an observation as the result of many small, independent errors. This is a powerful thing that lets us apply the central limit theorem, and treat the errors as normally distributed.

We mentioned Galton earlier, on and his work not only included giving name to the mode or indeed advancing fingerprints as evidence in court or even guessing the weight of a fat ox and the statistical implications of the estimates provided[22]. He also fitted normal curves to data and proposed the idea of regression to the mean by noticing the form by which a distribution is dispersed looking at the ideas of what we now call variance and standard deviation. His 1886 work on the relative size/height of children and their parents provided us with the name for *regression* and the use of correlation.

We cannot mention correlation without referring to Karl Pearson, whose work on the method of moments and correlation analysis provided a foundation for mathematical statistics. His work is also encapsulated in the use of *p*-values and principal component analysis. He is also

[21] Stahl, S. (2006). The evolution of the normal distribution. *Mathematics Magazine 79*(2), 96

We associate Gauss with the normal distribution, but a lot of it is due to Laplace. We discuss the normal distribution in Section 5.4.1.

[22] Rogel-Salazar, J. (2017). *Data Science and Analytics with Python*. Chapman & Hall/CRC Data Mining and Knowledge Discovery Series. CRC Press

Pearson correlation is discussed in Section 6.4.1.

See Section 5.5.

credited[23] with introducing the histogram as a tool to visualise data. His chi-square test of goodness of fit is one of the main ways to test for significance in statistics. There is no doubt that both Galton and Pearson made great contributions to the field, but it is also important to reflect on the impact that their views on eugenics have had in the world. It is great that University College London decided to rename three facilities that bore their names. UCL's president and provost, Prof Michael Arthur, is quoted saying[24]

> "This problematic history has, and continues, to cause significant concern for many in our community and has a profound impact on the sense of belonging that we want all of our staff and students to have. Although UCL is a very different place than it was in the 19th century, any suggestion that we celebrate these ideas or the figures behind them creates an unwelcoming environment for many in our community."

In terms of statistical testing, we need to mention William Sealy Gosset, aka *Student*, who proposed the famous Student's *t* distribution in 1908[25]. Gosset published his work under the pseudonym of Student to appease his employer, the Guinness Brewery in Dublin, who were reluctant for his work to be published in case competitors came to realise they were relying on *t*-tests to determine the quality of their raw materials.

Perhaps the Guinness brewers were happy with the initial reception of what could be a dry piece of mathematical writing without much fizz. Except, that is, if you are Ronald Aylmer Fisher, who considered how certain a result would

[23] Ioannidis, Y. (2003). The history of histograms (abridged). www.vldb.org/conf/2003/papers/S02P01.pdfo. Accessed: 2021-02-14

See Section 6.3 for the chi-square test.

[24] PA Media (2020). UCL renames three facilities that honoured prominent eugenicists. www.theguardian.com/education/2020/jun/19/ucl-renames-three-facilities -that-honoured-prominent-eugenicists. Accessed: 2021-02-14

[25] Student (1908). The probable error of a mean. *Biometrika* 6(1), 1–25

See Section 5.5.1 for the *t* distribution and Section 6.5.1 for the *t*-test.

I guess, similar to Guinness stout. Not much fizz, but lots of flavour!

be compared to chance and if those chances are low we can consider the result to be *significant*. Fisher introduced techniques such as the analysis of variance and estimation theory. He also contributed to the development of better experimental design. Some even consider him to have founded modern statistics. The Rothamsted Research[26] released in 2020 a statement condemning Fisher's involvement with eugenics and distancing themselves from his views. Similarly, Gonville and Caius College[27] of the University of Cambridge announced the removal of a stained-glass window commemorating his work.

The traditional use of statistics up until Fisher had been mainly inferential where hypothesis testing and *p*-values take centre stage. A different focus was brought in by John Tukey who considered the importance of exploring the data at hand to see what it is telling us and with that exploratory data analysis was born[28]. He is also the inventor of the box plot, contributed to the development of fast Fourier transform algorithms and is even credited with coining the term "bit" as a contraction of "binary digit" and now widely used in computer science and beyond. The influence that he has had in the field can be felt in the more recent world of data science. For an account of the trials and tribulations of the jackalope data scientist, take a look at Chapter 1 of *Data Science and Analytics with Python* and for techniques and algorithms see the rest of the book and its counterpart *Advanced Data Science and Analytics with Python*[29].

Let us now turn our attention to the field of data visualisation. We have mentioned above the contributions by

[26] Rothamsted Research (2020). Statement on R. A. Fisher. www.rothamsted.ac.uk/news/statement-r-fisher. Accessed: 2021-02-14

[27] Busby, M. (2020). Cambridge college to remove window commemorating eugenicist. www.theguardian.com/education/2020/jun/27/cambridge-gonville-caius-college -eugenicist-window-ronald-fisher. Accessed: 2021-02-14

[28] Tukey, J. W. (1977). *Exploratory Data Analysis*. Number v. 2 in Addison-Wesley Series in Behavioral Science. Addison-Wesley Publishing Company

You will need to consult the book for more on jackalopes and data science.

[29] Rogel-Salazar, J. (2020). *Advanced Data Science and Analytics with Python*. Chapman & Hall/CRC Data Mining and Knowledge Discovery Series. CRC Press

Pearson and Tukey in the form of histograms and box plots, but there are a couple more people that we would like to mention in this sampled history. The first is the Scottish engineer William Playfair, whose background ranges from engineering through economics, banking, and even espionage[30]. In this account of contributions he gets a mention for having invented different types of data representation that we use to this day. Examples include the line chart, the area plot and the bar chart, even the infamous pie chart. All that without the aid of modern plotting software!

[30] Berkowitz, B. D. (2018). *Playfair: The True Story of the British Secret Agent Who Changed How We See the World.* George Mason University Press

We will cover why infamous in Section 8.6.

Cartography has always been a rich ground for data depiction and the use of maps overlaying other information has been with us for a long time. A pioneer of these sort of maps is the French engineer Charles Joseph Minard. The flow maps he created depict the traffic of existing roads in the Dijon area in 1845; this may have helped with laying the railroad infrastructure in the area later on. Even more famous is his graphical representation of the Napoleonic Russian campaign of 1812 showing the deployment and eventual demise of Napoleon's army on their way to and back from Moscow. This is effectively a predecessor of what we now refer to as Sankey diagrams. They are named after Matthew Hery Phineas Riall Sankey, who used them to depict energy efficiency in a steam engine.

Dijon in France, famous for its mustard of course.

A notable entry is that of Florence Nightingale who not only founded modern nursing[31] but was also a social reformer, statistician and data visualiser. Building on work from Playfair, she was able to use charts effectively in her

[31] Bostridge, M. (2015). *Florence Nightingale: The Woman and Her Legend.* Penguin Books Limited

publications to draw attention to important results. An excellent example is her use of polar area charts or coxcombs to elucidate the actual causes of death by month in the Crimean War. In 1859 she was elected the first female member of the Royal Statistical Society.

Around the same time that Nightingale was persuading Queen Victoria and Members of Parliament of the need to improve conditions in military hospitals, John Snow was mapping the locations of cholera cases[32], in particular deaths, showing a clear concentration around a now infamous water pump in Broad Street in Soho, London. He was able to use this information not only to stop the outbreak but also to change the way we understand the cause and spread of disease.

Talking about maps, a well-deserved mention goes to Pierre Charles François Dupin[33] for the creation of the choropleth map to illustrate the illiteracy rate in France in 1826. This kind of thematic map uses shadings in proportion to the variable that represents an aggregate summary for each area.

There is much more we can cover in this sampled history. However, we will finish this section with the mention of Jacques Bertin and his 1967 book *Sémiologie Graphique*[34]. We can think of his work to be to data visualisation what Mendeleev's periodic table did for chemistry. In Chapter 7 we will cover some of this organisation of the visual and perceptual elements of graphics according to the features and relations in data. Can't wait!

[32] Vinten-Johansen, P., H. Brody, N. Paneth, S. Rachman, M. Rip, and D. Zuck (2003). *Cholera, Chloroform, and the Science of Medicine: A Life of John Snow.* Oxford University Press

[33] Bradley, M. *Charles Dupin (1784 - 1873) and His Influence on France.* Cambria Press

[34] Bertin, J. and M. Barbut (1967). *Sémiologie graphique: Les diagrammes, les réseaux, les cartes.* Gauthier-Villars

1.4   Statistics Today

As we have already seen, the field of statistics has an interesting and varied history. Today, the field has seen a renewed interest in light of the data availability that we discussed in Section 1.1. In a way, we can think of statistics as a way to describe the methods and ideas dealing with the collection, presentation, analysis and interpretation of data. All this with the purpose of using data to understand a variety of phenomena.

The renewed interest in statistics is fuelled by more widespread availability of data.

Largely speaking we can consider two different approaches to statistical analysis and both can be used in conjunction with each other. We mentioned them in the previous section and surely you have heard about descriptive and inferential statistics. Descriptive statistics, as the name suggests, is used to describe data from a group of observations, usually referred to as a population. In that way, descriptive statistics deals with the aggregation and summarisation of data. The use of tables, charts, or graphical displays is the norm in this area, as well as the calculation of some measures that provide information about the bulk of the data and how spread the observations are. Descriptive statistics enables us to see data in a meaningful way and provides us with clues not only about the shape of the data, but also about what to do next with it.

Usually a sample of that data.

Descriptive statistics enable us to see our data in a meaningful way.

And some of those things include going beyond the aggregations and reach conclusions from the evidence provided by the data although it may not be made explicit.

This is the role of inferential statistics. The methods and estimations made with inferential statistics lets us make inferences about the population from a sample. In this way we can study relationships between different attributes or values, called variables and make generalisations or predictions. It is then possible for us to test a hypothesis, in other words a proposed explanation for the phenomena we are seeing. Our aim is therefore to accept or reject the hypothesis based on the data at hand. Typically we would consider a quantity to be measured and propose that its value is zero. This is called the **null hypothesis**. We can then look at the results of two models for example, and we deem our results to be **statistically significant** if data would be unlikely to occur if the null hypothesis were true given a significance level provided by a threshold probability.

Finally, we are here talking about inferential statistics. I hope it was worth the wait.

Accepting or rejecting the null hypothesis is part and parcel of inferential statistics.

There are other classifications of statistics you may hear from time to time, for example, whether it is parametric or nonparametric. In the parametric methods, we work under the idea that there is a set of fixed parameters that describe our model and therefore its probability distribution. Parametric statistical methods are typically used when we know that the population is near normal, or we can approximate such a distribution. The normal distribution has two parameters: The mean and the standard deviation. If you are able to determine those two parameters, you have a model.

Parametric methods try to determine parameters to describe the data. Hence the name.

What about nonparametric statistics? Well, these are methods that do not need to make assumptions on parameters to describe the population at hand. This means

This is in contrast to nonparametric methods.

that the distribution is not fixed and sometimes we refer to these models as distribution-free. These methods are usually applied when we have ordinal data, in other words, data that relies on ranking or a certain order. A good example of a simple descriptive nonparametric statistic is a histogram plot.

Another distinction you may encounter from time to time regards the approach to making inference. This may be even thought of as "philosophies" behind the approach: You can do frequentist inference or Bayesian. The differences between frequentist and Bayesian statistics is rooted in the interpretation of the concept of probability. In frequentist statistics, only repeatable random events have probabilities. These are equal to the long-term frequency of occurrence of the events in which we are interested. In the Bayesian approach, probabilities are used to represent the uncertainty of an event and as such it is possible to assign a probability value to non-repeatable events! We are then able to improve our probability estimate as we get more information about an event, narrowing our uncertainty about it. This is encapsulated in Bayes' theorem.

Another distinction appears between the frequentist and Bayesian approaches to stats.

Think of the typical coin flipping experiment.

In a nutshell, the main goals of inferential statistics can be summarised as follows:

- Parameter estimation: If we are using parametric methods, we are interested in determining the distribution from which our samples came.

- Data prediction: Given the distribution obtained from the previous goal, we are now interested in predicting

The goals of inferential statistics.

the future. With our model under our arm, we are able to apply it to tell us something about observations outside our sample.

- Model comparison: If we have a couple of models that can be applied, we are interested in determining which one explains the observed data better.

In general, statistics is interested in a set of observations describing a population and not about a single particular observation. In statistics we are interested in the uncertainty of a phenomenon and make a distinction between the uncertainties we can control and those we cannot. That uncertainty is framed in the context of probability. We need to be mindful not only about the methods that we use and the interpretation of the results obtained, but also about the reliability of the data collection, processing and storage.

Accounting for uncertainty is a big part of doing statistics.

1.5 *Asking Questions and Getting Answers*

As we have seen above, statistics is a general discipline that can be applied to a varied range of questions. It is a great tool to have under our belt to design laboratory and field experiments, surveys or other data collection tasks. It supports our work in planning inquiries and enables us to draw conclusions as well as making predictions.

What is not to like about stats?

The use of statistics can be seen in every branch of knowledge, from physics to biology, genetics to finance, marketing to medicine. Any businessperson, or engineer, marketer or doctor can employ statistical methods in their

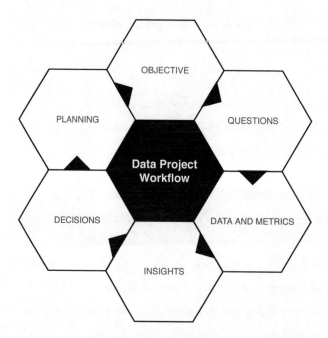

Figure 1.1: Diagrammatic representation of the data project workflow.

work. A key to this use is the generation of suitable questions that can seek for an answer based on data. There may be different approaches to tackle data-driven work and a few steps are represented in the diagram shown in Figure 1.1.

I always advocate[35] for strong foundations to support successful data-related projects. This includes the three pillar roles of:

- Project manager

- Lead statistician or data scientist

- Lead data architect

A very important step for the team above is to establish a clearly defined objective and explore how it informs the

[35] Rogel-Salazar, J. (2017). *Data Science and Analytics with Python*. Chapman & Hall/CRC Data Mining and Knowledge Discovery Series. CRC Press; and Rogel-Salazar, J. (2020). *Advanced Data Science and Analytics with Python*. Chapman & Hall/CRC Data Mining and Knowledge Discovery Series. CRC Press

Variations of these titles are welcome!

questions we might ask. A great starting point is to ask
ourselves what it is we are trying to learn. In this way we
are able to provide a direction and a goal to work towards.
At the same time it helps us and our team to stay the course
and clear out any noise. Similarly, it lets us plan the best
way to use our budget and resources.

A clear objective helps the team
stay the course.

Once we have clarity in the questions the need answering,
it becomes much easier to determine what datasets may
be useful in tackling those questions. I do despair when
someone approaches me with a given dataset and asks to
tell them "something they don't know"... In any case, if you
find yourselves in that situation, use the diagram above to
take them through the workflow. Alongside the datasets it is
also important to determine what metrics we are interested
in calculating and/or driving. In the first part of this book
we will cover some of the statistical methods that will
enable us to use data to answer questions that meet our
objectives. We will use Python as the main programming
language to carry out the analysis. In the next chapter we
will give a concise introduction to the language and in
the next chapters we will use it in the context of statistical
analysis.

The next step is to source data that
can help answer the questions we
formulated.

In this book we will use Python
to help us in our statistical
adventures.

An important consideration at this point in our workflow is
the distinction between outcomes and outputs. These
should be driven by the objectives we have set out. In other
words, once we have a clear aim for what we want to learn,
we need to develop the specific questions we will be
answering with our analysis, and agree how we will assess
the answers we obtain. For instance, our output may be

Remember that outcomes $\neq$
outputs.

related to the number of products we offer in the form of a
report, whereas the outcome we expect is related to an
increase in revenue and usage of those products. The
distinction between outcomes and outputs may be a subtle
one, but it is an important one to bear in mind particularly
during conversations with interested parties who need the
results or the actions stemming from them. Some examples
of outcomes and outputs are shown in Table 1.3.

The distinction is subtle but
important.

Outcomes	Outputs
Increase revenue	Reports
Change in cost	Spreadsheets
Rate of growth	Dashboards
Increased customer satisfaction	Infographics
Retain more customers	Brochures
Etc.	Etc.

Table 1.3: Examples of outcomes
and outputs.

Think of it this way: Outputs tell the story of what we have
produced or indeed the activities of our team or
organisation. Outputs themselves do not measure the
impact of the work done, that is done by the outcomes. An
outcome indicates the level of performance or achievement
that occurred because of the activities carried out. In a way,
the outcome should be contained in the output. Outcomes
often focus on changing things and they let us take a look at
what may be the variables that impact our figures and
provide us with insights. In turn, this leads us to making
better decisions based on evidence. Finally, we can close the
circuit by enabling the decisions made to plan for the next
iteration in the workflow.

In a way, the outcome should be
contained in the output.

A key component of the workflow described above is the formulation of good data questions. A good data question is one that covers the following points:

- It uses simple and direct language

- It is sharp and specific

The marks of a good data question.

- It asks technical teams to predict or estimate something

- It indicates what type of data is needed

- It involves data modelling or analysis

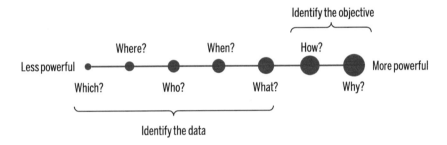

Figure 1.2. The power of questions on a scale.

Learning to ask better questions helps us make better requests to our teams and also enables us to clarify requirements. The way in which we formulate our questions can lead us to the answers we are looking for. Although all questions are important, in the workflow outlined above, some question words are more powerful than others. See the scale presented in Figure 1.2. As we can see, "why" questions are more powerful than others. This is because they are more open-ended and allow for more exploration. At the opposite side of the spectrum we have question

Some question words are more powerful than others. Use the scale above to help you.

words such as "which, where, who". These tend to be more specific and hence more directive.

Do not be fooled into thinking that because they are marked as "less powerful" these questions are not important and should not be used. On the contrary, since they are more specific they help us narrow on specifics and may enable us to identify the data needed. The questions on the right-hand side of our diagram are more open and therefore can help us identify the objective of our data analysis.

But less powerful does not mean less important!

Finally, I would like to mention the potential that we can tap into by realising what data we are missing. This is something that David Hand[36] has called *dark data* in analogy to the dark matter that composes much of the universe. The data we have and measure does not necessarily capture all the information that is required to answer the questions we have. I would like to think that this is also reflected in the models we create with that data. Remember the data we do have. that there are not perfect models, just good enough ones. And we can extend that maxim by saying, "just good enough given the data we do have". Be mindful of this!

[36] Hand, D. J. (2020). *Dark Data: Why What You Don't Know Matters.* Princeton University Press

There are no perfect models, just good enough ones ... given the data we have.

1.6   Presenting Answers Visually

I WOULD LIKE TO FINISH this chapter by talking about the use of visuals to present the answers we have obtained from the data analysis workflow we talked about in the previous section. Many outputs we may generate such as reports or dashboards do end up making use of visual representations

We will talk about data visualisation in the last two chapters of this book.

of the analysis done. This includes tables, charts, graphics and other visual cues that tell the story of the outcomes we have generated.

Representing data in tables can be a good way to drive a summary of the data. However, you would not like your audience to hunt for the patterns that drive your analysis in a long list of numbers. Instead, you may want to present a nice, elegant chart that is easy to understand and drives the point you want to make.

This would be the equivalent of trying to figure out where Waldo is in one of those super detailed illustrations.

Our data and the statistical analysis we perform on it does tell a story. Presenting the answers to our questions should fit the audience that we are addressing. This can be made a much easier task by asking the following three questions:

1. **What** is the purpose of generating a visual output for our data?

2. **Who** are we intending to communicate that purpose to?

3. **How** can we visualise that purpose in the best possible way?

Answer these questions when trying to visualise or present your data and results.

The answers to those questions will start shaping up the visual outputs we need to design. However, that is just the beginning of the story. It is not uncommon to see some very cluttered visualisations, and this is because there may be a tendency to present anything and everything. The end result is not only a busy visual but also one that misses the point of the message we are trying to create, leaving our audience trying to figure out what we are trying to convey at best, or utterly confused at worst.

Whenever possible avoid cluttered visualisations, your audience will appreciate it.

Our visuals are not about us, but instead about two things:

1. the data analysis performed, and more importantly

2. making sure our audience gets our message in a clear and concise manner.

Remember that the aim is to communicate, not obfuscate.

That is why we should avoid the temptation of including everything, and instead make sure that we are using the visuals that are in line with the purpose of our communication.

In the latter part of this book we will look at some aspects of data visualisation that will help us make decisions about the best way to present our results. Bear in mind that this part of the statistical work has a firm overlap with design and as such it may be a good opportunity to add your own creative flare to the work you do. Having said that, be mindful of adding extra design elements that may end up distorting or adding ambiguity to the statistical message.

OK, let us get started with a bit of Python!

2

Python Programming Primer

PYTHON PROGRAMMING IS A LOT of fun. No wonder
the language is becoming ever more popular and used
in academic and commercial settings. As programming
languages go, Python is versatile and with a very gentle
learning curve. The emphasis it puts on readability and
productivity does help its cause.

Python was created around 1989 by Guido van Rossum
who continued to be Python's *Benevolent Dictator for Life*
until his "permanent vacation" announcement in 2018. He
named the language after the British comedy troupe *Monty
Python* and it has nothing to do with the snake that bears
the same name. In this chapter we will cover some of the
most important aspects of programming with Python. As a
modern language, Python exploits the paradigms of object
orientation and a lot can be said about this. However, we
are not going to cover those aspects of the language here,
instead we will concentrate on the basics that enable the use
of programming in an interactive way.

This is a title given to some open-
source software development
leaders who have the final say in
disputes or arguments within the
community.

Python's attention to readability means that almost anyone can pick up a piece of code and understand what the programme is doing. We mentioned above that Python can be used interactively which is enabled by the fact that Python is an interpreted language. This means Python executes code without having to translate it into machine-language instructions. In contrast, compiled languages such as C/C++, FORTRAN or Java get executed by the computer's CPU. It can be argued that interpreted code may run less quickly than compiled code, but by the same token we can execute the same programme on multiple platforms without modification.

Readability is an important part of Python.

The Python programmer community has the advantage that the standard library of the language is quite powerful and comprehensive. Sometimes this is referred to as having "batteries included". Some of those batteries are things such as working with file system directories and reading files, manipulating strings, parsing JSON and XML, handling CSV files and database access, multiprocessing, mathematics, etc. Some of the more idiosyncratic features of the language include the use of indentation to mark blocks of data, the lack of punctuation to mark the code statements and the use of idiomatic shorthand notation known as "pythonic style".

We call ourselves a Pythonistas.

The use of indentation is an important feature of Python.

If you are a seasoned ninja Pythonista you may want to skip this chapter. You may be interested in a refresher and if so you are more than welcome to continue reading. If you are a newcomer to the Pythonista community, you are welcome. Please do take a look at this chapter and enjoy the party.

2.1   Talking to Python

HAVING A DIALOGUE IS AN enriching experience, from talking to friends and family to interacting with colleagues and collaborators. Performing data analysis as a form of dialogue with our data is a more rewarding exercise that can tell us where to move next depending on the answers we are getting. The capabilities that Python offers us in this regard are well suited. Not only are we able to run batch scripts to perform an established pattern of analysis and even produce reports programmatically, but we are also able to establish a dialogue with the data we are analysing thanks to the flexibility and interactivity provided by the Python ecosystem.

> Python is a very versatile general-purpose programming language.

Python in an interpreted language. This means that the programmes we write are executed one statement at a time. In a simplified way, we are asking the computer to read the statements provided, evaluate them, provide us with an answer and move to the next statement. This cycle is sometimes called REPL:

> Python is an interpreted language.

1. **R**ead the user input.

2. **E**valuate the commands provided.

3. **P**rint any results if available.

4. **L**oop back to step 1.

> The all-important REPL enables interactivity.

The REPL is one of the most attractive features of Python. One implementation that has gained the hearts of many data scientists and statisticians, as well as scientists in general, is the Jupyter notebook. The notebook gives us a fully fledged IDE that lives in a plain JSON file and is rendered as a website. We can use the REPL to ask Python to extract, load and transform our data in an interactive manner, executing code in each of the cells in the notebook. Interactivity is not exclusive of the Jupyter notebook, indeed this can be achieved even with an interactive terminal such as the iPython shell, but it may not be an experience rated highly by all.

> IDE stands for Integrated Development Environment.

Another important feature that is often cited as an advantage of the Python ecosystem is the plethora of modules that are readily available to the Pythonista community. We will be discussing in more detail the use of some of those modules or libraries, but as a starter we can mention a few of the more popular ones used for statistical analysis and data science. For example, NumPy is a module that lets us carry out numerical analysis work extending Python to use multidimensional arrays and matrices. With this we can do computational linear algebra and other mathematical operations needed in statistical work. Further to that, we have the SciPy module which builds on the functionality provided by NumPy extending library to include implementations of functions and algorithms used in many scientific applications.

> This is sometimes described as having "batteries included".

> NumPy stands for Numerical Python.

> SciPy stands for Scientific Python.

As you can see, Python programmers are able to use the modularity of Python to extend existing libraries or modules. A great example of the power of that extensibility is the pandas module. It uses, among other modules,

NumPy and SciPy to enable us to carry out panel data analysis with the use of dataframes, i.e. extensions to the arrays used in NumPy for example. Within pandas we are able to do data manipulations and analysis including plotting. This is thanks to the use of a library widely used for visualisation purposed in Python: Matplotlib. In terms of statistical analysis, there are some useful implementations of algorithms used in the area within NumPy and SciPy. More targeted approaches are provided by modules such as Statsmodels for statistical modelling and Seaborn for statistical data visualisation.

Panel data analysis give pandas its name.

We have mentioned that Python is an interpreted language and this brings about another aspect that makes code written in Python flexible and portable. This means that unlike compiled programmes, the scripts we develop in Python can be executed in machines with different architectures and operating systems. Python interpreters are available in Windows, Mac and Unix/Linux systems and your work can be run in any of them, provided you have the correct version installed.

Python code is flexible and portable.

Talking about Python versions, in this book we are working with version 3.x. Remember that Python 2 was sunset on January 1, 2020. This means that there will be no more releases for that version and should there be any security patches needed or bugs that need fixing, there will not be any support from the community. If you or your organisation, school, university, or local Pythonista club are using Python 2, consider upgrading to the next version as soon as you can.

We will be working with version 3 of the Python distribution.

Python 2 was released in 2000, and was supported for 20 years, not bad!

If you want an easy way to install the latest version of the language, I usually recommend looking at the Anaconda distribution[1], built by Continuum Analytics. It offers an easy way to install Python and a number of modules that can get you ready to go in no time. You may also want to look at Miniconda in case you want a streamlined version of the distribution. If you do use it, please remember that you may have to install individual modules separately. You can do that with the help of package managers such as pip, easy-install, homebrew or others. As you can imagine, there are other ways to obtain Python and any of them should be suitable for the explanations and code that will be used in the rest of the book.

[1] Anaconda (2016, November). Anaconda Software Distribution. Computer Software. V. 2-2.4.0. https://www.anaconda.com

2.1.1   Scripting and Interacting

WE NOW UNDERSTAND THAT PYTHON can be used in an interactive manner. This can be done for instance in a terminal or shell to establish a dialogue with Python. This is only one part of the story. We can actually use Python in a more traditional way by writing the entire sequence of commands we need to execute and run them in one go without interrupting the computer. Depending on the type of analysis, you have the flexibility of using one approach or the other. In fact you can start with an interactive session and once you are happy with the results, you can save the commands in a stand-alone script.

You do not have to choose one over the other as Python is flexible enough to enable you to do both.

We mentioned above using a terminal or shell to interact with Python. A shell lets us access the command line interface, where we can input text to let our computer know what to do using text. In the case of Python we may want to use something like an iPython shell to run Python commands. Within the shell we can see the result of the commands we issue and be able to take the output of the latest code executed as input for the next. This is very useful in prototyping and testing.

iPython is an interactive command shell to write programmes in various languages including Python.

One disadvantage of using the shell directly is that, although we can interact with Python, we are not able to persist or save the programmes we write. In many cases you would like to save your programmes so that you can use them at a later point in time. In those cases you may want to use scripts. These are simple text files that can be executed with the Python interpreter. If you have saved your script with the name `myprogramme.py`, you can execute it from the terminal as follows:

Python scripts have the extension `.py`.

```
> Python myprogramme.py
```

We are assuming that the script has been saved in the local path. In this way we can run the programme as many times as we want; we can also add instructions and extend our analysis.

The command above is launched directly from the terminal; no need for the iPython shell.

For the purposes of the explanations and implementations shown in this book, we will make the assumption that you are using an interactive shell such as iPython. This will let us break the code as we go along, and when appropriate, we can see the output we are generating. You may decide to save the commands in a single script for reuse. The code will be presented with a starting diple (>) to indicate that a command has been entered In the shell. Here is an example:

```
>  365  -  323

42
```

We assume that you are using an interactive shell.

As you can see, when running this command Python prints out the answer. Remember that we are using the REPL and Python is printing the result of the operation for us.

See Section 2.1.

In other cases we may need to show more than one command in our explanations. In those cases we will be presenting the code in a script format and we will not show the diple. The same will be done for the cases where the REPL is not expected to print the result. For example, in the case of assigning a value to a variable, the interactive shell does not print anything. In this case the code will be presented as follows:

```
result = 365  -  323
```

If the REPL has nothing to print we will not show the shell prompt.

The commands we issue to communicate with Python are enough for the interpreter to know what it is required to do. However, with the principle of readability in mind, human interpreters or our code are better off when we provide extra explanations for what we are trying to achieve. This is where comments come in handy. A comment in Python is created with a hash symbol, #. Here is an example:

```
> pi = 3.141592    # An approximation of pi
```

A comment in Python is entered with the hash symbol, #.

In the example above we have assigned the value 3.141592 to the variable called pi and have done so with the help of the = sign. Note that Python is ignoring everything after the hash symbol. The most typical way to enter comments is to start a line with a hash. Including comments in our programme makes it easier for other programmers to understand the code. An added advantage of using comments is that we can remove some lines of code from execution without deleting them from our script. We simply comment them out, and if we need them again, we can always remove the hash.

See Section 2.6 for a better way of referring to π.

Please include comments in all your programmes, your future self will appreciate it!

2.1.2   Jupyter Notebook

HAVING INTERACTIVE SHELLS IS GREAT as we can see the outcome of the code we have written as it executes. In many cases this is enough but sometimes we would like a bit more than readability in a plain-looking terminal. Wouldn't it be great to be able to have that interactivity together with a way in which the comments we add are formatted nicely and even include pictures or plots as well as being able to share the script not only with other programmers but a more general audience?

Interactivity is the name of the game with Jupyter.

Well, all that and more is possible with the Jupyter notebook. As the name indicates, a notebook provides us with a way to keep our programmes or scripts annotated and we are able to run them interactively. Code documentation can be

Jupyter notebooks used to be called iPython notebooks.

done beyond the simple use of comments as the notebook understands markdown and it is presented as part of a a web-based interface.

A Jupyter notebook is effectively a JSON file and it lets us include plain text, mathematical expression and inline graphics as well as other rich media such as websites, images or video. The notebook format has the extension .ipynb so you can easily recognise one. In many cases though, it is not possible to open a notebook directly by double-clicking in the file. Instead, you open it via the Jupyter web interface. Portability is the name of the game with Jupyter notebooks and this means that we can convert our files into plain Python scripts or even create presentations, export to PDF or HTML and even LATEX files. Furthermore, the Jupyter project supports the use of other programming languages. We recommend that you use notebooks as you work through the content of the book. We will not show a Jupyter interface to facilitate readability for the book.

A notebook is effectively a JSON file.

Jupyter gets its name from for **Ju**-lia, **Py**-thon and **R**; some of the languages supported by the interface. Other kernels are available too.

2.2   *Starting Up with Python*

UP UNTIL NOW WE HAVE been talking about the benefits of using Python and how the interactive capabilities of an interpreted language are well suited to our needs in data analysis and statistics. Furthermore, in the brief examples above we have seen how Python uses well-known notation to perform arithmetic operations such as subtraction (-) and I am sure you can see how other operators fit in within that

Python can be used as a glorified calculator, but there is more to it than that!

syntax. These operators are shown in Table 2.1, perhaps the one operator that needs some attention is the exponentiation, which is represented with a double asterisk, **. These operators are available to be used with numbers, and like many other programming languages Python has types. Let us take a look.

Exponentiation is denoted with ** in Python.

Operation	Operator
Addition	+
Subtraction	-
Multiplication	*
Division	/
Exponentiation	**

Table 2.1: Arithmetic operators in Python.

2.2.1   Types in Python

IN PYTHON WE DO NOT need to declare variables before we use them and furthermore, we do not have to tell the interpreter what type the variables or objects are. Each variable we create is automatically a Python object. Instead, Python is a dynamically typed language. This means that the type of an object is checked as the code runs and the type is allowed to change over its lifetime. However, we still need to know some of the basic types supported in Python so that we can build other objects. Let us take a look.

Remember that Python is an object oriented language.

Python is a dynamically typed language: We do not need to specify the variable type in advance.

2.2.2   Numbers: Integers and Floats

AS YOU CAN IMAGINE, PYTHON can be used as a calculator and therefore supporting numbers is part and parcel of this use case. Python supports two basic number types: Integers and floating point numbers, in Python called floats. In that way it is possible for us to assign an integer value to a variable as follows:

Python supports integers and floating point numbers.

```
> magic = 3
```

Remember that assignation does not require Python to print anything as a result. It is possible for us to check the type of an object with the command type:

```
> type(magic)

int
```

The command type lets us see the type of an object.

Python will let us know what type of object we are dealing with; in this case the object magic is of type integer. Let us see an example for a floating point number:

```
> trick = 1.5
> type(trick)

float
```

We can see that this is a float object.

In this case we can see that the type of the object trick is float. Notice that since Python is dynamically typed we can mix integers and floats to carry out operations and the Python interpreter will make the appropriate conversion or casting for us. For example:

```
> trick2 = magic / trick
> print(trick2)


2.0
```

Python is able to make appropriate conversions or casting.

You can check that the result of the operation above results in a float:

```
> type(trick2)


float
```

The result has the expected type.

We can cast the type of a variable too. For example, if we require the result stored in trick2 to be an integer we can do the following:

```
> trick2 = int(trick2)
> type(trick2)


int
```

We can also request Python to cast values into the appropriate type.

We can see that if we print the value assigned to trick2 after the casting operation above, we get an integer. We can see that as it has no decimal part:

```
> print(trick2)


2
```

We are using functions to do the casting for us, these include:

- `int()` creates an integer number from an integer literal, a float literal by removing all decimals, or a string literal (so long as the string represents a whole number)

  A literal is a notation for representing a fixed value in source code.

- `float()` creates a float number from an integer literal, a float literal or a string literal (so long as the string represents a float or an integer)

- `str()` creates a string from a wide variety of data types, including strings, integer literals and float literals

Take a look at these examples:

```
x = float(1)   # x will be 1.0
y = int('2') # y will be 2 (an integer number)
z = str(6.3)  # z will be '6.3' (a string)
```

Applying casting in Python is easy.

We mentioned strings above, but we have not said what they are. Not to worry, let us string along.

2.2.3   *Strings*

A SEQUENCE OF CHARACTERS IS called a string. Strings in Python are defined by enclosing the characters in question in either single (' ') or double quotes ('' ''). Here are a couple of examples:

A string is a sequence of characters or text.

```
> example1 = 'This is a string'
> example2 = ''And this is also a string''
```

Strings can be used to print messages to the standard output with the help of the `print` function:

```
> print(example1)

'This is a string'

> print(example2)

'And this is also a string'
```

Strings in Python can be defined with single or double quotes.

We can check the type of example1 as we have done before:

```
> type(example1)

str
```

The type of a string is str.

As we can see the type of the variable is reported to be a str or a string.

Python knows how to add to numbers, and should we use the + operator between two strings, Python knows what to do. Instead of giving an error, it overloads the operator to concatenate the two strings:

```
> vulcan, salute = ''Live Long'', ''Prosper''
> print(vulcan + '   and   ' + salute)

Live Long and Prosper
```

Concatenation of strings can be achieved with the + symbol.

If you program in other languages, the statement above may look surprising. In Python is it possible to assign multiple values to multiple variables in one single line of code. This is part of the pythonic style of coding mentioned

at the beginning of this chapter. In the statement above
we are assigning the value "Live Long" to the variable
vulcan, whereas the variable salute has the value Prosper.
Furthermore, in the concatenation we have added the string
' and ' to get the traditional salute made famous by Mr.
Spock.

It is important to note that the operator would not work if
we were to mix strings and either floats or integers. Let us
take a look:

```
> print(vulcan + magic)

...

TypeError: can only concatenate str (not ''int'')
to str
```

We can see that Python is telling us in the error message
that we cannot concatenate the two values. Instead, we can
use casting to correct for this as follows:

```
> print(vulcan + str(magic))

'Live Long3'
```

Note that there is no space between the g and the 3
characters as we never asked for one!

Python also overloads the multiplication operator ∗ to be
used with strings and in this case it replicates the string. For
example:

```
> print(vulcan + ' and ' + 3*(salute + ' '))


'Live Long and Prosper Prosper Prosper '
```

Finally, it is possible to create strings over multiple lines
with the use of triple single or double quotes. This is also
useful to define docstrings for functions

```
> space = ''''''Space:
the final frontier.
These are the voyages of
the Starship, Enterprise.
''''''
```

More about docstrings in Section
2.5.

There are a few other tricks that strings can do and we will
cover some of those later on. One more thing to mention
about strings is that they are immutable objects. This means
that it is not possible to change individual elements of a
string. We shall discuss more about immutable objects in
the context of tuples in Section 2.3.3.

Strings in Python are immutable.

2.2.4 Complex Numbers

WE HAVE SEEN THAT PYTHON understands the use of
numbers such as integers and floats. If you are interested in
doing mathematical operations, we may also be interested in
using complex numbers too, and Python has you covered.
In a very engineering style, Python denotes the imaginary
number $i = \sqrt{-1}$ as j, and so for a number m, mj is
interpreted as a complex number.

Python calls the imaginary
number i j.

Let us see an example: If we want to define the complex number $z = 42 + 24i$ we simply tell Python the following:

```
> z = 42+24j
> print(z)


(42+24j)
```

As any complex number, we can get its real and imaginary parts. Let us take a look:

```
> print('The real part is {0}, \
  the imaginary part is {1}' \
.format(z.real, z.imag) )


The real part is 42.0, the imaginary part is 24.0
```

You can see that Python is casting the integer numbers used to define z as floats. The curious among you may have noticed a few interesting things in the string above. First, we have broken out our statement into several lines of code with the use of a backslash (\). This helps with readability of the code. Furthermore, we have used a string method called format that helps format specified values and insert them in the given placeholders denoted by the number inside curly brackets. In that way, the value of z.real is replaced in the {0} placeholder for example.

You may also have noticed that we have referred to the real and imaginary parts with .real and .imag. These are methods of the complex type. This makes sense when we remember that each entity in Python is an object. Each

Complex numbers in Python are not complicated!

The backslash allows us to break a line.

The method of an object can be invoked by following the name of object with a dot (.) and the name of the method.

object has a number of possible actions they are able to perform, i.e. methods.

There is an alternative way to define a complex number in Python: The complex() function:

```
> x, y = complex(1, 2), complex(3, 4)
```

We can also create complex numbers with complex().

As you can imagine, Python knows how to do complex arithmetics:

```
print('Addition =', x + y)
print('Subtraction =', x - y)
print('Multiplication =', x * y)
print('Division =', x / y)


print('Conjugate =', x.conjugate())


Addition = (4+6j)
Subtraction = (-2-2j)
Multiplication = (-5+10j)
Division = (0.44+0.08j)
Conjugate = (1-2j)
```

Complex arithmetics in Python.

Python has a couple of modules that extend its functionality to define mathematical functions. For real numbers we can use math and for complex numbers we have cmath.

2.3   Collections in Python

AN ORGANISED GROUP OF OBJECTS acquired and maintained for entertainment, study, display or simply for fun is known

as a collection. I am sure you have one yourself, even if
you do not know it or want to admit it. Some of us collect
stamps, mugs, frogs or cats. Whatever you collect, each item
in your collection is important. The collection itself may get
bigger or smaller over time, and sometimes you would like
to know where each item is. Well, Python has a pretty good
idea of what collections are too and in fact they work in a
similar manner to the collection of ornamental plates you
keep in the attic.

Any similarities with actual
collections you may have are
purely coincidental.

A collection in Python is effectively a container type that is
used to represent different data type items as a single unit.
Depending on the use case, different collection types have
ways to manipulate data and manage storage. Python has
four collection types: **Lists, sets, tuples** and **dictionaries**.
Let us take a look at each of them. Collections are said to be
iterables. In Python an iterable is an object that can be used
as a sequence. We are able to loop over an iterable and thus
access the individual items. This, as we shall see, is a very
useful feature of the language.

Python has four collection types:
Lists, sets, tuples and dictionaries.

We talk about while loops in
Section 2.4.3 and for loos in
Section 2.4.4.

2.3.1   Lists

A LIST IS A USEFUL collection that I am sure you already
know how to use. We all maintain a list of things to do, or
a shopping list, or a list of friends and foes. In Python a list
is a very versatile type that puts items in a sequence. The
items in a Python list can be of different types and they can
be accessed one by one, they can be added or deleted, and
you can sort them or loop through them.

Python lists can have items of
different types.

STATISTICS AND DATA VISUALISATION WITH PYTHON 53

A list in Python is defined with square brackets, [ ]. Lists are mutable objects and therefore it is possible to change individual elements in a list. Furthermore the items in a list are ordered and we can have duplicates. Let us create a few simple lists:

A list is defined with square brackets [ ].

```
numbers = [1, 2, 3, 4, 5]
vulcan = [''wuhkuh'', ''dahkuh'', ''rehkuh'',
    ''kehkuh'', ''kaukuh'']
starships = [1701, ''Enterprise'', 1278.40,
    1031, ''Discovery'', 1207.3]
```

Yes, those are the numbers 1 to 5 in Vulcan!

We mentioned above that you can look at the individual items in our collection, and a list is no different. Since order is important in a list, we can refer to each of the elements in the list by their position. This is given by an index that is part of the list. We can do this as follows:

```
> print(numbers[0])

1

> print(vulcan[2:4])

['rehkuh', 'kehkuh']
```

We can refer to elements in a list with an index.

Note that we are referring to the first element in the list numbers with the index 0. If you were playing hide and seek with Python it would start counting as: "0, 1, 2, 3, . . .". In the second command above you can also see how we can refer to a sub-sequence in the list. This is often referred

Indexing in Python starts at zero.

to as slicing and dicing the sequence. We refer to the sub-
sequence with the help of a colon as start:end, where
start refers to the first element we want to include in
the sub-sequence and end is the last element we want to
consider in the slice.

Since Python counts from 0, the slicing notation means that
we are requesting for the last entry in our sub-sequence to
be the end-1 element of the original list. In our example, we
are asking for the sub-list to read item 2 and up to 4, but not
including 4. That is why only the third and fourth elements
of the vulcan list are returned.

> Slicing refers to the subsetting of an array-like object such as lists and tuples.

A more general way to obtain a slice of a list L sequence is
as follows:

$$L[\text{start} : \text{end} : \text{step}], \qquad (2.1)$$

which lets us traverse the list with an increment given by
step, which by default has the value 1. We can also omit the
start and/or end to let Python know that we want to start
at the beginning of the list and/or finish at the end of it.

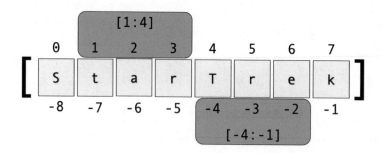

Figure 2.1: Slicing and dicing a list.

We can use negative indices to slice our list from the end. In
this case the last item has the index -1, the next one -2 and
so on. We can see how the indices and the slicing operator

work in the picture shown in Figure 2.1. We can think of each of the letters shown to be individual items in a list. However, you may be surprised to find out that strings can actually be sliced and diced in the same way as lists. Let us look at slicing the word shown in Figure 2.1:

```
> L = 'StarTrek'
> print(L)
'StarTrek'


> L[0]
'S'


>L[1:4]
'tar'


> L[-4:-1]
'Tre'
```

Strings are sequences of characters and we can slice them and dice them too.

List are mutable objects and this means that we can change individual items in the list. Let us create a list to play with:

Remember, however, that strings are immutable! In this case we have a list of characters and that can be modified.

```
> scifi = ['S','t','a','r','T','r','e','k']
> scifi[4]


'T'
```

Let us change the name of our favourite Sci-Fi saga by changing the last four items in our list:

```
> scifi[4:] = 'W','a','r','s'
> print(scifi)


['S', 't', 'a', 'r', 'W', 'a', 'r', 's']
```

Here we are changing the last 4 items in our list.

We have changed the item with index 4 to be the letter "W", index 5 to "a" , 6 with "r" and 7 with "s".

Immutability also means that we can add elements to a list. We can do this with the append method:

```
> scifi.append('.')
> print(scifi)


['S', 't', 'a', 'r', 'W', 'a', 'r', 's','.']
```

append lets us add elements to a list.

The new element (a period .) is added to the scifi list at the end, increasing the length of the list by one element.

Concatenation of lists is easily achieved with the + operator. Let us concatenated the numbers and vulcan lists:

```
> print(numbers + vulcan)


[1, 2, 3, 4, 5, 'wuhkuh', 'dahkuh',
'rehkuh', 'kehkuh', 'kaukuh']
```

The + symbol lets us carry out list concatenation.

Since the order of elements in a list is important, the concatenation of lists is not commutative. In other words numbers + vulcan is not the same as vulcan + numbers. Another important thing to note is that lists are not arrays and this means that the + operator will not sum the elements of the list. We will talk about arrays in the next chapter.

We know that lists have order and as they are mutable we are able to change that order. In particular, we can sort the items in our collection. We do this with the sort method. Let us take a look:

Order is important in a list. sort is used to order a list *in place*.

```
> l1 = [21, 0, 3, 1, 34, 8, 13, 1, 55, 5, 2]
> print(l1)


[3, 6, 9, 2, 78, 1, 330, 587, 19]
```

We can now call the sort method as follows:

```
> l1.sort()
> print(l1)


[0, 1, 1, 2, 3, 5, 8, 13, 21, 34, 55]
```

Using sort orders a list in ascending order.

Note that since this is a method, we call it with the dot (.) notation. The sorting is done in place and this means that now our list has changed. We can see that when we print the list we get the Fibonacci numbers from our original list in ascending order. If we wanted them in reverse order we simply pass this as a parameter as follows:

```
> l1.sort(reverse=True)


[55, 34, 21, 13, 8, 5, 3, 2, 1, 1, 0]
```

We can use reverse to order in reverse.

58   J. ROGEL-SALAZAR

Python also has functions that can act on objects. In this
case there is a function for lists that can help us order the
items. This is the sorted function and the difference is that
the function will create a new object rather than changing
the original:

Lists have a sorted function.

```
> l1 = [21, 0, 3, 1, 34, 8, 13, 1, 55, 5, 2]
> print(sorted(l1))


[0, 1, 1, 2, 3, 5, 8, 13, 21, 34, 55]
```

A new object is created, the
original list is not changed.

We can check that the original object has not been modified
by printing it:

```
> print(l1)


[21, 0, 3, 1, 34, 8, 13, 1, 55, 5, 2]
```

In principle we could have assigned the result of applying
the sorted function to a new variable. In that way we can
refer to the newly created object at a later point in time.

As before, if we need the elements in descending order we
can simply pass the reverse parameter to the function:

```
> sorted(l1, reverse=True)


[55, 34, 21, 13, 8, 5, 3, 2, 1, 1, 0]
```

Once again we can use reverse to
obtain a list ordered in reverse.

The elements of a list can be other types of objects, for
example they can be other lists. Let us define a short list of
lists as follows:

```
> m = [[1,2], [2,3], [3,4]]
```

The items in a list can be other collections, such as lists.

We can select items in the list:

```
> print(m[2])

[3,4]
```

and continue drilling down to obtain the sub-elements in the lists that comprise the main list:

The same slicing and dicing operations can be applied to them.

```
> m[2][1]

4
```

We can obtain the length of a list with the len function. For example:

```
> print(len(m))

3
```

The length of a list can be obtained withe len function.

In this case we can see that the list m has 3 elements.

Please note that it is not possible to simply copy a list by assignation. In other words list2 = list1 does not result in a copy of list1. Instead it is a reference to it and any changes made to list1 will be made to list2. If you require a copy, you need to use the copy() method. Other methods you can use with lists can be seen in Table 2.2.

We cannot copy a list by assignation. We use the copy() method instead.

List method	Description
append(item)	Add item at the end of the list
clear()	Remove all items
copy()	Copy the list
count(value)	Number of items with the given value
extend(iterable)	Add items of an iterable at the end of the current list
index(value)	Index of the first item with the given value
insert(position, item)	Add item at the specified position
pop(position)	Remove item at given position
remove(value)	Remove item with given value
reverse()	Reverses the order of the list
sort(reverse=True|False, key=func)	Sort the list, func is a function to specify sorting

Table 2.2: List methods in Python.

2.3.2   List Comprehension

THERE IS A VERY PYTHONIC way of creating lists. This is known as *list comprehension* and it lets us create a new list based on the items of an existing one. For example, we can take a list of numbers and create a new one whose elements are the square of the original items:

List comprehension is a very pythonic way of creating lists.

```
> l2 = [x**2 for x in l1]
> print(l2)


[441, 0, 9, 1, 1156, 64, 169, 1, 3025, 25, 4]
```

In a more traditional way, the code above could be written in an explicit for loop using a counter. As we shall see, we do not need counters in Python when using an iterator and this can be used to our advantage as we can include the for loop inside the list definition as shown above.

We will cover the use of for loops in Section 2.4.4.

Moreover, the syntax can accommodate the use of a condition too. The full syntax is as follows:

$$\text{newlist} \quad = \quad [\text{ expression } \textbf{for} \text{ item } \textbf{in} \text{ iterable}$$
$$\textbf{if} \text{ condition == True]}. \qquad (2.2)$$

We will cover conditional statements in Section 2.4.2.

Let us look at an example:

```
> l3 = [ [x, x**2] for x in l1 if x <= 3]
> print(l3)


[[0, 0], [3, 9], [1, 1], [1, 1], [2, 4]]
```

In this case we are telling Python to create a list of lists. Each element in our list l3 is a list whose elements are a number and its square. We are reading the elements of list l1 and only applying the operation if the item from l1 is smaller or equal to 3. All that in a single line of pythonic code!

List comprehension is a compact way to do things in a single line of code.

2.3.3   Tuples

WE HAVE SEEN THAT A list is an ordered sequence that we can change. What happens if we want to use a sequence where order is important, but we also require it to be immutable? Well, the answer is that we need to use a tuple. The items of a tuple can also be of different types but immutability means that we are not able to change the items. Tuples support duplicate values too and we define a tuple in Python with round brackets, ( ), and each element in the tuple is separated with a comma.

Tuples are defined with round brackets ( ).

Let us take a look at some tuples:

```
numbers_tuple = (1, 2, 3, 4, 5)
vulcan_tuple = (''wuhkuh'', ''dahkuh'', ''rehkuh'',
    ''kehkuh'', ''kaukuh'')
starships_tuple = (1701, ''Enterprise'', 1278.40,
    1031, ''Discovery'', 1207.3)
```

These tuples contain the same items as the lists created in the previous section.

The items in the variables defined above are the same as in the previous section. The main difference is that these variables are tuples instead of lists. We can see this as they have been defined with round brackets. We can ask for the type to make sure:

```
> type(vulcan_tuple)

'tuple'
```

We know that tuples are iterables where order is important. This means that we can use the colon notation we learned in Section 2.3.1 to slice and dice our tuples:

```
> starships_tuple[1]
'Enterprise'


> numbers_tuple[3]
4


> vulcan_tuple[1:4]
('dahkuh', 'rehkuh', 'kehkuh')
```

Tuples can also be sliced with the help of an index.

Notice that in the example above, the result of the slicing command returns a sub-tuple. You can also use negative indices as we did for lists and the diagram shown in Figure 2.1.

As we have mentioned above, immutable objects cannot be changed. In other words, we cannot add or remove elements and thus, unlike lists, they cannot be modified in place. Let us see what happens when we try to change one of the elements of a tuple:

Tuples are immutable objects.

```
> starships_tuple[0] = 'NCC-1701'

...

TypeError: 'tuple' object does not support item
assignment
```

We are not able to change elements of a tuple as they are immutable objects.

Similarly we are not able to apply a method to sort a tuple in place. However, we can create a new list whose elements are the sorted items from the original tuple. We can do this with the sorted function. Let us define a tuple as follows:

```
> t1 = (21, 0, 3, 1, 34, 8, 13, 1, 55, 5, 2)
```

We can now apply the sorted function to the tuple:

```
> t2 = sorted(t1)
> print(t2)

[0, 1, 1, 2, 3, 5, 8, 13, 21, 34, 55]
```

The result of the sorted function on a tuple is a list.

We mentioned above that the result would be a list and we can see that, as the object above is printed with square brackets. We can check this with the type command:

```
>  type(t2)


list
```

The result of the function is a list.

This behaviour is due to the immutability of tuples. Since we cannot change the tuple directly we transform it into a list. This also means that the number of methods available for tuples is limited too, as shown in Table 2.3.

Tuple method	Description
count(value)	Number of items with the given value
index(value)	Index of the first item with the given value

Table 2.3: Tuple methods in Python.

Let us look at a couple of examples:

```
> t1.count(1)
2


> t1.index(1)
3
```

We can see that there are two items with the value 1 in the tuple t1, and that the first item with value 1 is in the position with index 3, i.e. the fourth element in the tuple. We can obtain the length of a tuple with the len function:

```
> len(vulcan_tuple)

5
```

The immutability of tuples may be a strange thing if you are coming from other programming languages. You may be asking yourself, why do they exist? Well, the answer is that their use indicates to other programmers, and indeed to the Python interpreter, that the programme contains an object that will never change, which means that they also offer some performance optimisations.

These are some reasons to use tuples.

A useful way to create a tuple is via the `zip()` function. It takes one or more iterables as input, and merges them item by item based on their indices. The result is a tuple **iterator**. An iterator is an object used to iterate over an iterable object. The iterator that results from the application of `zip()` yields tuples on demand and can be traversed only once. Let us zip the list `numbers` with the tuple `vulcan_tuple` as follows:

An iterator is an object used to iterate over an iterable object.

```
> translate = zip(numbers, vulcan_tuple)
> type(translate)

'zip'
```

The `zip()` function merges iterables by index.

As you can see, the result is an object of class `zip`. If you try to print the object directly, you get a strange result:

```
> print(translate)

<zip object at 0x7fd41092f380>
```

A zip object yields each item one at a time until the iterable is exhausted.

This is because we are trying to print an iterator. Instead, we need to ask Python to yield the items one by one until the iterable is exhausted. We can do this with a for loop as we will see in Section 2.4.4 or by passing the request to a list as follows:

```
> list_translate = list(translate)

[(1, 'wuhkuh'), (2, 'dahkuh'), (3, 'rehkuh'),
(4, 'kehkuh'), (5, 'kaukuh')]
```

We can cast the zip object into a list if required.

We can see how the association worked and we can use this as a form of dictionary to get the name of the numbers in vulcan. Perhaps though, we can use an actual dictionary for these purposes. Let us take a look.

2.3.4   Dictionaries

HOW DO WE GO ABOUT counting from 1 to 3 in Vulcan? Well, it is only logical to ask the Enterprise computer to give you some information and what we will get is effectively a dictionary. Like a human dictionary, a Python one lets us find the information associated with a key. We do not have to iterate over every entry in the dictionary to find the information, we simple search for it by key. A dictionary in Python is made out of *key* and *value* pairs.

Although the universal translator used by Starfleet command will make this unnecessary.

We define a dictionary in Python with the use of curly brackets, { }. Each key-value pair is constructed with a colon (:) between the key and the value and pairs are

We define a dictionary with curly brackets { }.

separated from each other by a comma. Let us take a look at some examples:

```
> enterprise = { 'James T. Kirk': 'Captain',
   'Spock': ['First Officer', 'Science Officer'],
   'Nyota Uhura': 'Communications Officer',
   'Pavel Chekov': ['Navigator',
     'Security/Tactical Officer'] }
```

With the dictionary above we can check the rank of each of the senior command officers on the Enterprise. The keys in this case are strings, and that is the typical case. In general the keys of a dictionary can be any immutable Python object including numbers, strings and tuples. The value associated with a particular key can be changed by reassigning the new value to the dictionary item with the correct key. This means that dictionaries are mutable and duplicate keys are not allowed.

> The keys can be any immutable object: Numbers, strings or tuples for example.

We can obtain the value for a given key as follows:

```
> enterprise['Spock']

['First Officer', 'Science Officer']
```

> We can query a dictionary by key.

In this case the result is a list. In general, the value associated with a key can be any object. Since the result of that particular entry is a list, we can ask for the n-th element of the list:

```
> enterprise['Spock'][1]


'Science Officer'
```

We can use nested slicing and dicing as required.

If we attempt to search for a key that does not exist, Python will let us know that there is an error.

```
> enterprise['Montgomery Scott']


...

KeyError: 'Montgomery Scott'
```

As expected, we cannot query for keys that do not exist.

However, as dictionaries are mutable we are able to add new key-value pairs:

```
> enterprise['Montgomery Scott'] = 'Engineer'
```

However, we can create new entries on the go.

Furthermore, we can change the value associated with a key simply by reassigning the new value. We can, for example, correct the rank of Scotty:

```
> enterprise['Montgomery Scott'] = 'Chief Engineer'
> enterprise['Montgomery Scott']


'Chief Engineer'
```

The values in a dictionary can be modified.

You may be interested in getting to see all the keys in the dictionary and there is a method that lets us do just that: keys():

```
> names = enterprise.keys()
> print(names)


dict_keys(['James T. Kirk', 'Spock', 'Nyota Uhura',
'Pavel Chekov', 'Montgomery Scott'])
```

A list of dictionary keys can be obtained with the keys() method.

The object created is a view object which provides a dynamic view of the dictionary's entries. They can be iterated over and work in a similar way to a list. Let us update our dictionary and print the content of names:

```
> enterprise['Leonard McCoy']='Chief Medical' \
  ' Officer'
> print(names)


dict_keys(['James T. Kirk', 'Spock', 'Nyota Uhura',
'Pavel Chekov', 'Montgomery Scott',
'Leonard McCoy'])
```

The keys() method creates a dynamic view that updates as the dictionary object changes.

As we can see, the addition of Mr McCoy to the dictionary was immediately picked up by the viewer object names, no need to update it separately. The same behaviour happens for two other methods, one to see all the values values() and one for the key-value pairs items():

```
> enterprise['Hikaru Sulu'] = 'Helmsman'
> rank = enterprise.values()
> pairs = enterprise.items()
```

The same behaviour is obtained with the values() and items() methods.

In the code above we have added Mr Sulu to our dictionary and created two new view objects, one with the values associated with the keys in the dictionary and a second one with the associated pairs. Let us look at the contents:

```
> print(names)

dict_keys(['James T. Kirk', 'Spock', 'Nyota Uhura',
'Pavel Chekov', 'Montgomery Scott',
'Leonard McCoy', 'Hikaru Sulu'])


> print(rank)

dict_values(['Captain', ['First Officer',
'Science Officer'], 'Communications Officer',
['Navigator', 'Security/Tactical Officer'],
'Chief Engineer', 'Chief Medical Officer',
'Helmsman'])


> print(pairs)

dict_items([('James T. Kirk', 'Captain'),
('Spock', ['First Officer', 'Science Officer']),
('Nyota Uhura', 'Communications Officer'),
('Pavel Chekov', ['Navigator',
'Security/TacticalOfficer']),
('Montgomery Scott', 'Chief Engineer'),
('Leonard McCoy', 'Chief Medical Officer'),
('Hikaru Sulu', 'Helmsman')])
```

The contents of the dynamic views created with keys(), values() and pairs() are kept up-to-date.

Note that the entries of the pairs() dynamic view are tuples containing the keys and values.

You can see that the view object that corresponds to the items in the dictionary is made of tuples containing the key and value for each entry.

In Section 2.3.2 we saw how list comprehension can help us create lists in a streamlined manner. We can apply the same logic to the creation of new dictionaries in Python. In this case we also use the pythonic style of multiple assignation. Dictionary comprehension is also able to take a condition if necessary. Let us create a dictionary out of the zipped translate object we created in Section 2.3.3:

We can create dictionaries with some dictionary comprehension.

```
> translate = zip(numbers, vulcan)
> vulcan_dict = {k:v for (k, v) in translate}
> print(vulcan_dict)


{1: 'wuhkuh', 2: 'dahkuh', 3: 'rehkuh',
4: 'kehkuh', 5: 'kaukuh'}
```

We use a zipped object to create a dictionary by comprehension.

We are taking each item in the zip object and assigning the values to two variables: k for the key and v for the value. We then use these variables to construct the entries of our new dictionary as k:v. The result is a new dictionary that works in the usual way.

```
> vulcan_dict[3]


'rehkuh'
```

With a zip object there is another more succinct way to create the dictionary without comprehension. We could have simply used the dict() function:

Remember that zip objects can only be used once! You may need to re-create translate to make this work.

```
vulcan_dict = dict(translate)
```

Dictionary method	Description
clear()	Remove all Items
copy()	Copy the dictionary
fromkeys(keys, val)	Dictionary with the given keys. val is optional and is applied to all keys
get(key)	Value of given key list
items()	View of all key-value pairs
keys()	View of all keys
pop(key)	Remove entry with given key
popitem()	Remove last inserted entry
setdefault(key, val)	Returns the value of specified key. If key does not exist it inserts it with the specified val
update(dict)	Inserts dict into the dictionary
values()	View of all the values

Table 2.4: Dictionary methods in Python.

In Table 2.4 we can see some of the dictionary methods we have described along with others that can be useful in your work.

2.3.5   Sets

A SET IS A COLLECTION that covers some aspects that are not included in the collections we have discussed so far. If you remember your set theory course from school, using Venn diagrams and things like intersections, unions and differences, then you are ready to go. No worries if that is not the case, we shall cover this below.

A set is an unordered collection without duplicates.

In Python, a set is an unordered collection whose elements are unique and they cannot be changed, although we can add new ones. We can create a set with the use of curly brackets, { }. We used them to create dictionaries, but in this case we have single elements separated by commas

We can create a set with curly brackets { }. Do not confuse this with dictionaries!

instead of key-value pairs. Let us create an initial set based on Cylons:

```
significant_seven = {1, 2, 3, 4, 5,
    6, 6, 6, 6, 6, 6,
    8, 8}
> type(significant_seven)

set
```

Here we have several copies of each Cylon model.

We can see that the type of the object `significant_seven` is a `set`. You can see that the definition above has multiple copies of some of our favorite antagonist characters in Sci-Fi. However, it does not matter how many copies we have of each model, there are only 7 models in this set. So, there may be a Sharon "Boomer" Valerii as a sleeper agent in Galactica, or a Sharon "Athena" Agathon in Caprica, but both are a Cylon 8 model. The same with the many copies of Cylon model 6: Caprica Six talking to Baltar, or Gina Inviere in *Pegasus* or Natalie leading the rebels versus Cylon model 1. All of them are instances of the same model and the set should only contain one entry for them. Let us see if that is the case in our set:

No matter how many copies there are, there are only 7 significant models.

Other notable 6s include Shelly Godfrey, Lida and Sonja.

```
> print(significant_seven)

{1, 2, 3, 4, 5, 6, 8}
```

Here is the set of the Significant Seven Cylons.

An alternative way to create a set is via the `set()` method. All we have to do is pass an iterable with the elements that need to be included in the set. Let us create some sets with the rest of the Cylon models. First, there is of course the extinct model 7 dubbed "Daniel":

```
> extinct = set([7])
```

We can create sets with set().

Finally, we cannot forget to mention the final five:

```
> final_five = set(['Saul Tigh', 'Galen Tyrol',
    'Samuel T. Anders', 'Tory Foster',
    'Ellen Tigh'])
```

Let us create a set with the Final Five Cylons.

Please note that the items that we use to create a set have to be immutable, otherwise Python will complain. For example, if you pass a list an error is returned:

```
> error = {'end', ['of', 'line']}

...

TypeError: unhashable type: 'list'
```

The input to create sets must be immutable objects. Otherwise we get an error.

However, we are able to pass a tuple, because they are immutable:

```
> noerror = {'end', ('of', 'line')}
> noerror

{('of', 'line'), 'end'}
```

Using tuples as input is fine.

If we pass a string to the set() method we obtain a set of characters in the string:

```
> species = 'cylon'
> letters = set(species)
> print(letters)


{'c', 'l', 'n', 'o', 'y'}
```

Creating a set with a string results in a set of characters.

However, items placed in curly brackets are left intact:

```
> {species}


{'cylon'}
```

Note that passing a string directly inside curly brackets leaves the object intact.

We can have empty sets; we simply pass no arguments to the set() method, or include no elements in between the curly brackets:

```
> human_model = {}
```

Empty sets are easily created.

We can check the size of a set with the len() method:

```
> len(final_five)


5
```

We can check for membership using the in keyword:

```
> 'Laura Roslin' in final_five
False


>'Galen Tyrol' in final_five
True
```

The in keyword lets us check for membership.

Phew! So we know that President Roslin is not a Cylon but Senior Petty Officer Galen Tyrol is indeed a Cylon!

Spoiler alert!!!

A lot of the operations that we have used for other collections are not possible for sets. For instance, they cannot be indexed or sliced. Nonetheless, Python provides a whole host of operations on set objects that generally mimic the operations that are defined for mathematical sets.

One of the most important operations to carry out over a set is the union. A union contains all the items of the sets in question and any duplicates are excluded. We can create the union of sets with the union method:

A union contains all the items of the sets in question.

```
> humanoid_cylons = significant_seven.union(
    final_five)
```

Another way to obtain the union of sets is with the pipe operator |. Note that it lets us get the union of more than two sets:

```
> cylons=significant_seven | final_five | extinct

{1, 2, 3, 4, 5, 6, 7, 8,
 'Ellen Tigh',  'Galen Tyrol',
 'Samuel T. Anders',  'Saul Tigh',
 'Tory Foster'}
```

We can obtain the union with .union() or |.

Let us create a new set containing some of the officers in Galactica:

```
> officers = set(['William Adama',
   'Saul Thigh', 'Kara Thrace',
   'Lee Adama', 'Galen Tyrol',
   'Sharon Valerii'])
```

Another important operation is the intersection of sets. The operation results in the items that exist simultaneously in each of the sets in question. We can use the intersection() method or the & operator. Let us see who are the Cylons in our officers set:

The intersection gives us the items that exist simultaneously in each of the sets in question.

```
> officers & cylons


{'Galen Tyrol', 'Saul Tigh'}
```

We can obtain the intersection with .intersection() or &.

This will give us a set that contains those who are officers in Galactica and who are also Cylons. In this case, this corresponds to Chief and Galactica's XO. Well, our Cylon detector needs to be better, right? We could detect the presence of two of the final five, but a copy of model number 8 has infiltrated Galactica. Let us try to rectify this situation.

Our Cylon detector needs to be improved!

We can do this by adding elements to the set. Although the elements in a set are immutable, sets themselves can be modified. We can add elements one by one with add() or update the set with the union of sets using update():

```
> cylons.update(['Sharon Valerii',
   'Sharon Agathon'])
```

We can add elements to a set with .update().

Let us see if our Cylon detector is working a bit better. We can run the intersection operation on the updated set and officers:

```
> officers & cylons

{'Galen Tyrol', 'Saul Tigh', 'Sharon Valerii'}
```

We can now detect the Cylon infiltrator!

There you go, we can now detect the presence of the Cylon infiltrator!

It is possible to check for humans in the officers set by taking out the Cylons. We can do this with the difference() method, which will return the set of elements that are in the first set but not in the second. The same operation can be done with the minus sign (-):

The difference is the set of elements that are in the first set but not in the second.

```
> officers - cylons

{'Kara Thrace', 'Lee Adama', 'William Adama'}
```

We can use .difference() or -.

With the difference operation we go through the sets from left to right. This means that the operation is not commutative. Let us take a look:

```
> cylons - officers

{1, 2, 3, 4, 5, 6, 7, 8,
'Ellen Tigh', Samuel T. Anders',
'Sharon Agathon', 'Tory Foster'}
```

The set difference is not commutative.

We may be interested in getting all the elements that are in either of two sets but not in both. In this case we can use the symmetric_difference operation. This is effectively equivalent to subtracting the intersection of the sets in question. For more than two sets we can use the ^ operator too. Let us take a look at the symmetric difference of officers and cylons:

The symmetric difference gives us the elements that are in either of two sets but not in both.

```
> officers ^ cylons

{1, 2, 3, 4, 5, 6, 7, 8, 'Ellen Tigh',
'Kara Thrace', 'Lee Adama',
'Samuel T. Anders', 'Sharon Agathon',
'Tory Foster', 'William Adama'}
```

We can use symmetric_difference or ^.

Set method	Description
add(item)	Add item to the set
clear()	Remove all elements
copy()	Copy the set
difference(set)	Difference between sets
discard(item)	Remove item from set. If item not in set return None
intersection(set)	Intersection of sets
isdisjoint(set)	Check if two sets have a intersection
issubset(set)	Check if another set contains this one
issuperset(set)	Check if this set contains another one
pop(item)	Return and remove item from set
remove(item)	Remove item from set. If item not in set raise an error
symmetric_difference(set)	Symmetric difference between sets
union(set)	Union of sets
update(set)	Update set with the union of this set and others

Table 2.5: Set methods in Python.

There are a number of other methods that we can use with sets and some of them are shown in Table 2.5.

2.4   *The Beginning of Wisdom: Logic & Control Flow*

WE HAVE NOW A BETTER understanding of how Python works and some of the types and objects that are available to us out of the box. However, as Mr. Spock has said, *"Logic is the beginning of wisdom, not the end,"* and indeed we are able to use some wisdom in Python thanks to the logical operators available to us. With them we are able to control the flow of a programme to construct algorithms.

algorithm = logic + control flow

In Python, line breaks and indentation define blocks of code. This means that in Python, whitespace is important. Unlike other programming languages, there are no curly brackets to define blocks, or there is no need for other extra symbols like semicolons. There is, however, the need to use a colon to start classes, functions, methods, and loops as we shall see. It is only logical to get started.

Whitespace is a meaningful character in Python.

2.4.1   *Booleans and Logical Operators*

WE HAVE DISCUSSED SOME OF the types in Python including integers, floats and strings. One type that we have not mentioned yet is the Boolean type. Boolean values represent one of two values: `True` or `False`. Please note that in Python we write these two values with capital letters. We get these values when we run comparisons between two values, for example:

Boolean values are `True` or `False`.

```
> print(42>10)

True

> print(2001<=1138)

False
```

The result of comparisons return Boolean values.

As we can see Python returns True for the first comparison and False for the second comparison. We can see that the type of the result is a bool:

```
> type(42>10)

bool
```

In Python we can combine our comparisons to perform logical operations such as and, or and not. In Table 2.6 we can see the comparison and logical operators available to us. We can use this to create more complex comparisons as in the next examples:

```
> a = 75 != 75
> (51 > 33) and a

False

> (72 > 32) and ((94 == 87) or not a)

True
```

We can combine our comparisons to perform logical operations such as and, or and not.

Operation	Operator
Equal	==
Different	!=
Greater than	>
Less than	<
Greater or equal to	>=
Less or equal to	<=
Object identity	is
Negated object identity	is not
Logical AND	and
Logical OR	or
Logical NOT	not

Table 2.6: Comparison and logical operators in Python.

Boolean operators are a must when having to write programmes in any language as they let us make decisions about the flow of our analysis or algorithm execution. This is what we call control flow. Let us look at controlling the flow of our programmes in Python.

We can use the result of logical operations to control the flow of our programmes.

2.4.2 Conditional Statements

BEING ABLE TO DECIDE WHAT to do next depending on the result of a previous operation is an important part of programming. We can do this with the help of the Boolean operations we discussed in Section 2.4.1. A conditional statement lets us decide what to do if a condition is fulfilled, otherwise we can take a different action or actions, as we can add other conditions too. In Python we can do this with the following syntax:

A conditional statement lets us decide what to do if a condition is True or not.

```
if expression1:
    block of code executed
    if expression1 is True
elif expression2:
    block of code executed
    if expression2 is True
...
elif expressionN:
    block of code executed
    if expressionN is True
else:
    block of code executed
    if no conditions are True
```

The if... elif... else... lets us test various conditions and create branches for our code.

We can see a diagram representing the control flow of a conditional statement in Figure 2.2.

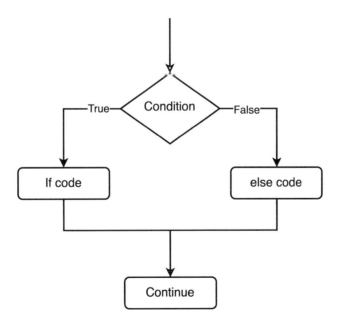

Figure 2.2: Conditional control flow.

Please note that each block of actions after each test expression is indented at the same level. The moment we go back to the previous indentation level, the block is automatically finished. Note that the colon (:) following each expression is required.

Indentation is important in Python.

The expressions we can test can be simple comparisons or more complex expressions that combine the logical operators and, or and not. We can test as many conditions as we require with the help of the "else if" operand elif. The conditions are tested in the order we have written them and the moment one condition is met, the rest of the conditions are not tested.

The conditions to test are logical expressions that evaluate to True or False.

```
> president = 'Laura Roslin'


> if president in cylons:
      print(''We have a problem!'')
  elif president in officers:
      print(''We need an election!'')
  else:
      print(''Phew! So say we all!'')


Phew! So say we all!
```

Hurrah!

In this case our expression is given by checking set membership. We are interested to know what to do if our Cylon detector tells us whether President Roslin is a Cylon, or whether she is part of the military and democracy has been put in jeopardy. In this case we can breathe as things are all good.

2.4.3   *While Loop*

REPEATING A SET OF ACTIONS is also a typical thing to do
in programming. Sometimes we do not necessarily know
how many times we need to repeat the actions and we only
stop when a condition is met. In this case we need to apply
a while loop.

A while loop is depends on the
result of a condition.

```
while condition:
    block of code to be executed
    don't forget to update the test variable
```

See Figure 2.3 for a diagrammatic representation of the
syntax above.

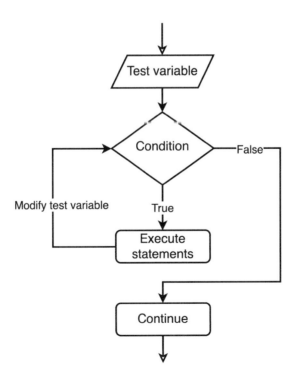

Figure 2.3: While loop control
flow.

You can see a couple of things that are similar to the syntax we saw for conditional statements. First, we need a colon after the condition. Second, the block of code that is executed as long as the condition is `True` is indented. One more example where whitespace is important in Python.

Please note that if the condition is not `True` at the beginning of the loop, the block of code will never execute. Also, you need to remember that the test variable in the condition needs to be updated as part of the block of code. Otherwise you end up with an infinite loop and Python will continue repeating the block forever.

The while loop requires a logical test at the beginning of the block.

We can see how this works for the Enterprise. So long as there is enough dilithium, Captain Picard is able to ask the crew to engage the engine:

```
> dilithium = 42
> while dilithium > 0:
      print('Engage!')
      dilithium -= 10


Engage!
Engage!
Engage!
Engage!
Engage!
```

Note that `dilithium -= 10` is a shorthand for `dilithium = dilithium - 10`.

As soon as the dilithium reserves are exhausted, we are not able to continue warping around space, the final frontier.

2.4.4   For Loop

WHEN WE KNOW HOW MANY times we need to repeat an
action, we are better off using a for loop. Either the number
of rounds is provided in advance or, as is typical in Python,
we traverse an iterable object such as a list, tuple or a string.
Since Python has access to the length of the iterable the
number of rounds is determined. In Figure 2.4 we can see
how this works. The syntax for a for loop is as follows:

In a for loop we know how
many times our code needs to be
repeated.

```
for item  in  sequence:
    block of code to be
    executed
```

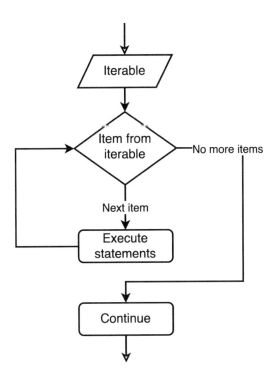

Figure 2.4: For loop control flow.

Once again we have the colon after defining the sequence to loop over and the indentation to define the actions that need repeating. Let us salute each of the Galactica officers we know:

```
> for officer in officers:
        print('Salute, {0}!'.format(officer))


Salute, Lee Adama!

Salute, Saul Tigh!

Salute, Kara Thrace!

Salute, William Adama!

Salute, Sharon Valerii!

Salute, Galen Tyrol!
```

This is the same basic structure used in list comprehension. See Section 2.3.2.

Let us rewrite the code for Captain Picard and define a range for the dilithium available to the Enterprise:

```
> for dilithum in range(42,0,-10):
        print('Engage!')


Engage!

Engage!

Engage!

Engage!

Engage!
```

range enables us to define a sequence of numbers as an object. This means that the values are generated as they are needed.

In the example above we used the range(start, end, step) function to generate a sequence of numbers from start to end−1 in steps given by step.

2.5   *Functions*

THAT HAS BEEN A WARP! Now that we have a good
understanding of the fundamentals of Python, we are able
to continue expanding our code to achieve specific goals we
have in mind. Many times those goals can be attained by
applying the same set of instructions. For instance, we know
that Captain Picard prefers his beverage to be *Tea. Earl Grey.
Hot* so we may be able to put together the steps in a block of
code under the name `picard_beverage` to get the Captain's
order right every time.

A function is a block of code
which can be run any time it is
invoked.

We are talking about creating a function with a given name.
The function may have input parameters and may be able to
return a result. In Python, the syntax to build a function is
as follows:

```
def my_function(arg1, arg2=default2,... \
                argn=defaultn):
    '''Docstring (optional) '''


    instructions to be executed
    when executing the function


    return result # optional
```

The function definition starts with
the word `def`.

We define a function with the keyword `def` at the beginning
of our block. As before, we need a colon at the end of the
first line and the block of code that forms the function is
indented. Here is what our `picard_beverage` function may
look like:

```
def picard_beverage():
    ''' Make Captain Picard's beverage '''
    beverage = 'Tea. '
    kind = 'Earl Grey. '
    temperature = 'Hot.'
    result = beverage + kind + temperature
    return result
```

Not quite a replicator, but hey!

We can run the code by calling the function:

```
> picard_beverage()

Tea. Earl Grey. Hot.
```

In this case our function is not taking any arguments and it returns a string as output. In general a function is able to take arguments arg1, arg2,... , argn that can be used in the block of code that makes up our function. It is possible to define default values for some of these parameters. Parameters with default values must be defined last in the argument list.

In the syntax shown above you can see a line of code that starts with triple quotes. This is called a *documentation string* and it enables us to describe what our function does. You can take a look at the contents as follows:

A documentation string enables us to provide information about what a function does. Make sure you use it!

```
> print(picard_beverage.__doc__)

Make Captain Picard's beverage
```

Let us define a function to calculate the area of a triangle given its base and height:

```python
def area_triangle(base, height=1.0):
    '''Calculate the area of a triangle'''
    area = base * height / 2
    return area
```

We are defining a default value for the parameter *height*.

Notice that height has been given the default value of 1. This means that we are able to call this function with one parameter, which will be used for the base, and the function will use the default value for height.

```python
> a = area_triangle(50)
> print(a)


25.0
```

The arguments are passed to the function in round brackets.

In this case we are giving the function only one argument such that the value of 50 is assigned to the base of the triangle and the height is automatically assumed to be 1. We can provide the second argument to override the default value for height:

```python
> a1 = area_triangle(50, 4)
> print(a1)


100.0
```

A function can be called simply using its name and any required input parameters.

The functions we define can make use of the control flow commands that we have discussed and make decisions depending on the parameters provided by the user. For example we can create a function to convert temperatures from centigrade to Fahrenheit and vice versa. We can convert from centigrade to Fahrenheit with the following formula:

$$F = \frac{9}{5}C + 32, \qquad (2.3)$$

and from centigrade to Fahrenheit with:

$$C = (F - 32)\left(\frac{5}{9}\right). \qquad (2.4)$$

This may be handy in determining the temperature of Captain Picard's beverage.

Let us take a look at creating a function to do the conversion:

```
def conv_temp(temp, scale):
  s = 'Converting {0} {1}'.format(temp, scale)
  if scale == 'C':
    print(s)
    result = (temp * 9/5) + 32
  elif scale == 'F':
    print(s)
    result = (temp - 32) * 5/9
  else:
    print('Please use C or F for the scale')
  return result
```

We are required to provide a temperature and the scale used for that temperature. When we pass the scale C, the temperature is measured in centigrade and we convert it to Fahrenheit. However, if the scale is F, we are converting from Fahrenheit to centigrade. Notice that if we use any

other character the function does not make any conversions
and instead it tells us what scales to use. Let us convert 451
Fahrenheit to centigrade:

```
> conv_temp(451, 'F')


Converting 451 F

232.77777777777777
```

We can try to improve the
presentation of the result... oh
well! We show how to do that
later.

In some cases we may not need to define a full function as
before and instead create an anonymous function that has
a single expression. This is called a lambda function and
there is no need to name the function, we simply use the
following syntax:

```
lambda arg1, arg2, ... : expression
```

A lambda function in Python is
an anonymous function created at
runtime.

where, as before, arg1, arg2,... are the input parameters
and expression is the code to be executed with the input
provided.

For example, if we require to calculate the square of a
number, we could try the following code:

```
sq = lambda n: n*n
```

In this case the object sq is a
lambda function that can be called
as any other function in Python.

We can then use the object sq as a function. For instance let
us calculate the square of 3:

```
> sq(3)


9
```

What about if we had a list of numbers and we require to obtain the square of the items in the list. Well, no problem, we can use our lambda function in a list comprehension.

```
> num = [4,14, 42, 451]
> [sq(n) for n in num]


[16, 196, 1764, 203401]
```

List comprehension with a lambda function, a pythonic way of writing code!

With functions we are able to create reusable pieces of code that can be used to carry out a specific task and make our programmes more readable. As we create more functions to do things for us we can put them together to create useful scripts and modules.

2.6   Scripts and Modules

WRITING COMMANDS TO ASK THE computer to do things for us is lots of fun. However, if we had to retype everything every time we need to execute the commands, things become rather tedious very quickly. Instead, we would prefer to have the capability of writing our commands and saving them for later use. We are able to do this with the help of scripts in Python. These scripts or programmes are plain text files with the extension .py. Furthermore, if we use the interactivity provided by Jupyter, it is also possible

A script is a way to save our programmes to be run any time we want.

to save our notebooks in a JSON formatted notebook with the extension .ipynb.

Python has the advantage of being cross-platform. This means that we can execute our script in any computer that has a Python interpreter with the correct version. All we need to do is open a terminal and invoke Python followed by the name of the file that contains our commands. In the example below we have a script that defines a function called main(). It asks users for a temperature and scale, then makes use of the function conv_temp we created earlier to convert the temperature from one scale to the other one. Finally, the main() function is executed in the same script. Let us tale a look:

We are not showing the conv_temp function in the code below. Make sure that you save both in the same script.

```
def main():
    '''Convert temperature provided
    by the user '''
    t = input('Give me a temperature: ')
    t = float(t)
    s = input('C or F? ')
    res = conv_temp(t, s)
    if s == 'C':
        print('{0} C is {1:.2f} F'.format(t, res))
    elif s == 'F':
        print('{0} F is {1:.2f} C'.format(t, res))
    else
        print('Try again!')


main()
```

We are defining a main function in this programme and calling it with the command main().

Note how we are formatting the result to show only two decimal places.

We can save this function together with the definition of
conv_temp in a file called convert_user_temperature.py.
In this case we are asking the user for a temperature t and
the scale (C or F). This is provided to us via the input()
command. We need to ensure that the value is cast as a float.
Finally, the conversion is made with the conv_temp function
and the result is printed.

input() stores values as strings.
In this case we need to ensure the
values are floats.

Now that we have saved the script we are able to execute it.
Open a terminal, navigate to the place where the script is
saved and type the following command:

```
> python convert_user_temperature.py


Give me a temperature: 451
C or F? F


Converting 451.0 F
451.0 F is 232.78 C
```

Here we have handled the number
of decimal places better than
before!

This is great, we can rerun this script over and over and
obtain the results required. We may envisage a situation
where other functions to transform different units are
developed and expand our capabilities until we end up with
enough of them to create a universal converter. We may
decide to put all these functions under a single umbrella
and make it available to others. This is what a module in
Python is.

In this case we want to convert 451
F to C.

A module is a collection of scripts with related Python
functions and objects to complete a defined task. Modules
let us extend Python and there are thousands of them. All

we need to do is install them and off we go. Furthermore, if you are using distributions such as Anaconda, many modules are already available to you. All we need to do is import them whenever we need to use them. This is not dissimilar to what Trinity and Neo do when they asked the Operator to import functionality to fly a helicopter or Kung-Fu fight! All the Operator would have to do is type import helicopter or import kungfu and presto, Trinity and Neo can save the day as they have now all the functionality of the helicopter or kungfu modules. Please note these two modules are purely fictional at this stage!

A module is a collection of scripts with related Python functions to achieve a specific task.

In an example closer to home, we may not want to Kung-Fu fight, but we can try to do some trigonometry. We can ask the Operator (in this case Python) to import the math module. In that way, we can ask for the value of π and just like that we can create a function to calculate the area of a circle of radius r for example:

The math module contains some common mathematical functions.

```
import math


def area_circ(r):
    '''Area of a circle of radius r'''
    area = math.pi * r**2
    return area


r = 7
ac = area_circ(r)
print('The area of a circle with ' \
    'radius {0} is {1:.2f}'.format(r, ac))
```

We can get the value of π with math.pi.

Running the programme will result in the following output
in a terminal:

```
> Python area_circ.py


The area of a circle with radius 7 is 153.94
```

We run the programme by typing
this in a terminal.

You may have seen in the code above that we require to tell
Python that the constant π is part of the math module. This
is done as math.pi. In the example above we are importing
all the functions of the math module. This can be somewhat
inefficient in cases where only specific functionality is
needed. Instead we could have imported only the value of π
as follows:

In some cases it may be more
efficient to load only the needed
functionality from a module.

```
from math import pi
```

With this syntax we can refer to π only as pi without the
dot notation. In many cases it is preferable to use the dot
notation to make it clear where functions, methods,
constants and other objects are coming from. This aids with
readability of our code and as you remember, this is an
important component of programming in Python.

We mentioned that there are many modules available to us.
A large number of modules are available from the Python
Standard Library and more information can be found
in https://docs.python.org/3/library/. We can create
our own modules and these modules can be organised
in packages. We will talk about some useful packages for
statistics in the rest of the book.

Check https://docs.python.
org/3/library/ for the Python
Standard Library modules.

3

Snakes, Bears & Other Numerical Beasts:

NumPy, SciPy & pandas

PROGRAMMING OFFERS ENDLESS POSSIBILITIES AND in the previous chapter we covered some of the basic aspects of programming with Python. We finished that chapter by looking at ways to break tasks into smaller, separate subtasks that can be imported into memory. It turns out that when we have created a large number of functions that support specific tasks in our workflow, it becomes much easier to put them together. This is called a module or package and there are many of them. In this chapter we are going to concentrate on a few that are useful in statistical analysis, namely NumPy, SciPy and pandas. For other packages you may want to check the Python Package Index (`https://pypi.org`). In the rest of the book we will deal with a few of these modules and packages.

In this chapter we will talk about NumPy, SciPy and pandas.

3.1   Numerical Python – NumPy

ONE OF THE MOST USEFUL packages in the Python ecosystem is NumPy[1]. It stands for "numerical Python" and it is widely used as an important component for many other packages, particularly for data analysis and scientific computing. It provides functionality for multidimensional arrays that lists cannot even dream of executing.

[1] Scientific Computing Tools for Python (2013). NumPy. http://www.numpy.org

To get a feeling of the capabilities of NumPy, let us take a look at some of the computations we would like to perform. A typical case is the use of linear algebra, as matrix calculations can facilitate the implementation of suitable statistical analysis workflows and treatments.

In that manner, the data analysis workflow, form processing to visualisation, benefits from the use of vectors and matrices. In Python we can define these as arrays. An array is a data type used to store multiple values under a single identifier and each element can be referenced by its index. This is similar to the collections we discussed in the previous chapter. However, in this case the elements are of the same type.

An array lets us store multiple values under a single identifier.

NumPy arrays are used to store numerical data in the form of vectors and matrices, and these numerical objects have a defined set of operations such as addition, subtraction, or multiplication, as well as other more specialised ones such as transposition, inversion, etc.

A straightforward application of NumPy arrays is vector and matrix algebra.

3.1.1   *Matrices and Vectors*

A MATRIX IS A RECTANGULAR array with m rows and n columns. We say that such an array is an $m \times n$ matrix. When $m = 1$ we have a column vector and when $n = 1$ we have a row vector. We can represent a matrix $\mathbf{A}$ with elements $a_{m,n}$ as follows:

$$\mathbf{A} = \begin{pmatrix} a_{1,1} & a_{1,2} & \cdots & a_{1,n} \\ a_{2,1} & a_{2,2} & \cdots & a_{2,n} \\ \vdots & \vdots & \ddots & \vdots \\ a_{m,1} & a_{m,2} & \cdots & a_{m,n} \end{pmatrix}. \tag{3.1}$$

A matrix is effectively a collection of row (or column) vectors.

We know that lists can be used to group elements in what may be row or column vectors. Consider the following two lists and let us push them to their computational limit:

```
list_a = [0, 1, 1, 2, 3]
list_b = [5, 8, 13, 21, 34]
```

On the surface these two objects may resemble a pair of vectors. After all, they are collections of numbers. However, Python considers these objects as lists, and for the interpreter these have specific operations. If we tried to add these two lists with the + symbol, Python will interpret the command as concatenation, not as the element-wise addition of the arrays:

We covered list concatenation in Section 2.3.1.

```
> list_a + list_b


[0, 1, 1, 2, 3, 5, 8, 13, 21, 34]
```

Using the + symbol with lists results in concatenation.

What happens if we try to carry out the multiplication of the two lists? Let us see:

```
> list_a * list_b


TypeError: can't multiply sequence by
non-int of type 'list'
```

Using other arithmetic symbols with lists results in an error.

Lists are excellent Python objects, but their use is limited for some of the operations we need to execute with numerical arrays. Python is able to use these lists as a starting point to build new objects with their own operations and functions letting us do the mathematical manipulations we require. In this case, modules such as NumPy and SciPy are already available to us for the use of *n*-dimensional arrays (i.e. ndarray) that can be used in mathematical, scientific, and engineering applications including statistical analysis.

3.1.2   N-Dimensional Arrays

THE POSSIBILITY OF CREATING OBJECTS that are suitable for the operations mentioned above is open thanks to NumPy. The module lets us define *n*-dimensional arrays for this purpose. An *n*-dimensional array is a multidimensional container whose elements are of the same type and size. In Python, the type of an *n*-dimensional array is ndarray. The

NumPy extends the types in Python by including arrays.

number of dimensions in an ndarray is its shape, which is a tuple of n integers specifying the sizes of each dimension. The type of the elements in an array is specified by a separate data-type object (called dtype) associated with each array. For convenience we will refer to ndarray objects as arrays in the rest of the text.

The shape of an array gives us its dimensions.

We can think of arrays as an enhancement on lists and you would not be surprised to know that we can create arrays with the help of lists:

```
import numpy as np


A = np.array(list_a)

B = np.array(list_b)
```

We define a NumPy array with np.array, where np is a convenient alias used for the NumPy package.

In the code above we are importing the NumPy package and using the alias np to refer to the module. With the help of the array command in NumPy we transform a list into an array object. Let us check the type of one of these new objects:

```
> type(A)


numpy.ndarray
```

The type of an array is ndarray.

As you can see, the type of object A is an n dimensional array. Since these are arrays, the sum is a well-defined operation now:

```
> C = A + B
> C


array([5, 9, 14, 23, 37])
```

The use of the + symbol with the arrays defined above results in their addition as expected.

This time Python has added the arrays element by element as expected for a vector operation. In this way the following vector operations are defined for NumPy arrays:

- Vector addition: +

- Vector subtraction: -

- Element-wise multiplication: *

- Scalar product: dot()

- Cross product: cross()

These are some of the vector operations that are supported by NumPy arrays.

3.1.3   N-Dimensional Matrices

NUMPY ALSO DEFINES MATRIX OBJECTS with np.matrix. Let us create a couple of them:

```
M1 = np.matrix([[1, 0], [0, 1]])


M2 = np.matrix([[0.5, 2.0], [-4.0, 2.5]])
```

Notice that the type of these objects is numpy.matrix:

```
> type(M1)


numpy.matrix
```

The type of a matrix is, surprise, surprise, matrix.

We can use apply arithmetic operations as defined for matrices. For example matrix addition:

```
> M1 + M2


matrix([[ 1.5,   2. ],
        [-4. ,   3.5]])
```

Matrix addition (and sustraction) works as expected.

or matrix multiplication:

```
> M1 * M2


matrix([[ 0.5,   2. ],
        [-4. ,   2.5]])
```

We can multiply NumPy matrices with the usual multiplication symbol.

In this case the result is the same as M2 because M1 is the 2×2 identity matrix. Note that we can also cast NumPy arrays as matrices with the mat command.

An operation that is specific to matrices is transposition. We can achieve this with the of the transpose method:

```
> M2.transpose()


matrix([[ 0.5, -4. ],
        [ 2. ,   2.5]])
```

Other operations, such as transposition, are also available.

We can check the shape of the vectors or matrices with the shape method as follows:

```
> A.shape
(5,)

> M2.shape
(2, 2)
```

Matrix dimensions can be
obtained with shape.

Similarly, we can obtain the types of the elements stored in
arrays and matrices. In this case, we use the dtype method:

```
> A.dtype
dtype('int64')

> M2.dtype
dtype('float64')
```

The elements inside matrices or
arrays also have types.

As you can see, array A has integer elements whereas the
matrix M2 has float elements.

We can create an array with all elements initialised to 0
using the function zeros():

```
> z1 = np.zeros((2,3))
> z1

array([[0., 0., 0.],
       [0., 0., 0.]])
```

zeros() creates a matrix whose
elements are all zero.

We can also create an array with all elements initialised to 1
using the function ones():

```
> o1 = np.ones((3,3))
> o1

array([[1., 1., 1.],
       [1., 1., 1.],
       [1., 1., 1.]])
```

ones() initialises a matrix with elements all equal to one.

3.1.4   Indexing and Slicing

ARRAY OBJECTS CREATED WITH NUMPY can also be indexed as well as sliced and even iterated over. The same notation we have used for lists and tuples is valid too. In other words start:end:step will extract the appropriate elements starting at start in steps given by step and until end-1. Let us create an array of the first 12 numbers and store it in a variable called a:

```
> a =  np.arange(12)
> print(a[1:4]); print(a[0:10:2])

[1 2 3]
[0 2 4 6 8]
```

Arrays and matrices can be indexed and sliced with the usual colon notation for lists and tuples.

In the example above we are first selecting the elements from 1 and up to but not including 4. We then ask for the elements from 0 through to 10 in steps of 2.

We can do the same for arrays with higher dimensions. For example, let us first create an array with two rows, one

containing the first 5 numbers and the second with the same
information but divided by 2:

```
> np.array([np.arange(5),0.5*np.arange(5)])
> print(b)


array([[0. , 1. , 2. , 3. , 4. ],
       [0. , 0.5, 1. , 1.5, 2. ]])
```

We have created a 2 × 5 array first.

This array has shape 2 × 5 and in this case we can select
elements from row 1 as follows:

```
> print(b[1, :])


[0.  0.5 1.  1.5 2. ]]
```

Remember that Python starts
counting from 0.

We can also get, for instance, the elements in column 2 of
the array:

```
> print(b[:, 2])


[2. 1.]
```

Slicing with : retrieves the entire
sequence.

This can be very useful when considering panel data that
can be put in the form of a table. Let us consider an
example where we have captured results for school tests in a
(very small) class of 5 students. See the results in Table 3.1

We can create a 5 × 3 array to capture the marks of the 5
students in each of the 3 subjects.

Name	Physics	Spanish	History
Antonio	8	9	7
Ziggy	4.5	6	3.5
Bowman	8.5	10	9
Kirk	8	6.5	9.5
María	9	10	7.5

Table 3.1: Student marks in three different subjects.

```
> marks = np.array([[8, 9 ,7],
    [4.5, 6, 3.5],
    [8.5, 10, 9],
    [8, 6.5, 9.5],
    [9, 10, 7.5]])
```

The results of each student are captured as rows in our array.

If we wanted to obtain the marks that Bowman got for Spanish, we need to obtain the element in row 2 for column 1. This can be done as follows:

```
> marks[2,1]

10.0
```

We are obtaining the element in row 2, column 1.

Similarly we can get the marks for Physics by requesting the values of row 0 for all the students:

```
> marks[:,0]

array([8. , 4.5, 8.5, 8. , 9. ])
```

Here, we get all the element in column 0.

3.1.5 Descriptive Statistics

NUMPY ALSO PROVIDES US WITH some functions to perform operations on arrays such as descriptive statistics including:

maximum, minimum, sum, mean and standard deviation. Let us see some of those for the Physics test marks:

```
> marks[:, 0].max(), marks[:, 0].min()
(9.0, 4.5)


> marks[:, 0].sum()
38.0


> marks[:, 0].mean(), marks[:, 0].std()
(7.6, 1.5937377450509227)
```

Descriptive stats such as the maximum, minimum, sum, mean and standard deviation are calculated easily with NumPy.

Furthermore, we can obtain these statistics for the entire frame or along rows or columns. For example, the mean of the marks across all subjects is:

```
> marks.mean()


7.733333333333333
```

We can obtain the average mark across all subjects for all students.

The average mark for each subject can be obtained by telling the function to operate on each column, this is axis=0:

```
> marks.mean(axis=0)


array([7.6, 8.3, 7.3])
```

Or for a specific subject, i.e. column, with slicing and dicing operations.

We can see that the average mark for Physics is 7.6 (which is the value we calculated above), for Spanish 8.3 and for History 7.3. Finally, we may be interested in looking at the average marks for each student. In this case we operate on each row. In other words axis=1:

```
> marks.mean(axis=1)

array([8.0, 4.6666667, 9.1666667, 8.0, 8.8333333])
```

The average mark for each student is also easily calculated.

The student with the best average mark is Bowman with 9.16, whereas the student that needs some support for the finals is Ziggy, with an average mark of 4.66.

It is possible to find unique elements in an array with the unique method. Consider the following array:

```
> m=np.array([3, 5, 3, 4, 5, 9, 10, 12, 3, 4, 10])
```

We can get the unique values as follows:

```
> np.unique(m)

array([ 3,  4,  5,  7,  9, 10, 12])
```

We can get unique elements with unique().

We can also obtain the frequency of each unique element with the return_counts argument as follows:

```
> np.unique(m, return_counts=True)

(array([ 3,  4,  5,  7,  9, 10, 12]),
array([3, 2, 1, 1, 1, 2, 1]))
```

It is also possible to get the frequency for each unique element.

In this way, we see that number 3 appears 3 times, number 4 twice, 5 once, and so on. The same also works for multidimensional arrays. Let us take a look at our table of student marks:

```
> np.unique(marks)

array([ 3.5,  4.5,  6. ,  6.5,  7. ,  7.5,
8. ,  8.5,  9. ,  9.5, 10. ])
```

If we are interested in finding entire unique rows or columns, we need to specify the axis. For rows we use `axis=0` and for columns `axis=1`.

Unique rows and columns in an array are obtained by specifying the axis.

Now that we have access to arrays, we can start expanding the type of operations we can do with these objects. A lot of those operations and algorithms are already available to us in the SciPy package.

3.2   Scientific Python – SciPy

THE COMPUTATIONAL DEMANDS OF SCIENTIFIC applications require the support of dedicated libraries available to us. In the case of Python, the SciPy[2] package provides us with implementations of algorithms and sub-modules that enables us to carry out calculations for statistics, use special functions, apply optimisation routines, and more. In this section we will cover only some of the richness of SciPy and you can explore some of the sub-packages that make up the library depending on your needs:

[2] Jones, E., T. Oliphant, P. Peterson, et al. (2001–). SciPy: Open source scientific tools for Python. http://www.scipy.org/

- `cluster` for clustering algorithms

- `constants` including physical and mathematical constants

- `fftpack` for Fast Fourier Transform routines

- integrate covering integration and ordinary differential equation solvers

- interpolate for interpolation and smoothing splines

- io for input and output

- linalg with linear algebra routines

- ndimage for N-dimensional image processing

- odr for orthogonal distance regression

SciPy sub-packages have you covered for (almost) any scientific computing needs you have.

- optimize with optimisation and root-finding routines

- signal for signal processing

- sparse to manage sparse matrices and associated routines

- spatial for spatial data structures and algorithms

- special with implementations of special functions

- stats for statistical analysis including distributions and functions

The SciPy package depends on NumPy for a lot of functionality. The typical way to import the required modules is to bring NumPy first, and then the required sub-module from SciPy. For instance, to use the stats sub-module we can import the following:

Importing SciPy and its sub-packages is straightforward.

```
import numpy as np
from scipy import stats
```

3.2.1   *Matrix Algebra*

LET US TAKE A LOOK at some things that we can do with
SciPy such as inverting a matrix. This is useful in solving
systems of linear equations, for example.:

Linear algebra methods are
included in linalg inside SciPy.

```
from numpy import array, dot
from scipy import linalg


x = array([[1, 10], [1, 21], [1, 29], [1, 35]])
y = array([[0.9], [2.2], [3.1], [3.5]])
```

We can now use these two arrays x and y to calculate the
following expression: $coef = (x^T x)^{-1} x^T y$. This gives us
the coefficients that define a line of best fit as given by a
linear regression. We can break down the calculation into
two parts. First $n = (x^T x)^{-1}$, where we need to calculate a
transpose and apply the inverse. The second part is given by
$k = x^T y$, such that $coef = nk$:

We can invert a matrix with the
.inv method.

```
n = linalg.inv(dot(x.T, x))
k = dot(x.T, y)


coef = dot(n,k)
```

Matrix multiplication with arrays
can be done with the dot()
function.

In Figure 3.1 we can see a scatter plot of the synthetic data
created and a line of best fit $y = 0.10612x - 0.09558$ given
by the coefficients we have calculated. In this case the
coefficients are stored in the coef object.

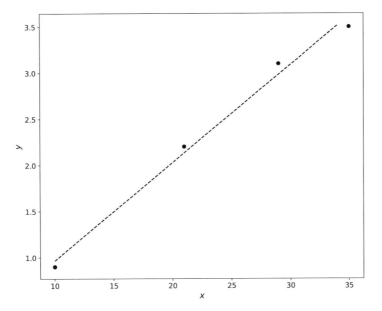

Figure 3.1: Scatter plot of synthetic data and a line of best fit obtained with simple matrix operations.

```
> print(coef)


[[-0.0955809 ]
 [ 0.10612972]]
```

We can use the linear algebra operations in SciPy to calculate other important quantities, for instance the determinant:

```
> a1 = np.array([[10, 30], [20, 40]])
> linalg.det(a1)


-200.0
```

We can also obtain the eigenvalues and eigenvectors of a matrix:

```
> l, v = linalg.eig(a1)
> print(l)


[-3.72281323+0.j 53.72281323+0.j]


> print(v)


[[-0.90937671 -0.56576746]
 [ 0.41597356 -0.82456484]]
```

We obtain the eigenvalues and eigenvectors with the .eig function.

3.2.2   Numerical Integration

SCIPY LETS US PREFORM NUMERICAL integration of integrals of the following kind:

$$I = \int_a^b f(x)dx. \qquad (3.2)$$

A number of routines are in the `scipy.integrate` library. One example is the `quad()` function, which takes the function $f(x)$ as an argument, as well as the limits a and b. It returns a tuple with two values: One is the computed results, and the other is an estimation of the numerical error of that result. We can, for instance, calculate the area under the curve for half of a Gaussian curve:

We can calculate definite integrals with SciPy.

$$\int_0^\infty e^{-x^2} = \frac{\sqrt{\pi}}{2}. \qquad (3.3)$$

```
> from scipy import integrate
> g = lambda x: np.exp(-x**2)
> integrate.quad(g, 0, np.inf)


(0.8862269254527579, 7.101318390472462e-09)
```

quad() lets us compute a definite integral.

3.2.3 Numerical Optimisation

WE CAN ALSO FIND ROOTS of functions with the optimize module in SciPy. Root finding consists in searching for a value x such that

$$f(x) = 0. \qquad (3.4)$$

Finding roots numerically is easy with SciPy.

Let us find (one) solution for the following transcendental equation:

$$\tan(x) = 1 \qquad (3.5)$$

We can rewrite our problem in the form: $f(x) = \tan(x) - 1 = 0$. We can now find the root with the fsolve() function in SciPy as follows:

```
> from scipy import optimize
> f = lambda x: np.tan(x)-1
> optimize.fsolve(f, 0)


array([0.78539816])
```

We can find roots with fsolve().

3.2.4   *Statistics*

AN IMPORTANT MODULE FOR US is stats, as it contains statistical tools and probabilistic descriptions that can be of great use in many statistical analyses. This, together with the random number generators from NumPy's random module, enables us to do a lot of things. For example, we can calculate a histogram for a set of observations of a random process:

The stats module in SciPy together with random from NumPy are a great combination for statistical work.

```
s = np.random.normal(size=1500)
b = np.arange(-4, 5)
h = np.histogram(s, bins=b, density=True)[0]
```

We get normally distributed random numbers with random.normal.

In this case we are drawing samples from a normal (Gaussian) distribution and calculate the histogram for b bins and we require the result to be the value of the probability density function at the bin (density=True).

A histogram gives us an approximation of the data distribution.

The histogram is an estimator of the probability density function (PDF) for the random process. We can use the stats module to calculate the probability density function for a normal distribution as follows:

PDF describes the relative likelihood for a random variable to take on a given value.

```
bins = 0.5*(b[1:] + b[:-1])
from scipy import stats
pdf = stats.norm.pdf(bins)
```

We talk about histograms in Section 8.7 and the normal probability distribution is addressed in Section 5.4.1.

We can estimate the parameters of the underlying distribution for a random process. In the example above,

knowing that the samples belong to a normal distribution
we can fit a normal process to the observed data:

```
> loc, std = stats.norm.fit(s)
> print(loc, std)


0.008360091147360452 0.98034848283625
```

Remember that we used random
samples, so the values shown here
may be different in your computer.

In this case this is close to a distribution with 0 mean and
standard deviation equal to 1.

We know that we can use NumPy to calculate the mean and
median:

```
> np.mean(s)


0.008360091147360452


> np.median(s)


0.030128236407879254
```

The mean and the median can
easily be obtained with the help of
NumPy as we saw in Section 3.1.

Other percentiles may be calculated too. We know that
the median is effectively the percentile 50, as half of the
observations are below it. We can calculate the percentiles
with scoreatpercentile:

The n-th percentile of a set of data
is the value at which n percent of
the data is below it. We talk more
about them in Section 4.4.2.

```
> stats.scoreatpercentile(s, 50)


0.030128236407879254
```

Other percentiles are easily obtained, for instance the percentile 75:

```
> stats.scoreatpercentile(s, 75)


0.7027762265868024
```

The 75-th percentile is also known as the third quartile.

We can also carry out some statistical testing. For example, given two sets of observations, which are assumed to have been generated from Gaussian processes, we can use a *t*-test to decide if the means are significantly different:

See Section 6.5.1 for more information on *t*-tests.

```
> process1 = np.random.normal(0, 1, size=100)
> process2 = np.random.normal(1, 1, size=50)
> stats.ttest_ind(process1, process2)


Ttest_indResult(statistic=-7.352146293288264,
pvalue=1.2290311506115089e-11)
```

The result comes in two parts. First the so-called *t*-statistic value tells us about the significance of the difference between the processes. The second is the *p*-value, which is the probability that the two processes are identical. If the value is close to 0, the more likely the processes have different means.

A *t*-test is used to determine if there is a significant difference between the means of two groups.

We will explore some of the concepts discussed above in greater detail later in the book. In the meantime, we can see that the arrays, matrices and vectors we have been playing with all contain numerical data. In many cases, data comes in different formats and we should not expect all of it to have the same type. NumPy and SciPy are unrivalled for

We start discussing hypothesis testing in Section 5.5.

numerical calculations, but we need other modules to be able to deal with different data types coming from a variety of sources. This is where packages such as pandas come to the rescue.

NumPy and SciPy are great to deal with numerical data.

3.3   *Panel Data = pandas*

PANDAS, MORE SPECIFICALLY, GIANT PANDAS are indeed those charismatic mammals with distinctive black-and-white markings that give part of its scientific name. Giant pandas, unlike most bears, do not have round pupils. Instead, they have vertical slits, similar to those of cats! There is of course the red panda, which may not be as famous, but it is equally endangered. Here, we will be talking about a different kind of panda, a numerical beast that is friends with Python, and no, not the snake, but the programming language.

Ailuropoda melanoleuca means "black and white cat footed animal'.'

Pandas[3] started life as a project by Wes McKinney in 2008 with the aim to make Python a practical statistical computing environment. Pandas is now used in a wider range of applications including machine learning and data science[4]. It is a powerful Python package that makes it easy for us to work with panel data. Panel data is typically encountered in economics, social science or epidemiology and the term is used to refer to datasets that have observations about different cross sections across time.

[3] McKinney, W. (2012). *Python for Data Analysis: Data Wrangling with Pandas, NumPy, and IPython,* O'Reilly Media

[4] Rogel-Salazar, J. (2017). *Data Science and Analytics with Python.* Chapman & Hall/CRC Data Mining and Knowledge Discovery Series. CRC Press; and Rogel-Salazar, J. (2020). *Advanced Data Science and Analytics with Python.* Chapman & Hall/CRC Data Mining and Knowledge Discovery Series. CRC Press

With the help of pandas, we can read data from a variety of sources and have it ready in a dataframe that can be easily manipulated. Pandas supports indexed, structured data with many columns and has functions to deal with missing values, encoding, manage multiple dataframes, etc.

3.3.1   Series and Dataframes

THE MOST BASIC TYPE OF data array in pandas is called a series, which is a 1-D array. A collection of series is called a dataframe. Each series in a dataframe has a data type and, as you can imagine, pandas builds these capabilities on top of NumPy and SciPy. A NumPy array can be used to create a pandas series as follows::

We are using the spelling of pandas with lowercase as used in its documentation, except in cases where is at the beginning of a sentence.

```
import numpy as np
import pandas as pd
a1 = np.array([14.75, 18.5, 72.9, 35.7])
s1 = pd.Series(a1)
```

A typical alias for the pandas library is pd.

We can check the type of the object s1 in the usual way:

```
> type(s1)

pandas.core.series.Series
```

The type of a pandas series is a Series.

As you can see the type of the object is a series, and each series (and dataframe) has a number of methods. The first thing to do is get to grips with the tabular data that we are able to manipulate with pandas. Let us look at some data published[5] in 2016 by the Greater London Authority about population density. In Table 3.2 we show the population and area (in square kilometres) for four global cities contained in the report.

[5] Three Dragons, David Lock Associates, Traderisks, Opinion Research Services, and J. Coles (2016). Lessons from Higher Density Development. Report to the GLA

City	Population	Area (sq km)
Greater London	8,663,300	1572
Tokyo	9,272,565	627
Paris	2,229,621	105
New York	8,491,079	784

Table 3.2: Population and area of some selected global cities.

We can load this data into Python by creating lists with the appropriate information about the two features describing the cities in the table:

```
names = ['Greater London', 'Tokyo', 'Paris',
    'New York']
population = [8663300, 9272565, 2229621,
    8491079]
area = [1572, 627, 105, 784]
```

We can use lists to create a pandas dataframe.

Let us use the DataFrame method in pandas with a dictionary as input. The keys will become our column names and the values will be the lists we created above:

```
df = pd.DataFrame({'cities': names,
    'population': population,
    'area': area})
```

We can pass a dictionary to .DataFrame to create our table of data.

We can see that the type of the df object is a pandas dataframe:

```
> type(df)

pandas.core.frame.DataFrame
```

The type of a pandas dataframe is DataFrame.

3.3.2   Data Exploration with pandas

NOW THAT THE DATA IS loaded into a pandas dataframe we can start exploring it. The first couple of entries in the dataframe df can be seen with the command .head():

```
> df.head(2)

          cities  population  area
0  Greater London    8663300  1572
1           Tokyo    9272565   627
```

The .head() method lets us see the first few rows of a dataframe.

We can also see the last few rows with .tail():

```
> df.tail(2)

      cities  population  area
2      Paris     2229621   105
3   New York     8491079   784
```

Similarly, .tail() will show the last few rows.

We can get information about our dataframe with some useful methods. For example, we can see the size of our dataframe with .shape:

```
> df.shape

(4, 3)
```

The dimension of our dataframe can be seen with .shape.

The result is a tuple that contains the dimensions of the rectangular table. The first number corresponds to the number of rows and the second the number of columns.

3.3.3   *Pandas Data Types*

WE CAN ALSO TAKE A look at the type of data that is stored
in each of the columns of our dataframe:

```
> df.dtypes

cities          object

population      int64

area            int64

dtype: object
```

We can easily check the types in
our columns with .dtypes.

This tells us that the population and area columns have
integers, and the cities one is either made out of strings or
mixed data. We can see the overlap between pandas, Python
and NumPy data types in Table 3.3.

More information about the dataframe can be obtained with
the .info() method:

```
> df.info()
<class 'pandas.core.frame.DataFrame'>
RangeIndex: 4 entries, 0 to 3
Data columns (total 3 columns):
 #   Column      Non-Null Count  Dtype
---  ------      --------------  -----
 0   cities      4 non-null      object
 1   population  4 non-null      int64
 2   area        4 non-null      int64
dtypes: int64(2), object(1)
```

The .info() method gives us
information about a dataframe
such as the index and column
dtypes, non-null values and
memory usage.

Pandas dtype	Python type	NumPy Type	Description
object	string or mixed	string_, unicode_, mixed types	Text or mixed numeric and non-numeric values
int64	int	int_, int8, int16, int32, int64, uint8, uint16, uint32, uint64	Integer numbers
float64	float	float_, float16, float32, float64	Floating point numbers
bool	bool	bool_	True/False values
datetime64	datetime	datetime64[ns]	Date and time values
timedelta[ns]	NA	NA	Differences between two datetimes
category	NA	NA	Finite list of text values

Table 3.3: Pandas data types.

We may have situations where we require to change the type of the data held in a column. In those cases, we can use the astype() function. Let us change the area column from integers to floats:

We can cast columns into other types with .astype().

```
> df['area'] = df['area'].astype('float')
```

3.3.4   Data Manipulation with pandas

LET US NOW LOOK AT some easy data manipulation we can perform with the help of pandas. You may recall that a dictionary can be used to create a pandas. The keys become the column names in our table. We can check the column names as follows:

```
> df.columns

Index(['cities', 'population', 'area'],

dtype='object')
```

The columns method returns the names of the columns in a dataframe.

This means that we can use these names to refer to the data in each of the columns. For example, we can retrieve the data about the population of the cities in rows 2 and 3 as follows:

```
df['population'][2:4]


2      2229621

3      8491079
```

We can view the contents of a dataframe column by name, and the data can be sliced with the usual colon notation.

Notice that we have referred to the name of the column as a string. Also, we have used slicing to select the data required.

You may notice that there is an index running along the left-hand side of our dataframe. This is automatically generated by pandas and it starts counting the rows in our table from 0. We can use this index to refer to our data. For example, we can get the city name and area for the first row in our table:

Pandas automatically assigns an index to our dataframe.

```
> df[['cities','area']][0:1]

          cities   area
0  Greater London  1572.0
```

We may want to define our own unique index for the data we are analysing. In this case, this can be the name of the cities. We can change the index with the set_index() method as follows:

We can assign our own index with set_index().

```
df.set_index('cities', inplace=True)
```

In this way, we are able to locate data by the index name with the help of the loc method:

```
> df.loc['Tokyo']

population    9272565.0
area              627.0
Name: Tokyo, dtype: int64
```

We can locate data by index name or label with loc. If you need to locate data by integer index use iloc instead.

In the example above, we looked at all the entries for Tokyo. We can also specify the columns we require. For instance, we can search for the population of Greater London as follows:

```
> df.loc['Greater London','population']

8663300
```

With loc we need to specify the name of the rows and columns that we want to filter out.

As we have seen, there are various useful commands in pandas that facilitate different tasks to understand the contents in a dataframe. A very handy one is the `describe` method. It gives us a fast way to obtain descriptive statistics for numerical columns in our dataframe. Instead of having to calculate the count, mean, standard deviation, and quartiles for our data, we can simply ask pandas to give us a description, and in one line of code we get a wealth of information:

```
> df.describe()

          population            area
count    4.000000e+00        4.000000
mean     7.164141e+06      772.000000
std      3.306720e+06      607.195191
min      2.229621e+06      105.000000
25%      6.925714e+06      496.500000
50%      8.577190e+06      705.500000
75%      8.815616e+06      981.000000
max      9.272565e+06     1572.000000
```

The `describe` method provides us with descriptive statistics of numerical data.

Note that using the `describe` method with categorical data provides a count, number of unique entries, the top category and frequency.

It is very easy to add new columns to a dataframe. For example, we can add a column that calculates the population density given the two existing columns in our dataframe:

Creating new columns out of existing ones is as easy as operating over the input columns.

```
> df['pop_density'] = df['population']/df['area']
```

The operation above is applied to each entry of the columns in question, and the result is added as a new column such that the result of the operation is aligned with the inputs used for the calculation. Let us take a look:

```
> df

                 population    area     pop_density
cities
Greater London    8663300    1572.0     5511.005089
Tokyo             9272565     627.0    14788.779904
Paris             2229621     105.0    21234.485714
New York          8491079     784.0    10830.457908
```

And our new column is part of the pandas dataframe.

3.3.5   Loading Data to pandas

IN THE SECTIONS ABOVE WE have entered our data by typing the entries. However, in many real situations, the data that we need to analyse has already been captured and stored in a database, a spreadsheet or a comma-separated-value (CSV) file. Since pandas was created to facilitate data analysis work, it is not surprising to hear that there are a number of ways we can bring data into a pandas dataframe. Table 3.4 lists some of the sources that we can use as data input.

We can import data into a pandas dataframe from a variety of sources.

Let us look at an example: The cities in Table 3.2 is only a small part of the actual data from the Greater London

Source	Command
	read_table()
Flat file	read_csv()
	read_fwf()
Excel file	read_excel()
	ExcelFile.parse()
JSON	read_json()
	json_normalize()
	read_sql_table()
SQL	read_sql_query()
	read_sql()
HTML	read_html()

Table 3.4: Some of the input sources available to pandas.

Authority report. The full dataset is available at[6]

`https://doi.org/10.6084/m9.figshare.14657391.v1` as a

comma-separated value file with the name

"`GLA_World_Cities_2016.csv`". Once you have downloaded

the file and saved it in a known location in your computer,

you can read the data into pandas as follows:

[6] Rogel-Salazar, J. (2021a, May). GLA World Cities 2016. https://doi.org/ 10.6084/m9.figshare.14657391.v1

```
import numpy as np
import pandas as pd
gla_cities=pd.read_csv('GLA_World_Cities_2016.csv')
```

We are reading a CSV file with read_csv()

The `read_csv()` function can take a number of parameters,

such as `sep` for the separator or delimiter used in the file,

`header` to define the rows that should be used as column

names, or `encoding` to tell Python what encoding to use for

UTF when reading or writing text.

Let us look at some of the rows in our dataset. For printing

purposes we will only show some limited information here:

```
> gla_cities.head(3)


            City    Country  ...   Constraint

0             NaN       NaN  ...          NaN

1  Greater London   England  ...           4%

2     Inner London   England  ...           5%
```

We are only showing a portion of the dataset. The ellipses (...) indicate columns not shown.

You can see that row 0 has NaN as entries. This means that the row has missing data, and in this case, it turns out that there is an empty row in the table. We can drop rows with missing information as follows:

```
> gla_cities.dropna(how='all', inplace=True)
```

Dropping rows from the table is achieved with dropna().

The dropna method also has a number of parameters to use. In this case have used how='all' to drop rows whose rows have all NaN values. The second parameter we used indicates to pandas that the dropping of rows should be done in the same dataframe object. We now have a table with 17 rows and 11 columns:

```
> gla_cities.shape


(17, 11)
```

For convenience we can rename the columns of our dataframe. This is easily done with the help of a dictionary whose keys are the existing column names and the values of the new names:

```
> renamecols = {'Inland area in km2': 'Area km2'}
> gla_cities.rename(columns=renamecols,
   inplace=True)
```

Renaming columns is an important manipulation that can be done with `rename(()`.

Let us look at the column names we have after the change above:

```
> gla_cities.columns

Index(['City', 'Country', 'Population',
   'Area km2', 'Density in people per hectare',
   'Dwellings', 'Density in dwellings per hectare',
   'People per dwelling', 'Approx city radius km',
   'Main topographical constraint', 'Constraint'],
   dtype='object')
```

We will now create a new column to capture the population density per square kilometre. If you do the following, you will get an error:

```
> gla_cities['pop_density'] = \
   gla_cities['Population']/gla_cities['Area km2']

TypeError: unsupported operand type(s) for /:
   'str' and 'str'
```

We get an error because the data was read as strings, not as numbers.

The reason for this is that the data for the `Population`, `Area Km2` and `Dwellings` columns has been read as strings and, as we know, we are not allowed to divide strings. We can fix this issue by changing the type of our columns. We will also

need to get rid of the commas used to separate thousands
in the file provided. All this can be done by chaining the
changes as follows:

```
gla_cities['Population']=gla_cities['Population'].\
    str.replace(',', '').astype(float)
```

Recasting the data type solves the
issue.

First we use the replace() method for strings to remove
the comma, and then we apply the astype() function to
transform the data into a float. We do the same for the other
two columns:

```
gla_cities['Area km2']=gla_cities['Area km2'].\
    str.replace(',', '').astype(float)
gla_cities['Dwellings']=gla_cities['Dwellings'].\
    str.replace(',', '').astype(float)
```

First we replace the commas in
the strings and then we recast the
column data as float.

We can now create our new column:

```
> gla_cities['pop_density'] = \
    gla_cities['Population']/gla_cities['Area km2']
> gla_cities['pop_density'].head(3)


1     5511.005089
2    10782.758621
3     4165.470494
```

Let's see what's out there... The
operation can now be completed
correctly!

It is also easy to make calculations directly with the
columns of our dataframe. For instance, we can create a
column that shows the population in units of millions:

```
> gla_cities['Population (M)'] =
    gla_cities['Population']/1000000
```

As before, we can create new columns out of existing ones.

This can make it easier for us and other humans to read the information in the table. The important thing is to note that pandas has effectively vectorised the operation and divided each and every entry in the column by a million. If we need to apply a more complex function, for instance one we have created ourselves, it can also be applied to the dataframe. First, let us create a function that categorises the cities into small, medium, large and mega. Please note that this categorisation is entirely done for demonstration purposes and it is not necessarily a real demographic definition:

```
def city_size(x):
    if x < 1.5:
        s = 'Small'
    elif 1.5 <= x < 3:
        s = 'Medium'
    elif 3 <= x < 5:
        s = 'Large'
    else:
        s = 'Mega'
    return s
```

Creating functions to manipulate our data is the same as discussed in Section 2.5.

We can now use the apply method of a series to categorise our cities:

```
> gla_cities['City Size'] = \
    gla_cities['Population (M)'].apply(city_size)
```

We can then apply those functions to our dataframe.

Pandas enables us to filter the data by simply making comparisons on the values of columns directly. For example, we can ask for the rows in the table for the cities classified as small:

```
> gla_cities[gla_cities['City Size']=='Small']

          City       ...   Population (M)  City Size
5         Lyon       ...        0.500715      Small
9       Sevilla      ...        0.693878      Small
12      Boston       ...        0.617594      Small
```

Boolean filtering is available directly on the dataframe.

We can also request a handful of columns instead of the entire table. For example, let us filter the data for the city name and population in millions for the cities with populations greater than 8 million:

```
> gla_cities[['City', 'Population (M)']] \
    [gla_cities['Population (M)']>8]

                             City  Population (M)
1                   Greater London        8.663300
10                New York (City)        8.491079
16      Tokyo (Special Wards Area)        9.272565
```

We can combine Boolean filtering with column selection.

3.3.6 Data Grouping

HAVING DATA ORGANISED IN A table makes it possible to ask for aggregations and groupings given the values of some columns of interest. Pandas makes it easy for us to create groups and apply aggregations to our dataframes with functions such as `.groupby()` and `.agg()`. Let us look at counting the number of cities that are in each of the classifications we created in the previous section. First, let us group the cities by the `City Size` column:

Data grouping and aggregation is readily available with pandas.

```
> gla_grouped = gla_cities.groupby('City Size')
```

Simply pass the column to group by to the `.groupby()` function.

We will now use the `size()` function to look at the size of the groups created:

```
> gla_grouped.size()

City Size
Large     4
Medium    5
Mega      5
Small     3
dtype: int64
```

We can see the size of the groups created.

We can also apply aggregation functions. Let us calculate the average population of the city classifications we created:

```
> gla_grouped['Population (M)'].mean()

City Size
Large     3.488562
Medium    2.324692
Mega      7.625415
Small     0.604062
Name: Population (M), dtype: float64
```

And get descriptive statistics for those groups too.

It is possible to apply multiple aggregations with the .agg() function we mentioned above:

```
> gla_grouped['Population (M)'].agg([np.mean,
    np.std])


              mean        std
City Size
Large      3.488562   0.313245
Medium     2.324692   0.453616
Mega       7.625415   1.705035
Small      0.604062   0.097290
```

We can also apply other aggregations with the .agg() function.

In this case, we are getting the mean and standard deviation with the help of NumPy.

There are many more things we can do with pandas. For example, it is possible to create plots directly from a dataframe. We can create a horizontal bar chart of the average population in our city classification as follows:

```
gla_grouped['Population (M)'].mean().\
    sort_values(ascending=True).plot.barh()
```

Pandas lets us create data visualisations directly from the dataframe. We cover this in further detail in Section 8.2.1.

We are sorting the values before passing the data to the plotting function. The result can be seen in Figure 3.2. We will cover data visualisation in more detail in Chapters 7 and 8.

As you can see, NumPy, SciPy and pandas provide us with a wide range of tools to analyse and manipulate data in

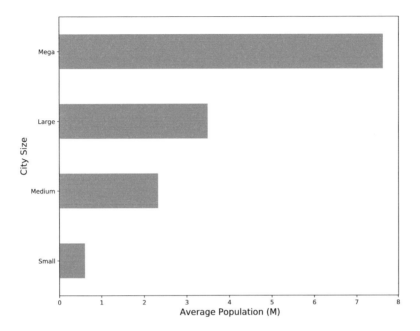

Figure 3.2: Average population in millions for the city classification created for the GLA report data.

a coherent ecosystem. Here, we have only covered some of the capabilities of these libraries, and we will continue using them in the rest of the book as we explore the world of statistics with Python.

4

The Measure of All Things – Statistics

WE MENTIONED IN CHAPTER 1 that statistics is the art
of learning from data. Statistics enables the creation of
new knowledge and a good statistical foundation will
help us understand a problem better and lead us to sound
conclusions.

Statistics is the art of learning
from data.

In that sense, statistics is not about simply looking at
numbers, but about understanding data. In other words,
statistics is all about numbers in context. We may take a
look at a list of numbers and be able to calculate things like
the mean or the standard deviation, but the context around
the numbers enables us to make interpretations about the
results we are seeing. Statistics lets us measure all sorts of
things and make sense of information around us and not be
overwhelmed or overloaded by it.

It is all about numbers in context
to enable understanding.

In order to do this we need to be methodical in the way
we acquire, organise and analyse available data. Given
a particular phenomenon of interest, we know that the

measurements we may record about it are varied. After all, if all measurements were exactly identical we would live in a very boring universe. Think of the students whose grades we encountered in Section 3.1.4, wouldn't it be strange if all af the grades were exactly the same for all students in all subjects?

A universe not worth exploring for strange new worlds or seek out new life and new civilisations.

Being methodical about our analysis is supported by having some definitions under our belt. We call a *population* the entire collection of things or subjects about which information is obtained for our analysis. A *sample* is a subset of the population, selected for study. Descriptive statistics help us describe data from our population, and we can use tables and graphs, as well as numerical aggregations to help us with our description. The data about our population may consist of a single or multiple characteristics, features or variables. In the case of a single variable, we are talking about a *univariate* dataset, and a *multivariate* one when we have two or more variables.

Population and sample are important concepts in statistics.

Our data can be univariate or multivariate.

The variables captured about our population can be *categorical* or *qualitative* if the individual observations correspond to categories or classes. If, however, the observations are numbers, the variables are said to be *numerical* or *quantitative*. In turn, numerical variables can be of different kinds. If the numbers resulting from the observation of our population are isolated points in the number line we have *discrete* data. If the observations can take any possible value along the number line we have *continuous* data.

The variables can be qualitative or quantitative. Quantitative data can be discrete or continuous.

With a phenomenon under study, for a sample in a population, we can set up an *experiment*, in other words set up a study where one or more *explanatory or independent variables* or *factors* are considered to observe the effects on a *response or dependent variable*. The former are the variables whose values are controlled, whereas the latter are measured as part of the experiment. An *experimental condition* or *treatment* is the name we give to a particular combination of values for the explanatory variables.

A experiment to observe the effects of explanatory variables on response ones.

The first thing to do after having collected the appropriate data is to explore it. Data exploration lets us build context around the data and in turn create suitable models. The source of the data is an important component of the exploration and whenever possible it is recommended to include any information that the data owners can provide about the data. For example, are the numbers we are seeing actually referring to categories, or are the dates provided in a specific format? The type of exploration may depend on the answers to some of those questions. Some of the typical things we would like to achieve during the exploration phase of a project include:

Data exploration lets us build context around the data.

Information about the data origin is as important as the data itself.

- Detecting erroneous data

- Determining how much missing data there is

- Understanding the structure of the data

- Identifying important variables in the data

- Sense-checking the validity of the data

- Determining any data refinement or cleaning required

Perhaps one of the most important outcomes of the data exploration step is the information that descriptive statistics gives us.

4.1   Descriptive Statistics

THINK OF YOUR FAVOURITE PLACE on Earth. Without telling Mr Spock the name of the place or its location, can you tell him about some of the most important things that distinguish this place? In other words, can you describe it? He can perhaps do the same about his home planet Vulcan. With some characteristics such as being a rocky planet, retaining a suitable atmosphere to sustain humanoid life, a surface abundant in water and with an orbit in the habitable zone of its system, the United Federation of Planets would consider both Earth and Vulcan as Class M worlds. Initial descriptions can let appropriate survey teams plan for further expeditions. The same is true of datasets.

Surely Mr Spock would use logic to determine where your favourite place on Earth is.

Suitable descriptions of data can let us plan for further explorations.

In the case of datasets, instead of using phrases for the description, we use numbers to summarise and describe the data. The descriptions provided by these summary figures is simply a description, they do not aim to generalise anything beyond the data points available and we refer to them as *descriptive statistics*. As the name says, descriptive statistics are just descriptive; their use does not generalise or tries to tell us anything beyond the data at hand.

Descriptive statistics do not generalise but let us understand.

When we use descriptive statistics for our data, we are interested in coming up with a number that is representative of the observations we have. Typically, we are interested to know where the data is located or "centred" and thus this is called a measure of central tendency. Let us take a look at some of them.

4.2   Measures of Central Tendency and Dispersion

THINK OF YOUR FAVOURITE DATASET. It may contain a few dozens of points, or thousands, even millions. Unless you are an Operator in the Matrix universe, you may not be able to look at a cascade of green neon figures, and make decisions accordingly. Instead, you will probably want to summarise the data and a useful aggregation is one that tells us something about the distribution of the data points. For that matter, locating where the data is centred is very useful. A second measure you will be interested in is how spread your data is.

Determining where our data is centred is an important step in descriptive statistics.

Consider the student marks we looked at in Chapter 3, shown in Table 3.1. A student with a given score may want to know how close they are to the maximum mark. They may also be interested in comparing their score to that of others. For example, María will be very pleased to have got 9/10 in Physics. Not only is it a mark close to the maximum, but is higher than the rest. However, her History mark of 7.5/10 is not as pleasing, but where is she compared to the rest of the class? This is where central tendency comes to the rescue.

Where does María stand compared to her classmates and to the class in general? Central tendency can help answer this questions.

4.3   Central Tendency

CENTRAL TENDENCY IS THE TREND that a given set of data
points have to pile up around a single value. That single
value is called a measure of central tendency and lets us
condense the dozens, thousands or millions of observations
into a single number. In the example above, it lets María
know how well she has performed compared to her
classmates, but also in comparison to other subjects, and as
a class in the school. Some common measures of central
tendency include:

We summaries a large number of
data points into a single value.

- Mode

- Median

- Arithmetic mean

- Geometric mean

- Harmonic mean

Some important measures of
central tendency.

We will cover these measures in the following sections. For
that purpose, we will use some data about car road tests[1]
from 1973 to 1974. The dataset comprises fuel consumption
and some information on automobile design and
performance for 32 cars. The data can be obtained from[2]
`https://doi.org/10.6084/m9.figshare.3122005.v1` as a
comma-separated value file with the name "cars.csv". The
variables included in this dataset are as follows:

[1] Henderson, H. V. and P. F.
Velleman (1981). Building multiple
regression models interactively.
Biometrics 37(2), 391–411

[2] Rogel-Salazar, J. (2016,
Mar).   Motor Trend Car
Road Tests. https://doi.org/
10.6084/m9.figshare.3122005.v1

1. mpg: Miles/(US) gallon

2. cyl: Number of cylinders

3. disp: Displacement (cu.in.)

4. hp: Gross horsepower

5. drat: Rear axle ratio

6. wt: Weight (1000 lbs)

These are the features contained in the "cars.csv" dataset.

7. qsec: 1/4 mile time

8. vs: Engine shape (0 = v-shaped, 1 = straight)

9. am: Transmission (0 = automatic, 1 = manual)

10. gear: Number of forward gears

11. carb: Number of carburettors

4.3.1 Mode

A GOOD WAY TO GET a sense of the values in a set of observations is to look for the value that is present in the data the most times. This is called the *mode* and it corresponds to the most common value in the dataset. In some cases we can even get more than one mode and this is called a multi-modal distribution.

The mode is the most frequent value observed in a dataset feature.

Let us look at an example. Consider the student marks we saw in Table 3.1. The mode for each subject is:

- Physics - 8

- Spanish - 10

- History - multiple values

For History we have a multi-modal distribution. This is because each of the values appears the same number of times. We can use SciPy to help us with the calculation:

```
> import numpy as np
> from scipy import stats
> marks = np.array([[8, 9 ,7],
                    [4.5, 6, 3.5],
                    [8.5, 10, 9],
                    [8, 6.5, 9.5],
                    [9, 10, 7.5]])
> stats.mode(marks)


ModeResult(mode=array([[ 8. , 10. ,  3.5]]),
   count=array([[2, 2, 1]]))
```

We can obtain the mode with the mode function in SciPy's stats.

In this case Python tells us the mode for each column in the NumPy array marks and also gives us the frequency. For the History column, the mode reported is the smallest value.

Let us look at the cars dataset, in particular we want to see the mode of the fuel consumption in miles per gallon.

```
> import pandas as pd
> cars = pd.read_csv('cars.csv')
> cars.loc[:, 'mpg'].mode()


0     10.4
1     15.2
2     19.2
3     21.0
```

We can apply the same function to a pandas dataframe.

```
4      21.4

5      22.8

6      30.4
```

In this case we also have a multi-modal distribution. We can apply the same measure of central tendency to different groups. For example, we may want to see the mode of fuel consumption for each of the cars with automatic (0) and manual (1) transmissions.

```
> ct = cars.groupby(['am'])

> ct['mpg'].apply(lambda x: x.mode())


   am
0   0     10.4

    1     15.2

    2     19.2

1   0     21.0

    1     30.4
```

The function can also be applied to a grouped dataframe. The result is provided for each of the groups. Note however that this needs to be done as a lambda function as mode does not reduce the dataset to a single number.

Once again we have more than one value. For the automatic cars we have three mode values, whereas for manual we have two. Note that since mode is not a function that reduces the dataset, like for example a sum of values, pandas does not have a method for grouped dataframes.

In a nutshell, to calculate the mode we need to tabulate how many times each of the values appear, i.e. we calculate their frequency. The entries with the highest frequency are the mode. The mode tells us what the most common value in a dataset is, but it may not be a good choice to summarise

The mode may not be the best way to summarise our data.

some data. Think for instance of the marks for Physics. The mode is 10 but it may not be a good choice to represent the rest of the marks for the class. Similarly, for the cars dataset, since we have a multi-modal distribution it may be difficult to discern a central value. Fear not, that is where other centrality measures come handy.

Other measures of central tendency are available.

4.3.2   *Median*

INSTEAD OF LOOKING AT THE most common values, we can summarise our data by looking at their position in our dataset. This is exactly what the median does; it corresponds to the middle-most value when our set of observations is arranged in ascending (or descending) order of magnitude. In the case of our student marks for Physics we have that the data would be sorted as follows:

The median is the middle-most value of an ordered dataset.

$$\text{Physics} = [\,4.5, 8, 8, 8.5, 9\,]$$

In this case, the middle value is 8 and that is our median. Note that here we have an odd number of observations and determining the middle value is easy. However, when the number of observations is even we sum the two values in the middle and divide the result by 2.

Depending on whether we have an odd or even number of observations, our median is either the middle value or the average of the central ones.

We can calculate the median of the three subjects our students have been studying with the help of NumPy as follows:

```
> np.median(marks, axis=0)

array([8. , 9. , 7.5])
```

The median for Physics is 8 as calculated above, for Spanish it is 9 and for History 7.5.

In a pandas dataframe we can use the .median() method as follows:

```
> cars.loc[:, 'mpg'].median()

19.2
```

Pandas dataframes have a median() method.

The median fuel consumption for the cars in our dataset is 19.2. We can see the median per transmission as follows:

```
> ct['mpg'].median()
am
0      17.3
1      22.8
```

The method can also be used for grouped dataframes.

In this case, pandas does have a method for us to apply directly. We can see that the median fuel consumption for automatic cars (17.3) is lower than that for manual ones (22.8). Also, note that the values are different from the median obtained for the entire dataset. One may start to wonder if there is a marked difference in fuel consumption for cars with different transmission, and this may help us decide what car is best for us.

We will answer this question in Section 6.6.1.

4.3.3   Arithmetic Mean

FINDING THE CENTRE OF A distribution, as we have seen, can be done from an actual position, and this has the great' advantage of being unbiased to having large or small values in the dataset. There are other ways to find the centre, and one of the most widely used methods is the arithmetic mean or simply the mean or the average.

The arithmetic mean is actually the average or mean value we all learn at school.

It is important to note that when we use the entire collection of data, i.e. the population, to calculate the mean, we refer to this as the **population mean** and denote it with the Greek letter μ. In contrast, when we use a sample we call it the **sample mean** and denote it as $\bar{X}$.

The population mean is μ and the sample mean is $\bar{X}$.

The arithmetic mean takes into account all the observations in the dataset (population or sample) and summarises them in a single number. Given a set of n values in an array **X**, the average is found by adding up all the observations $x_1, x_2, \ldots, x_n$ and dividing the result by the number of elements:

$$\bar{X} = \frac{1}{n} \sum_{i=1}^{n} x_i. \tag{4.1}$$

This is how to calculate the arithmetic mean, or average.

Unlike the median, the average is susceptible to the presence of large values in the data. Say we are at the Battlestar Galactica mess, and there are 5 human officers there. If we ask their ages, they may report the following values:

$$\text{ages} = [45, 30, 50, 26, 40]. \tag{4.2}$$

The average age would be given by:

$$\frac{1}{5}(45 + 30 + 50 + 26 + 40) = 38.2. \qquad (4.3)$$

Battlestar Galactica seems to have a young crew!

Suddenly, a Cylon arrives. It turns out to be one of the Final Five, and their age is, say, 2052. What happens to the average age? Let's take a look:

$$\frac{1}{6}(45 + 30 + 50 + 26 + 40 + 2052) = 373.833. \qquad (4.4)$$

The presence of the Cylon has skewed the average age to the point that it does not represent the majority of the values in the dataset. The median of this dataset is 42.5 and that may be a better description for this group of officers (and Cylon). This is because the median disregards the values present and concentrates on the most central value (in terms of ordered position).

The presence of a large number skews the average value. In this case an old Cylon turns our average into an impossible human age.

Let us take a look at the student marks we have been using to demonstrate how we use Python to calculate these central measures. The average for Physics is:

```
> physics = marks[:, 0]
> print('Physics Average: ', np.mean(physics))


Physics Average:  7.6
```

We use the mean function in NumPy.

We are using the mean function defined in NumPy for this task, and as we can see the mean is 7.6. We can calculate the mean for all the subjects in one go by passing the array of values and the axis:

```
> np.mean(marks, axis=0)


array([7.6, 8.3, 7.3])
```

The function can be applied to each column by providing the axis.

Note that NumPy arrays also have a mean method. This means that we can calculate the mean by the following means:

Pardon the alliteration.

```
> physics.mean()


7.6
```

This is very similar to what we would do for a pandas dataframe. Let us see the average of the fuel consumption for our cars dataset:

```
> print('MPG average: ', mpg.mean())


MPG average:   20.090624999999996
```

Pandas dataframes have the mean().

We know that we have two different types of transmission in our dataset. Let us see if the average fuel consumption is different between automatic and manual:

```
> ct['mpg'].mean()


am

0     17.147368

1     24.392308

Name: mpg, dtype: float64
```

The average fuel consumption is different between our automatic and manual transmission cars in our dataset.

The automatic cars have a mean fuel consumption of 17.15 miles per gallon, whereas the mean for manual is 24.4. Is this difference significant? Well, this is a question we shall tackle later on in the book.

See Section 6.6.1.

There may be some applications where each data point is given a weight such that each data point is contributing a different amount to the average. This is called a weighted arithmetic mean and is calculated as:

$$\bar{X} = \frac{\sum_{i=1}^{n} w_i x_i}{\sum_{i=1}^{n} w_i}. \tag{4.5}$$

Weighted arithmetic mean.

A weighted arithmetic mean is used for instance to calculate the return for a portfolio of securities[3].

[3] Rogel-Salazar, J. (2014). *Essential MATLAB and Octave*. CRC Press

4.3.4   Geometric Mean

AN ALTERNATIVE MEASURE OF CENTRAL tendency is the geometric mean. In this case, instead of using the sum of the observations as in the arithmetic mean, we calculate their product. The geometric mean is therefore defined as the n-th root of the product of observations.

The geometric mean is the n-th root of the product of observations.

In other words, given a set of n values in an array $\mathbf{X}$, with all elements $x_1, x_2, \ldots, x_n$ being positive, the geometric mean is calculated as follows:

$$GM = \left(\prod_{1=1}^{n} x_i \right)^{1/n}. \tag{4.6}$$

Geometric mean.

The geometric mean is suitable to be used for observations that are exponential in nature, for instance growth figures such as interest rates or populations. We can express Equation (4.6) as follows.

$$\left(\prod_{1=1}^{n} x_i\right)^{1/n} = \exp\left[\frac{1}{n}\sum_{i=1}^{n}\ln x_i\right]. \qquad (4.7)$$

An alternative formulation of the geometric mean.

It is clear from the expression above that we can calculate the geometric mean by computing the arithmetic mean of the logarithm of the values, and use the exponential to return the computation to its original scale. This way of calculating the geometric mean is the typical implementation used in computer languages.

This is the implementation used in many computer languages.

To calculate the geometric mean using NumPy we can define a function that implements Equation (4.7):

```
import numpy as np
def g_mean(x):
    avglnx = np.log(x)
    return np.exp(avglnx.mean())
```

Here is the implementation of Equation (4.7).

For the BSG officers list of ages we can then use this function to calculate the geometric mean:

BSG = Battlestar Galactica.

```
> bsg_ages = [45, 30, 50, 26, 40]
> g_mean(bsg_ages)

37.090904350447026
```

Including the 2052-year-old Cylon will result in a value of 72.4. A more human-like value for an age.

For a set of positive numbers, the geometric mean is smaller or equal to the arithmetic mean.

An alternative to creating our own function is using the gmean() function implemented in SciPy. For example, we can use this to calculate the geometric mean for the Physics marks:

```
> from scipy.stats import gmean
> gmean(physics)


7.389427365423367
```

Here we are using the gmean() function in SciPy.

We can also calculate the geometric mean for all the subjects as follows:

```
> gmean(marks, axis=0)


array([7.38942737, 8.11075762, 6.90619271])
```

We can calculate the geometric mean for the columns too.

Finally, for a pandas dataframe, we can continue using the SciPy function. For our fuel consumption column we have:

```
> gmean(mpg)


19.25006404155361
```

The function can also be used in pandas dataframes.

And for the car data grouped by transmission we have:

```
> ct['mpg'].apply(gmean)


am
0      16.721440
1      23.649266
Name: mpg, dtype: float64
```

For datasets containing positive values with at least a pair of unequal ones, the geometric mean is lower than the arithmetic mean. Furthermore, due to its multiplicative nature, the geometric mean can be used to compare entries in different scales. Imagine that we have the ratings shown in Table 4.1 for some Château Picard wine:

The geometric mean can let us compare values in different scales.

Vintage	Rater	Rate
2249	Commander Data	3.5
	Commander Raffi	80
	Musiker	
2286	Commander Data	4.5
	Commander Raffi	75
	Musiker	

Table 4.1: Ratings for some Château Picard wine.

In this case, Commander Data has provided his ratings in a scale from 1 to 5, whereas Commander Raffi Musiker has given her ratings in a scale of 100. If we were to take the arithmetic mean on the raw data we would have a biased view:

We have ratings for Château Picard wine in two different scales. The arithmetic mean is dominated by the larger numbers.

$$2249 \text{ vintage} \rightarrow (3.5 + 80)/2 = 41.75 \qquad (4.8)$$
$$2286 \text{ vintage} \rightarrow (4.5 + 75)/2 = 39.75 \qquad (4.9)$$

With the arithmetic mean, the 2249 vintage seems the better wine. However, the fact that we have ratings with different scales means that large numbers will dominate the arithmetic mean. Let us use the geometric mean to see how things compare:

The geometric mean lets us make a better comparison.

$$2249 \text{ vintage} \rightarrow \sqrt{3.5 * 80} = 16.73 \qquad (4.10)$$
$$2286 \text{ vintage} \rightarrow \sqrt{4.5 * 75} = 18.37 \qquad (4.11)$$

The better rated wine with the geometric mean seems to be the 2286 vintage. The geometric mean can help with the varying proportions, but notice that we lose the scaling. In other words, we can compare the values but we cannot say that we have an average rating of 16.73 out of neither 100 or 5. The other solution would be to normalise the data into a common scale first and then apply the calculations.

Although the geometric mean manages the proportion better, the scaling is lost.

We can also define a weighted geometric mean as follows:

$$WGM = \exp\left[\frac{\sum_{i=1}^{n} \ln w_i x_i}{\sum_{i=1}^{n} w_i}\right].$$ (4.12)

There is also a weighted version for the geometric mean.

This can be useful when we need to calculate a mean in a dataset with a large number of repeated values.

4.3.5 Harmonic Mean

ANOTHER ALTERNATIVE TO SUMMARISING OUR data with a single central number is the harmonic mean. In this case, instead of using the sum or the multiplication of the numbers like the arithmetic or the geometric means, we rely on the sum of the reciprocals.

To calculate the harmonic mean we need to do the following:

1. Take the reciprocal of each value in our data.

2. Calculate their arithmetic mean.

The harmonic mean uses the sum of reciprocals of the data points.

3. Take the reciprocal of the result and multiply by the number of values.

In other words:

$$HM = \frac{n}{\sum_{i=1}^{n} \frac{1}{x_1}} = n \left(\sum_{i=1}^{n} x_i^{-1} \right)^{-1}. \tag{4.13}$$

This is the formula to calculate the harmonic mean.

We can create a function in Python to obtain the harmonic mean as follows:

```
def h_mean(x):
    sum = 0
    for val in x:
        sum += 1/val
    return len(x)/sum
```

Beware that this implementation cannot handle zeroes.

Note that the code above, as indeed shown in Equation (4.13), is not able to handle zeroes in the list on numbers x. For our age list of Battlestar Galactica officers we have that the harmonic mean is given by:

```
> bsg_ages = [45, 30, 50, 26, 40]
> h_mean(bsg_ages)

35.96679987703658
```

Note that the harmonic mean is always the least of the three means we have discussed, with the arithmetic mean being the greatest. If we include the 2052-year-old Cylon the harmonic mean is 43.

The harmonic mean is the least of the three means discussed.

The harmonic mean is a useful centrality measure when we are interested in data that relates to ratios or rates. In financial applications, for example in price-to-earnings (P/E) ratios in an index. Let us see an example.

The harmonic mean is useful to compare ratios or rates.

Say for instance that you have two companies, Weyland Corp and Cyberdyne Systems. Each with a market capitalisation of $60 billion and $40 billion respectively. Their earnings are $2.5 billion and $3 billion each. With this information we have that Wayland Corp has a P/E ratio of 24, and Cyberdyne systems of 13.33.

An example of the use of the harmonic mean for ratios.

Consider now that we have an investment that has 20% in Wayland and the rest in Cyberdyne. We can calculate the P/E ratio of the index with a weighted harmonic mean defined as follows:

$$WHM = \frac{\sum_{i=1}^{n} w_i}{\sum_{i=1}^{n} w_i x_i^{-1}}. \tag{4.14}$$

For the index mentioned above we have that the weighted harmonic mean is given by:

The harmonic mean provides a fair comparison for the ratios.

$$PE_{WHM} = \frac{0.2 + 0.8}{\frac{0.2}{24} + \frac{0.8}{13.33}} = 14.63. \tag{4.15}$$

If we were to use the weighted arithmetic mean we will overestimate the P/E ratio:

$$PE_{wAM} = (0.2)(24) + (0.8)(13.22) = 18.93. \tag{4.16}$$

The arithmetic mean would overestimate the result.

This is because the arithmetic mean gives more weight to larger values.

For another example where the harmonic mean is used is in the context of rates, think for example speed. Consider a trip performed by Captain Suru of the *USS Discovery* to rescue Commander Michael Burnham:

An example of the use or the harmonic mean for rates.

- On the way to the rescue, *USS Discovery* travelled 180 Light Years in 2.6 seconds

- After the successful rescue, due to damaged sustained to the spore drive, *USS Discovery* made the trip back in 8 seconds

A successful trip to rescue Commander Michael Burnham.

- Captain Suru instructed Lieutenant Commander Stamets to use the same route both ways

If we are interested in determining the average speed across the entire trip, back and forth, we can use the arithmetic mean and make the following calculation:

$$0.5\left[\left(\frac{180}{2.6}\right) + \left(\frac{180}{8}\right)\right] = 45.86\frac{LY}{sec}. \qquad (4.17)$$

The arithmetic mean will give us a result that implies that we travelled more slowly on the first leg of the rescue.

This would be a good estimate if we had travelled different distances at different speeds. However, given that we used the same route, the arithmetic mean would imply that we actually travelled more slowly on the way there. However, we know that the spore drive was in spotless condition to start with. Let us use instead the harmonic mean:

$$2\left[\left(\frac{2.6}{180}\right) + \left(\frac{3.4}{180}\right)\right]^{-1} = 33.96\frac{LY}{sec}. \qquad (4.18)$$

The harmonic mean provides a more accurate picture as we travelled the first leg faster than the second one.

In this case we take into account that we covered the first 180 Light Years quicker and therefore spent less time travelling compared to the second leg. The harmonic mean does this for us at lightning speed.

We should also note that the harmonic mean is used in the definition of the F1 score used in classification modelling[4].

[4] Rogel-Salazar, J. (2017). *Data Science and Analytics with Python*. Chapman & Hall/CRC Data Mining and Knowledge Discovery Series. CRC Press

It is effectively the harmonic mean of precision and recall, both of which are actually rates, and as we have seen, the harmonic mean is helpful when comparing these sorts of quantities.

4.4   Dispersion

KNOWING WHERE OUR DATA IS centred is of great help. However, that is not the end of the tale. There is much more we can tell from the tail, quite literally. If we know how far our values are from the centre of the distribution, we get a better picture of the data we have in front of us. This is what we mean by dispersion, and it helps us understand variability. If all the values in our data are very close to the central value, we have a very homogeneous dataset. The wider the distribution, the more heterogeneous our data is. Let us take a look at some useful dispersion measures.

> Looking at how close or far the values is from the centre tells us something about our data.

4.4.1   Setting the Boundaries: Range

A VERY STRAIGHTFORWARD MEASURE OF dispersion is the width covered by the values in the dataset. This is called the range and it is simply the difference between the maximum and minimum values in the dataset.

> The range is the difference between the maximum and minimum values.

The first step in calculating the range is to obtain the boundaries. In other words, we need to find the maximum and minimum values. For our Physics marks from Table 3.1 we can do this as follows:

```
> physics.max()


9.0


> physics.min()


4.5
```

We are using the max and min methods for NumPy arrays.

We can then simply calculate the difference:

```
> physics_range = physics.max() - physics.min()
> print(physics_range)


4.5
```

This is such a common thing to do that NumPy has a method for arrays called .ptp() or peak-to-peak:

```
physics.ptp()

4.5
```

Or we can use the peak-to-peak or ptp method instead.

With it we can also calculate the range for the marks array in one go:

```
> marks.ptp(axis=0)


array([4.5, 4. , 6. ])
```

We can see that the marks for History are more spread than for the other two subjects.

We can see from the results above that History (6) has a wider range and this means that the variability in the marks is higher than for Spanish (4).

For our pandas dataframe we can use pretty much the same methods as above. Let us take a look at the maximum and minimum values of the fuel consumption column we have been analysing:

```
> mpg.max(), mpg.min()

(33.9, 10.4)

> mpg_range = mpg.max() - mpg.min()
> print(mpg_range)

23.5
```

For pandas dataframes we can use the max and min methods to calculate the range.

We can actually apply the NumPy peak-to-peak function to the pandas series too:

```
> np.ptp(mpg)

23.5
```

Or apply the peak-to-peak method instead.

For the car data grouped by transmission type we can calculate the range as follows:

```
> ct['mpg'].apply(np.ptp)

am
0     14.0
1     18.9
```

In this case we are using the apply method to calculate the range for our grouped dataframe.

4.4.2   Splitting One's Sides: Quantiles, Quartiles, Percentiles and More

IN MANY CASES IT IS useful to group observations into several equal groups. This is effectively what we are doing with the median: It represents the middle position of our data when dividing it into two parts. Half of the data has values lower than the median and the other half is higher. Positions like the median are useful as they indicate where a specified proportion of our data lies. These landmark points are known as *quantiles* and they split our observations into equal groups.

> The median splits a dataset into two halves.

> Quantiles split our data into equal groups.

We may want to create not only two groups, but for example four groups, such that the values that split the data give 25% of the full set each. In this case these groups have a special name: *quartiles*. Note that if we partition our data into n groups, we have $n - 1$ quantiles. In the case of quartiles we have therefore 3 of them, with the middle one being equal to the median. Other quantiles with special names include deciles, which split the data into 10 groups, and percentiles split it into 100 groups. In this case the 50th percentile corresponds to the median.

> Quartiles split the data into 4 groups. The median is therefore also called the second quartile.

> Percentiles partition the data into 100 equal groups. The median is thus the 50th percentile.

We find our $n - 1$ quantiles by first ranking the data in order, and then cutting it into $n - 1$ equally spaced points on the interval, obtaining n groups. It is important to mention that the terms quartile, decile, percentile, etc. refer to the cut-off points and not to the groups obtained. The groups should be referred to as quarters, tenths, etc.

> We need to order our data to obtain our quantiles.

As we mentioned before, quantiles are useful to specify the position of a set of data. In that way, given an unknown distribution of observations we may be able to compare its quantiles against the values of a known distribution. This can help us determine whether a model is a good fit for our data. A widely used method is to create a scatterplot known as the Q-Q plot or quantile-quantile plot. If the result is (roughly) linear, the model is indeed a good fit.

We can compare the distribution of quantiles to known distributions.

See Section 6.2.1 to learn more about Q-Q plots.

Let us take a look at the quantiles for the Physics marks in Table 3.1. We will use the quantile method in NumPy, where we pass the array we need to analyse as a first argument, followed by the desired quantile. In the case of quartiles we want to partition our data into $n = 4$ groups and thus we require $n - 1 = 3$ quartiles, namely 0.25, 0.5 and 0.75:

```
print('Physics Q1: ', np.quantile(physics, 0.25))
print('Physics Q2: ', np.quantile(physics, 0.50))
print('Physics Q3: ', np.quantile(physics, 0.75))


Physics Q1: 8.0
Physics Q2: 8.0
Physics Q3: 8.5
```

We are using the quantile method for NumPy arrays.

The quantile method can take a sequence for the quantiles required and we can indicate which axes we are interested in analysing. In this way, we can obtain the quartiles for each subject in a single line of code:

```
np.quantile(marks, [0.25, 0.5, 0.75], axis=0)


array([[ 8. ,  6.5,  7. ],
       [ 8. ,  9. ,  7.5],
       [ 8.5, 10. ,  9. ]])
```

The quantile method can take a list of values to calculate the appropriate quantiles.

In a pandas dataframe we can do pretty much the same as above as there is also a quantile method for dataframes:

```
mpg = cars.loc[:, 'mpg']
print('MPG Q1: ', mpg.quantile(0.25))
print('MPG Q2: ', mpg.quantile(0.50))
print('MPG Q3: ', mpg.quantile(0.75))


MPG Q1:   15.425
MPG Q2:   19.2
MPG Q3:   22.8
```

Pandas dataframes also have a quantile method.

The method can also take an array of quantile values as the NumPy one. Let us get, for example, the first and 100-th percentile for the miles per gallon column in our dataset:

```
> print(mpg.quantile([0.1, 1]))


0.1    14.34
1.0    33.90
```

Similarly, we can also provide a list of the desired quantiles for a pandas dataframe.

Note that we can use the describe method in a pandas dataframe to obtain some measures such as the quartiles:

```
> print(mpg.describe())


count    32.000000

mean     20.090625

std       6.026948

min      10.400000

25%      15.425000

50%      19.200000

75%      22.800000

max      33.900000
```

The describe method of a pandas dataframe provides a list of useful descriptive statistics, including the quartiles.

We get the quartiles as calculated above and we also get other information such as the maximum and minimum we described in the previous section. We also get the count of data and mean as defined in Section 4.3.3 and the standard deviation (std), which we will discuss in Section 4.4.4.

4.4.3   Mean Deviation

THINK OF HOW YOU WOULD describe the departure from an established route or course of action, even an accepted standard. The larger that gap, the bigger the departure or *deviation*. We can use this idea to consider the variation of all the observations of a dataset from a central value, for example the mean. If we calculate the mean of the deviations of all values from the arithmetic mean, we are obtaining the mean deviation of our dataset.

The mean deviation is the average departure of our data points from a central value.

By definition the chosen measure of central tendency is indeed central, and so we expect to have values larger and lower than it. In order for our mean deviation to avoid cancelling out positive and negative values, we take the absolute value of the deviations, in this case given by the difference from the point x_i from the mean μ, in other words $|x_i - \mu|$. The mean deviation for n observations is therefore given by:

$$MD = \frac{1}{n} \sum_{i=1}^{n} |x_i - \mu|. \qquad (4.19)$$

An alternative name is therefore mean absolute deviation.

The mean deviation provides us with information about how far, on average, our observations are spread out from a central point, in this case the mean. We can create a function to calculate the mean deviation:

```
def md(x, axis=None):
    avg = np.mean(x, axis)
    dev = np.absolute(x - avg)
    return np.mean(dev, axis)
```

Here is an implementation of Equation (4.19).

With that function in place, we can calculate the mean absolute deviation for our Physics marks:

```
> md(physics)

1.24
```

We can also apply it to our array of marks:

```
> md(marks, axis=0)

array([1.24, 1.64, 1.64])
```

Note that the mean deviation for Spanish and History marks is the same.

Notice than the mean deviation for Spanish and History marks is the same. This means that on average, the marks for these two subjects are 1.64 units from their respective means; 8.3 for Spanish and 7.3 for History. Notice that the interpretation of the mean deviation requires, therefore, the context of the average value.

The interpretation of the mean deviation requires the context of the mean value.

In pandas we have a dataframe method called mad that calculates the mean absolute deviation of the values in the dataframe. For our cars observations, the mean absolute deviation for fuel consumption is:

In pandas the mean absolute deviation can be calculated with the mad method.

```
> mpg.mad()

4.714453125
```

Similarly, for the mean absolute deviation for fuel consumption by transmission is:

```
> ct['mpg'].mad()

am
0    3.044875
1    5.237870
Name: mpg, dtype: float64
```

The mad method can be used for grouped dataframes too.

4.4.4   Variance and Standard Deviation

WE HAVE SEEN THAT WE can get a measure of the dispersion from a central value by calculating the difference from it. In the previous section we took the differences and used the absolute value to avoid the cancelling out of positive and negative values. Another possibility is to take the square of each difference. We ensure in that way that we obtain positive values, and have the advantage that we make the measure more sensitive. Let us take a look.

We can use the square of the differences.

Variance

This new measure of dispersion is called the *variance* and for a population with mean μ, the population variance is given by:

$$\sigma^2 = \frac{1}{n} \sum_{i=1}^{n} (x_i - \mu)^2 .$$

(4.20)

The variance is also called the mean square deviation.

For a sample, the variance is calculated as follows:

$$s^2 = \frac{1}{n-1} \sum_{i=1}^{n} (x_i - \bar{X})^2 .$$

(4.21)

Notice that the only difference between the population and sample variances is the factor used in the calculation. We use $n-1$ for the sample variance to obtain an unbiased estimate of the variability. This is because for a sample we would tend to obtain a lower value than the real variance for the population. The factor $n-1$ makes the sample variance larger.

See Appendix A for more information.

In many cases we are interested in calculating the sample variance to estimate the population variance, or we may be interested in saying something about the sampling error of the mean. If the sample size is n and the population mean μ is known, then the most appropriate estimation of the population variance is given by Equation (4.20). And we are done.

We estimate the population variance with the sample variance.

However, it is usually the case that we do not know the value of μ. Instead we can estimate it by using the sample mean $\bar{X}$. With a fixed value of $\bar{X}$ we need to know $n - 1$ of the elements in the sample to determine the remaining element. That element, therefore, cannot be freely assigned; and although we have used n elements to calculate the mean, we need to reduce the number by one to obtain the mean squared deviation. The number of values that are free to vary is called the *degrees of freedom* of a statistic.

The degrees of freedom are the values that can vary in a statistical analysis.

Standard Deviation

Calculating the square of the difference is helpful, but it leaves us with much larger units and in some cases units that are difficult to interpret as they would be the square of the unit. If we are interested in expressing the dispersion measurement in the same units as the original values, we need to simply take the square root of the variance. This measure of dispersion is called the *standard deviation*.

The standard deviation is the square root of the variance.

The population standard deviation is therefore given by:

$$\sigma = \sqrt{\frac{1}{n} \sum_{i=1}^{n} (x_i - \mu)^2}. \qquad (4.22)$$

The sample standard deviation is calculated as:

$$s = \sqrt{\frac{1}{n-1} \sum_{i=1}^{n} (x_i - \bar{X})^2}. \qquad (4.23)$$

We can calculate the population variance and standard deviation with the help of NumPy. For our Physics marks we can do the following:

```
> np.var(physics)
2.54


> np.std(physics)
1.5937377450509227
```

You can check that the variance is the square of the standard deviation.

If we need to calculate the sample variance and standard deviation, we simply use the delta degrees of freedom parameter ddof, and we use n - ddof in the calculation. For our Physics marks we have:

```
> np.var(physics, ddof=1)
3.175


> np.std(physics, ddof=1)
1.7818529681205462
```

ddof is the delta degrees of freedom.

We can apply the same functions to the array of marks too. For the population variance and standard deviation:

```
> np.var(marks, axis=0)
array([2.54, 2.96, 4.46])


> np.std(marks, axis=0)
array([1.59373775, 1.72046505, 2.11187121])
```

We can apply the functions to the columns of a NumPy array.

You may remember that when calculating the mean deviation for our student marks we obtained the same value for Spanish and History. With the standard deviation above we obtain markedly different values for the variance and standard deviation. From the values obtained we can see that the marks for History are spread wider than those for Spanish.

We can use the delta degrees of freedom parameter for the sample variance and standard deviation:

```
> np.var(marks, axis=0, ddof=1)
array([3.175, 3.7  , 5.575])


> np.std(marks, axis=0, ddof=1)
array([1.78185297, 1.92353841, 2.36114379])
```

The variance and standard deviation provide a better view of the dispersion of a dataset.

For a pandas dataframe we can use the .var and .std methods provided. However, please note that these two methods provide by default the sample variance and standard deviation measures. If we are interested in the population variance and standard deviation we need to pass the parameter ddof=0. Let us take a look. For the fuel consumption variable in our cars dataset we have:

The pandas .var and .std methods provide the sample variance and standard deviation by default.

```
> mpg.var(ddof=0)
35.188974609375


> mpg.std(ddof=0)
5.932029552301219
```

We need to pass ddof=0 to obtain the population values.

Since the default is ddof=1 for these methods, to obtain the sample variance and standard deviation we simply do the following:

```
> mpg.var()
36.32410282258065


> mpg.std()
6.026948052089105
```

The sample values are obtained by default.

For our grouped data by transmission we get the following sample variance and standard deviation measures:

```
> ct['mpg'].var()
am
0      14.699298
1      38.025769


> ct['mpg'].std()
am
0      3.833966
1      6.166504
```

The methods can be applied to grouped dataframes too.

4.5   Data Description – Descriptive Statistics Revisited

AS WE HAVE SEEN, WE can summarise a lot of information from a dataset using the descriptive statistics discussed so far. The mean and standard deviation are the most common measures that are quoted in many data description tasks. This is because they can provide a good view of what our data looks like and these measures, as we shall see, can be used to compare against well-known distributions.

The mean and standard deviation are the most widely used descriptive statistics.

When the data does not match a distribution, or there it is skewed, it is sometimes preferable to use the median and the centiles such as the 10th and 90th. We know that the .describe() method in pandas quotes the first and third quartiles. This is useful as it lets us define the interquartile range.

The median and percentiles are used when the distribution is skewed.

Although descriptive statistics tell us a lot about our data, they do not tell us everything. We may look at the mean or median value, but we cannot say anything about the outliers that happen to be in the data for example. We may want to look at the dispersion too and even then, different distributions have very different shapes and still have the same mean and standard deviation.

Descriptive statistics are not the full story; we need to consider the overall distribution of the data.

If we know that the data matches a known distribution we can use this information to our advantage. If the mean and the standard deviation are known, we can for instance express the values in our dataset as deviations from the mean as a multiple of the standard deviation. This is called a Z-score or standard score:

Z-scores let us compare the data from a test to a normal population (in the statistical sense).

$$Z = \frac{x - \mu}{\sigma}.$$ (4.24)

See Section 5.4.1 for information about the normal distribution.

The advantage of using these scores is that the values are effectively normalised, enabling us to make comparisons.

Other times, we may have two distributions that have similar average values and thus we can compare the standard deviations. However, if the units are different, or the average value is different, we need a variability measure that is independent of the units used and takes into account the means. In this case we can use the following transformation.

$$CV = \frac{100\sigma}{\mu}, \tag{4.25}$$

and it is called the coefficient of variation. It is expressed as a percentage, and is defined as the ratio of the standard deviation to the mean. It encapsulates the degree of variability in relation to the mean of the population.

As you can imagine, we need other tools to continue making sense of the data we are analysing, and having a better view of different distributions is our next step.

The coefficient of variation measures the variability in relation to the mean.

5

Definitely Maybe: Probability and Distributions

THE TYPE STATISTICAL ANALYSIS WE have seen in the previous chapters has concentrated on describing our data. However, we are also interested in making predictions based on it. In order to do that, we rely on the probability that certain phenomena will occur. We can quantify that probability with a number between 0 and 1, where the former is equivalent to saying that the phenomenon is impossible, and the latter that the phenomenon will occur for certain.

Probability is a good companion of statistical analysis.

We can define probability in terms of relative frequency. In other words, from the number of times that an event happens, divided by the total number of trials in an actual experiment. Think of flipping a coin; the theoretical probability of getting a head is 1/2. If we flipped the coin 100 times we may not get exactly 50 heads, but a number close to it. Relative frequencies let us estimate the probability we are after based on the outcomes of an experiment or trial.

We can define probability based on the relative frequency of an event happening.

5.1   *Probability*

WHEN WE TALK ABOUT UNCERTAINTY we tend to use the
language of probability. Capturing data about the specific
phenomena of interest provides us with important
information to understand the randomness in the results
obtained. This is known as empirical probability and it is
obtained from experimental measurement. We call Ω the set
of all possible events that may occur around the
phenomenon we are interested in studying. There are some
important properties that probabilities follow.

*Empirical probability is measured
by experimentation.*

1. In the sample space (Ω) for an experiment, the
   probability of $P(\Omega)$ is 1.

*Some important properties of
probabilities.*

2. For an event A, the probability of the event happening is
   given by $P(A) = |A|/|\Omega|$ where $|\cdot|$ is the cardinality of
   the event.

3. Given the statement above, for any event A, the
   probability $P(A)$ is between 0 and 1.

4. For an any event A and its complement A',
   $P(A) + P(A') = 1$.

Think of A' as "not A".

5. If two events, A and B, are independent from each other,
   the probability of them occurring simultaneously is
   $P(A \cup B) = P(AB) = |AB|/|\Omega| = P(A)P(B)$.

6. If two events, A and B, cannot occur at the same time, we
   say they form a disjoint event. The probability of A or B
   occurring is given by $P(A \cap B) = P(A) + P(B)$.

7. If two events, A and B, are not mutually exclusive, the probability of both occurring is $P(A \cup B) = P(A) + P(B) - P(A \cap B)$.

We may also be interested in knowing the probability of an event A happening based on the occurrence of another event B. This is known as the conditional probability and is denoted as $P(A|B)$. This is read as the probability of A given B and is calculated as:

Conditional probability is the probability of an event happening based on the occurrence of another event.

$$P(A|B) = \frac{|AB|}{|B|} = \frac{\frac{|AB|}{|\Omega|}}{\frac{|B|}{\Omega}}. \tag{5.1}$$

It is possible to ask about the conditional probability of B given A and the expression for this is given by:

$$P(B|A) = \frac{|BA|}{|A|}. \tag{5.2}$$

We can substitute Equation (5.2) into Equation (5.1) and we obtain the following expression:

$$P(A|B) = \frac{P(B|A)P(A)}{P(B)}, \tag{5.3}$$

Bayes' theorem.

and this is known as Bayes' theorem. It is named after the 18th-century English statistician and Presbyterian minister Thomas Bayes based a posthumous publication[1] presented to the Royal Society in 1763. There is an alternative interpretation of the concept of probability known as Bayesian probability. Instead of using the relative frequency of an event, probability is thought of as reasonable expectation representing a state of knowledge or as

[1] Bayes, T. (1763). An essay towards solving a problem in the doctrine of chances. *Philosophical Transactions* 53, 370–418

quantification of a personal belief. This expectation can be updated from prior ones.

The probability $P(A|B)$ in Equation (5.3) is known as the *posterior* probability, and $P(A)$ is the *prior*. $P(B|A)$ is called the likelihood. Bayes' theorem can be thought of as a rule that enables us to update our belief about a hypothesis A in light of new evidence B, and so our posterior belief $P(A|B)$ is updated by multiplying our prior belief $P(A)$ by the likelihood $P(B|A)$ that B will occur if A is actually true.

$P(A|B)$ is the posterior probability and $P(A)$ is the prior.

This rule has had a number of very successful applications, for example, in machine learning classification[2] problems where the Naïve Bayes Classifier is a favourite. It can also be applied to a variety of things, even in space, the final frontier. An example I enjoy of the use of this approach is the account of Laplace determining the mass of Saturn[3]. Let us know talk about the role that random variables have in the calculation of probabilities and their distribution.

[2] Rogel-Salazar, J. (2017). *Data Science and Analytics with Python.* Chapman & Hall/CRC Data Mining and Knowledge Discovery Series. CRC Press

[3] Laplace, P. S. and A. Dale (2012). *Pierre-Simon Laplace Philosophical Essay on Probabilities: Translated from the Fifth French Edition of 1825 with Notes by the Translator.* Sources in the History of Mathematics and Physical Sciences. Springer New York

5.2   *Random Variables and Probability Distributions*

WE HAVE BEEN REFERRING TO important concepts in statistics, for instance in Chapter 4 we talked about population and sample. We know that the idea of taking samples is to draw conclusions about the population. We may be interested in understanding a given characteristic of the population, but we may not have the entire data. This can be solved by estimating a parameter from the sample statistic to determine a parameter that describes the

Sample statistic is the value calculated from the sample data.

population. The samples can be taken at random and thus we need to understand some ideas behind random variables.

5.2.1   Random Variables

LET US CONSIDER THE FOLLOWING example. You are faced with Harvey Dent, aka Two-Face, and Batman is nowhere to be seen. Mr Dent uses his coin to wield his weapon of choice: Decisions. Depending on whether the coin lands on the scarred or the clear face, we may end with different outcomes, evil or less so. Say that the coin is flipped twice and it can land on either the scarred face (S) or the clear face (C). For this situation, we have the following possible outcomes:

Mr Dent could be using a normal coin too, with heads and tails instead.

- SS

- SC

- CS

- CC

In the encounter with Mr Dent above, we have managed to create a random variable. A random variable is a variable that takes on different values determined by chance.

A random variable has values determined by chance.

If we are interested in the number of times that the coin leads Two-Face to act evilly, we need to count the number of times the coin lands on the S face. We will call our variable of interest X, and according to the information above, it can take the values 0, 1, or 2.

We can use this information to build a table that tells us how frequent the outcomes may be. In particular, we can look at the relative frequency of the outcomes, which in turn can be interpreted as the probability of a particular outcome to be realised. For example, there is only one time in four that no S occurs in our experiment. The relative frequency of this outcome is 1/4. This means that we have a 0.25 probability of getting this result.

The relative frequency gives us the probability of different events.

Table 5.1 shows the probabilities for all outcomes and it represents the probability distribution of our statistical experiment.

X	Probability $P(X = x)$	Cumulative Probability $P(X \leq x)$
0	0.25	0.25
1	0.50	0.75
2	0.25	1.00

Table 5.1: Probability of our coin flipping experiment.

We can now ask about the probability that the value of our random variable X falls within a specified range. This is called the cumulative probability. For example, if we are interested in the probability of obtaining one or fewer S outcomes, we can calculate the probability of obtaining no S, plus the probability of getting one S:

A cumulative probability is the probability that the value of a random variable falls within a specified range.

$$
\begin{aligned}
P(X \leq 1) &= P(X = 0) + P(X = 1), \\
&= 0.25 + 0.50 = 0.75. \quad (5.4)
\end{aligned}
$$

For our coin experiment with Two-Face, the cumulative probability distribution for $P(X \leq x)$ is in the last column of Table 5.1.

5.2.2   *Discrete and Continuous Distributions*

THE VARIABLE X IN OUR experiment with Two-Face's coin can only take four possible outcomes and thus we refer to its probability distribution as a discrete probability distribution. The frequency function that describes our discrete random variable experiment is called the probability mass function or PMF.

Discrete probability distribution refers to the occurrence of discrete or individually countable outcomes.

If the random variable we are studying can take any value between two specified values, then the variable is called continuous and, imaginatively enough, its probability distribution is called a continuous probability distribution.

Continuous probability distributions can take any value in a given range.

The probability that a continuous random variable will take a particular value is zero and this means that we cannot express the distribution in the form of a table. We require instead a mathematical expression. We refer to this expression as the probability density function or PDF. The area under the curve described by the PDF is equal to 1 and it tells us the probability:

$$\int_{-\infty}^{\infty} p(x)dx = 1, \tag{5.5}$$

The area under the PDF gives us the probability.

and the probability that our random variable takes a value between two values a and b is given by the area under the curve bounded by a and b.

Sometimes it is useful to go the other way around. In other words, given a distribution, we may want to start with a probability and compute the corresponding x for the cumulative distribution. This can be done with the percent point function (PPF). We can think of the PPF as the inverse of the cumulative distribution function.

5.2.3   Expected Value and Variance

GIVEN THE SCENARIO ABOVE WITH Mr Dent, we can ask what value we should expect to obtain. To answer this question we need to find the expected value of our random variable. For a discrete random variable the expected value $E(X)$ is given by:

We also call this the mean.

$$E(X) = \mu = \sum x_i p_i, \qquad (5.6)$$

where p_i is the probability associated with the outcome x_i. This is effectively a weighted average as described in Section 4.3.4. For our experiment above we have that the mean value is:

The expected value is a weighted average.

$$\mu = E[X] = 0(0.25) + 1(0.5) + 2(0.25) = 1. \qquad (5.7)$$

This means that if we flip a fair coin 2 times we expect 1 S face; or equivalently the fraction of heads for two flips is one half. But what about the variability in our experiment. Well, we are therefore interested in looking at the variance of our discrete random variable which is given by:

$$Var(X) \;\; = \;\; \sigma^2 = E\left[(X - E[X])^2\right],$$

We can express the variance in terms of expected values.

$$= \;\; = E\left[X^2 - 2XE[X] + E[X]^2\right],$$

$$Var(X) \;=\; E[X^2] - 2E[X]E[X] + E[X]^2,$$

$$\;=\; = E[X^2] - E\,[X]^2. \tag{5.8}$$

In other words, the variance of X is equal to the mean of the square of X minus the square of the mean of X. For our coin experiment this can be written as:

$$\sigma^2 = \sum x_i^2 p_i - \mu^2. \tag{5.9}$$

An alternative notation for the variance.

Substituting the values we have that:

$$\sigma^2 = 0^2(0.25) + 1^2(0.5) + 2^2(0.25) - 1^2 = 0.5. \tag{5.10}$$

In the case of a continuous variable with PDF $f(x)$, we have that the expected value is defined as:

$$E(X) = \mu = \int_{-\infty}^{\infty} x f(x)dx, \tag{5.11}$$

The expectation value for a continuous variable is given by the integral of its PDF, $f(x)$, multiplied by x.

and the variance is given by:

$$Var(X) \;=\; E[X^2] - \mu^2,$$

$$\;=\; \int_{-\infty}^{\infty} x^2 f(x) - \left[\int_{-\infty}^{\infty} x f(x) \right]^2. \tag{5.12}$$

The results obtained in Equations (5.7) and (5.10) are suitable for two flips of Mr Dent's coin. However, we are now curious to know about the probability distribution for the fraction of S faces we get if we were to increase the number of flips to, say, 100. We can ask Python to help us.

We are now interested in repeated trials of our coin flip.

```
import numpy as np

import random


def coinFlip(nflips=100):

    flips = np.zeros(nflips)

    for flip in range(nflips):

        flips[flip] = random.choice([0,1])

    return flips
```

We can use this function to simulate repeated coin flips for our experiment.

With the help of the random.choice function in the random module in Python, we can choose values at random from the list provided, in this case between the discrete values 0 or 1. Let 1 be the S face we are interested in. We throw the fateful coin 100 times by default (nflips=100), and we store the results in a list called flips. Let us see the result of a few of instances of the 100 flips:

```
> t1, t2, t3 = coinFlip(), coinFlip(), coinFlip()
> np.sum(t1), np.sum(t2), np.sum(t3)


(57.0, 46.0, 54.0)
```

Remember that the numbers are random, so your list may look different.

We have performed 100 flips on three different trials. In the first trial we obtained 57 scar faces, 46 in the second trial and 54 in the third. The fraction of scar faces is close to 50, but to be able to assert the expected value we may need to do the experiment several more times. Perhaps 100, 250, 1000 or even 10000 times. Once again, lets get Python to help:

```
def coinExperiment(ntrials):

    results = np.zeros(ntrials)

    for trial in range(ntrials):

        f = coinFlip()

        results[trial] = np.sum(f)

    return results
```

This function will let us simulate repeated trials of our coin flipping experiment. We are throwing the coin nflips=100 times.

Here, we store the number of S faces obtained in each trial in the array called results. We can now ask Python to throw the coins:

```
ntrials = [100, 250, 1000, 10000]

r = []

for i, n in enumerate(ntrials):

    r.append(coinExperiment(n))
```

We repeat our experiment with an increasing number of trials.

We can look at the mean, variance and standard deviations obtained in each of the experiments:

```
> for i in r:

    print(i.mean()/100, i.var()/100, i.std()/10)


0.49369999999999997 0.183731 0.428638542364

0.49723999999999996 0.293358 0.541625553311

0.49988999999999995 0.262368 0.512219474444

0.50110199999999999 0.252276 0.502271400340
```

We are looking at the fraction of S faces obtained, hence the division by 100. Remember that the standard deviation is the square root of the variance.

We are looking at the fraction of S faces obtained and that is why we are dividing by the total number of flips, i.e. $nflips = 100$. We can look at the frequency of each result. This can be seen in the histogram shown in Figure 5.1. We

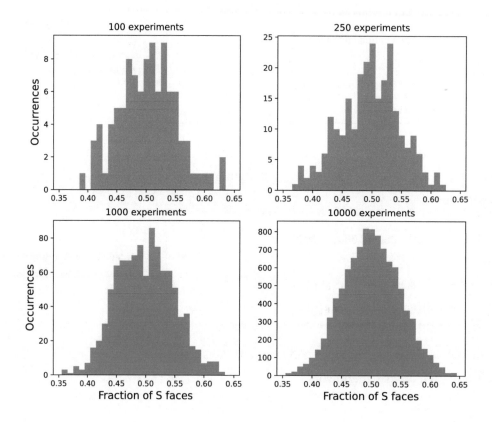

Figure 5.1: Probability distribution of the number of S faces in Two-Face's fair coin flipped 100 times.

can see that as the number of experiments increases, we get a better defined distribution.

The distribution that emerges as the number of experiments grows is called the normal distribution and this is the result of taking a random sample of size n from any distribution. For sufficiently large n, the sample mean $\bar{X}$ follows approximately the normal distribution with mean μ and standard deviation $\sigma/\sqrt{n}$ where μ and σ are the mean and

See Section 5.4.1 for more information about the normal distribution.

standard deviation of the population from which the sample
was selected. This is the central limit theorem and we will
look at this in more detail later on in Section 5.4.4.

See Section 5.4.4 for information
about the central limit theorem.

5.3   Discrete Probability Distributions

Now that we are better acquainted with what a
probability distribution is, we will take a look at a few of the
most widely used discrete probability distributions.

5.3.1   Uniform Distribution

Let us start with one of the most straightforward
probability distributions, the uniform distribution. As the
name implies, it describes the case where every possible
outcome has an equal likelihood of happening. An example
of this is the casting of a fair die: Each face is equally likely
to be obtained with a probability of 1/6. Another example
is drawing any card from a standard deck of cards, where
each card has a probability of 1/52 to be drawn.

In the uniform distributions,
all outcomes are equally likely.
Examples include the casting of
a die, or drawing a card from a
deck.

The probability mass function (PMF) for the uniform
distribution is given by:

$$f(x) = \frac{1}{n},$$

(5.13)

The PMF of the uniform
distribution.

where n is the number of values in the range. It is also
possible to use upper and lower bounds, denoted as U and
L respectively. In this way we can express the number of
values in the range as $n = U - L + 1$.

In terms of upper and lower bounds, the probability mass function for the uniform distribution can be written as:

$$f(x) = \begin{cases} \frac{1}{U-L+1} & \text{for } L \le x \le U+1, \\ \\ 0 & \text{for } x < L \text{ or } x > U+1. \end{cases} \quad (5.14)$$

The PMF of the uniform distribution in terms of upper and lower bounds.

The cumulative distribution function for the uniform distribution is given by:

$$F(x) = \begin{cases} 0 & \text{for } x < L, \\ \\ \frac{x-L}{U-L+1} & \text{for } L \le x \le U+1, \\ \\ 1 & \text{for } x > U+1. \end{cases} \quad (5.15)$$

The cumulative distribution function of the uniform distribution.

The mean of the uniform distribution can be calculated as follows:

$$\begin{aligned} \mu &= \sum_{1}^{n} x_i f(x_i) = \frac{1}{n} \sum_{i=0}^{n-1} i, \\ \\ &= \frac{1}{n} \frac{n(n-1)}{2}, \\ \\ &= \frac{n-1}{2}, \end{aligned} \quad (5.16)$$

The mean of the uniform distribution.

where we have used the following identity:

$$\sum_{i=0}^{n-1} i = \frac{n(n-1)}{2}. \quad (5.17)$$

See Appendix B for more information.

Equation (5.16) is the standard version of the mean for the uniform distribution where the lower bound is 0. Recalling

that $E[X + c] = E[X] + c$, where c is a constant, we can write
our mean as follows:

$$\mu = \frac{n-1}{2} + L = \frac{L+U}{2}, \qquad (5.18)$$

The mean of the uniform
distribution in terms of upper
and lower bounds.

where the last expression is obtained by substituting $n =$
$U - L + 1$. This shows that the mean value of the uniform
distribution is the arithmetic mean of the upper and lower
bounds.

The variance of the uniform distribution is given by $\sigma^2 =$
$E[X^2] - E[X]^2$ and thus:

$$\sigma^2 = \frac{1}{n} \sum_{i=0}^{n-1} i^2 + \left(\frac{n-1}{2}\right)^2. \qquad (5.19)$$

The second term of the expression above is given by
Equation (5.16), whereas the first term can be calculated
with the identity:

See Appendix C for more
information.

$$\sum_{i=0}^{n-1} i^2 = \frac{n(n-1)(2n-1)}{6}. \qquad (5.20)$$

Substituting Equation (5.20) into Equation (5.19) and
expanding:

$$\sigma^2 = \frac{1}{n} \frac{n(n-1)(2n-1)}{6} + \frac{n^2 - 2n + 1}{4},$$

The variance of the uniform
distribution.

$$= \frac{2n^2 - 3n + 1}{6} + \frac{n^2 - 2n + 1}{4},$$

$$= \frac{4n^2 - 6n + 2 - 3n^2 + 6n - 3}{12} = \frac{n^2 - 1}{12}. \qquad (5.21)$$

Let us go back to the idea of throwing a die. We can model
the PMF of the uniform distribution in Python with the help
of uniform from scipy.stats as follows:

```
> import numpy as np
> from scipy.stats import uniform
> x = np.arange(1,7)
> print(x)


array([1, 2, 3, 4, 5, 6])
```

The uniform distribution is
implemented in SciPy's uniform.

The array x in the code above represents our random
variable. Here, the values refer to the faces of our die. We
can now call the pdf(x, loc, scale) method, where x is
the random variable. The distribution is uniform on $[0, 1]$. If
we use the parameters loc and scale, we obtain the
uniform distribution on [loc, loc + scale]. We can see
the depiction of the uniform distribution PDF in the upper
left-hand panel of Figure 5.2.

The implementation of the
uniform distribution in SciPy is
described as continuous, hence the
use of PDF in the implementation
name.

```
> pdf = uniform.pdf(x, 0, 6)
> print(pdf)

array([0.16666667, 0.16666667, 0.16666667,
   0.16666667, 0.16666667, 0.16666667])
```

We obtain the PDF of the uniform
distribution with the pdf method.

The cumulative distribution function can be obtained with
cdf(x, loc, scale) as shown in the code below. We can
see a depiction for our die rolls in the upper right-hand side
panel of Figure 5.2.

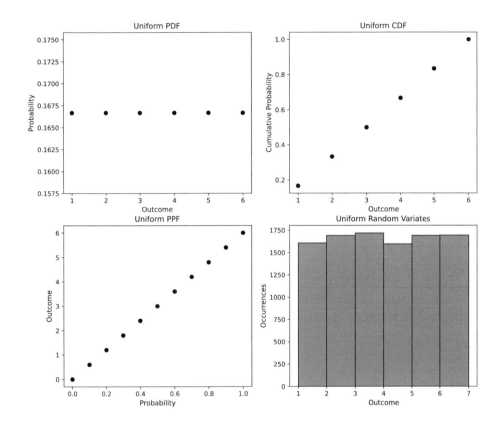

Figure 5.2: The uniform distribution.

```
> cdf = uniform.cdf(x, 0, 6)

> print(cdf)


array([0.16666667, 0.33333333, 0.5,

    0.66666667, 0.83333333,

        1.         ])
```

We get the CDF of the uniform distribution with the cdf method.

As we can see, the probabilities add up to 1 as expected. Let us now look at the percent point function (PPF). We start by postulating some probabilities and calculate the corresponding random variables:

```
> probs = np.arange(0, 1.1, 0.1)
> ppf = uniform.ppf(probs, 0, 6)
```

We get the PPF of the uniform distribution with the ppf method.

We store the probabilities from 0.1 to 1 in steps of 0.1 in the probs array. We then calculate the PPDF with the ppf method. The result is shown in the lower left-hand side panel of Figure 5.2.

Finally, let us look at generating random variates that follow the uniform distribution. We can do this with the help of rvs(loc, scale, size), where the last parameter specifies the shape of the arrays requested. Let us look at generating 10000 random variates. Please note that the entries will be of type float, so we will cast them as integers to get a better feel for the actual throw of a die:

We generate random variates that follow the uniform distribution with the rvs method.

```
> x1 = uniform.rvs(1, 6, 10000)
> x1 = x1.astype(int)
```

Since in our example we can only obtain integer numbers from our dice, we are casting the random variates given by rvs as integers. A histogram of these random variates is shown in the lower right-hand side panel of Figure 5.2.

Remember that in SciPy the uniform distribution is implemented as continuous.

Let us see what the mean and population variance for the random variables above are:

```
> x1.mean(), x1.var(ddof=1)


(3.5154, 2.9080536453645367)
```

Using the Equations (5.18) and (5.21) we can check the values from the theoretical distribution:

```
> n=6, L=1
> u_mean = (n-1)/2 + L
> u_var = (n**2-1)/12
> print(u_mean)
3.5


> print(u_var)
2.9166666666666665
```

We can corroborate that the mean and variance of the variates generated correspond to the values we expect for a uniform distribution.

5.3.2   Bernoulli Distribution

REMEMBER OUR ENCOUNTER WITH MR Dent and his fateful coin? Provided that his coin is fair, for a single coin flip we have one of two outcomes each with a probability of 50%. This scenario can be described by the Bernoulli distribution.

And that fairness remains to be proven. Where is Batman by the way?

The distribution bears the name of the 17-th century mathematician Jacob Bernoulli who defined what we now call a Bernoulli trial: An experiment with only two possible outcomes. His posthumous book *Ars Conjectandi*[4] is perhaps one of the first textbooks on formal probability, and in it the probabilistic folklore of trials with outcomes described as "success" or "failure" started getting cemented.

[4] Bernoulli, J., J. Bernoulli, and E. D. Sylla (2006). *The Art of Conjecturing, Together with Letter to a Friend on Sets in Court Tennis.* Johns Hopkins University Press

Coin flipping is a classic example of the Bernoulli distribution as there are only two possible outcomes. In the case of Mr Dent's coin we have the scarred and the clear faces. One could argue that for a fair coin the distribution could be a uniform distribution too. Similarly, the case of rolling a die can be cast as a Bernoulli distribution if we fold the outcomes into 2, for instance getting an odd or an even number. The two outcomes of our Bernoulli trial are such that a success (1) is obtained with probability p and a failure (0) with probability $q = 1 - p$. This is therefore the PMF of the Bernoulli distribution:

A Bernoulli experiment is one where there are only two possible outcomes.

$$f(x) = p^x(1-p)^{1-x}, \text{ for } x \in \{0,1\}. \qquad (5.22)$$

For our coin $p = q = 0.5$, but the probabilities need not be equal. The coin may be biased, or the Bernoulli trial may be the outcome of a fight between me and Batman... He is much more likely to win! My success may be 0.12 and his 0.88.

The probabilities p and q may be different. Perhaps Mr Dent's coin is indeed biased.

The mean of the Bernoulli distribution is:

$$\mu = (1)(p) + 0(1-p) = p. \qquad (5.23)$$

The mean of the Bernoulli distribution.

For our coin flipping experiment the mean is $\mu = 0.5$. The variance of the Bernoulli distribution is:

$$\begin{aligned} \sigma^2 &= (p-1)^2 p + (p-0)^2(1-p), \\ &= p - p^2, \\ &= p(1-p). \qquad (5.24) \end{aligned}$$

The variance of the Bernoulli distribution.

The variance is the multiplication of the two possible outcomes. For our coin flipping experiment the variance is $\sigma^2 = 0.25$.

Python has us covered with the `bernoulli` implementation in SciPy. Let us create a distribution for the encounter between me and Batman. The outcomes are failure (0) or success (1) and $p = 0.12$ for my success. The PMF can be seen in the top left-hand panel of Figure 5.3 and we calculate it with Python as follows:

KA-POW!!!

```
> x = np.array([0, 1])

> pmf = bernoulli.pmf(x, 0.12)

> print(pmf)


array([0.88, 0.12])
```

Probability distribution implementations in SciPy all have similar methods for calculating PMFs/PDFs, CDF, PPF and random variates. Here we use bernoulii module.

The CDF for the Bernoulli distribution is easily obtained:

```
> cdf = bernoulli.cdf(x, 0.12)

> print(cdf)


array([0.88, 1.  ])
```

See the CDF of the Bernoulli distribution in the top right-hand panel of Figure 5.3.

The PPF, as you expect, will return the outcome given certain probabilities:

```
> probs = np.array([0.88, 1.0])

> ppf = bernoulli.ppf(probs, 0.12)

> print(ppf)


array([0., 1.])
```

See PPF in the bottom left-hand panel of Figure 5.3.

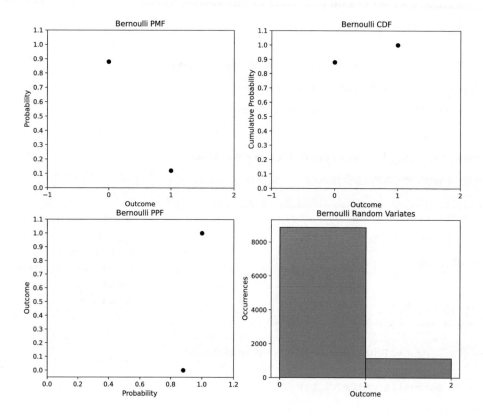

Figure 5.3: The Bernoulli distribution.

We can obtain random variates that follow the Bernoulli distribution as follows:

```
> x1 = bernoulli.rvs(0.12, size=10000)

> print(x1.mean(), x1.var(ddof=1))


0.1144 0.10132277227722773
```

See a histogram of Bernoulli variates in the bottom right-hand panel of Figure 5.3.

Let us compare the result obtained versus theoretical values:

```
> print(bernoulli.mean(0.12))

> print(bernoulli.var(0.12))


0.12

0.1056
```

5.3.3 Binomial Distribution

LET US REVISIT OUR COIN toss encounter with Two-Face, where we know that flipping a coin one time has one of two possible outcomes: Either the scarred face or the clear one. What if we were to challenge our villainous friend to make his decision on 2 out of 3 flips, or 4 out of 5 or many more throws, say k out of n flips. Well, we are facing a situation similar to that encountered in Section 5.2.3 where we tested with 100 trials and went up to 10000.

Enemy? Frenemy perhaps?

Each of the coin flips follows a Bernoulli distribution as explained in Section 5.3.2. The repeated trials imply the sum of these Bernoulli random variables. This sum will follow the binomial distribution. We require though that each of the trials has the same probability of success (and therefore of failure). Also, each trial is independent from any other trial, in other words, the previous flip does not influence the outcome of the next one.

A binomial distribution is given by a sequence of n independent Bernoulli experiments.

Back to the challenge to Two-Face. We may be interested in the way we obtain k results out of n items, irrespective

of their order. We can calculate this with the help of the
binomial coefficient[5].

[5] Scheinerman, E. A. (2012).
Mathematics: A Discrete Introduction.
Cengage Learning

$$\binom{n}{k} = \frac{n!}{(n-k)!k!},$$ (5.25)

where $n!$ stands for n factorial, and we can read the

$n! = n(n-1)(n-2)\ldots(2)(1).$

binomial coefficient as "choose k out of n" or "n choose k".
Check Appendix D for a derivation of the binomial
coefficient, and there are no prizes for guessing why this
distribution is called binomial.

The probability mass function for the binomial distribution
is given by:

$$f(k,n,p) = \binom{n}{k}p^k q^{(n-k)},$$ (5.26)

The PMF of the binomial
distribution.

where p is the probability of success in each trial, $q = 1 - p$
is the probability of failure, n is the number of trials and k is
the number of successes that can occur among the n trials.
Remember that the values for p and q should remain the
same from one trial to the next, and they do not need to be
equal to each other.

We can use Equation (5.26) to determine the probability of
getting no (0) scar faces in 3 flips:

$$f(0,3,0.5) = \frac{3!}{3!0!}(0.5)^0(1-0.5)^{3-0},$$

This is the probability of getting
no scar faces in 3 flips of Mr
Dent's coin.

$$= (1)(1)(0.5)^3,$$

$$= 0.125.$$ (5.27)

The mean of the binomial distribution can be obtained as follows:

$$\mu = \sum_{k=1}^{n} k \cdot \binom{n}{k} p^k q^{(n-k)}, \tag{5.28}$$

Some preliminary steps to calculate the mean of the binomial distribution.

$$= n \sum_{k=1}^{n} \binom{n-1}{k-1} p^k q^{(n-k)}, \tag{5.29}$$

$$= np \sum_{k=1}^{n} \binom{n-1}{k-1} p^{(k-1)} (1-p)^{(n-k)}. \tag{5.30}$$

In Equation (5.28) we start the sum from 1 as the case $k = 0$ does not have a contribution. In Equation (5.29) we have used the binomial property:

$$k \cdot \binom{n}{k} = n \cdot \binom{n-1}{k-1}, \tag{5.31}$$

See Appendix D for more information.

We have taken the factor n out of the sum as the latter does not depend on n. Now, we are going to do some re-writing and express $n - k$ as $(n-1) - (k-1)$:

$$\mu = np \sum_{k=1}^{n} \binom{n-1}{k-1} p^{(k-1)} (1-p)^{(n-1)-(k-1)}, \tag{5.32}$$

$$= np \sum_{j=0}^{m} \binom{m}{j} p^j (1-p)^{m-j}, \tag{5.33}$$

$$= np. \tag{5.34}$$

The mean of the binomial distribution.

Here, we have made some substitutions in Equation (5.33), such that $n - 1 = m$, and $k - 1 = j$. The sum in Equation (5.33) is equal to 1 as it is the sum of all probabilities for all outcomes.

The variance of the binomial distribution is given by:

$$\sigma^2 \;=\; E[X^2] - \mu^2,$$

$$= \sum_{k=1}^{n} k^2 \binom{n}{k} p^k (1-p)^{n-k} - (np)^2, \qquad (5.35)$$

Some preliminary steps to calculate the variance of the binomial distribution.

$$= n \sum_{k=1}^{n} k \binom{n-1}{k-1} p^k (1-p)^{n-k} - (np)^2. \qquad (5.36)$$

The sum in Equation (5.35) runs from 1 as the case $k = 0$ does not contribute to it. In Equation (5.36) we have used the following property:

$$k^2 \binom{n}{k} = kk \binom{n}{k} = kn \binom{n-1}{k-1}. \qquad (5.37)$$

See Appendix D.

Let us now use the following identity $p^k = pp^{k-1}$:

$$\sigma^2 = np \sum_{k=1}^{n} k \binom{n-1}{k-1} p^{k-1} (1-p)^{n-k} - (np)^2, \qquad (5.38)$$

and we can simplify the expression above:

$$\sigma^2 = np \sum_{k=1}^{n} k \binom{n-1}{k-1} p^{k-1}.$$
$$(1-p)^{(n-1)-(k-1)} - (np)^2, \qquad (5.39)$$

Almost there...

$$= np \sum_{j=0}^{m} (j+1) \binom{m}{j} p^j (1-p)^{m-j} - (np)^2, \qquad (5.40)$$

$$= np \left((n-1)p + 1 \right) - (np)^2, \qquad (5.41)$$

$$\sigma^2 = (np)^2 + np(1-p) - (np)^2, \qquad (5.42)$$

$$= np(1-p). \qquad (5.43)$$

The variance of the binomial distribution.

In Equation (5.40) we have distributed the sum and expressed it as two terms, the first being the expected value of the binomial distribution and the second the sum of all probabilities:

$$\sum_{j=0}^{m} j \binom{m}{j} p^j (1-p)^{m-j} + \sum_{j=0}^{m} \binom{m}{j} p^j (1-p)^{m-j}, \qquad (5.44)$$

$$mp + 1, \qquad (5.45)$$

$$(n-1)p + 1. \qquad (5.46)$$

Note that the binomial distribution for the case where $n = 1$ is actually a Bernoulli distribution. You can check the mean and variance for the Bernoulli distribution is recovered when only one trial is run.

The case $n = 1$ recovers the Bernoulli distribution.

In Python, the binomial distribution can be calculated with binom. For our several attempts with our coin, we can check the probability obtained in Equation (5.27) as follows:

```
> from scipy.stats import binom
> binom.pmf(0, 3, 0.5)

0.125
```

The binomial distribution is implemented in the binom module in SciPy.

Let us calculate the probability mass function (PMF) and the cumulative distribution function for obtaining 0, 1, ... , 100 scar faces in 100 attempts. The results can be seen in the top panels of Figure 5.4:

```
import numpy as np

x = np.arange(0, 100, 1)

pmf = binom.pmf(x, 100, 0.5)

cdf = binom.cdf(x, 100, 0.5)
```

The PMF and CDF of the binomial distribution are shown in the top panels of Figure 5.4.

The PPF for our experiment can be seen in the bottom left-hand side of Figure 5.4 and is calculated as follows:

```
probs = np.arange(0, 1, 0.01)

ppf = binom.ppf(probs, 100, 0.5)
```

The PPF is shown in the bottom left-hand side of Figure 5.4.

Finally, let us obtain 10000 random variates that follow the binomial distribution as shown in the bottom right-hand side of Figure 5.4:

```
> x1 = binom.rvs(n=100, p=0.5, size=10000)

> print(x1.mean(), x1.var(ddof=1))


49.9683 25.216416751675165
```

A histogram of binomial variates is shown in the bottom right-hand side of Figure 5.4.

We can see what the mean and variance are for our experiment and compare with the sample mean and sample variance above:

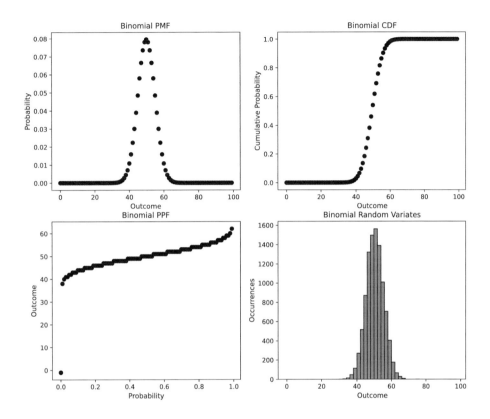

Figure 5.4: The binomial distribution.

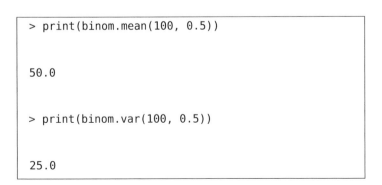

We can calculate the mean and variance for a binomial process with Python's help.

5.3.4   *Hypergeometric Distribution*

STARBUCK HAS BEEN CHASING CYLONS that jumped well into our quadrant and she is now stranded in our planet. After recovering for a few days, to pass the time she talks to us about an interesting card game popular among the Twelve Colonies: Triad. In the game, hexagonal cards show a large star surrounded by a border with smaller stars. After trying to explain the rules to us, and realising that we do not have a triad deck of cards, we teach her some of the card games we play in this planet, like poker or Texas hold 'em. Let us play: Starbuck starts with a deck of 52 cards, and she is dealt 4 cards. If those 4 cards are returned to the deck, the next time we deal the probabilities remain the same, but if we hold those cards, the deck now has only 48 cards. What happens then?

Playing triad or poker with Starbuck may prove to be a futile way to try to earn money, but a good way to pass the time.

Let us go through a first deal with Starbuck by considering the probability of getting an ace of any suit. There are 4 aces in a deck and for the first card we have 4/52, or 1/13, chance of getting an ace. Starbuck is a lucky person and she gets an ace! For the second card, since the ace obtained is no longer in the deck, the probability of getting an ace is now different. In the case where an ace is drawn in the first hand, the probability would be 3/51, but if Starbuck did not get an ace in the first hand, the chances would be 4/51. The game continues and, as you can see, the outcome of the next trial depends on the outcome of the previous one, and one of the key assumptions behind the binomial distribution is broken.

In this case, the outcome of the next trial depends on the outcome of the previous one, breaking one of the assumptions behind the binomial distribution.

For repeated trials where the probabilities remain constant, or when replacement is enabled, the distribution is binomial. For a single trial, we recover the Bernoulli distribution. But what about a different type trial, like the simple game with our Battlestar Galactica officer? The outcome may still be either success or failure, but without replacing the cards, the probabilities shift. This type of trial is called a hypergeometric experiment and its distribution is called a hypergeometric distribution.

In a hypergeometric experiment, the probabilities from one trial to the next change depending on the outcome of previous trials.

It sounds like a grandiose name, and perhaps a little bit scary, but there is a reason behind the it. Consider first a sequence where each succeeding term is produced by multiplying the previous term by a fixed number, called the common ratio. This type of sequence is called a geometric progression and they have been studied for centuries. Simply take a look at Euclid's Elements[6]. An example of a geometric progression with common ratio $1 - p$ is:

[6] Heath, T. L. (2017). *Euclid's Elements (The Thirteen Books)*. Digireads.com Publishing

$$p, \ p(1-p), \ p(1-p)^2, \ldots, p(1-p)^n. \qquad (5.17)$$

Generalisations of these types of progressions have been used in a variety of applications from quantum mechanics to engineering[7] for the description of elliptic curves or solving differential equations. The idea behind the generalisation is that successive terms, say k and $k + 1$, get applied different proportions that vary relative to each other, all this determined by a rational function. Since these progressions go beyond the geometric one described above, they are referred to as hypergeometric.

[7] Seaborn, J. B. (2013). *Hypergeometric Functions and Their Applications*. Texts in Applied Mathematics. Springer New York

A rational function is the quotient of two polynomials.

The probability mass function for the hypergeometric distribution in a population of size N is given by the number of samples that result in k successes divided by the number of possible samples of size n:

$$f(k, N, K, n) = \frac{\binom{K}{k}\binom{N-K}{n-k}}{\binom{N}{n}},$$

(5.48)

The PMF of the hypergeometric distribution.

where K is the number of successes in the population. As mentioned above, the denominator is the number of samples of size n. The numerator is made out of two factors, the first one is the number of combinations of k successes observed out of the number of successes in the population (K). The second corresponds to the failures, where $N - K$ is the total number of failures in the population.

Remember that $\binom{a}{b}$ stands for the binomial coefficient. See Appendix D.

Let us go back to our card game with Starbuck, and we can now consider the probability of getting 2 aces when 4 cards are dealt. This means that $k = 2$, $N = 52$, $K = 4$ and $n = 4$:

$$f(2, 52, 4, 4) = \frac{\binom{4}{2}\binom{52-4}{4-2}}{\binom{52}{4}},$$

$$= \frac{(6)(1128)}{270725},$$

The probabilities of the card game with Starbuck are easily obtained with the PMF above.

$$= 0.02499954.$$

(5.49)

In other words, there is about 2.5% chance of Starbuck getting 2 aces when dealt 4 cards. In Python, we can use the SciPy implementation of the hypergeometric PMF as follows:

```
> from scipy.stats import hypergeom

> hypergeom.pmf(2, 52, 4, 4)


0.024999538276849162
```

SciPy provides the hypergeom module.

For cases where the population N is large, the hypergeometric distribution approximates the binomial. Let us go catch some Pokémon with Ash Ketchum and Pikachu. We have a large container of Poké Balls; the container has two types of balls, 575 Poké Balls and 425 Beast Balls. Pikachu will take 10 balls out of the container for us. What is the probability that we will get 3 Beast Balls? Well, we can use the hypergeometric PMF to get the result:

See Appendix E.1.

Or to use their actual name モンスターボール or Monster Ball.

$$
\begin{aligned}
f(3, 1000, 425, 10) &= \frac{\binom{425}{3}\binom{1000-425}{10-3}}{\binom{1000}{10}}, \\[2mm]
&= \frac{(1.2704 \times 10^{7})(3.9748 \times 10^{15})}{2.6340 \times 10^{23}}, \\[2mm]
&= 0.19170.
\end{aligned}
\tag{5.50}
$$

Using Python we have that:

```
> from scipy.stats import hypergeom

> hypergeom.pmf(3, 1000, 425, 10)


0.19170588792109242
```

When the population N is large, the hypergeometric distribution approximates the binomial.

We can compare this to a binomial point estimate:

$$
\binom{10}{3}(0.425)^{3}(0.575)^{7} = 0.19143.
\tag{5.51}
$$

The results are pretty close and the idea behind this proximity is that as the population N grows to be larger and larger, although we do not replace the Poké Balls, the probability of the next event is nearly the same as before. This is indeed because we have a large population. We can now go and "catch 'em all".

Although we do not replace the balls, the probability of the next event remains nearly the same.

We are now interested in describing the mean and variance for the hypergeometric distribution. Let us start with the mean; let $P[X = k] = f(k, N, K, n)$ and we calculate the expectation value for X^r:

$$E[X^r] = \sum_{k=0}^{n} k^r \frac{\binom{K}{k}\binom{N-K}{n-k}}{\binom{N}{n}}. \tag{5.52}$$

We will use this expression to obtain the mean of the hypergeometric distribution.

We can use some useful identities of the binomial coefficient:

$$k\binom{K}{k} = K\binom{K-1}{k-1}, \tag{5.53}$$

See Appendix D.1 for more information

$$\binom{N}{n} = \frac{1}{n} \cdot n\binom{N}{n} = \frac{1}{n} \cdot N\binom{N-1}{n-1}. \tag{5.54}$$

Substituting Expressions (5.53) and (5.54) into Equation (5.52) and writing k^r as $k \cdot k^{r-1}$:

$$E[X^r] = \frac{nK}{N} \sum_{k=1}^{n} k^{r-1} \frac{\binom{K-1}{k-1}\binom{N-K}{n-k}}{\binom{N-1}{n-1}}. \tag{5.55}$$

We are writing the sum from $k = 1$ as the case for 0 does not contribute to the sum. If we define $j = k - 1$ and $m = K - 1$

we can rewrite the above expression as:

$$E[X^r] = \frac{nK}{N} \sum_{j=0}^{n-1} (j+1)^{r-1} \frac{\binom{m}{j}\binom{(N-1)-m}{(n-1)-j}}{\binom{N-1}{n-1}}. \qquad (5.56)$$

The sum in Expression (5.56) can be seen as the expectation value of a random variable Y with parameters $N-1$, K and $n-1$ and we end up with the following recursion formula:

$$E[X^r] = \frac{nK}{N} E[(Y+1)^{r-1}], \qquad (5.57)$$

and therefore the mean is given by:

$$\mu = \frac{nK}{N}. \qquad (5.58)$$

The mean of the hypergeometric distribution.

For the variance, remember that $Var[X] = E[X^2] - E^2[X]$. We can use the recursion formula obtained above to get the first term in the variance and thus:

$$\sigma^2 = \frac{nK}{N} \left(\frac{(n-1)(K-1)}{N-1} + 1 \right) - \left(\frac{nK}{N} \right)^2,$$

$$= \frac{nK}{N} \left(\frac{(n-1)(K-1)}{N-1} + 1 - \frac{nK}{N} \right),$$

$$= \frac{nK}{N} \left(\frac{N^2 - Nn - NK + nK}{N(N-1)} \right),$$

$$= \frac{nK}{N} \left(\frac{N-n}{N-1} \right) \left(1 - \frac{K}{N} \right). \qquad (5.59)$$

The variance of the hypergeometric distribution.

Let us play a different card game with Starbuck. This time it is Bridge, where a hand is such that 13 cards are selected at random and without replacement. We can use the hypergeom implementation in SciPy to understand this game better. Let us look at the distribution of hearts in a bridge hand. Let us see what Starbuck may experience. First, let us see the PMF and CDF for our experiment:

```
> x = np.arange(0, 14, 1)
> pmf = hypergeom.pmf(x, 52, 13, 13)
> cdf = hypergeom.cdf(x, 52, 13, 13)
```

hypeprgeom provides pmf and cdf methods.

The PMF can be seen in the upper left-hand panel of Figure 5.5, and the CDF in the upper right-hand one. Notice that there are 13 cards for each of the suits in the deck. If we were to ask for the distribution of red cards, the distribution will start looking more and more like a binomial.

See the upper panels of Figure 5.5 for the PMF and CDF of the hypergeometric distribution.

The PPF for our game of bridge can be seen in Figure 5.5 in the lower left-hand panel and here is the code for that:

```
> probs = np.arange(0, 1, 0.1)
> ppf = hypergeom.ppf(probs, 52, 26, 13)
```

The PPF of the hypergeometric distribution is shown in the lower left-hand panel of Figure 5.5.

Finally, let us create a set of 1000 observations following this hypergeometric distribution:

```
> x1 = hypergeom.rvs(52, 13, 13, size=1000)
> print(x1.mean(), x1.var(ddof=1))


3.241 1.9808998998999
```

A histogram of hypergeometric variates is shown in the lower right-hand panel of Figure 5.5.

A histogram of these values can be seen in the lower right-hand panel of Figure 5.5. We can compare these values with the mean and variance for the hypergeometric distribution:

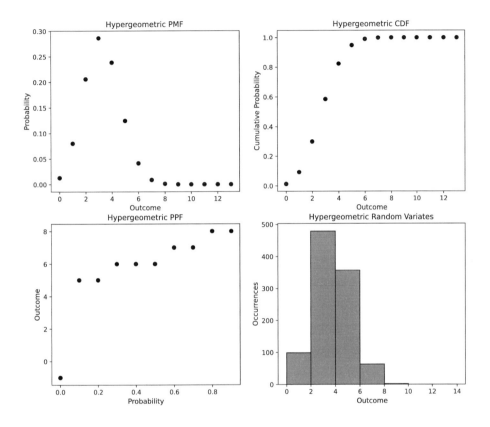

Figure 5.5: The hypergeometric distribution.

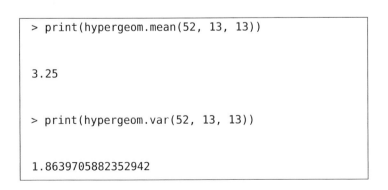

5.3.5   *Poisson Distribution*

AFTER HAVING PLAYED CARDS WITH Starbuck in the previous section, we start talking about the number of Cylon Raptors that she had experienced in the day prior to landing on our planet. For some time, nothing seemed to appear, and then two of them may show up in succession. A bit like waiting for a bus at your local bus stop.

We have all been there.

Events like these may be described, within their context, as rare in the sense that they do not happen that often. Some examples include: The release of an electron by the change of a neutron to a proton in radioactive beta decay[8], the number of hits to your website over a period of time, the number of births in a hospital during a given day, the number of road accidents occurring at a particular interval, the number of single photons detected[9] in an experiment, or as mentioned, the number of buses arriving to your local bus stop, and even the number of Cylon Raptors scouting for Battlestar Galactica.

[8] Melissinos, A. C. and J. Napolitano (2003). *Experiments in Modern Physics*. Gulf Professional Publishing

[9] McCann, L. I. (2015). Introducing students to single photon detection with a reverse-biased LED in avalanche mode. In E. B. M. Eblen-Zayas and J. Kozminski (Eds.), *BFY Proceedings*. American Association of Physics Teachers

These phenomena can be described with the Poisson distribution. It is named after the French mathematician Siméon Denis Poisson, and it was derived in 1837. It was famously used by Bortkiewicz to describe the number of deaths by horse kicking in the Prussian army[10]. A Poisson experiment is such that the following conditions are met:

[10] Good, I. J. (1986). Some statistical applications of Poisson's work. *Statistical Science 1*, 157–170

- The number of successes can be counted

- The mean number of successes that occurs in a specific interval is known

- Outcomes are independent of each other

- The probability that a success occurs is proportional to the size of the interval

Consider the time interval t in which Starbuck is looking for Cylon Raptors. We can break that time in smaller intervals, δt, small enough so that no two events occur in the same interval. We find an event with probability $P(1, \delta t) = l\delta t$ and its complement, i.e. no event with probability $P(0, \delta t) = 1 - l\delta t$. We are interested in determining the probability of getting n Cylon Raptor sightings in the interval t.

Our "success" event here is a Cylon Raptor sighting.

Let us assume that we know $P(0, t)$. We can reasonably ask about the probability of observing a Cylon Raptor in the interval $t + \delta t$. Since the events are independent the probability is given by the product of the individual probabilities:

See the probability properties described in Section 5.1.

$$P(0, t + \delta t) = P(0, t)(1 - l\delta t) \qquad (5.60)$$

We can rewrite the expression above as a rate of change as follows:

$$\frac{P(0, t + \delta t) - P(0, t)}{\delta t} = \frac{dP(0, t)}{dt} = -lP(0, t). \qquad (5.61)$$

It becomes a differential in the limit $\delta t \to 0$.

The solution of this differential equation is $P(0, t) = Ce^{-lt}$. At $t = 0$ we have no sightings and thus the probability $P(0, 0) = 1$ which means that $C = 1$:

$$P(0, t) = e^{-lt}. \qquad (5.62)$$

What is the probability for the case where there are Cylon Raptor sightings, i.e. $n \neq 0$. We can break this into two parts as follows:

1. The probability of having all n sightings in the interval t and none in δt, and

Breaking the probability of Cylon sightings into two parts.

2. Having $n - 1$ sightings in t and one in δt.

Let us take a look:

$$P(n, t + \delta t) = P(n,t)(1 - l\delta t) + P(n-1,t)l\delta. \qquad (5.63)$$

The probability of n events at $t + \delta t$.

In the limit $\delta t \to 0$, the expression above is given by the following differential equation for $P(n,t)$:

$$\frac{dP(n,t)}{dt} + lP(n,t) = lP(n-1,t). \qquad (5.64)$$

From Equation (5.64) it is possible to show that the probability of finding n events in the interval t is given by the following expression:

See Appendix F.1.

$$P(n, \mu) = \frac{\mu^n}{n!}e^{-\mu}, \qquad (5.65)$$

The PMF of the Poisson distribution.

where $\mu = lt$. The expression above is the probability mass function for the Poisson distribution. We can now turn our attention to obtaining the mean and variance for the Poisson distribution.

The mean or expected value of the Poisson distribution can be calculated directly from the probability mass function obtained in Equation (5.65):

$$E[X] = \sum_{n=0}^{\infty} nP(n,\mu) = \sum_{n=0}^{\infty} n\frac{\mu^n}{n!}e^{-\mu},$$

$$= e^{-\mu}\sum_{n=1}^{\infty} n\frac{\mu^n}{n!} = \mu e^{-\mu}\sum_{n=1}^{\infty}\frac{\mu^{n-1}}{(n-1)!},$$

The $n = 0$ term is zero, hence the change in the sum.

$$= \mu e^{-\mu}\sum_{m=0}^{\infty}\frac{\mu^m}{m!}. \qquad (5.66)$$

We relabelled the index so that $m = n - 1$.

We can recognise the Taylor expansion for e^μ in expression (5.66) and thus:

$$E[X] = \mu e^{-\mu}e^{\mu} = \mu. \qquad (5.67)$$

The mean of the Poisson distribution.

The parameter μ in the Poisson distribution is therefore the mean number of successes that occur during a specific interval.

For the variance, we know that $Var[X] = E[X^2] - E^2[X]$. The second term can be easily obtained from the mean value above. For the first term we can use the following identity: $E[X^2] = E[X(X-1)] + E[X]$. For this expression, the second term is known, and we can use a similar approach to the one used for calculating the mean to obtain the value of $E[X(X-1)]$:

$$E[X(X-1)] = \sum_{n=0}^{\infty} n(n-1)\frac{\mu^n}{n!}e^{-\mu} = \mu^2 e^{-\mu}\sum_{n=2}^{\infty}\frac{\mu^{n-2}}{(n-2)!},$$

The cases for $n = 0$ and $n = 1$ do not contribute to the sum.

$$= \mu^2 e^{-\mu}\sum_{m=0}^{\infty}\frac{\mu^m}{m!} = \mu^2 e^{-\mu}e^{\mu} = \mu^2. \qquad (5.68)$$

We used $m = n - 2$ to relabel the sum.

Hence the variance is given by:

$$Var[X] = \mu^2 + \mu - \mu^2 = \mu. \qquad (5.69)$$

The variance of the Poisson distribution.

As we can see, the variance of the Poisson distribution is equal to the mean value μ.

Let us say that Starbuck has experienced an average of $\mu = 2$ Cylon Raptors per hour. We can use Equation (5.65) to determine the probability of getting 0, 1, 2 or 3 sightings:

$$P(0,2) = 2^0 \frac{e^{-2}}{0!} = 0.1353,$$

$$P(1,2) = 2^1 \frac{e^{-2}}{1!} = 0.2707,$$

$$P(2,2) = 2^2 \frac{e^{-2}}{2!} = 0.2707,$$

$$P(3,2) = 2^3 \frac{e^{-2}}{3!} = 0.1805.$$

For $\mu = 2$, we can get the probability of different number of Cylon Raptor sightings.

Let us see what Python returns for the example above. We can use the poisson implementation in SciPy and calculate the PMF as follows:

```
> from scipy.stats import poisson
> print('The probability of seeing Cylon Raptors:')
> for r in range(0, 4):
    print('{0}: {1}'.format(r, poisson.pmf(r, 2)))


The probability of seeing Cylon Raptors:
0: 0.1353352832366127
1: 0.2706705664732254
2: 0.2706705664732254
3: 0.18044704431548356
```

We can use the poisson module in SciPy.

The Poisson distribution can be obtained as a limit of the binomial distribution we discussed in Section 5.3.3. This can be done by letting n be a large number of trials, in other words $n \to \infty$. We also fix the mean rate $\mu = np$. Equivalently, we can make the probability p be very small such that $p \to 0$. In doing so, we are effectively saying that there is no longer a fixed number of events in the interval in question. Instead, each new event does not depend on the number of events already occurred, recovering the statistical independence for the events. The PMF for the binomial distribution given by Equation (5.26) can be written as follows:

The Poisson distribution can be obtained as a limit of the binomial distribution.

$$P(X) = \lim_{n \to \infty} \frac{n!}{k!(n-k)!} \left(\frac{\mu}{n}\right)^k \left(1 - \frac{\mu}{n}\right)^{n-k}, \quad (5.70)$$

See Appendix F.2.

$$= \frac{\mu^k}{k!} e^{-\mu}. \quad (5.71)$$

which is the Poisson PMF we obtained before.

Let us go back to the SciPy implementation of the Poisson distribution. We know that the PMF can be calculated with poisson.pmf. If the average number of Cylon Raptors were 4, the PMF will be given by the top leff-hand panel of Figure 5.6 and can be calculated as follows:

```
mu = 4
x = np.arange(0, 14, 1)
pmf = poisson.pmf(x, mu)
```

The PMF of the Poisson distribution is shown in the top left-hand panel of Figure 5.6.

The PMF shows the probability of sighting between 0 and 14 Cylon Raptors in the same time interval.

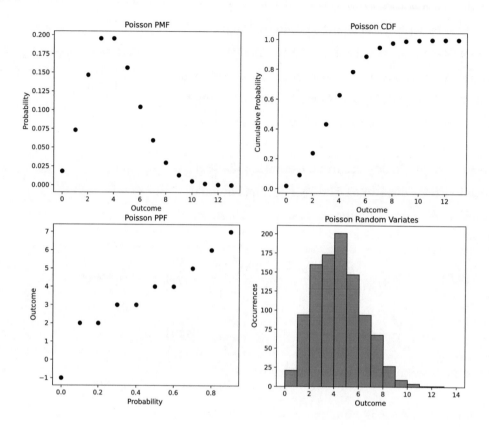

Figure 5.6: The Poisson distribution.

The cumulative distribution function can be seen in the top right-hand panel of Figure 5.6 and is calculated as follows:

```
cdf = poisson.cdf(x, mu)
```

The CDF is shown in the top right-hand panel of Figure 5.6.

We can calculate the occurrences for a given probability with the PPF:

```
probs = np.arange(0, 1, 0.1)

ppf = poisson.ppf(probs, mu)
```

The PPF is shown in the lower left-hand panel of Figure 5.6.

and the result is shown in the lower left-hand panel of Figure 5.6.

Finally, we can generate random variates that follow the Poisson distribution as follows:

```
> x1 = poisson.rvs(mu, size=1000)

> print(x1.mean(), x1.var(ddof=1))


4.004 4.054038038038038
```

Random Poisson variates can be seen in the lower right-hand panel of Figure 5.6.

Here, we started with $\mu = 4$, which in the Poisson distribution corresponds to the mean and variance. As we can see, the values obtained from the 1000 random variates we generated are close to that parameter. The histogram of these values can be seen in the lower right-hand panel of Figure 5.6.

5.4   Continuous Probability Distributions

THE PROBABILITY DISTRIBUTIONS WE HAVE discussed so far have all been discrete. We now turn our attention to continuous distributions. Remember that if the random variable of interest can take any value between two specified values, then the variable is called continuous, and imaginatively enough, its probability distribution is called a continuous probability distribution.

See Section 5.2.2 for the distinction between discrete and continuous distributions.

5.4.1   Normal or Gaussian Distribution

NO SELF-RESPECTING BOOK ON STATISTICS would avoid talking about the normal distribution. It can be argued that it would be better to simply call it Gaussian as it seems that normal is not the norm. Gaussian alludes to the description of the famous bell-shaped curve by Carl Friedrich Gauss. As a matter of fact its original name was *law of errors* as given that Gauss[11] used it to model errors in astronomical observations in 1823 as we mentioned in Section 1.3.

One may argue that there is nothing normal about the normal distribution. As we will see, the distribution runs from minus infinity to infinity, and never ever touches or crosses the x-axis. If we were to use this to describe, for example, the height of "normal" people, we would not be surprised to find that Gulliver's discovery of tiny Lilliputians, or Jack's encounter with a bone-bread-making giant are real. The term "normal" has become a moniker to mean typical or common. The use became more popular thanks to Karl Pearson who later clarified[12] the use of "normal" in the sense of being typical, as opposed to being normative:

> "Many years ago I called the Laplace–Gaussian curve the normal curve, which name, while it avoids an international question of priority, has the disadvantage of leading people to believe that all other distributions of frequency are in one sense or another 'abnormal'. That belief is, of course, not justifiable. It has led many writers to try and force all frequency by aid of one or another process of distortion into a 'normal' curve."

What is normal anyway?

[11] Gauss, C. F. (1823). *Theoria combinationis observationum erroribus minimis obnoxiae*. Number V. 2 in Commentationes Societatis Regiae Scientiarum Gottingensis recentiores: Classis Mathemat. H. Dieterich

Values range in the $(-\infty, \infty)$. interval, enabling for tiny Lilliputians and enormous giants.

[12] Pearson, K. (1920). Notes on the history of correlation. *Biometrika* 13(1), 25–45

We mentioned that Gauss used the normal distribution to model errors in astronomy. We can motivate our discussion with a StarTrek example: Consider the use of *kellicams* or *qellqams* by the Klingon empire to measure distance.

Space is still the final frontier.

Lieutenant Commander Worf informs us that a kellicam is roughly equal to two kilometers. But, how close is that correspondence? As good lower decks, we take the mission and make some measurements. The first measurement is 1.947 metres. For the second we get 2.099 metres. So what is it? The first or the second? Well, let us measure it again and then again and again. As it happens, each measure gives us a different answer and we end up with the following list of measures:

We are obtaining empirical measures for a quantity of interest, go stats!

2.098	2.096	2.100
2.101	2.099	2.098
2.099	2.098	2.099
2.099	2.100	2.100
2.100	2.099	2.099

Different measures of a standard imperial Klingon kellicam in metres.

A histogram of this data, shown in Figure 5.7, indicates that the "true" value for a kellicam in metres is 2.099 to the nearest millimetre. We can think of the measurements above in terms of errors: If there is a true value for the metres in a kellicam, as we measure the distance, we may incur some errors, but we are likely to obtain a measure close, or on target, for that value. As we get farther and farther from the true value, our chances of obtaining it are reduced. In other words, the rate at which the frequencies decrease is proportional to the distance from the true value.

We can think of our measurements in terms of errors.

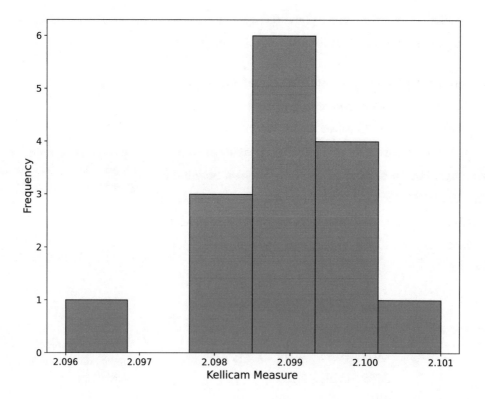

Figure 5.7: Measures of a standard imperial Klingon kellicam in metres.

This is, however, not the end of the story. If that was the only condition on the frequencies, we may end up with a distribution that follows a parabolic curve. In that case, as we move farther from the true value, the frequencies would become negative, and as Mr. Spock would remind us, that is highly illogical. We can get the frequencies to level off as they get closer and closer to zero by requiring that the rate at which they fall off is proportional to the frequencies themselves. We say that data is normally distributed if

Obtaining negative frequencies is highly illogical, as Mr Spock will surely tell us.

the rate at which the frequencies observed fall off 1) is proportional to the distance of the score from the central value, and 2) is proportional to the frequencies themselves. This can be expressed by the following differential equation:

A couple of conditions for frequencies to follow a normal distribution.

$$\frac{df(x)}{dx} = -k(x - \mu)f(x), \qquad (5.72)$$

where k is a positive constant. We can solve this equation as follows:

$$\int \frac{df(x)}{f(x)} = -k \int (x - \mu)dx,$$

$$f(x) = C\exp\left[-\frac{k}{2}(x - \mu)^2\right]. \qquad (5.73)$$

We can find the value of C by recalling that this is a probability distribution and therefore the area under the curve must be equal to 1:

We will deal with the value of k later on.

$$C\int_{-\infty}^{\infty} \exp\left[-\frac{k}{2}(x - \mu)^2\right] dx = 1. \qquad (5.74)$$

It can be shown that the constant $C = \sqrt{k/2\pi}$. Our probability distribution is thus far given by

See Appendix G.1 for more information.

$$f(x) = \sqrt{\frac{k}{2\pi}}\exp\left[-\frac{k}{2}(x - \mu)^2\right]. \qquad (5.75)$$

We can use Equation (5.75) to calculate the expected value. In order to simplify our calculation, let us consider transforming our variable such that $v = x - \mu$ and therefore

This means that $dx = dv$.

$E[x] = E[v] + \mu$. The expected value of v is:

$$E[v] = \sqrt{\frac{k}{2\pi}} \int_{-\infty}^{\infty} v e^{-\frac{k}{2}v^2} dv. \qquad (5.76)$$

Let $w = -\frac{k}{2}v^2$, and therefore $dw = -kv dv$. Substituting into (5.76):

$$E[v] = \sqrt{\frac{1}{2\pi k}} \int_{-\infty}^{\infty} e^w dw = 0$$

The expected value of the normal distribution.

$$E[x] = E[v] + \mu = 0 + \mu = \mu. \qquad (5.77)$$

As expected, the expected value for the normal distribution is μ.

Pun definitely intended!

For the variance we have:

$$\sigma^2 = \int_{-\infty}^{\infty} (x - \mu)^2 f(x) dx,$$

$$= \sqrt{\frac{k}{2\pi}} \int_{-\infty}^{\infty} (x - \mu)^2 \exp\left[-\frac{k}{2}(x - \mu)^2 \right] dx.$$

Let us now look at the variance of the normal distribution.

Let us make the following change of variable: $w = x - \mu$ and $dw = dx$. The variance of the normal distribution can then be expressed as:

$$\sigma^2 = \sqrt{\frac{k}{2\pi}} \int_{-\infty}^{\infty} w^2 e^{-\frac{k}{2}w^2} dw. \qquad (5.78)$$

We can integrate the (5.78) by parts with:

$$u = w, \qquad v = -\frac{1}{k} e^{-\frac{k}{2}w^2},$$

$$du = dw, \qquad dv = w e^{-\frac{k}{2}w^2} dw.$$

Useful variable changes to integrate our expression by parts.

Substituting into our integral, we have:

$$\sigma^2 = \sqrt{\frac{k}{2\pi}} \left[-\frac{we^{-\frac{k}{2}w^2}}{k} \right]_{-\infty}^{\infty} + \frac{1}{k}\sqrt{\frac{k}{2\pi}} \int_{-\infty}^{\infty} e^{-\frac{k}{2}w^2} \, dw. \quad (5.79)$$

The first term is zero, and the second one contains the PDF
of the normal distribution multiplied by $1/k$ and therefore
we have that:

Compare with Equation (5.75).

$$\sigma^2 = \frac{1}{k},$$

$$k = \frac{1}{\sigma^2}. \quad (5.80)$$

This is because the area under the
curve is equal to 1.

This gives meaning to the constant k in terms of the variance
of the normal distribution. As such, we are able to write our
PDF in terms of the mean μ and the standard deviation σ
as:

$$f(x) = \frac{1}{\sigma\sqrt{2\pi}} \exp\left[-\frac{1}{2}\left(\frac{x-\mu}{\sigma}\right)^2 \right]. \quad (5.81)$$

The PDF of the normal
distribution.

We can determine the maximum of the probability
distribution function of the normal distribution and show
that the peak corresponds to the mean value μ.
Furthermore, the points of inflection for the PDF are given
by $\mu \pm \sigma$. In other words, the points where the PDF changes
concavity lie one standard deviation above and below the
mean. Given the importance of the parameters μ and σ to
define the normal distribution, we sometimes use the
notation $N(\mu, \sigma)$ to refer to a normal distribution with mean
μ and standard deviation σ.

The points of inflection for the
normal PDF are given by $\mu \pm \sigma$.

The notation $N(\mu, \sigma)$ stands for a
normal distribution with mean μ
and standard deviation σ.

Let us go back to our measurements of the Klingon kellicam. Our Starfleet colleagues have amassed an impressive collection of measurements that follow a normal distribution with mean $\mu = 2.099$ and standard deviation $\sigma = 0.2$. We can use this information to calculate the probability distribution function with Python as follows:

We have kellicam measurements that follow a $N(2.099, 0.2)$ distribution.

```
from scipy.stats import norm

mu = 2.099
sigma = 0.2
x = np.arange(1, 3, 0.01)
pdf = norm.pdf(x, mu, sigma)
```

We can use the norm module in SciPy.

A graph of the probability distribution function can be seen in the top-left hand panel of Figure 5.8.

As the normal distribution is continuous, obtaining the cumulative distribution function is as easy as calculating the following integral:

$$F(x) = \int_{-\infty}^{a} \frac{1}{\sigma\sqrt{2\pi}} \exp\left[-\frac{1}{2}\left(\frac{x-\mu}{\sigma}\right)^2\right]. \qquad (5.82)$$

The probability is given by the area under the normal curve.

Unfortunately, there is no simple closed formula for this integral and the computation is best done numerically. Python is well suited to help with this. Another alternative is to use probability tables. In Python we can obtain the CDF as follows:

We prefer to use a computer for this!

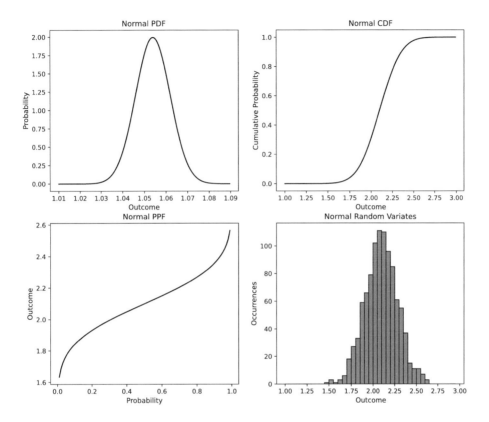

Figure 5.8: The normal or Gaussian distribution.

```
cdf = norm.cdf(x, mu, sigma)
```

The graph of the CDF for the normal distribution can be seen in the top right-hand panel of Figure 5.8. We can use the CDF to find the probability that a measurement is below 2 metres for example:

The normal CDF is shown in the top right-hand panel of Figure 5.8.

```
> norm.cdf(2, mu, sigma)


0.3103000602544874
```

The prob of having a measurement below 2 metres for $N(2.099, 0.2)$.

Similarly, we can ask for the probability that a measurement is between one standard deviation above and below the mean:

```
> lower = norm.cdf(mu-sigma, mu, sigma)
> upper = norm.cdf(mu+sigma, mu, sigma)
> p = upper - lower
> print(p)


0.6826894921370861
```

The probability of having a measurement above and below one standard deviation.

In other words, the probability of a kellicam measurement being between 1.89 and 2.299 metres is:

$$P(1.89 \leq X \leq 2.299) = 0.6826, \qquad (5.83)$$

or equivalently, 68.2% of the observations are within 1 standard deviation of the mean. We will revisit this fact in the next section when we talk about the empirical rule and the standard normal distribution Z.

We discuss the "empirical rule" for the normal distribution in Section 5.4.2.

Now, given a normal distribution with parameters μ and σ, we can use Python to calculate the percent point function (PPF):

```
probs = np.arange(0, 1, 0.01)
ppf = norm.ppf(probs, mu, sigma)
```

The normal PPF is shown in the bottom left-hand panel of Figure 5.8.

and the result is shown in the bottom left-hand panel of Figure 5.8.

Another useful thing that we can do with Python is to create random variates that follow a normal distribution with parameters μ and σ.

```
x1 = norm.rvs(mu, sigma, size=1000)
print(x1.mean(), x1.var(ddof=1))
```

Normal variates are shown in the bottom right-hand panel of Figure 5.8.

A histogram of these random variates is shown in the bottom right-hand panel of Figure 5.8. Let us compare the mean and standard deviations obtained with our randomly generated values and the parameters of our Gaussian function:

```
> print(x1.mean(), x1.var(ddof=1))


2.096088672876906 0.035225815987363816


> print(norm.mean(mu, sigma))
> print(norm.var(mu, sigma))


2.099
0.04000000000000001
```

Remember that the variance is the square of the standard deviation.

The Binomial Distribution Approximated by a Normal Distribution

In Section 5.2.3 we looked at the repeated flipping of a coin in a growing number of experiments. As suggested by the last panel of Figure 5.1, the binomial distribution that describes our experiment can be approximated by a Gaussian curve with the same mean and standard deviation, i.e. $\mu = np$ and $\sigma = \sqrt{npq}$. This works well under the following conditions:

1. the number of trials n is large,

2. the probability of success is sufficiently small, and

3. the mean $\mu = np$ is a finite number.

Conditions for the binomial distribution to approximate a normal curve.

What does "sufficiently small" probability mean though? Well, to start with, if the underlying binomial distribution is skewed, the approximation is not going to be that good, so the closer the probability is to 0.5 the better. Let us consider the bulk of the Gaussian distribution to be two standard deviations from its mean and use this information to determine some bounds for the number of trials. We can express this in terms of the following inequalities:

$$\mu - 2\sigma > 0, \qquad \mu + 2\sigma < n, \qquad (5.84)$$

We consider the bulk of the normal distribution to be $\pm 2\sigma$ away from the mean.

substituting the mean and standard deviation for the binomial we have that:

$$np > \sqrt{npq}, \qquad np + 2\sqrt{npq} < n,$$
$$np > 4q, \qquad 2\sqrt{npq} < n(1-p),$$
$$np > 4 - 4p, \qquad 4 - 4q < nq,$$
$$np \geq 5, \qquad 5 \leq nq. \qquad (5.85)$$

Since p and q are probabilities, their values must stay between 0 and 1, and therefore the inequalities are satisfied if np and nq are greater than 5.

Remember that the normal distribution is a continuous probability distribution, however the binomial is discrete. If we want to use the approximation we need to apply a continuity correction. The simplest thing to do is to add or subtract 0.5 to or from the discrete value.

Remember that the binomial distribution is discrete.

5.4.2   Standard Normal Distribution Z

IN THE PREVIOUS SECTION, WE motivated the discussion of the normal distribution from measurements obtained by our Starfleet colleagues to determine the length of a Klingon kellicam in metres. This gave us information to calculate the mean and standard deviation of the measures obtained. Depending on the mean and standard deviation, the shape of the probability distribution is different but the characteristics are the same. For instance, the inflection points will be given by $\mu \pm \sigma$, no matter what the individual values of μ and σ are. This means that we can use these characteristics to help us understand our data.

The general characteristics of a normal distribution are the same.

Consider for example a case where we need to compare different distributions. If we are able to bring them under the same footing, we have a better chance of comparing them. This is called standardisation, and the standard normal distribution is what we end up with. Think of the standard normal distribution as a special case of the normal distribution where the mean is 0 and the standard deviation is 1. We can standardise our data by taking each raw measurement, subtracting the mean from it and dividing the

The standard normal is given by $N(0, 1)$.

result by the standard deviation. In other words:

$$z = \frac{X - \mu}{\sigma}. \tag{5.86}$$

The standard or z-score.

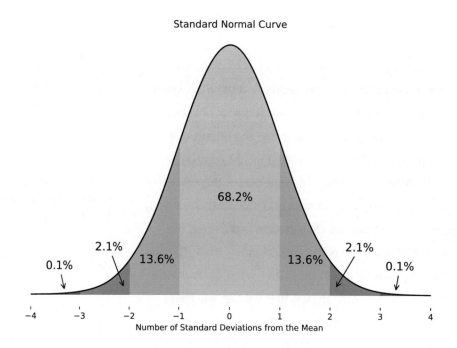

This is usually referred to as the z-score and the values represent the number of standard deviations a specific observation is away from the mean. For example, if a z-score is −1.2 it means that the observation is 1.2 below the mean. This turns out to be a very effective way to understand each observation relative to the full distribution. It also helps with the comparison of distributions that have different parameters.

Figure 5.9: The empirical rule gives us approximations about the percentage of data observations within a number of standard deviations from the mean.

Furthermore, if our data is well described by a normal curve, we can use the standard normal to tell us something about the observations we have. In Equation (5.83) we calculated the probability that our Klingon kellicam measurement fell within a standard deviation of the mean obtaining a probability of around 68.2%. This is the case for any normal curve and this part of what we call the Empirical Rule. On a normal distribution:

About 68.2% of the observations in a normal distribution are within one standard deviation of the mean.

- about 68.2% of data will be within one standard deviation of the mean,

- about 95.4% will be within two standard deviations of the mean, and

The Empirical Rule of the standard normal distribution.

- about 99.7% will be within three standard deviations of the mean

This is shown schematically in Figure 5.9. This information lets us make predictions about the probabilities of the phenomena we are studying, provided that the data is normally distributed. It is also a great way to identify outliers. Since 99.7% of the observations are supposed to be within three standard deviations of the mean, any value that is outside can be considered as a potential outlier. We can even use the Empirical Rule as a simplistic test for normality of our data: If more than 0.3% of the data is outside the three standard deviations from the mean, the data may not follow a normal distribution.

We can use the Empirical Rule to look for potential data outliers.

In Python, using SciPy, the standard normal distribution is obtained with the same methods used in the previous section. The default values for the mean and standard deviation are $\mu = 0$ and $\sigma = 1$. We can get the probability distribution for the standard normal as follows.

```
from scipy.stats import norm
x = np.arange(-5, 5, 0.01)
zdist = norm.pdf(x)
```

We do not need to specify the mean and standard deviation.

Notice that we do not need to specify the values for the mean or the standard deviation. Alternatively, we could have written this as norm.pdf(x, 1, 0). Similarly, we can use norm.cdf to obtain the cumulative distribution. Let us see the values obtained for the empirical rule:

```
> sigma1 = 100*(norm.cdf(1)-norm.cdf(-1))
> sigma2 = 100*(norm.cdf(2)-norm.cdf(-2))
> sigma3 = 100*(norm.cdf(3)-norm.cdf(-3))

> print('{0:.2f}%, {1:.2f}%, {2:.2f}%'.
        format(sigma1, sigma2, sigma3))

68.27%, 95.45%, 99.73%
```

The Empirical Rule values obtained using Python.

5.4.3   Shape and Moments of a Distribution

AN IMPORTANT FEATURE IN THE description of the empirical rule discussed above is the symmetry of the normal distribution around the mean. The shape of the distribution is a helpful measure of the normality of a distribution, and a way to characterise the shape is through the moments of the distribution. The k-th moment is

The shape of a normal distribution is distinctive enough to characterise how close data is to being normally distributed.

defined as the expectation of the k-th power of the random variable X, i.e. $m_k = E[X^k]$. As a matter of fact, we have already dealt with some of the moments of a distribution. The first moment is the expectation value or mean, whereas the second moment is the standard deviation.

The first moment of a distribution is the mean. The second is the variance.

The k-th moment of a distribution can be expressed as:

$$m_k = \frac{\mu_k}{\sigma_k} = \frac{E\left[(X-\mu)^k\right]}{E\left[(X-\mu)^2\right]^{k/2}}. \tag{5.87}$$

The k-th moment of a distribution.

Thinking of our standard normal distribution, we can see that the first moment is indeed $\mu = 0$:

$$m_1 = \frac{\mu_1}{\sigma} = \frac{E\left[(X-\mu)\right]}{E\left[(X-\mu)^2\right]^{1/2}},$$

$$= \frac{\mu - \mu}{\left(E\left[(X-\mu)^2\right]\right)^{1/2}} = 0 \tag{5.88}$$

The first moment of the normal distribution is $m_1 = \mu = 0$.

We said that the second moment of a distribution corresponds to the variance, and for a standard normal this has the value 1:

$$m_2 = \frac{\mu_2}{\sigma^2} = \frac{E\left[(X-\mu)^2\right]}{E\left[(X-\mu)^2\right]^{2/2}} = 1 \tag{5.89}$$

The second moment is $m_1 = \sigma^2 = 1$.

The mean tells us where our distribution is centred and the variance tells us about the dispersion in our distribution. It is clear that obtaining the moments of a distribution is a useful task and there is an easier way to generate them. We can do this with moment generating functions.

We can obtain the moments with the help of generating functions.

If X is a random variable, its moment generating function is given by:

$$\phi(t) = E[e^{tX}],$$

The moment generating function.

$$= \begin{cases} \sum_x e^{tx} P(X = x) & \text{discrete case,} \\ \int_{-\infty}^{\infty} e^{tx} f(x) dx & \text{continuous case.} \end{cases} \quad (5.90)$$

The name of this mathematical object should be clear enough to explain what it does. Nonetheless, let us take a further look and write its Taylor expansion:

$$E(e^{tX}) = E[1 + tX + \frac{1}{2}t^2 X^2 + \frac{1}{3!}t^3 X^3 + \cdots]$$

The Taylor expansion of the moment generating function.

$$= 1 + tEX + \frac{1}{2}t^2 E[X^2] + \frac{1}{3!}t^3 E[X^3] + \cdots$$

As we can see we can generate the k-th moment $m_k = E[X^k]$ out of this series and we note that:

$$\frac{d}{dt} E\left[e^{tX}\right]\Big|_{t=0} = E[X],$$

We can obtain the moments from the Taylor expansion above.

$$\frac{d^2}{dt^2} E\left[e^{tX}\right]\Big|_{t=0} = E[X^2].$$

We can compute the moment generating function for a standard normal random variable as follows:

$$\phi(t) = \frac{1}{\sqrt{2\pi}} \int_{-\infty}^{\infty} e^{tx} e^{-x^2/2} dx,$$

The moment generating function of the normal distribution.

$$= \frac{1}{\sqrt{2\pi}} e^{t^2/2} \int_{-\infty}^{\infty} e^{(x-t)^2/2} dx = e^{t^2/2}, \quad (5.91)$$

where we have used the following expression:

$$tx - \frac{1}{2}x^2 = -\frac{1}{2}(-2tx + x^2) = \frac{1}{2}((x-t)^2 - t^2).$$

We can obtain the moments of the normal distribution carrying out an integration by parts. For the standard normal we have that:

$$\int_{-\infty}^{\infty} x^n e^{-\frac{x^2}{2}} dx = \frac{x^{n+1}}{n+1} e^{-\frac{x^2}{2}} \Big|_{-\infty}^{\infty} - \int_{-\infty}^{\infty} \frac{x^{n+1}}{n+1} \left(-xe^{-\frac{x^2}{2}}\right) dx,$$

$$= \frac{1}{n+1} \int_{-\infty}^{\infty} x^{n+2} e^{-\frac{x^2}{2}} dx.$$

We can calculate the moments of the standard normal with this expression.

In terms of moments, we therefore have the following recurrence relation:

$$m_{n+2} = (n+1)m_n. \tag{5.92}$$

Now that we are able to obtain moments of a distribution in a more expeditious way, let us return to our description of the shape of our distributions: **Skewness** and **kurtosis**. Let us look first at skewness. Consider the distributions shown in Figure 5.10, as we can see, the symmetry shown by the standard normal distribution is broken and the tails of each distribution taper differently.

Skewness and kurtosis are measures that help us characterise the shape of our distribution.

In a positive skewed distribution, the right tail is longer and thus the mass of the distribution is concentrated on the left of the curve. For a negative skewed distribution, the left tail is longer and the mass is concentrated on the right of the curve.

The skewness describes the shift of the centre of mass of the distribution.

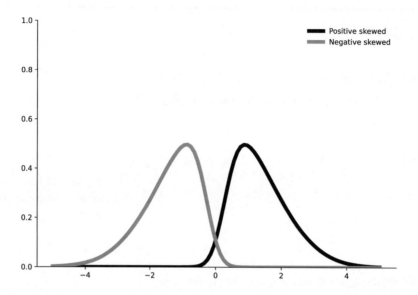

Figure 5.10: Positive and negative skewed distributions.

The third moment provides us with a way to measure the **skewness**. We denote it as g_1 and it is usually referred to as the Fisher-Pearson coefficient of skewness:

$$g_1 = m_3 = \frac{\mu_3}{\sigma^3}. \qquad (5.93)$$

The third moment or skewness.

To correct for statistical bias, the adjusted Fisher-Pearson standardised moment coefficient is given by:

$$G_1 = \frac{\sqrt{n(n-1)}}{n-1} g_1. \qquad (5.94)$$

For data that is normally distributed, the skewness must be close to zero. This is because the skewness for the standard normal is 0:

Normally distributed data has skewness close or equal to 0.

$$E[X^3] = m_3 = (1+1)m_1 = 0. \qquad (5.95)$$

If the Fisher-Pearson coefficient of skewness is greater than zero, we have a positive skewed dataset; if the value is smaller than zero we have a negative skewed dataset. We can calculate the Fisher-Pearson coefficient of skewness in Python with the help of skew in the statistics module of SciPy. Note that we can obtain the unbiased value with the bias=False parameter. Let us see the skewness of our kellicam measurements:

Positive skewed data has skewness greater than 0; negative skewed data has skewness lower than 0.

```
from scipy.stats import skew
kellicam = np.array([2.098, 2.101, 2.099, 2.099,
    2.1, 2.096, 2.099, 2.098, 2.1, 2.099, 2.1,
    2.098, 2.099, 2.1, 2.099])
skew(kellicam)
skew(kellicam, bias=False)


-0.7794228634063756
-0.8688392583242721
```

In this case our sample data is negatively skewed.

Another measure about the shape of the normal distribution is the **kurtosis**. It tells us how curved the distribution is and whether it is heavy-tailed or light-tailed compared to the normal. The normal distribution is said to be mesokurtic. If a distribution has lighter tails than a normal curve it will tend to give us fewer and less extreme outliers than the normal. These distributions are called leptokurtic. Finally, if a distribution has heavier tails than a normal curve, we have a platykurtic distribution and we tend to have more outliers than with the normal. The three different kurtoses mentioned above are depicted in Figure 5.11.

From the Greek $\kappa \upsilon \rho \tau \acute{o} \varsigma$ meaning curved or arched.

From the Greek $\lambda \epsilon \pi \tau \acute{o} \varsigma$, meaning thin or slender.

From the Greek $\pi \lambda \alpha \tau \acute{u} \varsigma$, meaning flat.

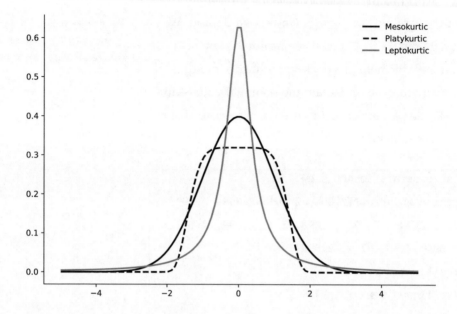

Figure 5.11: Kurtosis of different distributions.

The kurtosis is measured with the fourth standard moment and defined therefore as:

$$g_2 = m_4 = \frac{\mu_4}{\sigma^4}. \tag{5.96}$$

The fourth moment or kurtosis.

Let us see the value of the kurtosis for the standard normal:

$$E[X^4] = m_4 = (2+1)m_2 = 3. \tag{5.97}$$

The kurtosis of a normal distribution is 3 and therefore platykurtic distributions have values lower than 3, whereas leptokurtic ones have values greater than 3. Sometimes it is useful to subtract 3 from the value obtained and thus a normal distribution has a kurtosis value of 0. This makes it

A normal distribution has kurtosis equal to 3.

easier to compare. This is known as the Fisher definition of kurtosis.

In Python we can use kurtosis in the statistics module of SciPy. Note that we can obtain the unbiased value with the bias=False parameter. By default, the implementation used Fisher's definition of kurtosis. If you need the value in terms of the fourth moment, simply use the fisher=False parameter. Let us see the kurtosis of our kellicam measures:

The SciPy implementation used the Fisher definition of kurtosis, where the normal kurtosis is 0.

```
from scipy.stats import kurtosis
kurtosis(kellicam)
kurtosis(kellicam, fisher=False)


0.89999999999992
3.89999999999992
```

5.4.4   *The Central Limit Theorem*

THE EXPECTED VALUE AND VARIANCE are concepts we are now familiar with. In particular, we looked at an experiment with a fair coin performed multiple times. We observed that the distribution starts resembling a normal distribution as the number of trials increases. Let us consider this in light of what we know now about the standard normal distribution.

We covered them in Section 5.2.3.

As the number of trials increases, the distribution becomes normal.

What we did for our experiment consists of getting a sequence of independent and identically distributed (i.i.d.) random variables $X_1, X_2, \ldots X_n$. Let us consider that each of these observations has a finite mean such that $E[X_i] = \mu$ and variance σ^2. The central limit theorem tells us that the sample mean $\bar{X}$ follows approximately the normal distribution with mean μ and standard deviation $\frac{\sigma}{\sqrt{n}}$. In other words $\bar{X} \simeq N(\mu, \frac{\sigma}{\sqrt{n}})$. We can even standardise the values and use $z = \sqrt{n}(\bar{x} - \mu)/\sigma$.

The central limit theorem.

Let us look at this in terms of the moment generating function. Let X_n be a random variable with moment generating function $\phi_{X_n}(t)$, and X be a random variable with moment generating function $\phi_X(t)$. The central limit theorem therefore tells us that as n increases:

$$\lim_{n \to \infty} \phi_{X_n}(t) = \phi_X(t), \tag{5.98}$$

The central limit theorem in terms of moment generating functions.

and thus the CDF of X_n converges to the CDF of X.

Let us use the information above to look at the central limit theorem. Assume that X is a random variable with mean μ and standard deviation σ. If, as in our experiment, $X_1, X_2, \ldots X_n$ are independent and identically distributed following X, let $T_n = \frac{\sum_i X_i - n\mu}{\sigma\sqrt{n}}$. The central limit theorem says that for every x, the probability $P(T_n \leq x)$ tends to $P(Z \leq z)$ as n tends to infinity, where Z is a standard normal random variable.

Having independent and identically distributed random variables is important.

To show this, let us define $Y = \frac{X-\mu}{\sigma}$ and $Y_i = \frac{X_i-\mu}{\sigma}$. Then Y_i are independent, and distributed as Y with mean 0 and standard deviation 1, and $T_n = \sum_i Y_i/\sqrt{n}$. We aim to prove that as n tends to infinity, the moment generating function of T_n, i.e. $\phi_{T_n}(t)$, tends to the moment generating function of the standard normal. Let us take a look:

$$\phi_{T_n}(t) = E\left[e^{T_n t}\right],$$

$$= E\left[e^{\frac{t}{\sqrt{n}}Y_1}\right] \times \cdots \times E\left[e^{\frac{t}{\sqrt{n}}Y_n}\right],$$

$$= E\left[e^{\frac{t}{\sqrt{n}}Y}\right]^n,$$

$$= \left(1 + \frac{t}{\sqrt{n}}E[Y] + \frac{t^2}{2n}E[Y^2] + \frac{t^3}{6n^{3/2}}E[Y^3] + \cdots\right)^n,$$

$$= \left(1 + 0 + \frac{t^2}{2n} + \frac{t^3}{6n^{3/2}}E[Y^3] + \cdots\right)^n,$$

$$\simeq \left(1 + \frac{t^2}{2n}\right)^2,$$

$$\to e^{t^2/2}. \tag{5.99}$$

As $n \to \infty$, $\phi_{T_n}(t) \to e^{t^2/2}$.

As we showed in Equation (5.91), $\phi_Z(t) = e^{t^2/2}$ and therefore the limiting distribution is indeed the standard normal $N(0,1)$.

Remember that $e^{t^2/2}$ is the moment generating function of the standard normal distribution.

5.5   Hypothesis and Confidence Intervals

OUR MEASUREMENTS FOR THE LENGTH of a standard Klingon kellicam has proved so useful that the Vulcan Science Academy has asked us to take a look at an issue that has been puzzling Starfleet for quite some time and we are eager to help. It turns out that there has been a report of a gas leakage whose properties seem to be similar to hexafluorine gas, used in starship and sensor construction. The possibilities of an alternative gas for anti-intruder systems that is less lethal to non-Vulcans or non-Romulans seem exciting. We have been tasked with finding more

We are not about to decline a request by the Vulcan Science Academy!

about this gas, particularly after some reports have come about the potential anti-gravity effects that it seems to have on some Starfleet officers.

Since the gas is still under strict Federation embargo, we are not able to get the full details of all the population that has been exposed to the gas, but we have a sample of the crew members that first encountered it. We select 256 crew members that provide a good sample for what happened in the starship, and although we may not be able to account for all systematic variables, we are in a position to account for the hexafluorine-like substance. All in all, if we do find differences between crew that has been affected by this gas and those who have not, we may have a good case to continue with a more complete investigation. The mild anti-gravity effect the gas has is reflected in the mass of the person affected. We obtain a mean of 81.5 kg. Measuring the average weight of the crew seems to be around the right track, but this may tell us nothing about the comparison of the affected population with those who were not. For instance, a difference may be due to having selected heavier, non-affected crew members.

Selecting a suitable sample is a good first step.

Having a target variable for our analysis is required.

However, we are able to compare a score to a population of scores, in this case the mean. In other words, we can consider selecting every possible sample of size 256 of the unaffected population and calculate each sample mean. This will give us a distribution that can be used as a benchmark. We already have the sample from the affected starship and we can now compare these two populations of sample means. If we find a difference, we are now onto something.

Having every possible sample of size n from the population is a monumental task. We need a different approach.

Sadly, we currently only have the mean of our 256 gravity-challenged colleagues!

What should we do? Well, it is only logical to look at what we have been discussing in this chapter. We do not need to go out of our way to obtain every possible sample of the unaffected population. We know that for a large enough sample we obtain a normal distribution. We can use this information to test the hypothesis that the gas has an anti-gravity effect and we need to ascertain a significance level for this hypothesis, find the z-score, and obtain the probability to make our decision.

How very Vulcan!

We test our hypothesis based on what we know about the normal distribution.

If we consider that we have a population with mean μ and standard deviation σ, and provided that we have a large number of observations for the central limit theorem to apply, we can define a confidence interval as:

$$\bar{x} \pm (z \text{ critical value }) \left(\frac{\sigma}{\sqrt{n}} \right). \tag{5.100}$$

Confidence interval.

A typical critical value is to consider a 95% confidence interval. In terms of z-scores, the probability of randomly selecting a score between -1.96 and $+1.96$ standard deviations from the mean is around 95%. Let us check this with Python's help:

For the standard normal distribution, a 95% confidence interval corresponds to z-scores between ± 1.96.

```
CIlower = norm.cdf(-1.96)
CIupper = norm.cdf(1.96)
print(CIupper - CIlower)

0.950004209703559
```

We can use this information to say that if we have less than
a 5% chance of randomly selecting a raw score, we have
a statistically significant result. We call this the **level of
significance** and is denoted as α.

The level of significance, α.

Back to our gravity-defying effect, let us say that the mean
of our sampling distribution is 83 kg with a standard
deviation 4.3. The 95% confidence interval will be:

$$83 \pm (1.96)\left(\frac{4.3}{\sqrt{256}}\right) = (82.47325, 83.52675). \quad (5.101)$$

As we saw above a 95% confidence
interval requires z-scores between
± 1.96.

In other words, plausible values of the mean are between
82.4 and 83.5 kg.

What about our measurement for the affected population?
Well, let us take a look: The score we are after is calculated
as:

$$Z = \frac{\bar{X} - \mu}{\frac{\sigma}{n}} = \frac{81.5 - 83}{\frac{4.3}{\sqrt{256}}} = -5.5813.$$

Let us ask Python to give us the probability p of obtaining a
sample mean as low or even lower than 81.5 kgs:

```
> norm.cdf(-5.5813)

1.1936373019551489e-08
```

We call this the p-value.

This is well below a significance level of $\alpha = 0.05$, or
similarly well below the bottom 5% of the unaffected
sampling distribution. We can conclude that a sample mean
of 81.5 kg is so uncommon in the unaffected Starfleet
population that the distribution obtained from our
colleagues who encountered this gas is not the same as the

We compare the p-value to the
significance level α to determine
whether we reject (or not) our
hypothesis.

benchmark, and hence the hypothesis that the hexafluorine-like gas may indeed have some anti-gravity effects.

The hypothesis that proposes that there are no differences between the characteristics of two populations of interest is called the **null hypothesis** and is usually denoted as H_0. The counterpart of the null hypothesis is called the **alternative hypothesis**. In our example above we can therefore say that we accept or reject the null hypothesis with a level of significance $\alpha = 0.05$. Please note that there is nothing special about the value chosen, but it is a common value to use. In the next chapter we will expand our discussions about hypothesis testing.

H_0 is the null hypothesis and it typically proposed that there is no difference between two populations.

The significance value is arbitrarily chosen.

The probability p mentioned above to help us reject (or not) the null hypothesis is imaginatively called the p-value and it tells us how likely it is that our data could have occurred under the null hypothesis. The calculation of a p-value depends on the statistical test we are using to check our hypothesis. Sometimes we refer to statistical significance and that is a way to say that the p-value for a given statistical test is small enough to reject the null hypothesis. There are some criticisms about the misuse and misinterpretation of p-values. The debate is a long one, and part of the problem is the interpretation of the meaning of these values. It is not unusual to think that the p-value is the probability of the null hypothesis given the data. Actually it is the probability of the data given the null hypothesis.

Statistical significance refers to having a p-value small enough to reject the null hypothesis.

The American Statistical Association released a statement[13] on the use of statistical significance and p-values. The statement addresses six principles around the use of p-values:

[13] Wasserstein, R. L. and N. A. Lazar (2016). The ASA statement on p-values: Context, process, and purpose. *The American Statistician* 70(2), 129–133

1. p-values can indicate how incompatible the data are with a specified statistical model.

2. p-values do not measure the probability that the studied hypothesis is true, or the probability that the data were produced by random chance alone.

3. Scientific conclusions and business or policy decisions should not be based only on whether a p-value passes a specific threshold.

Six principles about the use of p-values.

4. Proper inference requires full reporting and transparency

5. A p-value, or statistical significance, does not measure the size of an effect or the importance of a result.

6. By itself, a p-value does not provide a good measure of evidence regarding a model or hypothesis.

We are entering the realm of statistical inference, where we are interested in performing hypothesis tests. The comparison of statistical models is said to be statistically significant if, according to the threshold probability chosen, the observations obtained would be unlikely to occur if the null hypothesis were true. In order to do this, we have a variety of tests and distributions that can be used. In this section we are going to talk about two particular distributions that are commonly used in statistical inference.

We will expand this discussion in Chapter 6.

5.5.1   Student's t Distribution

IMAGINE YOU ARE A WORKING at your local brewery in Dublin, Ireland and your employer is highly interested in bringing some quality control to the brewing of your famous stouts. As a connoisseur of beer, you already know that brewing has an element of uncertainty, and you have been tasked with eliminating that uncertainty as much as possible. The ingredients that make your beer do have an inherent variability: From the malted barly you buy to the hops and yeast the brewer has cultivated over the years. Your task involves not only the assessment of these ingredients but also doing so in a cost-effective manner. Instead of wasting a lot of valuable ingredients in tests, you are looking at carrying out experiments with small samples to come to some conclusions.

From Guinness to Romulan Ale, brewing is both science and art.

Unlike the example of the fictitious hexafluorine-like gas, this is an actual historical one. William Sealy Gosset was indeed working at the Guinness brewery in Ireland, and his work led to the effective use of small samples to show that the distribution of the means deviated from the normal distribution. This meant that he could not rely on methods devised under the assumption of normality to draw valid conclusions. He therefore could not use conventional statistical methods based upon a normal distribution to draw his conclusions.

Remember Gosset next time you enjoy a Guinness beer!

We will cover those in Chapter 6.

In 1908 Gosset published[14] a paper about his work under the pseudonym of Student. In this paper, he shows how having n observations, within which lays the mean of the

[14] Student (1908). The probable error of a mean. *Biometrika* 6(1), 1–25

sample population, can be used to determine within what limits the mean of the sampled population lay. He provides values (from 4 to 10) which become the cumulative distribution function of what now we know as the Student's *t*-distribution. The *t*-distribution can be used to describe data that follow a normal-like curve, but with the greatest number of observations close to the mean and fewer data points around the tails. As shown by Gosset, it is useful in cases where we have smaller sample sizes, and where the standard deviation of the data is not known. Instead, the standard deviation is estimated based on the degrees of freedom of the dataset, in other words, the total number of observations minus one.

The *t*-distribution is useful in cases where we have smaller sample sizes, and where the standard deviation of the data is not known.

As you would expect, as the degrees of freedom increase, the *t*-distribution converges to the normal distribution. Anecdotally, this happens to be the case above 30 degrees of freedom, at which point we can use the standard normal distribution *z*.

Remember the central limit theorem.

For a series of independently and identically distributed random variables $X_1, X_2, \ldots, X_n$, let $\bar{X} = \frac{1}{n}\sum_i X_i$ be the sample mean and let $S^2 = \frac{1}{n-1}\sum_i(X_i - \bar{X})^2$ be the sample variance. The random variable $Z = \frac{\bar{X}-\mu}{\sigma/\sqrt{n}}$ has a standard normal distribution, and the variable:

$$t = \frac{\bar{X} - \mu}{\frac{S}{\sqrt{n}}}, \tag{5.102}$$

This is called the *t*-score.

has a Student *t*-distribution with $\nu = n - 1$ degrees of freedom. The value of S may not be close to σ, particularly for small n and this introduces more variability in our

We denote the degrees of freedom as ν, for the Student *t*-distribution $\nu = n - 1$.

model. The t-distribution tends to be more spread than the standard normal.

The probability density function of the t-distribution is given by:

$$f(t) = \frac{\Gamma\left(\frac{v+1}{2}\right)}{\sqrt{v\pi}\,\Gamma\left(\frac{v}{2}\right)} \left(1 + \frac{t^2}{v}\right)^{-\frac{v+1}{2}}, \qquad (5.103)$$

The PDF of the t-distribution.

where $v = n - 1$ is the degrees of freedom and $\Gamma(\cdot)$ is the gamma function. For a positive integer n, the gamma function is related to the factorial:

$$\Gamma(n) = (n-1)!. \qquad (5.104)$$

We can also define the gamma function[15] for all complex numbers, except non-positive integers:

$$\Gamma(z) = \int_0^\infty x^{z-1} e^{-x} dx. \qquad (5.105)$$

[15] Arfken, G., H. Weber, and F. Harris (2011). *Mathematical Methods for Physicists: A Comprehensive Guide*. Elsevier Science

Expressions for the cumulative distribution function can be written in terms of the regularised incomplete beta function[16], I:

[16] Pearson, K. (1968). *Tables of the Incomplete Beta-Function: With a New Introduction*. Cambridge University Press

$$F(t) = \int_{-\infty}^t f(u)\,du = 1 - \frac{1}{2}I_{x(t)}\left(\frac{v}{2}, \frac{1}{2}\right), \qquad (5.106)$$

where $x(t) = v/(t^2 + v)$. For some values of the degrees of freedom we have some simple forms for the PDF and CDF of the Student's t-distribution as shown in Table 5.2.

As we saw in Equation (5.102) we can define a t-score for the t-distribution similar to the z-score for the standard

The t-score helps us to define the t-test describe in Section 6.5.1.

ν	PDF	CDF
$\nu = 1$	$\dfrac{1}{\pi(1+t^2)}$	$\dfrac{1}{2} + \dfrac{1}{\pi}\arctan(t)$
$\nu = 2$	$\dfrac{1}{2\sqrt{2}\left(1+\frac{t^2}{2}\right)^{3/2}}$	$\dfrac{1}{2} + \dfrac{t}{2\sqrt{2}\left(1+\frac{t^2}{2}\right)^{2/2}}$
$\nu = 3$	$\dfrac{2}{\pi\sqrt{3}\left(1+\frac{t^2}{3}\right)^2}$	$\dfrac{1}{2} + \dfrac{1}{\pi}\left[\dfrac{t}{\sqrt{3}\left(1+\frac{t^2}{3}\right)} + \arctan\left(\dfrac{t}{\sqrt{3}}\right)\right]$
$\nu = 4$	$\dfrac{3}{8\left(1+\frac{t^2}{4}\right)^{\frac{5}{2}}}$	$\dfrac{1}{2} + \dfrac{3}{8}\dfrac{t}{\sqrt{1+\frac{t^2}{4}}}\left[1 - \dfrac{1}{12}\dfrac{t^2}{1+\frac{t^2}{4}}\right].$
$\nu = 5$	$\dfrac{8}{3\pi\sqrt{5}\left(1+\frac{t^2}{5}\right)^3}$	$\dfrac{1}{2} + \dfrac{1}{\pi}\left[\dfrac{t}{\sqrt{5}\left(1+\frac{t^2}{5}\right)}\left(1 + \dfrac{2}{3\left(1+\frac{t^2}{5}\right)}\right) + \arctan\left(\dfrac{t}{\sqrt{5}}\right)\right]$
$\nu = \infty$	$\dfrac{1}{\sqrt{2\pi}}e^{-t^2/2}$	$\dfrac{1}{2}\left[1 + \operatorname{erf}\left(\dfrac{t}{\sqrt{2}}\right)\right]$

Table 5.2: Special cases of the PDF and CDF for the Student's t-distribution with different degrees of freedom.

normal one. It represents the number of standard deviations from the mean and we can use this to define upper and lower bounds for our confidence interval and obtain p-values for t-tests.

As we mentioned above, the Student t-distribution is useful when the standard deviation is not known. If the sample size is large, we can use the confidence interval definition used for the normal distribution shown in Equation (5.100). Otherwise, we need to rely on the sample data to estimate the standard deviation and thus our confidence interval is given by:

$$\bar{x} \pm (t \text{ critical value})\left(\frac{S}{\sqrt{n}}\right), \qquad (5.107)$$

Confidence interval for the t-distribution.

where the t critical value is defined in terms of v, the degrees of freedom. Remember that if n is large, we can use the normal distribution for our estimation. The confidence interval above is suitable only for small n provided that the population distribution is approximately normal. If that is not the case, a different estimation method should be considered. In Figure 5.12 we can see a comparison of the probability density of the normal distribution versus Student's t-distributions for different values of the degrees of freedom v.

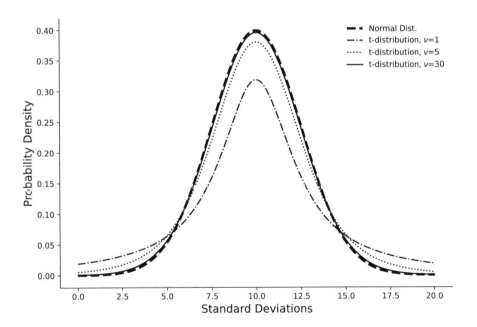

Figure 5.12: Probability distributions for the Student's t-distribution for $v = 1, 5, 30$. For comparison we show the normal distribution as a dashed curve.

For $v = 1$, the t-distribution is much flatter and has flatter tails than the standard Gaussian curve. This is advantageous in the case of smaller sample sizes as it provides a more conservative estimate of the probability density compared to using the normal distribution. As the degrees of freedom increase, we can see that the curves match quite well.

Python lets us calculate the Student's t-distribution in much the same way as we have seen for others. The PDF can be calculated with the t.pdf method and we need to provide the degrees of freedom as a required parameter. Note that you are also able to provide a parameter loc to shift the distribution and use the parameter scale to scale it. Otherwise, Python will assume you are requesting a standardised t-distribution. Let us calculate the PDF for standard t-distribution for the $v = 3$ case which can be seen in the top left-hand panel of Figure 5.13:

We use the t module in SciPy.

```
from scipy.stats import t
x = np.arange(-5, 5, 0.01)
nu = 3
pdf = t.pdf(x, nu)
```

Python will calculate a standard t distribution by default.

The CDF for the Student's t-distribution also requires us to provide the degrees of freedom. The CDF for the case $v = 3$ can be seen in the top right-hand panel of Figure 5.13:

```
cdf = t.cdf(x, nu)
```

The PDF and CDF of the t distribution are shown in the top panels of Figure 5.13.

As before, the PPF can easily be obtained too:

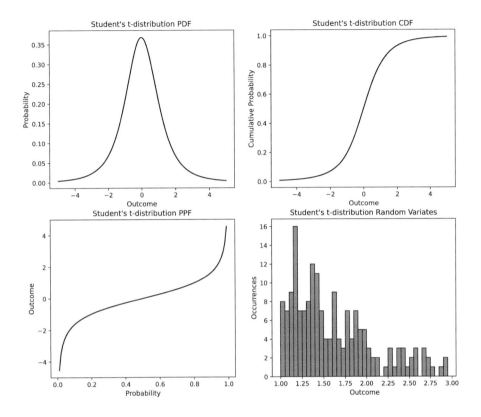

Figure 5.13: The Student's *t*-distribution for $\nu = 3$.

```
probs = np.arange(0, 1, 0.01)

ppf = t.ppf(probs, nu)
```

and the result is shown in the bottom left-hand panel of Figure 5.13.

Finally, as we have done with other distributions, we are able to create random variates with the rvs method. In this case we are creating random variates following the Student's *t*-distribution for $\nu = 3$. The results are shown in the bottom right-hand panel of Figure 5.13.

```
x1 = t.rvs(nu, size=1000)
```

5.5.2   Chi-squared Distribution

A NEW REPLICATOR HAS FINALLY been delivered to our
ship, the *USS Cerritos*. We, along with Mariner, Rutherford,
Boimler and Tendi and 94 other Starfleet colleagues, are
trying to decide whether the enchiladas or the tacos are
the best choice of Mexican food. In the best democratic
style, a vote is required and we have 60 colleagues going
for enchiladas, whereas the rest, i.e. 40, are voting for the
tacos. The requirement here has been a tally of frequency
counts on categorical data, in this case enchiladas and tacos.
We can extend our sample to the rest of the ship and the
frequency data collected can be used to determine a test
for the hypothesis that there is a preference for replicator
enchiladas, hmmm!

Yes, you and me, making it a
group of 100 Starfleet officers.

It seems that we for the next
squad meal we are going to have
enchiladas. Yay!

A way to analyse frequency data is the use of the
chi-squared distribution and we can use it to test if the
variables are independent. We arrange the data to the
expectation that the variables are independent. If the data
does not fit the model, the likelihood is that the variables
are dependent and thus rejecting the null hypothesis. We
start our analysis based on the z-score and we obtain our χ^2
statistic simply by squaring z:

χ-squared or even χ^2

See Section 6.3 for more
information on the chi-square
test.

$$\chi^2 = z^2 = \frac{(X - \mu)^2}{\sigma^2}. \tag{5.108}$$

As you can see, the values are always positive. In any event, if the categories we are selecting things from are mutually independent, then the sum of individual χ^2 follows a chi-square distribution, i.e. $\sum x^2 = \chi^2$. This means that we can find a chi-square for each of the categories and their sum will also be a chi-square. If that is not the case, the categories are not independent!

If the distribution of observation follows a chi-square, the categories are independent.

The shape of the chi-square distribution depends on the degrees of freedom, which in this case is the number of categories minus one. For our enchiladas and tacos vote, we have $k = 2 - 1 = 1$, in other words one degree of freedom. The probability distribution function of the chi-squared distribution is given by:

$$f(x) = \begin{cases} \dfrac{x^{\frac{k}{2}-1} e^{-\frac{x}{2}}}{2^{\frac{k}{2}} \Gamma\left(\frac{k}{2}\right)}, & x > 0; \\ 0, & \text{otherwise.} \end{cases} \tag{5.109}$$

The PDF of the chi-squared distribution.

where k corresponds to the degrees of freedom and $\Gamma(\cdot)$ is the gamma function.

For each chi-squared variable of degree k, the mean is actually k and its variance is $2k$. Using the central limit theorem, we can see that as n tends to infinity, the chi-square distribution converges to a normal distribution of mean k and standard deviation $\sqrt{2k/n}$. In practical terms, for k greater than 50 the normal distribution can safely be used. We can see the probability density function of the chi-square distribution for different degrees of freedom in Figure 5.14.

As $n \to \infty$, $\chi^2(k) \to N\left(k, \sqrt{\frac{2k}{n}}\right)$

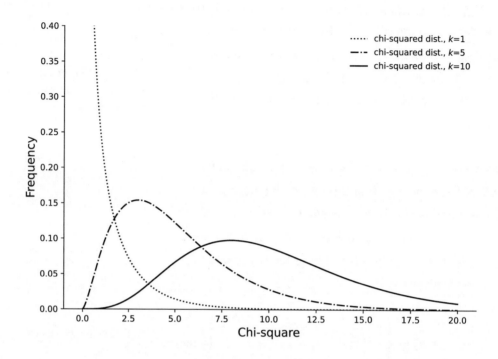

Figure 5.14: Probability density function for the chi-square distribution for different degrees of freedom.

When $k = 1$ we expect that, if the categories are indeed independent, most of the results will be close to 0 as we can see in Figure 5.14. As we add more and more degrees of freedom we are effectively adding together independent chi-distributions each with $k = 1$. Although they individually bunch close to 0, when added together the centre of the distribution starts shifting. The more values we add, the more symmetrical the distribution becomes, until we converge to a normal distribution.

The cumulative distribution function is expressed in terms of the gamma function, $\Gamma(\cdot)$, we encountered in the previous section, and the lower incomplete gamma

function[17] $\gamma(\cdot)$:

$$F(x) = \frac{\gamma\left(\frac{k}{2}, \frac{x}{2}\right)}{\Gamma\left(\frac{k}{2}\right)}. \tag{5.110}$$

[17] Abramowitz, M. and I. Stegun (1965). *Handbook of Mathematical Functions: With Formulas, Graphs, and Mathematical Tables*. Applied Mathematics Series. Dover Publications

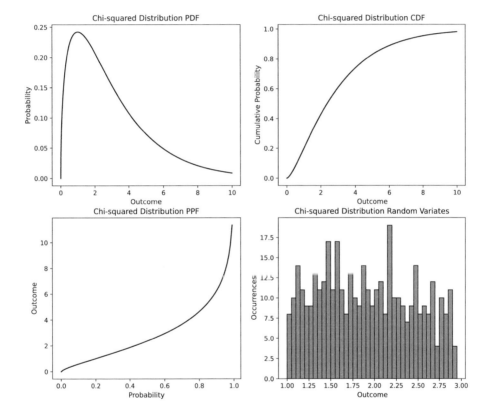

Figure 5.15: The chi-squared distribution for $k = 3$.

We can obtain values for the PDF with Python with the help of the chi2 implementation in SciPy:

```
from scipy.stats import chi2
x = np.arange(0, 10, 0.01)
k = 3
pdf = chi2.pdf(x, k)
```

We use the chi2 module in SciPy.

The distribution can be seen in the top left-hand panel of Figure 5.15. You need to provide the degrees of freedom as a parameter. As before the distribution can be shifted with loc and scaled with scale.

The CDF is calculated in Python as follows:

```
cdf = chi2.cdf(x, k)
```

You know the drill by now.

We can see the shape of the CDF in the top right-hand panel of Figure 5.15. The PPF can be seen in the bottom left-hand panel of Figure 5.15 and obtained as follows:

```
probs = np.arange(0, 1, 0.01)
ppf = chi2.ppf(probs, k)
```

The CDF and PPF of the chi-squared distribution is shown in the top-right and bottom-left panels of Figure 5.15.

Finally, we can get random variates following the chi-squared distribution with $k = 3$ with rvs:

```
x1 = chi2.rvs(k, size=1000)
```

A histogram of the values obtained is shown in the bottom right-hand panel of Figure 5.15.

Let us go back to our initial survey of preferred Mexican food. From our data, we have that the probability for enchiladas is $p_e = 0.6$ and the probability for tacos is $p_t = 0.4$. We could explore whether obtaining 72 and 28 is significantly different from the values obtained. There are therefore two χ^2 distributions we need to add up:

$$\chi^2 = \frac{(72-60)^2}{60} + \frac{(28-40)^2}{40} = 6. \qquad (5.111)$$

We can use the chi-square to devise a suitable test.

Let us find the critical value for a chi-squared distribution for 95% confidence with $k = 1$. We can use the PPF to find the value:

```
chi2.ppf(0.95,1 )


3.841458820694124
```

As the value obtained is larger than the one shown by the chi-distribution we can conclude that there is indeed a strong preference for enchiladas! In this case we may not need to resort to a test, but as the number of categories increases, the chi-square is a good friend to have.

See Section 6.3.1 for more on the goodness-of-fit test.

6

Alluring Arguments and Ugly Facts – Statistical Modelling and Hypothesis Testing

WE HAVE COME A LONG way in our journey; with the
knowledge we have now, we are in a position to start
interrogating our data a bit more. In this chapter we will
introduce the idea of statistical modelling as a way to
understand and interpret the observations we have gathered.
This will let us identify potential relationships between
variables and make predictions.

Statistical modelling lets us
understand and interpret our data.

We will first expand on our discussion of hypothesis testing
from the previous chapter and look at the difference
between one-tailed and two-tailed tests. This will give us
the opportunity to talk about testing for normality, i.e. to
check if a set of data follow a normal distribution. We will
apply hypothesis testing to more specific tests that will help
us tease out ugly facts in alluring arguments, and
sometimes the other way around too.

Check Section 5.5.

6.1   Hypothesis Testing

IN THE PREVIOUS CHAPTER WE talked about the characteristics of various probability distributions and we also looked at how these distributions can help us with determining whether we should accept or reject a hypothesis. We now understand that for us to absolutely determine if a hypothesis is true or false, we need absolute knowledge and hence we will have to examine a full population or populations. This is clearly not possible in many cases. Instead, we use a random sample, and use its properties to see if there is enough evidence to support the hypothesis or not.

We cannot absolutely have absolute knowledge about the population.

Let us recall from Section 5.5 that we have two hypotheses:

- H_0: the null hypothesis, and

- H_a: the alternative hypothesis.

We may want to test if the alternative hypothesis is likely to be true and hence we have two possible results:

- we reject the null hypothesis and accept the alternative one as we have enough evidence in favour of H_a, or

- we do not reject the null hypothesis because we do not have enough evidence in favour of the alternative.

Not rejecting the null hypothesis does not mean that H_0 is necessarily true!

Note that not rejecting the null hypothesis does not necessarily mean that H_0 it is true. It only means that we do not have enough evidence to support H_a.

Let us consider an example. The toaster manufacturer in Caprica City has issued a technical statement saying that their Model-5 artificially intelligent toasters are really good. However, they mentioned that their defective rate is 5%. We would like to investigate if the true probability, p, of a toaster being defective is indeed equal to the value mentioned by the manufacturer, or actually greater than that. Our hypothesis can be formulated as follows:

We know how good the A.I. in these toasters is, particularly in the Model-5.

- H_0: $p = 0.05$,

- H_a: $p > 0.05$.

Note that the null hypothesis test is for equality.

We take a sample of 100 Model-5 toasters and perform some quality control tests to determine if the toasters are defective or not. Let us denote the number of defective toasters X, and it is our **test statistic**. We will reject the null hypothesis if $X \geq 10$, with 10 being our **critical value**. The region that provides evidence about the rejection of the null hypothesis is called the **critical region**. Look at Figure 6.1 to give you an idea of what we are dealing with. You may be thinking, why 10? Well, as we said, the value is arbitrary, but not random. Let us take a look.

We chose the critical value arbitrarily, but not randomly.

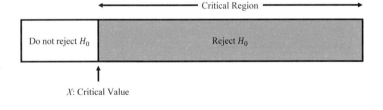

Figure 6.1: A schematic way to think about hypothesis testing.

The result of our quality testing on each Model-5 toaster is effectively a Bernoulli process. As discussed in Section

5.3.2, there are only two outcomes for each trial, either the Model-5 toaster is defective or it is not. If the probability of defect is $p = 0.05$, in a sample of 100 toasters we expect to have $100 \times 0.05 = 5$ defective toasters. If we find 10 defective ones, we have strong evidence to reject the null hypothesis.

Our test results in a Bernoulli process as we have only two outcomes: defective or non-defective toaster.

Taking measurements is not an exact science, and we need to come to terms with the idea that we may make some errors. If we reject the null hypothesis when the alternative one is actually correct we are good! That is also the case when we do not reject the null hypothesis when it is in fact true. But, what happens when we make an error. We can use Table 6.1 to think of the possible situations.

	H_0 is true	H_a is true
Do not reject H_0	Correct decision True Negative $1 - \alpha$	Type II error False Negative β
Reject H_0	Type I error False Positive α	Correct decision True Positive $1 - \beta$

Table 6.1: Types of errors when performing hypothesis testing.

As we can see, we have a Type I error when we have a false positive. In other words, we reject the null hypothesis when in fact it is true. If this was a courtroom case, this is equivalent to convicting a defendant when in fact they are innocent. The probability of committing a Type I error is called the **level of significance**, and we denote it with the letter α. The lower the value of α, the less likely we are to commit a Type I error. As discussed in the Section 5.5 we generally choose values smaller than 0.05.

Type I errors correspond to false positives.

The lower the value of α, the less likely we are to erroneously convict an innocent person.

We know from Section 5.3.3 that repeated Bernoulli trials follow a binomial distribution. We can therefore use the probability mass function (PMF) of the binomial to determine the level of significance for our test, i.e. $\alpha = Pr(X \geq 10)$ when $p = 0.05$. Let us use Python to do this:

The distribution of our data helps us determine the values we need to test for.

```
from scipy.stats import binom

alpha = 0


for n in range(10, 101):
    alpha += binom.pmf(n, 100, 0.05)
```

We are calculating the probability in a range greater than 10, hence the use of range(10, 101).

And we can see the significance value calculated:

```
> print(alpha)

0.028188294163416106
```

Let us now turn our attention to Type II errors. These come about when we fail to reject the null hypothesis when in fact the alternative hypothesis is true. This is a false negative and the probability of committing a Type II error is denoted as β. If we have a true positive when rejecting H_0, the probability is $1 - \beta$ and this is called the **power** of a test.

Type II errors correspond to false negatives.

In order to compute β, we need to look at specific alternative hypotheses. In our example, since we do not know the true value of p, all we can do is compute β for specific cases, for example $H_a : p = 0.08$. In other words, $\beta = Pr(X < 10)$ when $p = 0.08$:

We calculate β for specific H_a's.

```
beta = 0
for n in range(0, 10):
    beta += binom.pmf(n, 100, 0.08)
print(beta)


0.7219779808448744
```

Note that there is an interplay between α and β. If we reduce the critical region, we reduce α but this will increase β. The inverse is also true, we can reduce β by increasing the critical region, but then α increases. There is a way to reduce both α and β simultaneously: We need to increase the sample size!

> We can reduce α and β simultaneously by increasing the sample size.

Hang on a minute! Increasing the sample size implies that we can make use of the central limit theorem as discussed in Section 5.4.4 and we can approximate our distribution with a Gaussian curve. For our example with a binomial distribution, we have that the mean is np and the standard deviation is $np(1-p)$. We can use this information to obtain our z-score:

> Increasing the sample size gives us the opportunity of using the central limit theorem.

$$z = \frac{X - np}{\sqrt{np(1-p)}}. \qquad (6.1)$$

> We are using the mean and standard deviation of the binomial distribution. See Section 5.3.3.

Let us say that we increase our sample to 550 toasters to test, and our critical value to 45. We can use Python to calculate α with the help of the CDF of the normal distribution for our z-score:

```
X = 45

n = 550

p = 0.05

zs= (X-n*p)/np.sqrt(n*p*(1-p))

alpha=1-norm.cdf(zs)

print(alpha)


0.00030874671173 17555
```

We are reducing α, and thus our chances of committing a Type I error.

With these values, we are very unlikely to commit a Type I error! This is such a common thing that Python has a shortcut for us in the form of the so-called survival function sf=1-cdf:

```
> print(norm.sf(zs))


0.0003087467117317515
```

We are using the survival function for the normal distribution.

6.1.1 Tales and Tails: One- and Two-Tailed Tests

So, you have a hypothesis? Now what? Well, let us recap a few of the things we mentioned in the previous section. After having identified your null hypothesis H_0, and your alternative hypothesis H_a, you are interested in determining if there is enough evidence to show that the null hypothesis can be rejected.

So, you have a hypothesis? Let us test it!

- H_0 assumes that there is no difference between a parameter and a given value, or that there is no difference between two parameters

H_0 assumes there is no difference.

- H_a assumes that there is a difference between a parameter and a given value, or that there is a difference between two parameters

H_a assumes there is a difference.

- The critical region is the range of values that indicate that a significant difference is found, and therefore the null hypothesis should be rejected

The critical region helps us reject the null hypothesis.

- The non-critical region is the range of values that indicates that the difference is probably due to chance, and we should not reject the null hypothesis

- The critical value separates the critical and non-critical regions

- The significance level is the maximum probability of committing a Type I error, or in other words getting a false positive i.e $P(\text{Type I error})|H_0 \text{ is true}) = \alpha$.

In the previous section, we considered an example where the Model-5 toaster manufacturer in Caprica City claimed that their defective rate was equal to a given value, θ_0. The alternative hypothesis in that example was to assume that the probability was bigger than θ_0. In other words:

We used p before, and we adopt θ_0 here to avoid confusion with p-values.

- $H_0: \quad \theta = \theta_0$

The hypotheses of a right-tailed test.

- $H_a: \quad \theta > \theta_0$

In this case the critical region was only on the right-hand side of the distributions. This is why we call tests like these **one-tailed tests**; here we have a right-tailed test. We can see a depiction of this situation in the top panel of Figure 6.2.

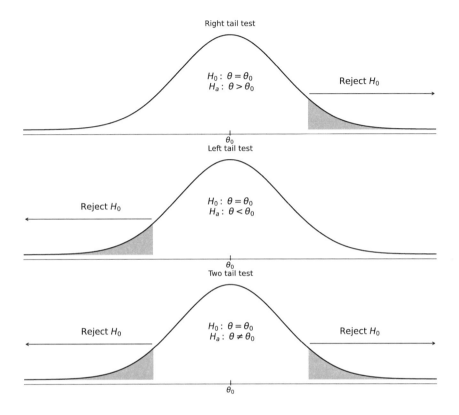

Figure 6.2: One- v Two-Tail Tests.

We could have formulated a one-tailed test where the tails is located on the left-hand side.

- $H_0: \quad \theta = \theta_0$

  The hypotheses of a left-tailed test.

- $H_a: \quad \theta < \theta_0$

This left-tailed test is depicted in the middle panel of Figure 6.2. Finally, we have the case where we check for differences:

- $H_0:$ $\theta = \theta_0$

- $H_a:$ $\theta \neq \theta_0$

The hypotheses of a two-tailed test.

Here, we have a situation where the critical region is on both sides of the distribution and hence we call this a **two-tailed test**. Note that the significance level is split so that the critical region covers $\alpha/2$ on each side.

Let us go back to our Model-5 toaster manufacturer in Caprica City for an example of a two-tailed test. This time the statement is that their toasters have a resistor of 48Ω. We take a sample of 100 toasters and look at the resistors obtaining a sample mean of 46.5Ω. Let us assume that we have a known population standard deviation of 9.5, following a normal distribution. The steps that we need to complete in hypothesis testing can be summarised as follows:

I assume a lecture on the futility of resistance would result in a wrong-SciFi pun.

1. State the hypotheses and identify the claim. This helps formulate H_0 and H_a.

2. Find the critical value or values.

Hypothesis testing steps.

3. Compute the test value.

4. Decide whether to reject the null hypothesis or not.

5. Explain the result.

For the first step, we have that our hypothesis is that the manufacturer used a 48Ω resistor. Our null hypothesis corresponds to the claim made. If we reject the null hypothesis we are saying that there is enough evidence to reject the claim. When the alternative hypothesis is the

Stating clearly our hypothesis, let us better interpret the results.

claim, rejecting the null hypothesis means that there is enough evidence to support the claim. In our Model-5 toaster case, our hypothesis test is given by:

- $H_0: \quad \mu = 48$

- $H_a: \quad \mu \neq 48$

Note that we have a two-tailed hypothesis.

Since we have information about the population standard deviation, we are going to use as our test statistic a z-test:

Note that we are assuming that we know the standard deviation of the population.

$$z = \frac{\bar{X} - \mu_0}{\frac{\sigma}{\sqrt{n}}}. \tag{6.2}$$

Let us select a significance level $\alpha = 0.05$. We can then calculate a critical value, cv. Since this is a two-tailed test, we need to check that the test statistic given by our z-score value is between $-cv$ and cv, otherwise we will reject the null hypothesis:

In a two-tailed test, we split the significance level to have $\alpha/2$ on each side.

```
alpha=0.05

print(norm.ppf(alpha/2))


-1.9599639845400545
```

Remember the magic z-scores of ± 1.96 for a 95% confidence level? If not, take a look at page 249.

We can now use the information from our data to calculate our test value:

```
> n = 100
> sigma = 9.5
> mu = 48
> X = 46.5
> zs = (X-mu)/(sigma/np.sqrt(n))
```

Let us calculate our z-score.

Let us take a look:

```
> print(zs)

-1.5789473684210527
```

Since the test value is between -1.96 and 1.96, we cannot reject the null hypothesis and conclude that the sample data support the claim that the resistors in the Model-5 toasters are 48Ω at a 5% significance level. In this example we have made use of a standard normal distribution, however, in many cases a Student's t-distribution is used for this type of test.

See Section 6.5 for running tests with the t-distribution.

In the example above we selected the significance value first. We can also employ a p-value to test our hypothesis. Remember that a p-value is the probability of getting a sample statistic, for example the mean, or a more extreme sample statistic pointing toward the alternative hypothesis when the null hypothesis is considered to be true. In other words, the p-value is the lowest level of significance at which the observed value of a test statistic is significant. This means that we are calculating the minimum probability of a Type I error with which the null hypothesis can still be rejected. Let us see what the p-value is for our Model-5 toasters:

See Section 5.5.

The smaller the p-value, the stronger the evidence against H_0.

```
> pval = 2*(1-norm.cdf(zs))
> print(pval)

1.8856518702577993
```

We can also use the survival function to obtain pval.

This *p*-value is such that we would not be able to reject the null hypothesis, as the minimum significance is $p = 1.8856$. In this case the claim from the manufacturers of the Model-5 toasters holds.

Now that we have a better understanding of how hypothesis testing works, we will concentrate on more specific ways in which this general methodology can be applied to make sure that ugly facts are not hidden behind alluring arguments, and vice versa.

Hypothesis testing works along these lines for different tests. We will discuss this in the rest of this chapter.

6.2   Normality Testing

THERE IS NO DOUBT OF the importance of the normal or Gaussian distribution. It arises in many situations and applications. Thanks to the central limit theorem many variables will have distributions that approximate the normal. Furthermore, given its mathematical closed form, it is easy to manipulate and consequently it underpins many statistical tests. Many statistical analyses start with some exploratory data analysis as described in Chapter 4, followed by some normality testing. This will let us decide if other tests described in this chapter are suitable to be applied.

Testing if our data follows a normal distribution is a typical step in statistical analysis.

The Gaussian distribution can be fully determined by two parameters: The mean and the standard deviation. In terms of shape, we know that it is a symmetrical distribution and the empirical rule indicates the percentage of data observations within a number of standard deviations from

Review Sections 5.4.1 and 5.4.2 for more information about the normal distribution.

the mean. One way to assess the normality of our data is to do it graphically. We shall see how to use Python to create a histogram in Section 8.7 and a box plot in Section 8.8. Let us start with a graphical test call the Q-Q plot and we will then discuss some more formal tests.

Histograms and box plots are other ways to check for normality in a graphical way.

6.2.1   Q-Q Plot

A Q-Q PLOT, OR QUANTILE-QUANTILE plot, is a graphical way to assess if a dataset resembles a given distribution such as the normal. The idea is to look at the distribution of data in each of the quantiles. In Section 4.4.2 we discussed the grouping of observations into quantiles, and in this graphical test we create a scatterplot that shows the quantiles of two sets of data, the dataset in question and that of a theoretical distribution such as the normal.

Q-Q is short for quantile-quantile. Nothing to do with the extra-dimensional being with immeasurable power.

See Section 8.3 for more information on scatterplots.

The idea is that if both sets of quantiles come from the same distribution, the plot will show a straight line. The further the plot is from a straight line, the less likely it is that the two distributions are similar. Note that this is only a visual check and it is recommended to use a more formal test as discussed in the rest of this section.

A straight line indicates that the data follows a normal curve.

Let us take a look at some example data containing random samples taken from a normal distribution, and compare them to some that are skewed. The data can be obtained[1] from https://doi.org/10.6084/m9.figshare.17306285.v1 as a comma-separated value file with the name "normal_skewed.csv". Let us read the data into a pandas dataframe:

[1] Rogel-Salazar, J. (2021b, Dec). Normal and Skewed Example Data. https://doi.org/10.6084/m9.figshare.17306285.v1

```
import pandas as pd

df = pd.read_csv('normal_skew.csv')
```

The data contains data for two series, one normally distributed and one skewed.

We now can call the `probplot` method from the `stats` module in SciPy. It lets us generate a Q-Q plot of sample data against the quantiles of a specified theoretical distribution. The default is the normal distribution and in the example below we explicitly say so with `dist='norm'`. Note that we request for a plot to be produced with the help of matplotlib. Let us look at the normal example first:

```
from scipy import stats
import matplotlib.pyplot as plt


stats.probplot(df['normal_example'], dist='norm',
    plot=plt)
```

We create a Q-Q plot with the probplot method.

We are directly passing the pandas series to the `probplot` method and indicate the reference distribution via `dist`. The result can be seen in the left-hand side of Figure 6.3. The plot shows a reference diagonal line. If the data come from the same distribution, the points should align with this reference. For this example, we can see that the data in question is normally distributed.

We provide the reference distribution via `dist`.

The more the data points depart from the reference line in the Q-Q plot, the greater the chance the datasets come from different distributions. We can see the Q-Q plot for the skewed dataset by using the corresponding pandas series:

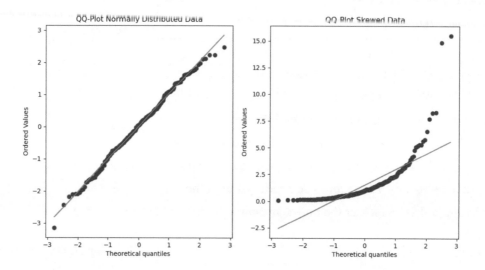

Figure 6.3: Q-Q plots for a normally distributed dataset, and a skewed dataset.

```
stats.probplot(df['skewed_example'], dist='norm',
    plot=plt)
```

The result is shown in the right-hand side of Figure 6.3. As we can see, the points deviate from the reference line significantly. In this case, we can visually assess that the dataset in question is not normally distributed.

6.2.2 Shapiro-Wilk Test

TESTING FOR NORMALITY IN A visual way as done in the previous section provides us with a quick way to assess our data. However, in many cases this subjective approach requires more robust ways to test our hypothesis. With that in mind, one of the most widely used tests for normality is the one proposed by Samuel Sanford Shapiro and Martin

Graphical testing is subjective, and we need a more robust method.

Wilk in 1965[2]. The Shapiro-Wilk test statistic is called W and is given by:

[2] Shapiro, S. S. and Wilk, M. B. (1965, 12). An analysis of variance test for normality (complete samples)†. *Biometrika* 52(3-4), 591–611

$$W = \frac{\left(\sum_i a_i x_{(i)} \right)^2}{\sum_i (x_i - \bar{x})^2},$$ (6.3)

where $\bar{x}$ is the sample mean and $x_{(i)}$ is the i-th order statistic, in other words the i-th smallest number in the sample.

In order to compare to the normal distribution, the test takes samples from a normal distribution and calculates expected values m_i of the order statistics of normally distributed samples. We denote $m = (m_i, \ldots, m_n)^T$ the vector of these expected values, and V the covariance matrix of those normal order statistics. These mathematical objects enable us to calculate the coefficients a_i in Equation (6.3):

We calculate the coefficients a_i with the help of expected values m.

$$(a_i, \ldots, a_n) = \frac{m^T V^{-1}}{|V^{-1}m|}.$$ (6.4)

See Section 6.4.1 for a formal definition of the covariance.

The test makes the null hypothesis that a random sample is independent and identically distributed (i.i.d) and came from a normal distribution $N(\mu, \sigma)$ for some unknown μ and $\sigma > 0$. If the p-value obtained from the test is less than the chosen level of significance α, the null hypothesis is rejected, indicating that the data is not normally distributed. In Python we can use the implementation of the test in the statistics module in SciPy. The function is called `shapiro` and takes an array of sample data. It returns the test statistic and a p-value. Let us import the function:

The null hypothesis is that the data is normally distributed.

```
from scipy.stats import shapiro
```

We use the `shapiro` function in SciPy.

Now that we know how the test considers the null and alternative hypotheses, we can create a function that takes the sample data and returns the result of the test:

```
def shapiro_test(data, alpha=0.05):
    stat, p = shapiro(data)
    print('stat = {0:.4f}, p-value= {1:.4f}'.
          format(stat, p))
    if p > alpha:
      print(''Can't Reject the null hypothesis. The
             data seems to be normally distributed.'')
    else:
      print(''Reject the null hypothesis. The data
             does not seem to be normally
             distributed.'')
```

A function that helps us interpret our results for a given value of α.

Let us take a look at applying the Shapiro-Wilk test to the example data used in the previous section:

```
> shapiro_test(df['normal_example'])


stat = 0.9954, p-value= 0.6394


Can't reject the null hypothesis.
The data seems to be normally distributed.
```

We can test against the data we know is normally distributed.

For the skewed data we have the following:

```
> shapiro_test(df['skewed_example'])


stat = 0.6218, p-value= 0.0000


Reject the null hypothesis.
The data does not seem to be normally distributed.
```

As well as the skewed data.

6.2.3 D'Agostino K-squared Test

WE ARE ALL FAMILIAR WITH the shape of the Gaussian
distribution, and in Section 5.4.3 we discussed how the
moments of the normal distribution can help us characterise
the normality of sample data. We know that a normal
distribution has kurtosis equal to $g_2 = 3$, and skewness
$g_1 = 0$. Looking at these measures for our sample data
can help us formulate a test. This is where the D'Agostino
proposal [3] comes into play.

Or kurtosis $g_2 = 0$ if we use the
Fisher definition.

[3] D'Agostino, R. B. (1970, 12).
Transformation to normality
of the null distribution of g_1.
Biometrika 57(3), 679–681

Looking at the skewness, g_1, and kurtosis, g_2, of the sample
data is a good start. In fact, if the samples are drawn from
a population that is normally distributed, it is possible
to write down expressions of the skewness and kurtosis
in terms of their mean (μ_1), variance (μ_2), skewness (γ_1)
and kurtosis (γ_2). Unfortunately, the convergence of these
expressions to the theoretical distribution is slow. This
means that we may require a large number of observations.
In order to remedy this, D'Agostino's proposal is to use the

See Appendix H.

following transformation:

$$Z_1(g_1) = \delta \ \text{asinh} \left(\frac{g_1}{\alpha \sqrt{\mu_2}} \right),$$ (6.5)

where:

$$
\begin{aligned}
W^2 &= \sqrt{2\gamma_2 + 4} - 1, \\
\delta &= (\ln W)^{-1/2}, \\
\alpha^2 &= \frac{2}{W^2 - 1}.
\end{aligned}
$$

See Appendix H for expressions for μ_2 and γ_2.

A further proposal was explored by D'Agostino[4] to use an omnibus test that combines skewness and kurtosis. For this we define a statistic D such that:

[4] D'Agostino, R. B. (1971, 08). An omnibus test of normality for moderate and large size samples. *Biometrika* 58(2), 341–348

$$D = \frac{\sum_i \left(i - \frac{1}{2}(n+1) \right) X_{i,n}}{n^2 S},$$ (6.6)

where $X_{i,n}$ are the ordered observations derived from a random sample $X_1, \ldots, X_n$, and $S^2 = \sum (X_i - \bar{X})^2 / n$. An approximate standardised variable with asymptotically mean zero and variance one is:

An omnibus test is used to check if the explained variance in a set of data is significantly greater than the unexplained variance, overall.

$$Y = \left(D - \frac{1}{2\sqrt{\pi}} \right) \left(\frac{24\pi n}{12\sqrt{3} - 37 + 2\pi} \right).$$ (6.7)

If a sample is drawn from a non-normal distribution, the expected value of Y tends to be different from zero.

This approach and some empirical results[5] to test for the departure from the normal distribution have been used to implement a statistical test that combines skewness and kurtosis in SciPy. The null hypothesis is that the sample comes from a normal distribution and the implementation

[5] D'Agostino, R. and E. S. Pearson (1973). Tests for Departure from Normality. Empirical Results for the Distributions of b_2 and $\sqrt{b_1}$. *Biometrika* 60(3), 613–622

in the statistics module in SciPy is called the normaltest. The test is two-sided.

We will again create a function that makes it clearer when we are able to reject the null hypothesis and interpret the result:

```
from scipy.stats import normaltest


def dagostino_test(data, alpha=0.05):
    k2, p = normaltest(data)
    print('stat = {0:.4f}, p-value= {1:.4f}'.
        format(k2, p))
    if p > alpha:
      print(''Can't Reject the null hypothesis. The
            data seems to be normally distributed.'')
    else:
      print(''Reject the null hypothesis. The data
            does not seem to be normally
            distributed.'')
```

We first load the normaltest function.

We then create a function to help us interpret the results of the test.

Let us take a look at applying the Shapiro-Wilk test to the example data used in the previous section:

```
> dagostino_test(df['normal_example'])


stat = 1.0525, p-value= 0.5908


Can't reject the null hypothesis.
The data seems to be normally distributed.
```

We can test against the data we know is normally distributed.

For the skewed data we have the following:

```
> dagostino_test(df['skewed_example'])


stat = 253.0896, p-value= 0.00000


Reject the null hypothesis.
The data does not seem to be normally distributed.
```

As well as the skewed data.

6.2.4   Kolmogorov-Smirnov Test

ANOTHER METHOD FOR TESTING FOR normality is, given a set of random samples $X_i, \ldots, X_n$, we need to check if an empirical distribution, $F_n(x)$, is consistent with a theoretical known distribution $F(x)$. Note that the theoretical distribution does not need to be a Gaussian and the test can check for other distributions, but we assume that the population mean and standard deviation are known.

This approach can test for other distributions, not just Gaussian.

Consider the order statistics $y_z < y_2 < \cdots < y_n$ of the observed random samples, with no tied observations, then the empirical distribution is defined as:

Tied observations are data points with the same value.

$$
F_n(x) = \begin{cases} 0, & \text{for } x \leq y_1, \\ \frac{k}{n}, & \text{for } y_k \leq x < y_{k+1}, \quad k = 1, 2, \ldots, n-1, \\ 1, & \text{for } x \geq y_n. \end{cases}
$$

Empirical distribution given a set of order statistics.

We describe our empirical distribution as the fraction of sample values that are equal to, or less than x. We are using a step function that jumps by $1/n$ in height at each observation. When we have n_k tied observations the jump is n_k/n.

With this information we can justify creating a test statistic that helps us check whether a cumulative distribution function $F_n(x)$ equals a theoretical distribution function $F(x)$ such that:

$$D_n = \max_x \left[|F_n(x) - F(x)| \right].$$ (6.8)

The Kolmogorov-Smirnov test.

This is the Kolmogorov-Smirnov test, and the hypothesis testing can be summarised as:

- H_0: $F_n(x) = F(x)$, i.e. the distributions are the same,

- H_a: $F_n(x) \neq F(x)$, i.e. the distributions are different.

The Kolmogorov-Smirnov hypotheses.

If the p-value obtained is lower than the significance level α, we reject the null hypothesis and assume that the distribution of our data is not normal. If, on the other hand, the p-value is larger than the significance level, we fail to reject the null hypothesis and assume that our data is normally distributed.

The Kolmogorov-Smirnov test[6] is a non-parametric test. This means that we are not making any assumption about the frequency distribution of the variables. Instead, rely on order statistics. The test relies on the fact that as the sample size n tends to infinity, the empirical distribution function, $F_n(x)$, converges with probability 1 and uniformly in x, to the theoretical distribution function $F(x)$. If at any point there is a large difference between the two, we take this as evidence that the distributions are different.

[6] Kolmogorov, A. (1933). Sulla determinazione empirica di una legge di distribuzione. *Inst. Ital. Attuari, Giorn.* 4, 83–91; and Smirnov, N. V. (1939). Estimate of deviation between empirical distribution functions in two independent samples. *Bulletin Moscow University* 2(2), 3–16

In Python we are able to use the `kstest` implementation of
the Kolmogorov-Smirnov test in the `stats` module of SciPy.
It lets us perform both one- and two-sided tests with the
help of the `alternative` parameter. Notice that the default
is the two-sided test, and that is what we will be using here.
Let us write a function to test our hypothesis. Remember
that we are using the two-sided test:

> kstest implements the Kolmogorov-Smirnov test in Python.

```python
from scipy.stats import kstest


def ks_test(data, alpha=0.05):
  d, p = kstest(data, 'norm')
  print('stat = {0:.4f}, p-value= {1:.4f}'.
        format(d, p))
  if p > alpha:
    print(''Can't Reject the null hypothesis. The
          data seems to be normally distributed.'')
  else:
    print(''Reject the null hypothesis. The data
          does not seem to be normally
          distributed.'')
```

> We first load the kstest function.

> We create a function to help us interpret the results of the test.

We can apply this function to check the example normal
data we have used in the rest of this section:

```python
> ks_test(df['normal_example'])


stat = 0.0354, p-value= 0.8942


Can't reject the null hypothesis.
The data seems to be normally distributed.
```

> We can test against the data we know is normally distributed.

For the skewed example data we have that:

```
> ks_test(df['skewed_example'])


stat = 0.5420, p-value= 0.0000


Reject the null hypothesis.
The data does not seem to be normally distributed.
```

As well as the skewed data.

6.3   Chi-square Test

IN SECTION 5.5.2 WE INTRODUCED the chi-squared distribution as a way to analyse frequency data. Now that we have a better understanding of hypothesis testing, we can see how to use this distribution to look at the comparison of observed frequencies, O, with those of an expected pattern, E.

We were trying to decide whether enchiladas or tacos were the favourite Mexican food in our spaceship.

6.3.1   Goodness of Fit

WE CAN OBTAIN OBSERVED FREQUENCIES from collected data, and we may have an expectation of what these frequencies should be. As you may imagine, the expected frequencies are those corresponding to situations where the null hypothesis is true. In general, however, we can check if the observed frequencies match any pattern of expected frequencies we are interested in, and hence we call this a "goodness of fit". In this way, we can decide if the set of observations is a good fit for our expected frequencies.

The expected frequencies form our null hypothesis.

Let us then consider k different categories in our data and our hypotheses are as follows:

- H_0 :

  - p_1 - hypothesised proportion for category 1

  - p_2 - hypothesised proportion for category 2

  - ...

  - p_k - hypothesised proportion for category k

- H_a : the null hypothesis is not true

The hypotheses of the goodness-of-fit test.

Our test statistics is:

$$X^2 = \sum \frac{(O - E)^2}{E}. \qquad (6.9)$$

with degrees of freedom $\nu = k - 1$. In the example used in Section 5.5.2 we have that our colleagues in *USS Cerritos* are testing the new replicator and there is a vote for the chosen Mexican food for the evening meal, with 60 colleagues going for enchiladas, and 40 voting for tacos.

Check Section 5.5.2.

If we expected the proportions to be equally distributed, are the observed frequencies a good fit for our expected pattern? Well, let us take a look with Python's help. We can use the chisquare implementation in SciPy providing an array for the observed frequencies, and one for the expected ones:

You can see why this test is called that, right?

```
> expected = [50, 50]
> observed = [60, 40]
```

We can now pass these arrays to our `chisquare` function:

```
> from scipy.stats import chisquare
> chisq, p = chisquare(observed, expected)
> print('stat = {0:.4f}, p-value= {1:.4f}'.
  format(chisq, p))


stat = 4.0000, p-value= 0.0455
```

We use the `chisquare` function in SciPy.

With $p < 0.05$ there is a significant difference between the observed and expected frequencies and therefore the enchiladas and tacos are not equally preferred. Enchiladas for dinner it is!

6.3.2   Independence

WE MENTIONED IN SECTION 5.5.2 that independence can be inferred from the chi-squared distribution and our hypotheses are:

- H_0: Two variables are independent,

- H_a: Two variables are not independent.

Hypotheses to test for independence.

Our test statistic is the same as before, given by Equation (6.9).

In this case, it is convenient to organise the frequency table in a contingency table with r rows and c columns with the intersection of a row and a column called a cell. We can calculate the expected values for our table as:

A contingency table, or crosstab displays the frequency distribution of the variables facilitating the calculation of probabilities.

$$\text{Expected value of a cell} = \frac{\text{row total} \times \text{column total}}{\text{overall total}} \quad (6.10)$$

Suppose that we want to know whether or not the rank of a Starfleet officer is associated with their preference for a particular Mexican dish created by the new replicator delivered to the *USS Cerritos*. Table 6.2 has the result of a simple random sample of 512 officers and their choice for Mexican food for dinner.

Is the rank of a Starfleet officer associated with their choice of Mexican food?

	Tacos	Enchiladas	Chilaquiles	Total
Senior Officers	125	93	38	256
Junior Officers	112	98	46	256
Total	237	191	84	512

Table 6.2: Results from a random sample of 512 Starfleet officers about their preference for Mexican food and their rank.

In Python we can use the `chi2_contingency` function in SciPy stats where we provide as an input an array in the form of a contingency table with the frequencies in each category.

We will use the `chi2_contingency` function in SciPy.

```
mexican = np.array(
   [[125, 93, 38],
    [112, 98, 46]])
```

The result of the function comprises 4 objects:

- the test statistic,

- the *p*-value,

- the degrees of freedom, and

- an array with the expected frequencies.

The result comprises these 4 objects.

Let us create a function that helps us interpret the results:

```
def chi_indep(data, alpha=0.05):
  chisq, p, dof, exp_vals = chi2_contingency(data)
  print('stat = {0:.4f}, p-value= {1:.4f}'.
    format(chisq, p))
  print('Expected values are:')
  print(exp_vals)
  if p > alpha:
  print(''Can't reject the null hypothesis.
    The samples seem to be independent'')
  else:
  print(''Reject the null hypothesis.
    The samples are not independent.'')
```

We create a function to help us interpret the result of our independence test.

We can now apply our function to the contingency table above:

```
> chi_indep(mexican)

stat = 1.6059, p-value= 0.4480

Expected values are:
[[118.5  95.5  42. ]
 [118.5  95.5  42. ]]

Can't reject the null hypothesis.
The samples seem to be independent
```

We can use our function on our contingency table.

As we can see, with a $p > 0.05$ we fail to reject the null hypothesis and we conclude that we do not have sufficient evidence to say that there is an association between the rank of the officers and their preference for Mexican food. After all, who can resist the flavours of such fascinating cuisine.

6.4   Linear Correlation and Regression

TALL VULKAN PARENTS SEEM TO have tall Vulkan children, and shorter Vulkan parents, have shorter Vulkan children. There seems to be a relationship there, but every so often we find that some tall Vulkan parents have shorter kids and vice versa. We are interested to know if, despite the counter examples, there is a relationship. In other words, we would like to see whether the height of a Vulkan parent correlates to the height of their children.

The same may apply to other humanoid species, not just Vulkans.

We do not need to travel the galaxy to encounter a question like this; as a matter of fact Francis Galton asked that question about human parents and children and in the process he gave us the term *regression*[7]. If we are able to determine that there is a correlation between two variables, then we shall be able to create a regression model. In particular, if the relationship is linear we have a linear regression model. Our first task is therefore the quantification of the correlation. We can then take a look at performing a regression analysis.

[7] Rogel-Salazar, J. (2017). *Data Science and Analytics with Python.* Chapman & Hall/CRC Data Mining and Knowledge Discovery Series. CRC Press

6.4.1   Pearson Correlation

ONE WAY TO START LOOKING at the relationship between two random variables is to calculate the covariance. This will let us see if the change in one of the variables is proportional to the change in the other one. For observations $x_1, x_2, \ldots, x_n$ and $y_1, y_2, \ldots, y_n$ their covariance is given by:

$$Cov(x,y) \;=\; \frac{1}{n}\sum_{i=1}^{n}(x_i - \bar{x})(y_i - \bar{y})$$

$$=\; \frac{1}{n}\left(\sum_{i=1}^{n} x_i y_i - n\bar{x}\bar{y}\right). \qquad (6.11)$$

Covariance between variables x and y.

If the covariance is positive the two variables move in the same direction, if it is negative they move in opposite direction, and if it is 0 there is no relation between them.

Let us assume further that the data that we need to analyse follows a normal distribution. In that case, we know that we can standardise our values by subtracting the mean, and dividing by the standard deviation. We have therefore the following expression:

$$\rho \;=\; \frac{1}{n}\sum_{i}\left(\frac{x_i - \bar{x}}{\upsilon_x}\right)\left(\frac{y_i - \bar{y}}{\sigma_y}\right)$$

$$=\; \frac{Cov(x,y)}{\sigma_x \sigma_y} \qquad (6.12)$$

The Pearson correlation.

This is known as the Pearson correlation coefficient. If we express the Pearson correlation coefficient in terms of vectors $\mathbf{a} = (x_1 - \bar{x}, x_2 - \bar{x}, \ldots, x_n - \bar{x})$ and $\mathbf{b} = (y_1 - \bar{y}, y_2 - \bar{y}, \ldots, y_n - \bar{y})$ we can write it as:

$$\rho = \frac{\mathbf{a} \cdot \mathbf{b}}{|\mathbf{a}||\mathbf{b}|}, \qquad (6.13)$$

The Pearson correlation in terms of vectors.

and since $\mathbf{a} \cdot \mathbf{b} = |\mathbf{a}||\mathbf{b}|\cos\theta$ we can see that the Pearson coefficient is bounded between -1 and 1, the former value indicating perfect negative correlation and the latter perfect positive correlation.

We may want to look at testing the significance of the coefficient calculated and make the following hypotheses:

The hypotheses for correlation between two variables.

- H_0: The correlation between the variables is zero, i.e. $\rho = 0$

- H_a: The correlation between the variables is not zero, i.e. $\rho \neq 1$

Under the null hypothesis, the sample correlation is approximately normally distributed with standard error[8] $\sqrt{(1-\rho^2)/(n-2)}$ and the t-statistic is therefore:

$$t = \rho \frac{\sqrt{n-2}}{\sqrt{1-\rho^2}}. \qquad (6.14)$$

The p-value is calculated as the corresponding two-tailed p-value for the t-distribution with $n-2$ degrees of freedom.

[8] Bowley, A. L. (1928). The Standard Deviation of the Correlation Coefficient. *Journal of the American Statistical Association* 23(161), 31–34

It is time to look at some data and bring the ideas above to life. Let us use the cities data we looked at in Chapter 3. Remember that dataset is available at[9] https://doi.org/ 10.6084/m9.figshare.14657391.v1 as a comma-separated value file with the name "GLA_World_Cities_2016.csv". As before we read it into pandas for convenience:

[9] Rogel-Salazar, J. (2021a, May). GLA World Cities 2016. https://doi.org/ 10.6084/m9.figshare.14657391.v1

```
import numpy as np
import pandas as pd
gla_cities=pd.read_csv('GLA_World_Cities_2016.csv')
```

We will assume here that the data is cleaned up as before. We will create a copy of the dataframe to ensure we do not destroy the dataset. We drop the missing values as the Pearson coefficient implementation in SciPy does not work with them:

Refer to Section 3.3.5 for some required transformations on this dataset.

```
cities = gla_cities.copy()
cities.dropna(inplace=True)
```

Let us now calculate the Pearson correlation coefficient with pearsonr from scipy.stats for the population of the cities and their radius:

```
stats.pearsonr(cities['Population'],
               cities['Approx city radius km'])


(0.7913877430390618, 0.00026025429100622228)
```

We use the pearsonr module in SciPy.

The first number is the correlation coefficient and therefore we have that $\rho = 0.7913$. The second number given by Python is the p-value. For a 95% confidence, in the example above we can reject the null hypothesis as the value obtained is lower than 0.05 and say that the correlation coefficient we have calculated is statistically significant.

Let us check that we can obtain the p-value above. We have that $n = 16$ and $\rho = 0.7913$. We can therefore calculate our test statistic as:

The first number is the correlation coefficient, the second one is the p-value.

```
n = cities.shape[0]
rho = 0.7913877430390618
tscore = rho*np.sqrt(n-2) / np.sqrt(1-rho**2)
```

We can obtain the p-value with the help of Equation 6.14.

Let us see the result:

```
> print(tscore)


4.843827042161198
```

We are not done yet.

The one-tailed p-value can be obtained from the cumulative distribution function (CDF) of the t-distribution with $n - 2$ degrees of freedom. Since, we require the two-tailed value, we simply multiply by 2:

```
from scipy.stats import t
p1t = 1- t.cdf(tscore, n-2)
p2t = 2*p1t


> print(p2t)


0.0002602542910061789
```

We use our t-score to obtain our p-value.

This is effectively the same value reported by the pearsonr implementation. An alternative method to obtain the one-tailed p-value is to use the survival function, defined as 1-cdf:

```
> 2*t.sf(tscore,n-2)

0.00026025429100622294
```

We can also use the survival function.

Pandas is able to calculate the correlation coefficients too. Furthermore, we are able to obtain a correlation matrix between the columns provided, and we do not need to worry about missing values. Let us calculate the correlation coefficient of the population, radius of the city and the people per dwelling in the original gla_cities dataframe. All we need to do is use the corr method:

```
> gla_cities[['Population','Approx city radius km',
     'People per dwelling']].corr()
```

	Population	Approx city radius km	People per dwelling
Population	1.000000	0.791388	-0.029967
Approx city radius km	0.791388	1.000000	0.174474
People per dwelling	-0.029967	0.174474	1.000000

We can use the corr method in a pandas dataframe to calculate a correlation matrix.

Remember that the correlation coefficient is a measure of the existence of a linear relationship. It is possible that there is a non-linear relationship between variables, in which case the correlation coefficient is not a good measure. Another important thing to mention is that although correlation may be present, it does not necessarily imply that there is a causal relationship between the variables.

Remember that correlation does not imply causation.

6.4.2   *Linear Regression*

NOW THAT WE HAVE A way to quantify the correlation we may want to take a look at building a model to describe the relationship. We mentioned that if the relationship is linear we can build a linear regression model. Let us take a look at doing exactly that.

Our model needs to capture the relationship between the dependent variable **y** and the independent variables x_i. Since the relationship is assumed to be linear our model can be written as:

$$\mathbf{y} = \beta \mathbf{X} + \varepsilon, \qquad (6.15)$$

A linear regression model.

where $\beta = (\beta_0, \ldots, \beta_i)^T$ are the regression coefficients and we aim to find their value; ε are the residuals which are random deviations and are assumed to be independent and identically normally distributed.

One way to find the regression coefficients is to minimise the sum of squared residuals[10]:

$$
\begin{aligned}
SSR \;&=\; \varepsilon^2, \qquad\qquad (6.16)\\
&=\; |\mathbf{Y} - \mathbf{X}\beta|^2,\\
&=\; (\mathbf{Y} - \mathbf{X}\beta)^T (\mathbf{Y} - \mathbf{X}\beta),\\
&=\; \mathbf{Y}^T\mathbf{Y} - \beta^T\mathbf{X}^T\mathbf{Y} - \mathbf{Y}^T\mathbf{X}\beta + \beta^T\mathbf{X}^T\mathbf{X}\beta. \quad (6.17)
\end{aligned}
$$

[10] Rogel-Salazar, J. (2017). *Data Science and Analytics with Python.* Chapman & Hall/CRC Data Mining and Knowledge Discovery Series. CRC Press

Since we require the minimum of the SSR quantity above, we take its derivative with respect to each of the β_i parameters and equal the result to zero. This leads us to the following expression:

$$\frac{\partial(SSR)}{\partial \beta_i} = -\mathbf{X}^T\mathbf{Y} + \left(\mathbf{X}^T\mathbf{X}\right)\beta = 0. \qquad (6.18)$$

We take the derivative to obtain the minimum.

The regression coefficients are therefore given by:

$$\beta = \left(\mathbf{X}^T\mathbf{X}\right)^{-1}\mathbf{X}^T\mathbf{Y}. \qquad (6.19)$$

This is the solution to the linear model given in Equation (6.15).

We refer to Equation (6.19) as the normal equation associated with the regression model, and this method is known as Ordinary Least Squares or OLS for short.

OLS = Ordinary least squares.

To calculate the coefficients in Python we are able to use the Statsmodels package that has an implementation for OLS. Let us start by importing the module:

```python
import statsmodels.formula.api as smf
```

We first import the Statsmodels package. We will use the `formula.api` method to simplify our code.

We will be using the formula notation that uses a tilde (~) to show the dependency among variables. In this case we want to show the relationship between the city population and the radius of the city. Before we do that let us rename the city radius variable so that we can use the formula:

```python
> gla_cities.columns = gla_cities.columns.str.\
    replace('Approx city radius km',
    'City_Radius')
```

We are now able to fit our regression model:

```python
> results = smf.ols('Population ~ City_Radius',
    data=gla_cities).fit()
```

This is the OLS model for the population as a function of the city radius.

Let us look at the parameters we have obtained:

```python
> results.params

Intercept      -1.797364e+06
City_Radius     4.762102e+05
```

These are the coefficients of our regression model.

This indicates that the intercept of the model is $\beta_0 = -1.797364 \times 10^6$ and the slope of the line is $\beta_1 = 4.762102 \times 105$. The results object has further information for us and you can look at a summary with the following command:

Population $= \beta_0 + \beta_1 \times$ City_Radius.

```
results.summary()
```

We will select some of the entries in the summary report and explain what they mean:

```
OLS Regression Results

=====================================

Dep. Variable:          Population
Model:                         OLS
Method:              Least Squares
No. Observations:               16
Df Residuals:                   14
Df Model:                        1
R-squared:                   0.626
Adj. R-squared:              0.600
```

A regression model summary.

First we can see that the model is using the Population data as the dependent variable and that the model is the ordinary least squares we have discussed above. We have a total of $n = 16$ observations and we are using $k = 1$ predictive variable, denoted as Df Model. The Df residuals is the number of degrees of freedom in our model, calculated as $n - k - 1$.

Df residuals corresponds to the degrees of freedom.

R-squared is known as the coefficient of determination and is related to the Pearson correlation coefficient so that

See Section 6.4.1 for information on the Pearson correlation.

$\rho^2 = R^2$. This is perhaps the most important measure in the summary. In our case we have an $R^2 = 0.626$ indicating that around 62% of the total variance is explained with our simple model. However, we need to be careful when only looking at R^2. This is because it is known that when adding more explanatory variables to our regression model, this measure will be equal or higher. This may give the impression that the model is getting more accurate with more variables, but that may not be true.

Remember that the relationship does not mean causation!

In order to mitigate this risk, the adjusted R^2 introduces a penalty as extra variables are included in the model:

$$R^2_{Adj} = 1 - \frac{(1 - R^2)(n - 1)}{n - k - 1}. \qquad (6.20)$$

We are also interested in knowing if the global result of the regression is significant or not. One way to do that is to test the null hypothesis that **all** of the regression coefficients are equal to zero. If so, this would mean that the model has no predictive capabilities. This can be done with the help of an F test which compares our linear model to a model where only the intercept is present. This lets us decide if our coefficients are such that they make our model useful. The OLS results provide some information about the F test:

See Section 6.7.1 for more information on the F distribution and analysis of variance.

F-statistic:	23.46
Prob (F-statistic):	0.000260
Log-Likelihood:	-252.37
AIC:	508.7
BIC:	510.3

The F test summary for a regression model.

In this case the p-value is 0.000260. For a value of $\alpha = 0.05$ we can reject the null hypothesis. We also get a measure of the log-likelihood, $\ln(L)$, which is a way to measure the goodness-of-fit for a model. In general, the higher this value the better the model fits the data provided. It ranges from minus infinity to infinity though, and on its own the measure is not very useful. Instead you can use the value of the log-likelihood for a model and compare it to others. Other ways to compare and select models is via the comparison of the Akaike and Bayesian Information Criteria, AIC and BIC:

The log-likelihood gives us a goodness-of-fit for our model.

$$AIC = 2k_p - 2\ln(L), \tag{6.21}$$

These information criteria can help us select models.

$$BIC = k_p \ln(n) - 2ln(L). \tag{6.22}$$

where k_p is the number of estimated parameters.

	coef	std err	t	P>|t|	[0.025	0.975]
Intercept	-1.797×10^6	1.24×10^6	-1.453	0.168	4.45×10^6	8.56×10^5
City_Radius	4.762×10^5	9.83×10^4	4.844	0.000	2.65×10^5	6.87×10^5

Table 6.3: Results from the regression analysis performed on the brain and body dataset.

The summary of model also has a breakdown of the variables that have been included, and it helps us determine whether the components we have chosen have an impact in the predictability of the model. In Table 6.3 we present the results of the individual components in our model. We can see the coefficients for the Intercept and City_Radius in the column called "coef".

The standard deviation of the coefficients is shown in the "std err" column. The column "t" has the *t*-statistic helping us determine if our estimate is statistically significant. This is where the column " P>|t|" comes in: It shows the *p*-value for the estimate, and for a given significance value we can use this to reject (or not) the null hypothesis that the coefficient is equal to zero. Finally, the "[0.025" and "0.975]" columns give us the upper and lower values for our 95% confidence interval.

See Sections 5.5.1 and 6.5.1 for information on *t* tests.

There are a few other measures that are presented at the end of the summary:

```
=================================================
Omnibus:          9.560   Durbin-Watson:     2.192
Prob(Omnibus):    0.008   Jarque-Bera (JB):  6.136
Skew:             1.374   Prob(JB):          0.0465
Kurtosis:         4.284   Cond. No.          34.2
```

Other measures included in the linear regression model summary.

The omnibus measure describes a test of normality for the distribution of the residuals based on a chi-squared test using skewness and kurtosis, which are also shown in the summary. The *p*-value for the omnibus test is shown as `Prob(omnibus)`. Another measure of normality is given by the Jarque-Bera measurement and its *p*-value is given by `Prob(JB)`.

Please look at Section 6.3 for information on chi-squared testing.

One of the main assumptions in regression modelling is that there is no correlation between consecutive residuals, this is called autocorrelation of the residuals and the Durbin-Watson measurement is used to detect autocorrelation in the residuals of our model. The null hypothesis is that there is

The Durbin-Watson test detects autocorrelation in the residuals of our linear model.

no correlation among residuals, and the test is calculated as
follows:

$$d = \frac{\sum_{t=2}^{T} (\varepsilon_t - \varepsilon_{t-1})^2}{\sum_{t=1}^{T} \varepsilon_t^2},$$
(6.23)

The Durbin-Watson test statistic.

where T is the total number of observations and ε_t is the
t-th residual from the regression model. The statistic above
ranges between 0 and 4, and we can interpret the results as
follows:

- $d = 2$ indicates no autocorrelation

- $d < 2$ indicates positive autocorrelation

Values for d such that $1.5 \leq d \leq 2.5$ are considered to be no cause for concern.

- $d > 2$ indicates negative autocorrelation

Finally, another important assumption in linear regression
modelling is the fact that no multicollinearity should be
present. This refers to a situation where there is perfect
or exact relationship between the regression exploratory
variables. One way to measure for this is the use of the
condition number. For an object x, the condition number
is defined[11] as the norm of x times the norm of the inverse
of x. For a matrix, the condition number tells us whether
inverting the matrix is numerically unstable with finite-
precision numbers. If the condition number is above 30, the
regression may have severe multicollinearity.

[11] Strang, G. (2006). *Linear Algebra and Its Applications*. Thomson, Brooks/Cole

6.4.3   *Spearman Correlation*

WE HAVE DECIDED TO GET schwifty and join the famous
planetary Cromulon musical competition. Our song is a

Bear with me!

blast, and we think that we will win. However, there is a question hanging in the air: Are the scores of two of the head judges related? Since the scores provided are ordinal values between 0 and 10, it is not possible to use the Pearson correlation we described in the Section 6.4.1. Instead, we need to use the ranks that the ordinal values provide.

Pun definitely intended for Cromulon judges.

It is possible to find a correlation coefficient using the ranks of the data, and it is commonly known as the Spearman correlation coefficient, r_s. To calculate it, we need to rank the scores from lowest to highest and we simply calculate a Pearson correlation on the ranks rather than on the values. Note that since the ranks do not come from a normal distribution, we cannot use our standard normal, or for that matter, any other parametric distributions. Instead, we call this type of test non-parametric.

The Spearman correlation is a non-parametric test.

Similar to the Pearson correlation, the Spearman one varies between -1 and 1, with 0 indicating no correlation. In this way the hypothesis testing can be expressed as follows:

- H_0: The correlation between the variables is zero, i.e.
  $r = 0$

We have a two-tailed test!

- H_a: The correlation between the variables is not zero i.e.
  $r \neq 0$

For two variables that need to be checked for correlation, when using ranks they will have the same standard deviation $\sigma_x = \sigma_y = \sigma$ and so we can write the Spearman correlation as:

$$r = \frac{Cov(R(x), R(y))}{\sigma^2},$$

(6.24)

where $R(\cdot)$ denotes the rank. If there are no values that can be assigned the same rank, we say that there are no ties in our data. We can simplify our expression by noting that

Remember that tied observations have the same value and thus it is not possible to assign them a unique rank.

$$Cov(R(x), R(y)) = \sigma^2 - \frac{1}{2}\sum d^2, \qquad (6.25)$$

where d is the difference between a subject's ranks on the two variables in question. This may be easier to see with an example. Let us go back to our planetary musical competition. For Singer X, Judge 1 has given a mark that corresponds to rank 7, whereas the mark from Judge 2 corresponds to rank 4. The difference d for Singer X is $d = 7 - 2 = 5$.

I wonder if this is why they call it the X factor.

When using ranks, we have that the standard deviation is related to the number of observations n as $\sigma^2 = (n^3 - n)/12$. Substituting this expression in Equation (6.25), for the case of no ties, the Spearman correlation can be written as:

$$r = 1 - \frac{6}{n^3 - n}\sum d^2. \qquad (6.26)$$

The Spearman correlation for no ties.

Let us consider the results of the Cromulon competition considering two judges as shown in Table 6.4. If we were to calculate the Spearman correlation manually, we would have to order the scores for each judge separately and assign them a rank. This will let us calculate d. If there are no ties we can use the Equation (6.26), otherwise we need to calculate the covariances.

Instead, we are going to rely on Python and use the implementation of the Spearman correlation coefficient in

Singer	A	B	C	D	E	F	G	H	I	J
Judge 1	2	10	7	8	5	7	5	8	6	4
Judge 2	4	9	8	8	2	9	4	7	6	3

Table 6.4: Results of the planetary Cromulon musical competition.

SciPy called spearmanr. As with the Pearson correlation, the implementation will return the value of the coefficient and the *p*-value to help us test our hypothesis.

The Spearman correlation can be calculated with spearmanr.

Let us first create a pandas dataframe with the date from Table 6.4:

```
schwifty = pd.DataFrame({
    'singer': ['A', 'B', 'C', 'D', 'E', 'F', 'G',
               'H', 'I', 'J'],
    'judge1': [2, 10, 7, 8, 5, 7, 5, 8, 6, 4],
    'judge2': [4, 9, 8, 8, 2, 9, 4, 7, 6, 3]})
```

We can now simply pass the values to the spearmanr function:

```
> r, p = stats.spearmanr(schwifty['judge1'],
      schwifty['judge2'])
> print('r={0}, p={1}'.format(r, p))


r=0.8148148148148148, p=0.004087718984741058
```

We simply pass the columns of interest to spearmanr to obtain the Spearman correlation.

We can see that the Spearman rank correlation is $r(n - 2 = 8) = 0.8148$ with a *p*-value smaller than 0.05. Given this information, for a 95% confidence level, we reject the null hypothesis and say that the values in the data are monotonically correlated.

6.5   *Hypothesis Testing with One Sample*

WE HAVE A PRETTY GOOD idea about how hypothesis testing works, and in Section 6.1 we have covered a lot of the things we need to consider when formulating a hypothesis and testing it statistically. A good example for using hypothesis testing is when we want to check if the estimated parameter from a population is significantly different from a hypothesised population value. We call this type of test a one-sample test.

A one-sample test checks if an estimated parameter is significantly different from a hypothesised one.

This is similar to the treatment we addressed in Section 6.1 where we were using the standard normal z-distribution. For datasets where we know the population variance, or the sample size, n, is big we can use the z-distribution, but in cases where the sample size is smaller, we are better off using the t-distribution for our test.

For $n > 30$, we can use the z-distribution, although many computational packages implement a t-test.

6.5.1   *One-Sample t-test for the Population Mean*

A TYPICAL CASE FOR THE use of sample testing is to check the mean value of a normally distributed dataset against a reference value. Our test statistic is the Student t-distribution we encountered in Section 5.5.1 given by the following expression:

We covered the use of a z-test in Section 6.1.1.

$$t = \frac{\bar{X} - \mu}{\frac{s}{\sqrt{n}}},$$

(6.27)

with $\nu = n - 1$ degrees of freedom.

Our null hypothesis is that the mean is equal to a hypothesised value μ_0, i.e. $H_0 : \mu = \mu_0$. Our alternative hypothesis may be any of the following:

The hypotheses for the one-sample *t*-test.

- $H_a : \quad \mu > \mu_0$,

- $H_a : \quad \mu < \mu_0$,

- $H_a : \quad \mu \neq \mu_0$.

In the first two cases we have a one-tailed test, and in the last one, a two-tailed test.

Let us revisit our test for the Model-5 toaster: The Caprica City manufacturer is still claiming that their toasters have a resistor of 48Ω. This time we have a set of 12 measurements for the resistor:

See Section 6.1.

$$\begin{bmatrix} 54.79, & 59.62, & 57.33, \\ 48.57, & 51.14, & 25.78, \\ 53.50, & 50.75, & 43.34, \\ 45.81, & 43.88, & 60.47 \end{bmatrix}$$

Our null hypothesis is $H_0 : \mu = 48\Omega$, the alternative hypothesis is $H_a : \mu \neq 48$. We can calculate the mean and standard deviation of the sample with Python as follows:

```
data = np.array([54.79, 59.62, 57.33, 48.57,
    51.14, 25.78, 53.50,50.75, 43.34, 45.81,
    43.88, 60.47])
xbar = np.mean(data)
s= np.std(data, ddof=1)
```

We need the sample mean and standard deviation.

Let us take a look at the values:

```
> print(xbar)

49.58166666666668

> print(s)

9.433353624563248
```

Our test statistic is therefore given by:

$$t = \frac{49.58 - 48}{\frac{9.43}{\sqrt{12}}} = 0.58081. \qquad (6.28)$$

We use the values obtained to calculate our test statistic.

In Python we can calculate the statistic in one go, together with the corresponding p-value with the help of the test_1samp function is the stats module of SciPy:

```
from stats import t
mu = 48
n = len(data)
ts = (xbar-mu)/(s/np.sqrt(n))
pval = 2*t.sf(ts, n-1)
print(pval)

0.5730709487398256
```

We can obtain the p-value with the help of the survival function.

We have used the survival function for the t-distribution in the calculation above. We are multiplying the result by 2 as this is a two-sided test.

This is such a common process that there is a function in the stats module of SciPy to calculate the test statistic and its *p*-value. All we need to do is to call the `test_1samp` function, which takes an array of data and a `popmean` parameter for the expected value in the null hypothesis.

```
> from scipy.stats import ttest_1samp
```

We can calculate the one-sample *t* test with `test_1samp`.

We can also ask if we are doing a one- or two-sided test with the help of the `alternative` parameter which takes values `'two-sided'`, `'less'` or `'greater'`. In our case we have that:

```
> ttest_1samp(data, popmean=mu,
    alternative='two-sided')


Ttest_1sampResult(
statistic=0.5808172016728843,
pvalue=0.5730709487398256)
```

The values are the same that we obtained before.

The values obtained are the same as the ones we calculated above using the Student's t-distribution directly. Let us take a look at the results we have obtained: For a significance level of $\alpha = 0.05$, given the *p*-value obtained, we are not able to reject the null hypothesis. We can therefore conclude that there is no evidence in the data we have that the mean resistance for the resistor in the Model-5 toaster is different from 48Ω.

We can use the *p*-value to interpret our results.

We can build the following function to help us with the interpretation of the results for other *t*-tests:

```
def t_test(data, mu, alt='two-sided', alpha=0.05):
  stat, p =ttest_1samp(data, mu, alternative=alt)
  print('stat = {0:.4f}, p-value= {1:.4f}'.
      format(stat, p))
  if p > alpha:
    print(''Can't Reject the null hypothesis. There
      is no evidence to suggest that the mean is
      different from {0}.''.format(mu))
  else:
    print(''Reject the null hypothesis. The mean
      is different from {0}.''.format(mu))
```

A helpful function to interpret a one-sample *t* test.

We can use this function to solve our problem:

```
> t_test(data, mu)

stat = 0.5808, p-value= 0.5731

Can't reject the null hypothesis. There
is no evidence to suggest that the mean is
different from 48.
```

We see the results and interpretation in one go.

6.5.2   One-Sample z-test for Proportions

WE HAVE SEEN HOW WE can use a one-sample test for the mean of a population. Another useful thing for which we can use the test is the proportion of successes in a single population to a known or hypothesised proportion p_0. Let us motivate the discussion with an example: We have been assessing Dr Gaius Baltar's Cylon detector techniques and

We can use a one-sample test to check proportions.

he claims that the proportion of Cylons in any one ship of the convoy is 40%. We select a simple random sample of the crew and people aboard the Battlestar Galactica and test whether they are Cylon or not. The proportion in the sample population surely will be different from Dr Baltar's claim. The question is whether the difference is statistically significant or not.

We are not at liberty to disclose the details of the Cylon detector technique. Surely you understand...

Our null hypothesis is that the population proportion is the same as the hypothesised value p_0, i.e. $H_0 : p = p_0$. The alternative hypothesis can be any of the following:

- $H_a :$ $p > p_0$,

- $H_a :$ $p < p_0$,

- $H_a :$ $p \neq p_0$.

The hypotheses for a one-sample proportion test.

As before, the first two cases refer to one-tailed tests, and the third one is a two-tailed one.

Our test statistic is given by:

$$z = \frac{\bar{p} - p_0}{\sqrt{\frac{p_0(1-p_0)}{n}}},$$ (6.29)

Our one-sample proportion test statistic.

where $\bar{p}$ is the estimated proportion and n is the sample size. Going back to our Cylon detection example, after taking a look at our data, we find that the observed sample proportion is 36 in a sample of size $n = 100$. We can use the same logic for the testing done in Section 6.1.1. Instead we are going to look at the `proportions_ztest` function in the Statsmodels module for Python. The function takes the following parameters:

We are going to be using the `proportions_ztest` function in the Statsmodels module.

- count – The number of successes in the number of trials or observations

- nobs – The number of trials or observations, with the same length as count

- value – The value used for the null hypothesis

- alternative – Whether we require a two-sided or one-sided test. Options are 'two-sided', 'smaller' or 'larger'

The parameters used in proportions_ztest.

Let us take a look at our test:

```
> stat, pval = proportions_ztest(count=40,
  nobs=100, value=0.36)
> print('stat = {0:.4f}, p-value= {1:.4f}'.\
  format(stat, pval))


stat = 0.8165, p-value= 0.4142
```

Let us look at the Cylon detector values.

We can see that our test statistic is 0.816 and the corresponding p-value is 0.4142. Since this value is not lower than $\alpha = 0.05$, we are not able to reject the null hypothesis. In other words, we do not have enough evidence to say that the proportion of Cylons is different from 40%. We will find you out Baltar!

For a 95% confidence level, we cannot reject the null hypothesis.

Let us look at a second example. In this case we have received a report that 75% of Starfleet Academy applicants in general indicated that they have learnt Python in the past year. The recruiting officer wants to assess whether applicants from Vulkan have also learned Python in the

Great to see that Python has survived over centuries.

same proportion. A sample of 256 Vulkan applicants are surveyed, and the results indicate that 131 of them have knowledge of Python. Is there a significant difference in the Vulkan applicants compared to the overall population? Well, let us take a look:

```
> p0 = 0.75
> n = 256
> p = 131/n
> count = n*p0
> zscore = (p-p0)/np.sqrt((p0*(1-p0)/n))
> print(zscore)

-8.804591605141793
```

Is there a significant difference in the Vulkan applicants compared to the overall population?

We can use the z-score to assess our null hypothesis, or we can use the proportions_ztest. In this case let us create a function to help us with the interpretation:

```
def proportion_test(count, n, value, alpha=0.05):
    stat, p = proportions_ztest(count, n, value)
    print('stat = {0:.4f}, p-value= {1:.4f}'.
        format(stat, p))
    if p > alpha:
        print(''Can't reject the null hypothesis. There
            is no evidence to suggest that the proportion
            is different from {0}''.format(count/n))
    else:
        print(''Reject the null hypothesis. The
            proportion is different from {0}.''.format(
            count/n))
```

A helpful function to interpret our results for proportions.

Let us take a look using the values calculated above:

```
> proportion_test(count, n, p)


stat = 8.8046, p-value= 0.0000


Reject the null hypothesis.
The proportion is different from 0.75
```

We reject the null hypothesis in this case.

At a 95% confidence level we reject the null hypothesis as the p-value obtained is lower than 0.05. We can conclude that there is a statistically significant difference in the proportion of Vulkan applicants to Starfleet Academy that learn Python compared to the proportion in the overall population of applicants.

This is a result that may defy logic, particularly for a Vulkan!

6.5.3   Wilcoxon Signed Rank with One-Sample

UP UNTIL NOW OUR DISCUSSION has assumed that the data we have is normally distributed and we have therefore used parametric methods for our one-sample tests. If instead we have data that is not normally distributed, we make use of non-parametric methods and the equivalent of the t-test discussed in Section 6.5.1 is the one-sample Wilcoxon test.

We use non-parametric tests with data that is not normally distributed.

First proposed by Frank Wilcoxon[12] in 1945, the test does not assume that the samples are normally distributed and is typically is used to test if the samples come from a symmetric population with a specified median, m_0. The test is sometimes referred to as the Wilcoxon t-test.

[12] Wilcoxon, F. (1945). Individual comparisons by ranking methods. *Biometrics Bulletin* 1(6), 80–83

The null hypothesis is therefore that the median is the same as the hypothesised value m_0, i.e. $H_0 : m = m_0$. The alternative hypothesis can be any of the following:

- $H_a :$ $m > m_0$,

- $H_a :$ $m < m_0$,

- $H_a :$ $m \neq m_0$.

Note that in this case we test for the median. This is because we have non-normally distributed data.

Consider a set of X_i samples for our test. We calculate $|X_i - m_0|$ and determine the rank R_i for each observation in ascending order according to their magnitude. The Wilcoxon signed-rank test statistic is calculated as follows:

$$W = \sum_{i=1}^{n} \psi_i R_i, \qquad (6.30)$$

The Wilcoxon signed-rank test statistic.

where,

$$\psi_1 = \begin{cases} 1 & \text{if } |X_i - m_0| > 0, \\ \\ 0 & \text{if } |X_i - m_0| < 0. \end{cases} \qquad (6.31)$$

Let us stop for a moment to consider the distribution of the sum of a set of numbers U_i such that $U = \sum_i U_i$; each number has an equal chance of being included in the sum or not and thus $P(U_i = i) = P(U_i = 0) = \frac{1}{2}$. Our test statistic W has the same distribution as U. For a large number of samples, n, we have that the expected value is given by:

Our test statistic W has the same distribution as U.

$$E(W) = E(U) = \sum_{i=1}^{n} E(U_i).$$

With the information above we can calculate the expected value as follows:

$$E[W] = \sum_{i=1}^{} \left[0 \left(\frac{1}{2} \right) + i \left(\frac{1}{2} \right) \right],$$

$$= \frac{1}{2} \sum_{i=1}^{n} i = \frac{1}{2} \frac{n(n+1)}{2},$$

$$= \frac{n(n+1)}{4}. \tag{6.32}$$

The expected value of W.

Note that $Var(W) = Var(U) = \sum_i Var(U_i)$; this is because the U_i are independent from each other under the null hypothesis. The variance can be calculated as follows:

$$Var(U_i) = E(U_i^2) - E(U_i)^2,$$

$$= \left[0^2 \left(\frac{1}{2} \right) + i^2 \left(\frac{1}{2} \right) \right] - \left(\frac{i}{2} \right)^2,$$

$$= \frac{i^2}{2} - \frac{i^2}{4} = \frac{i^2}{4}. \tag{6.33}$$

We will use this information to calculate the variance of W.

We have therefore that:

$$Var(W) = \sum_{i=1}^{n} Var(U_i) = \frac{1}{4} \sum_{i=1}^{n} i^2,$$

$$= \frac{1}{4} \frac{n(n+1)(2n+1)}{6}. \tag{6.34}$$

The variance of W.

We can use this information to create our test statistic:

$$W' = \frac{W - E(W)}{\sqrt{Var(W)}}, \tag{6.35}$$

We can obtain a standard Wilcoxon test statistic.

which follows an approximate standard normal distribution.

The implementation of the Wilcoxon test in `scipy.stats` is called `wilcoxon` and it takes an array of data from which we need to subtract the hypothesised mean. It also can take an `alternative` parameter to identify whether we need a one-sided or a two-sided test. Note that the default is the two-sided test. Let us create a function to help with the interpretation:

We can use the `wilcoxon` implementation in SciPy.

```
from scipy.stats import wilcoxon


def wilcoxon1s(data, m0, alt='two-sided',
    alpha=0.05):
    stat, p = wilcoxon(data-m0, alternative=alt)
    print('stat ={0:.4f}, p-value= {1:.4f}'.
        format(stat, p))
    if p > alpha:
        print(''Can't reject the null hypothesis.
        There is no evidence to suggest that the
        median is different from {0}.''.format(m0))
    else:
        print(''Reject the null hypothesis.
        The median is different from
        {0}.''.format(m0))
```

A function to help us interpret the results of a Wilcoxon test.

Let us now see the Wilcoxon test in action using Python. We are continuing our study of Starfleet Academy applicants. We have heard that the median age at which Starfleet officers receive the rank of lieutenant is 41 years of age. We have collated the following information for recently promoted officers:

A very young commanding force at Starfleet.

$$
\begin{aligned}
[\,32.4, \quad &55.2, \quad 40.5, \quad 47.9, \quad 33.4, \\
34.3, \quad &28.1, \quad 43.0, \quad 34.8, \quad 60.2, \\
48.5, \quad &52.2, \quad 29.7, \quad 29.9, \quad 26.6, \\
44.4, \quad &43.6, \quad 50.4, \quad 47.3, \quad 34.2, \\
38.5, \quad &61.0, \quad 55.3, \quad 45.2, \quad 58.6\,].
\end{aligned}
$$

Ages at which Starfleet officers got promoted to the rank of lieutenant.

Let us enter the data into Python:

```
> lieutenants=np.array([
  32.4, 55.2, 40.5, 47.9, 33.4,
  34.3, 28.1, 43.0, 34.8, 60.2,
  48.5, 52.2, 29.7, 29.9, 26.6,
  44.4, 43.6, 50.4, 47.3, 34.2,
  38.5, 61.0, 55.3, 45.2, 58.6])
```

and let us check our hypothesis:

```
> wilcoxon1s(lieutenants, 41)


stat = 132.0000, p-value= 0.4261


Can't reject the null hypothesis.
There is no evidence to suggest that
the median is different from 41
```

We can use our function to test our hypothesis. It seems that we do indeed have a young Starfleet force!

6.6 Hypothesis Testing with Two Samples

IN THE PREVIOUS SECTION WE concentrated on testing whether an estimated parameter is significantly different from a hypothesised one. In many cases, we are interested in comparing two different populations, for example by estimating the difference between two population means or determining whether this difference is statistically significant. We require therefore to use notation that lets us distinguish between the two populations.

We can use hypothesis testing to compare two populations.

If the parameter to be compared is the mean, instead of simply using μ, we may need to refer to μ_1 for one population and μ_2 for the other one. The hypotheses we formulate can be recast in different manners, for example we can hypothesise that the population means are equal and test $\mu_1 = \mu_2$. This is equivalent to checking for the difference to be equal to zero, i.e. $\mu_1 - \mu_2 = 0$. In the same manner we can express the test that $\mu_1 > \mu_2$ as $\mu_1 - \mu_2 > 0$ and $\mu_1 < \mu_2$ as $\mu_1 - \mu_2 < 0$.

We can recast our test for $\mu_1 = \mu_2$ as $\mu_1 - \mu_2 = 0$.

One important consideration that we need to make is how the data for each population is sampled. We say that the samples are **independent** if the selection for one of the populations does not affect the other. Another option is to select the populations in a way that they are related. Think, for example, of a study of a "before" and "after" treatment. In this case the samples are said to be **paired**. In this section we will take a look at how to run hypothesis testing for independent and paired populations.

Independent populations do not affect each other's selection. Paired populations can be thought of as "before" and "after" situations.

6.6.1   Two-Sample t-test – Comparing Means, Same Variances

FOR INDEPENDENT SAMPLES, WE KNOW that we can estimate the population mean μ_i with the sample mean $\overline{x_i}$.

We can therefore use $\overline{x_1} - \overline{x_2}$ as an estimate for $\mu_1 - \mu_2$. The mean value of the sampling distribution $\overline{x_1} - \overline{x_2}$ is $\mu_{\overline{x_1} - \overline{x_2}} = \mu_{\overline{x_1}} - \mu_{\overline{x_2}} = \mu_1 - \mu_2$. Similarly, the standard deviation of $\overline{x_1} - \overline{x_2}$ is given by $\sigma^2_{\overline{x_1} - \overline{x_2}} = \sigma^2_{\overline{x_1}} + \sigma^2_{\overline{x_2}} = \frac{\sigma^2_1}{n_1} + \frac{\sigma^2_2}{n_2}$.

We use the sample to estimate the population parameters.

A typical test to perform is the comparison of two population means. The null hypothesis can be formulated as $H_0 : \mu_1 - \mu_2 = c$, where c is a hypothesised value. If the test is to check that the two population means are the same, we have that $c = 0$. Our alternative hypothesis may be any of the following:

The hypotheses for the comparison of two-sample means.

- $H_a :$ $\mu_1 - \mu_2 > c$,

- $H_a :$ $\mu_1 - \mu_2 < c$,

- $H_a :$ $\mu_1 - \mu_2 \neq c$.

When the number of observations n_1 and n_2 for our samples is large, their distributions are approximately normal, and if we know the standard deviations, we can calculate a z-distribution such that:

$$z = \frac{(\overline{x_1} - \overline{x_2}) - (\mu_1 - \mu_2)}{\sqrt{\frac{\sigma^2_1}{n_1} + \frac{\sigma^2_2}{n_2}}}.$$ (6.36)

The test statistic for our two-sample test.

However, in practice we may not know the standard deviations of the populations and instead we use the standard deviations, s_i, for the samples. If we are confident that the population variances of the two samples are equal, we can use a weighted average of the samples to estimate the population variance. For group 1 with sample variance

Homoscedasticity describes a situation where our random samples have the same variance. When the opposite is true we use the term heteroscedasticity.

s_1^2, and group 2 with sample variance s_2^2, the pooled variance can be expressed as:

$$s_p^2 = \frac{s_1^2(n_1 - 1) + s_2^2(n_2 - 1)}{n_1 + n_2 - 2}. \qquad (6.37)$$

We can use this information to calculate a t-distribution such that:

$$t = \frac{(\overline{x_1} - \overline{x_2}) - (\mu_1 - \mu_2)}{s_p \sqrt{\frac{1}{n_1} + \frac{1}{n_2}}}, \qquad (6.38)$$

A test statistic for two samples with pooled variance.

that approximates a t-distribution with $df = n_1 + n_2 - 2$ degrees of freedom.

Let us look at an example using Python. In this case we will revisit the cars dataset we used in Chapter 4 in Section 4.3. We saw that the fuel consumption in miles per gallon for cars in the dataset with automatic (0) and manual (1) transmissions had different means:

Check Section 4.3 for more info on the cars dataset used here.

```
import pandas as pd

cars = pd.read_csv(DATA/'cars.csv')

ct = cars.groupby(['am'])

ct['mpg'].mean()


am

0    17.147368

1    24.392308

Name: mpg, dtype: float64
```

We see a difference in the fuel consumption of manual and automatic cars in our dataset. Is that difference significant?

We are now better equipped to answer the question as to whether the difference is statistically significant and we can do this with a two-sample *t*-test! First let us create arrays for our automatic and manual observations:

```
automatic = cars[cars['am']==0][['mpg']]
manual = cars[cars['am']==1][['mpg']]
```

We create arrays with the data for clarity on the analysis.

Let us check whether the data is normally distributed. We can use the Shapiro-Wilk function described in Section 6.2.2 to test for normality.

```
> shapiro_test(automatic, alpha=0.05)


stat = 0.9768, p-value= 0.8987
Can't reject the null hypothesis.
The data seems to be normally distributed.


> shapiro_test(manual, alpha=0.05)


stat = 0.9458, p-value= 0.5363
Can't reject the null hypothesis.
The data seems to be normally distributed.
```

We can use the tests covered in Section 6.2 to test for normality.

We would like to see if the means are different and thus we use a two-sided test. Let us first take a look at the two-sample *t*-test implemented in SciPy. The function is called ttest_ind and it takes a parameter called alternative with the default value 'two-sided'. We can also specify heteroscedasticity with the parameter equal_var. In this case we use the value True.

In SciPy we have the ttest_ind function for a two-sample *t*-test.

```
import scipy.stats as sps


tstat, p = sps.ttest_ind(automatic, manual,
    alternative='two-sided', equal_var=True)
```

We need to pass each of the arrays to compare. We can also specify the type of test and whether the variances are assumed to be equal.

Let us look at the results:

```
> print('stat = {0:.4f}, p-value = {1:.4f}'.
    format(tstat, p))


stat = -4.1061, p-value= 0.0003
```

There is enough evidence to say that the difference in fuel consumption is statistically significant.

With a test statistic of -4.1061 we have a p-value less than 0.05. For a 95% confidence level we reject the null hypothesis. We have sufficient evidence to say that the difference in mean fuel consumption between automatic and manual transmission cars in our dataset are statistically significant.

We can also use the implementation of the two-sample t-test in the Statsmodels package. The name of the function is the same ttest_ind and we are distinguishing them with a method notation. The implementation also takes an alternative parameter and in this case the heteroscedasticity is defined with the parameter usevar='pooled':

Refer to Chapter 2 about the method notation in Python.

```
import statsmodels.stats.weightstats as smw
tstat, p, df = smw.ttest_ind(automatic, manual,
    alternative='two-sided',
    usevar='pooled')
```

Let us look at the results:

```
> print('stat = {0:.4f}, p-value = {1:.4f}, df =
    {2}'.format(tstat, p, df))


stat = -4.1061, p-value = 0.0003, df = 30.0
```

The Statsmodels implementation provides the degrees of freedom.

Note that the values obtained are the same, but we get the degrees of freedom with the Statsmodels implementation.

6.6.2   Levene's Test – Testing Homoscedasticity

WE MENTIONED IN THE PREVIOUS section that one of the assumptions used in the sample t-test is homoscedasticity. In other words, the implementation of the test relies on the assumption that the variances of the two groups are equal. It is therefore fair to consider a statistical test for this situation and this is the main objective of the Levene test. The test was introduced by Howard Levene[13] in 1960 for the mean and then extended by Morton B. Brown and Alan B. Forsythe[14] for the median and the trimmed mean.

The Levene test checks for homoscedasticity, i.e. equal variances.

[13] Howard, L. (1960). Robust tests for equality of variances. In I. Olkin and H. Hotelling (Eds.), *Contributions to Probability and Statistics: Essays in Honor of Harold Hotelling*, pp. 278–292. Stanford University Press

[14] Brown, M. B. and A. B. Forsythe (1974). Robust tests for the equality of variances. *Journal of the American Statistical Association* 69(346), 364–367

The hypotheses in the Levene test are:

- $H_0 : \sigma_1^2 = \sigma_2^2 = \ldots = \sigma_k^2$,

- $H_a : \sigma_i^2 \neq \sigma_j^2$, for at least one pair (i, j).

The test statistic W is defined for a variable Y with sample size N divided into k groups, with N_i being the sample size

of group i:

$$W = \frac{N-k}{k-1} \frac{\sum_{i=1}^{k} N_i (Z_{i\cdot} - Z_{\cdot\cdot})^2}{\sum_{i=1}^{k} \sum_{j=1}^{N_i} (Z_{ij} - Z_{i\cdot})^2}, \qquad (6.39)$$

where:

$$Z_{ij} = \begin{cases} |Y_{ij} - \overline{Y}_i|, & \overline{Y}_i \text{ is a mean of the } i\text{-th group,} \\ |Y_{ij} - \widetilde{Y}_i|, & \widetilde{Y}_i \text{ is a median of the } i\text{-th group,} \end{cases}$$

Levene test.

Brown-Forsythe test.

$$Z_{i\cdot} = \frac{1}{N_i} \sum_{j=1}^{N_i} Z_{ij} \text{ is the mean of the } Z_{ij} \text{ for group } i,$$

$$Z_{\cdot\cdot} = \frac{1}{N} \sum_{i=1}^{k} \sum_{j=1}^{N_i} Z_{ij} \text{ is the mean of all } Z_{ij}.$$

In Python we can use the implementation in SciPy called levene that takes a parameter called center which can be any of 'median', 'mean', 'trimmed', with the median being the default.

We can use the levene function in SciPy.

We can take a look at the cars data we used before and check if indeed our assumption of heteroscedasticity was correct:

```
> import scipy.stats as sps
> tstat, p = sps.levene(automatic, manual)
> print('stat ={0:.4f}, p-value= {1:.4f}'.
   format(tstat, p))


stat = 4.1876, p-value= 0.0496
```

The variances for manual and automatic cars are not equal. What do we do now? See the next section!

With $\alpha = 0.05$, we can see that we reject the null hypothesis in this case. Sadly the variances in our data appear to be different. So, what do we do in cases like this. Well, let us see in the next section.

6.6.3   Welch's t-test – Comparing Means, Different Variances

COMPARING TWO MEANS WHEN THE datasets are not homoscedastic requires a different approach to the one discussed in Section 6.6.1. Using a pooled variance, as we did before, works well to detect evidence to reject H_0 if the variances are equal. However, the results can lead to erroneous conclusions in cases where the population variances are not equal, i.e. we have heteroscedasticity. The test was proposed by Bernard Lewis Welch[15] as an adaptation to the Student t-test.

> We use Welch's test when comparing means of two samples with different variances.

The approach is still the same for our null and alternative hypotheses and the main difference is the consideration of the variances. In this case, since we do not assume equality, we have that the test statistic is

$$t = \frac{(\overline{x_1} - \overline{x_2}) - (\mu_1 - \mu_2)}{\sqrt{\frac{s_1^2}{n_1} + \frac{s_2^2}{n_2}}}, \qquad (6.40)$$

which approximates a t-distribution with degrees of freedom given by the Welch-Satterthwaite equation[16]:

$$\nu = \frac{(V_1 + V_2)^2}{\frac{V_1^2}{n_1 - 1} + \frac{V_2^2}{n_2 - 1}}, \qquad (6.41)$$

where $V_i = \dfrac{s_i^2}{n_i}$.

[15] Welch, B. L. (1947, 01). The generalization of 'Student's' problem when several different population variances are involved. *Biometrika* 34(1-2), 28–35

[16] Satterthwaite, F. E. (1946). An approximate distribution of estimates of variance components. *Biometrics Bulletin* 2(6), 110–114

One advantage of using this approach is that if the variances are the same, the degrees of freedom obtained with Welch's test are the same as the ones for the Student t-test. In a practical way, it is recommended to use the Welch test as you do not have to concern yourself with assumptions about the variance. Note that the degrees of freedom in Welch's t-test are not integers and they need to be rounded in case you are using statistical tables. Fortunately we are using Python.

I recommend using the Welch test as we do not have to concern ourselves with assumptions about the variance.

In Python, the implementation of Welch's test is done using the same methods used in Section 6.6.1. In the SciPy implementation we need to use the parameter equal_var=False. Let us see the results for our cars data:

```
> import scipy.stats as sps
> tstat, p = sps.ttest_ind(automatic, manual,
    alternative='two-sided', equal_var=False)
> print('stat = {0:.4f}, p-value= {1:.4f}'.
    format(tstat, p))


stat = -3.7671, p-value= 0.0014
```

The Welch test is implemented in ttest_ind with the parameter equal_var=False.

In the case of the Statsmodels implementation we have to use the parameter usevar='unequal' to apply Welch's test to our data:

```
import statsmodels.stats.weightstats as smw
tstat, p, df = smw.ttest_ind(automatic, manual,
    alternative='two-sided', usevar='unequal')
```

For the Statsmodels implementation we use usevar='unequal'.

Let us see the results:

```
> print('stat = {0:.4f}, p-value = {1:.4f},
    df = {2:.4f}'.format(tstat, p, df))


stat = -3.7671, p-value = 0.0014, df = 18.3323
```

We still reject the null hypothesis for our manual v automatic car comparison.

As before, we have a *p*-value smaller than 0.05 and we reject the null hypothesis. We have sufficient evidence to say that the difference in mean fuel consumption between automatic and manual transmission cars in our dataset are statistically significant.

6.6.4   Mann-Whitney Test – Testing Non-normal Samples

WHEN WE ARE INTERESTED IN comparing samples where we have a small number of observations, or the samples are not normally distributed, the tests described above are not suitable. Instead, we need to resort to non-parametric techniques. The Mann-Whitney test is a non-parametric test, proposed in 1947[17], that helps us compare the differences between two independent, non-normal, samples of ordinal or continuous variables.

[17] Mann, H. B. and D. R. Whitney (1947, Mar). On a test of whether one of two random variables is stochastically larger than the other. *Ann. Math. Statist.* 18(1), 50–60

The null hypothesis H_0 is that the distributions of the two populations are equal. The typical alternative hypothesis H_a is that they are not, in other words, we have a two-sided test. The main idea for the test is based on the comparison of the ranks of the data. If we are able to identify a systematic difference between the samples, then most of the high ranks

The Mann-Whitney test lets us compare non-normally distributed samples. It is a non-parametric test.

will be attached to one of the samples, and most of the lower ones to the other one. If the two samples are similar, then the ranks will be distributed more evenly.

For samples with sizes n_1 and n_2, the test involves pooling the observations from the two samples while keeping track of the sample from which each observation came. The ranks for the pooled sample range from 1 to $n_1 + n_2$. The Mann-Whitney test statistic is denoted as U and tells us about the difference between the ranks, and usually it is the smaller of U_1 and U_2

In the test we pool the observations of both samples and rank them keeping track of which sample the observation came from.

$$U_1 \;=\; n_1 n_2 + \frac{n_1(n_1 + 1)}{2} - R_1 \qquad (6.42)$$

$$U_2 \;=\; n_1 n_2 + \frac{n_2(n_2 + 1)}{2} - R_2 \qquad (6.43)$$

The Mann-Whitney test statistic. We can select the larger of U_1 and U_2 too.

with R_i being the sum of the ranks for group i. Note that $U_1 + U_2 = n_1 n_2$. The theoretical range of the test statistic U ranges between:

- 0: Complete separation of the two samples, and thus H_0 most likely to be rejected, and

The U statistic ranges between 0 and $n_1 n_2$.

- $n_1 n_2$: Suggesting evidence in support of H_a.

In Python we can use the `mannwhitneyu` implementation in SciPy's stats module. Note that this implementation always reports the U_i statistic associated with the first sample. As with other tests we can pass an `alternative` parameter to select whether we require a `'two-sided'` (default), `'less'`, or `'greater'` test.

SciPy provides the `mannwhitneyu` function.

Let us look at an example: In Section 5.5 we tackled the mystery posed to us by the Vulcan Academy regarding a gas similar to hexafluorine with alleged anti-gravity effects on some Starfleet officers. Although we found that the anti-gravity hypothesis was not supported, colleagues reported some headaches that turned out to be indeed caused by the gas. This presented us with a great opportunity to compare the effectiveness of some new pain killers: "Headezine" and "Kabezine". We found 15 volunteers to trial the medication and have randomly allocated them to one or the other treatment. We have asked them to report their perceived effectiveness in a scale from 0 (no effect) to 10 (very effective). The results are shown in Table 6.5.

Although the anti-gravity effects of hexafluorine-like gas did not have a lot of evidence, it turns out it does cause some headaches. Never a dull day at Starfleet.

Headezine		Kabezine	
Volunteer	Rating	Volunteer	Rating
1	4	1	8
2	2	2	7
3	6	3	5
4	2	4	10
5	3	5	6
6	5	6	9
7	7	7	8
8	8		

Table 6.5: Ratings for the perceived effect of two Starfleet pain relief medications.

We would like to know if there is a significant difference in the perceived effectiveness of the two pain relief medications. We can start by looking at the medians of the ratings provided:

Is there a difference in the perceived effectiveness of the treatments? We shall see!

```
> headezine = np.array([4, 2, 6, 2, 3, 5, 7, 8])
> kabezine = np.array([8, 7, 5, 10, 6, 9, 8])
> np.median(headezine)


4.5


> np.median(kabezine)


8.0
```

The medians of the two treatments seem to be different. Is this statistically significant?

We can see that the medians are different, but we want to know if the difference is statistically significant. We can use the Mann-Whitney test for this purpose:

```
> U, p = mannwhitneyu(headezine, kabezine)
> print('stat = {0:.4f}, p-value= {1:.4f}'.
    format(U, p))


stat = 8.5000, p-value= 0.0268
```

We use the Mann-Whitney test to check our hypothesis.

With a p-value lower than $\alpha - 0.05$, we can reject the null hypothesis and conclude that the difference is statistically significant. Note that since we carried out a two-tailed test we can only strictly conclude that there is a difference in the perceived effectiveness. If we wanted to assert that Kabezine is perceived to be more effective among the Starfleet volunteers, we can use a one-tailed test. Here, our alternative hypothesis being that Kabezine has a lower median:

We can reject the null hypothesis and conclude that there is indeed a difference.

```
> U, p = mannwhitneyu(headezine, kabezine,
    alternative='less')
> print('stat = 0:.4f, p-value= 1:.4f'.
    format(U, p))


stat = 8.5000, p-value= 0.0134
```

To assert which sample has a higher median, we conduct a new (one-tailed) test.

We can reject the null hypothesis and conclude that indeed Kabezine is perceived to be more effective.

6.6.5   Paired Sample t-test

WE HAVE A FOLLOW UP to the Starfleet challenge with the hexafluorine-like gas and the headaches reported by some of our colleagues. We are interested in the self-reported scores from volunteers taking "Kabezine" before and after treatment. Since we have a pair of measurements for each subject, we should take this relationship into account. This is a good scenario to use a paired sample t-test. Sometimes this is referred as a dependent samples t-test.

Since we have a before and after treatment case, we use a paired sample t-test. We assume the data is normally distributed.

The null hypothesis is that the population means are equal. This can be expressed in terms of the difference as follows: $H_0 : \mu_1 - \mu_2 = c$, where c is the hypothesised value. A typical case is for $c = 0$. The alternative hypothesis can be any of the following:

The hypotheses for a paired sample t-test.

- $H_a : \mu_1 - \mu_2 > c,$
- $H_a : \mu_1 - \mu_2 < c,$
- $H_a : \mu_1 - \mu_2 \neq c.$

Notice that we are interested in the difference between the values of each subject in the data. With n sample differences, our test statistic is therefore given by

$$t = \frac{\overline{x_d} - c}{\frac{s_d}{\sqrt{n}}},$$ (6.44)

The test statistic for a paired sample t-test.

where $\overline{x_d}$ is the mean of the sample differences and s_d is their standard deviation. The degrees of freedom are $v = n - 1$.

Volunteer	Pre-Treatment	Post-Treatment	Difference
1	6	7.3	1.3
2	7	8.3	1.3
3	5.4	5.7	0.3
4	7.3	8	0.7
5	6.8	5.3	−1.5
6	8	9.7	1.7
7	5.7	6.7	1
8	7	7.7	0.7
9	7.7	6.3	−1.3
10	6	6.7	0.7
11	4.7	5	0.3
12	4.1	5.1	1
13	5.2	6	0.8
14	6.3	8.8	2.5
15	6	6	0
16	6.7	8	1.3
17	4	6	2
18	7.3	8.3	1
19	5	6.4	1.4
20	5.7	5.7	0

Table 6.6: Pre- and post-treatment general health measures of Starfleet volunteers in the Kabezine study.

Let us go back to our Kabezine study. This time we have requested for volunteers affected by the hexafluorine-like gas to have a medical examination with Dr McCoy before and after treatment with Kabezine. The measures provided by the medical examination are numbers in the range 1-10 in a continuous scale, with 10 being great general health. The results are shown in Table 6.6. Let us look at entering our data in Python:

Dr McCoy has captured data in a continuous scale from 1 to 10, with the higher the number, the better the health of the volunteer.

```
pre = [6.0, 7.0, 5.4, 7.3, 6.8, 8.0,
    5.7, 7.0, 7.7, 6.0, 4.7, 4.1, 5.2,
    6.3, 6.0, 6.7, 4.0, 7.3, 5.0, 5.7]
post = [7.3, 8.3, 5.7, 8.0, 5.3, 9.7,
    6.7, 7.7, 6.3, 6.7, 5.0, 5.1, 6.0,
    8.8, 6.0, 8.0, 6.0, 8.3, 6.4, 5.7]
```

We can use our lists to create a pandas dataframe, which will let us create a new column for the differences:

```
df = pd.DataFrame('pre': pre, 'post': post)
df['difference'] = df['post']-df['pre']
```

We create a dataframe with the data from Table 6.6.

Let us see the mean and (sample) standard deviation for the differences:

```
> df['difference'].describe()
```

count	20.000000	25%	0.300000
mean	0.755000	50%	0.900000
std	0.980588	75%	1.300000
min	-1.500000	max	2.500000

These are the descriptive statistics for our Kabezine study.

Let us look at whether the data seems to be normally distributed. In this case we will use the Shapiro-Wilk test function from Section 6.2.2. First, the pre-treatment measurements:

```
> shapiro_test(df['pre'])

stat = 0.9719, p-value= 0.7944

Can't reject the null hypothesis.
The data seems to be normally distributed.
```

We are using the Shapiro-Wilk test to check for normality in our data.

And the post-treatment ones:

```
> shapiro_test(df['post'])

stat = 0.9453, p-value= 0.3019

Can't reject the null hypothesis.
The data seems to be normally distributed.
```

So far so good. We have that the mean of the differences is $x_d = 0.755$ with a sample standard deviation equal to 0.9805. We can use this to build our test statistic. In Python we can use the ttest_rel function in SciPy's stat module. The default for alternative is 'two-sided'.

We can use the ttest_rel function in SciPy to perform a paired sample t-test.

```
> from scipy.stats import ttest_rel
> tstat, p = ttest_rel(df['pre'], df['post'])
> print('stat = {0:.4f}, p-value= {1:.4f}'.
  format(tstat, p))

stat = -3.4433, p-value= 0.0027
```

With a p-value lower than 0.05 we can reject the null hypothesis and conclude that there is strong evidence that, on average, Kabezine does offer improvements to the headaches in Starfleet colleagues affected by the gas under investigation.

For a 95% confidence level, we reject the null hypothesis. Kabezine does offer improvements to Starfleet officers.

6.6.6   Wilcoxon Matched Pairs

AS YOU CAN IMAGINE, WE may have a situation when a parametric test is not suitable with paired data, either because we have a small dataset, or the data is not normally distributed. A non-parametric alternative to the paired t-test is the Wilcoxon matches pairs test.

The Wilcoxon matched pairs test is non-parametric.

The paired test follows the same logic as the single sample version we saw in Section 6.5.3. The null hypothesis is that the medians of the populations are equal. As before we can express this as $H_0 : m_1 - m_2 = c$. The alternative hypothesis can be any of the following:

- $H_a :$ $m_1 - m_2 > c$,

- $H_a :$ $m_1 - m_2 < c$,

- $H_a :$ $m_1 - m_2 \neq c$.

The hypotheses for a Wilcoxon matched pairs test.

In this case we consider a set of paired samples $(X_i, Y - i)$. For each observation we calculate $|X_i - Y_i|$ and determine the rank, R_i, compared to the other observations. The Wilcoxon signed-rank test statistic is calculated in the same way as before:

$$W = \sum_{i=1}^{n} \psi_i R_i, \tag{6.45}$$

The Wilcoxon test statistic is the same as in Section 6.5.3.

where,

$$\psi_1 = \begin{cases} 1 & \text{if } |X_i - Y_i| > 0, \\ 0 & \text{if } |X_i - Y_i| < 0. \end{cases} \qquad (6.46)$$

The normalised test statistic remains the same too:

$$W' = \frac{W - E(W)}{\sqrt{Var(W)}}. \qquad (6.47)$$

The normalised test statistic for the Wilcoxon matched pairs test.

Given the similarities with the one-sample test, in Python we actually use the same `wilcoxon` function. The main difference is that we pass two arrays instead of one. We can continue using the `alternative` parameter to identify whether we need a one-sided or a two-sided test.

Volunteer	Pre-Treatment	Post-Treatment	Difference
1	8.2	8.3	0.1
2	7.3	9.3	2.0
3	7.2	9.6	2.4
4	8.0	9.1	1.1
5	1.6	2.0	0.4
6	9.6	8.8	−0.8
7	4.0	9.9	5.9
8	4.7	4.0	−0.7
9	7.9	7.4	−0.5
10	2.9	3.5	0.6
11	5.0	8.5	3.5
12	2.0	5.8	3.8

Table 6.7: Pre- and post-treatment general health measures of *USS Cerritos* volunteers in the Kabezine study.

Let us consider an example: It turns out that Commander T'Ana of the *USS Cerritos* is interested in reproducing the results of our study of Kabezine and enlists a limited number of volunteers to assess the feasibility of a study.

With a small dataset, Commander T'Ana is better using a nonparametric test. The results of the small study are as shown in Table 6.7. Let us capture the data:

```
cerritos_pre = [8.2, 7.3, 7.2, 8, 1.6, 9.6,
   4, 4.7, 7.9, 2.9, 5, 2]
cerritos_post = [8.3, 9.3, 9.6, 9.1, 2, 8.8,
   9.9, 4, 7.4, 3.6, 8.5, 5.8]
cerritos_df = pd.DataFrame('pre': cerritos_pre,
   'post': cerritos_post)
```

We create a pandas dataframe. Make sure you import pandas.

Let us calculate the difference between post- and pre-treatment and look at the median:

```
> cerritos_df['difference'] = cerritos_df['post']-
   cerritos_df['pre']
> cerritos_df['difference'].median()


0.8999999999999999
```

We can calculate the median difference between post- and pre-treatment.

The null hypothesis is that the median of the differences is equal to 0. Let us test our hypothesis:

```
> tstat, p = wilcoxon(cerritos_df['pre'],
   cerritos_df['post'])
> print('stat = {0:.4f}, p-value= {1:.4f}'.
   format(tstat, p))


stat = 13.5000, p-value= 0.0425
```

We apply the wilcoxon function to test our hypothesis.

With a p-value of 0.0425 at $\alpha = 0.05$ level of significance, we can reject the null hypothesis and conclude that the difference is statistically significant. In this case we used a two-sided test as we left the `alternative` parameter out of the command, using the default value.

Commander T'Ana can now start thinking of a wider study including more subjects.

6.7   Analysis of Variance

UP UNTIL NOW WE HAVE looked at ways in which we can test for situations where our null hypothesis has been a comparison of two populations, i.e. $H_0 : \mu_1 = \mu_2$ or checking a single population against a hypothesised value, i.e. $H_0 : \mu_1 = c$. In many cases, we may need to carry out a comparison of more than two populations and running pairwise tests may not be the best option. Instead, we look at estimating the "variation" among and between groups.

We have seen how to compare two populations, but what happens when we need to compare more?

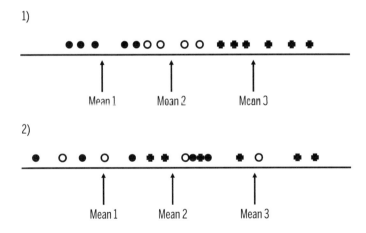

Figure 6.4: Two possible datasets to be analysed using analysis of variance. We have three populations and their means. Although the means are the same in both cases, the variability in set 2) is greater.

We may encounter some situations similar to those shown in Figure 6.4. We have three populations depicted by open circles, filled circles and plus signs. In each of the cases 1) and 2) we have a different distribution of the observations for each population. In both cases, however, we have that the population means are located in the same positions in our scale. In the first situation the samples of each population are more clearly separated and we may agree by initial inspection the three means are different from each other.

The samples in 1) are more clearly separated. The three means are different.

However, in the second case we can see that there is a wider spread in the samples for each population and there is even some overlap. The separation between the means may be attributed to the variability in the populations rather than actual differences in the mean.

The samples in 2) are more spread. The means may be better explained by the variability of the data.

In case 1) shown in Figure 6.4 the within-sample variability is small compared to the between-sample one, whereas in case 2) the overall variability observed is due to higher variability within-sample. If we can account for the differences between sample means by variability within-sample, then there is no reason to reject the null hypothesis that the means are all equal. Understanding the variation can be done with the so-called analysis of variance, or ANOVA for short. Not only did Ronald Fisher coin the term "variance"[18], but also popularised the ANOVA methodology in his book *Statistical Methods for Research Workers*[19] first published in 1925. We have never looked back and analysis of variance is a useful tool to understand.

ANOVA is a way of looking at different aspects that contribute to the overall variance of a variable.

[18] R. A. Fisher (1918). The correlation between relatives on the supposition of mendelian inheritance. *Philos. Trans. R. Soc. Edinb. 52*, 399–433
[19] Fisher, R. (1963). *Statistical Methods for Research Workers*. Biological monographs and manuals. Hafner Publishing Company

Let us consider a study where we need to compare two or more populations. Typically, we would be interested in a particular variable for the comparison. This would be a

variable that enables us to distinguish among the samples.
We call that variable a **factor** under investigation.
Sometimes we talk about **levels** to refer to values of a factor.

Let us say that we are interested in how one factor affects
our response variable; in this case we want to use a
one-factor ANOVA, also known as one-way ANOVA.
Similarly, we use a two-factor ANOVA, or two-way ANOVA,
to analyse how two factors affect a response variable. In this
situation, we are also interested in determining if there is an
interaction between the two factors in question, having an
impact on the response variable. Let us take a look.

A one-way ANOVA looks at the effect of one factor on the response variable. A two-way ANOVA looks at the effect of two factors.

6.7.1   One-factor or One-way ANOVA

A ONE-FACTOR ANALYSIS OF VARIANCE is used in the
comparison of k populations, or treatments, with means
$\mu_1, \mu_2, \ldots, \mu_k$ and our aim is to test the following
hypotheses:

- $H_0 : \mu_1 = \mu_2 = \cdots = \mu_k$,

One-way ANOVA hypotheses.

- H_a: at least two of the means are different.

As with other statistical tests we have seen, there are a
number of assumptions that are made in order to apply a
one-way ANOVA. We assume that:

1. The observations are independent and selected randomly
   from each of the k populations.

Assumptions behind a one-way ANOVA.

2. The observations for each of the k populations, or factor
   levels, are approximately normally distributed.

3. The normal populations in question have a common variance σ^2.

For a population with k levels such that each level has n_i observations we have that the total number of observations is $n = \sum_i^k n_i$. Let us now zoom in the levels themselves and say that the j-th observation in the i-th level is x_{ij} with $j = 1, 2, \ldots n_j$. The sum of n_i observations in level i is denoted as $T_i = \sum_j x_{ij}$ and thus the sum of all n observations is $T = \sum_i T_i = \sum_i \sum_j x_{ij}$.

This is important notation used in ANOVA.

As we did in Section 6.4.2, for a linear regression, we are interested in minimising a sum of squares. In this case we would like to compare the sum of squares between samples and within samples. Let us take a look. The total sum of squares is:

$$SS_T = \sum_i \sum_j x_{ij}^2 - \frac{T^2}{n},$$ (6.48)

The total sum of squares.

similarly, the sum of squares between samples is:

$$SS_B = \sum_i \frac{T_i^2}{n_i} - \frac{T^2}{n},$$ (6.49)

The sum of squares between samples.

and so we can calculate the sum of squares within samples by subtracting the two quantities above:

$$SS_W = SS_T - SS_B.$$ (6.50)

The sum of squares within samples.

Let us recall from Section 4.4.4 that a sample variance can be obtained by taking the sum of squares and dividing by the population minus one as shown in Equation (4.21). This means that we can obtain a mean square for the quantities above as follows:

$$MS_T = \frac{SS_T}{n-1}, \quad \text{total mean square,} \tag{6.51}$$

Note that the degrees of freedom $n-1=(k-1)+(n-k)$.

$$MS_B = \frac{SS_B}{k-1}, \quad \text{mean square between samples,} \tag{6.52}$$

$$MS_W = \frac{SS_W}{n-k}, \quad \text{mean square within samples.} \tag{6.53}$$

When the null hypothesis is true, the between- and within-sample mean squares are equal, i.e. $MS_B = MS_W$. Otherwise, $MS_B > MS_W$, and as the difference among the sample means is bigger, the greater MS_B will be compared to MS_W. We can therefore think of creating a test statistic that looks at the ratio of these two mean squares, or effectively, variances. This is called the F statistic:

$$F = \frac{MS_B}{MS_W} = \frac{\text{between sample variance}}{\text{within sample variance}}, \tag{6.54}$$

We encountered the F statistic in Section 6.4.2 in relationship to regression coefficients.

The F distribution with degrees of freedom v_1 and v_2 is the distribution described by:

$$X = \frac{S_1/v_1}{S_2/v_2}, \tag{6.55}$$

where S_1 and S_2 are independent random variables with chi-squared distributions with respective degrees of freedom v_1

See Section 5.5.2 about the chi-squared distribution.

and v_2. Its probability distribution function is given by:

$$f(x, v_1, v_2) = \frac{x^{\frac{v_1}{2}-1}}{B\left(\frac{v_1}{2}, \frac{v_2}{2}\right)} \left(\frac{v_1}{v_2}\right)^{\frac{v_1}{2}} \left(1 + \frac{v_1}{v_2}x\right)^{-\frac{v_1+v_2}{2}}, \quad (6.56)$$

for real $x > 0$, and where B is the beta function[20]. The expected value for the F distribution is given by:

$$\mu = \frac{v_2}{v_2 - 2}, \text{ for } v_2 > 2, \quad (6.57)$$

and its variance by:

$$\sigma^2 = \frac{2v_2^2(v_1 + v_2 - 2)}{v_1(v_2 - 2)^2(v_2 - 4)}, \text{ for } v_2 > 4. \quad (6.58)$$

The cumulative distribution function of the F distribution is given by:

$$F(x, v_1, v_2) = I_{\frac{v_1 x}{v_1 x + v_2}}\left(\frac{v_1}{2}, \frac{v_2}{2}\right), \quad (6.59)$$

where I is the regularised incomplete beta function[21].

It is important to note that for unbalanced data, there are three different ways to determine the sums of squares involved in ANOVA. If we consider a model that includes 2 factors, say A and B, we can consider their main effects as well as their interaction. We may represent that model as $SS(A, B, AB)$. We may be interested in looking at the sum of squares for the effects of A after those of the B factor and ignore interactions. This will be represented as: $SS(A|B) = SS(A, B) - SS(B)$. Another example: $SS(AB|A, B) = SS(A, B, AB) - SS(A, B)$ is the sum of squares for the interaction of A and B after the main

[20] Abramowitz, M. and I. Stegun (1965). *Handbook of Mathematical Functions: With Formulas, Graphs, and Mathematical Tables.* Applied Mathematics Series. Dover Publications

[21] Abramowitz, M. and I. Stegun (1965). *Handbook of Mathematical Functions: With Formulas, Graphs, and Mathematical Tables.* Applied Mathematics Series. Dover Publications

There are different ways to consider the effects of our factors.

individual effects. This bring us to the types mentioned above:

- Type I: Sequential sum of squares: First assigns maximum variation to A: $SS(A)$, then to B: $SS(B|A)$, followed by the interaction $SS(AB|B, A)$, and finally to the residuals. In this case the order of the variables makes a difference and in many situations this is not what we want.

Type I looks at the factors sequentially.

- Type II: Sum of squares no interaction: First assigns the variation to factor A taking into account factor B, i.e. $SS(A|B)$. Then the other way around, i.e. $SS(B|A)$. We leave the interaction out.

Type II ignores the interaction.

- Type III: Sum of squares with interaction: Here we look at the effect of factor A after the effect of B and the interaction AB, i.e. $SS(A|B, AB)$. Then the other way around for the main effects: $SS(B|A, AB)$. If the interactions are not significant we should use Type II.

Type II considers the interaction.

Let us take a closer look at the assumptions we are making about the model. First we are assuming that the observations in our dataset are normally distributed, i.e. $x_{ij} \sim N(\mu_i, \sigma^2)$ for $j = 1, 2, \ldots, k$. We can centre the distributions and thus $x_{ij} - \mu_i = \varepsilon_{ij} = N(0, \sigma^2)$, where ε_{ij} denotes the variation of x_{ij} about its mean μ_i and can be interpreted as random variations that are part of the observations themselves.

We exploit the normality of our data to express our model in terms of variations inherent to the observations.

Now, if the overall mean is $\mu = \sum_i \mu_i / k$, then we can assert that $\sum_i (\mu_i - \mu) = 0$. Let us denote the quantity in parenthesis

as L_i and thus $\mu_i = \mu + L_i$. The assertion above would
indicate that the sum of L_i is equal to 0. We can interpret
L_i as the mean effect of factor level i relative to the mean μ.
With this information we are able to define the following
model:

$$x_{ij} = \mu + L_i + \varepsilon_{ij}, \qquad (6.60)$$

for $i = 1, 2, \ldots, k$ and $j = 1, 2, \ldots, n_i$. For the case where the
null hypothesis holds, we have that $\mu_i = \mu$ for all i and this
is equivalent to having $L_i = 0$ for all i, implying that there
are no effects for any of the available levels. As you can see,
we can consider ANOVA as a regression analysis problem
with categorical variables such that for a response variable
Y we are interested to see how the levels $X_1, X_2, \ldots, X_k$
influence the response and so we have a model that can be
written as:

$$Y = \beta_0 + \beta_1 X_1 + \beta_2 X_2 + \cdots + \beta_k X_k + \varepsilon. \qquad (6.61)$$

Source of variation	Sum of Squares	Degrees of Freedom	Mean Square	F statistic
Between samples	SS_B	$k-1$	MS_B	$\frac{MS_B}{MS_W}$
Within samples	SS_W	$n-k$	MS_W	
Total	SS_T	$n-1$		

Table 6.8: Table summarising the results of an analysis of variance (ANOVA).

L_i is the mean effect of factor level i relative to the mean μ.

The null hypothesis in ANOVA is equivalent to having $L_i = 0$ for all i. In other words, we have no effects.

We can express ANOVA as a regression analysis.

Under the null hypothesis we have that $\beta_1 = \beta_2 = \cdots = 0$,
versus the alternative hypothesis that $\beta_j \neq 0$ for any j.

The results of the ANOVA analysis are conveniently presented as a summary in the form of a table as shown in Table 6.8. As usual the *p*-value obtained can help with our decisions to reject, or not, the null hypothesis.

Let us now consider an example to see ANOVA in action with Python. We will go back to our toaster manufacturer in Caprica City and we are interested in the performance of three models of toaster, including Model 5. The manufacturer has provided information of ours in excess of 1500 hours for three models as shown in Table 6.9.

Frakking toasters!

Model 5	Model Centurion	Model 8
14	17	24
17	19	33
12	19	28
14	22	22
22	18	29
19	17	32
16	18	31
17	19	28
15	17	29
16	16	30

Table 6.9: Performance of three Caprica City toasters in hours in excess of 1500 hours of use.

Let us capture this data into NumPy arrays and look at the means. Assuming we have already imported NumPy:

```
> five = np.array([14, 17, 12, 14, 22, 19, 16, 17,
   15, 16])
> centurion = np.array([17, 19, 19, 22, 18, 17, 18,
   19, 17, 16])
```

We enter our data into NumPy arrays and use the mean method to obtain the averages.

```
> eight = np.array([24, 33, 28, 22, 29, 32, 31,
  28, 29, 30])
> print(five.mean(), centurion.mean(),
  eight.mean())


16.2 18.2 28.6
```

We can see that the mean performance for toaster model 8 is larger than for the other 2 models. The question is whether this is a statistically significant difference. We can use ANOVA to look at the null hypothesis, that all the means are the same, and the alternative hypothesis, that at least one of them is different. In Python we can use the f_oneway implementation in SciPy:

Is the average value difference statistically significant?

```
> from scipy.stats import f_oneway
> fstat, p = f_oneway(five, centurion, eight)
> print('stat = {0:.4f}, p-value= {1:.4f}'.
  format(fstat, p))


stat = 59.3571, p-value= 0.0000
```

We use the f_oneway function in SciPy to carry out an ANOVA.

With an F statistic of 59.3571 we have a p-value lower than $\alpha = 0.05$, for a 95% confidence level we can reject the null hypothesis. We conclude at least one of the means is different from the others.

See Section 6.7.2 to see how Tukey's range test can help find the sample with the difference.

Note that the SciPy implementation only gives us the F statistic and the p-value, but none of the other information shown in Table 6.8. Furthermore, the function only uses the Type II sum of squares. If we require more information, we can resort to the fact that we can express our problem as a linear model and use Statsmodels to help us. The first thing to mention is that we may need to reorganise our data into a long form table. We will therefore create a pandas dataframe with the information from Table 6.9:

To obtain more information we use Statsmodels and recast our problem as a linear regression.

```
import pandas as pd
toasters = pd.DataFrame({
    'five': five,
    'centurion': centurion,
    'eight': eight})
```

We first create a dataframe with our observations.

To get a long form table, we melt the dataframe as follows:

```
toasters_melt = pd.melt(
    toasters.reset_index(),
    id_vars=['index'],
    value_vars=toasters.columns,
    var_name='toastermodel',
    value_name='excesshours')
```

We then melt the dataframe to obtain a long form table.

The result will be a long dataframe with a column containing the name of the toaster model and another one with the excess hours. We can use this to write a model such that:

$$excesshours = \beta_0 + \beta_1 * \texttt{toastermodel}, \qquad (6.62)$$

We can now recast our problem as a linear regression.

where the `toastermodel` variable contains three levels: `five, centurion, eight`. We can now use the ordinary least squares method we saw in Section 6.4.2 and apply the anova_lm function to get more information about our analysis of variance. Let us first import the modules:

```
import statsmodels.api as sm
from statsmodels.formula.api import ols
```

We can now implement our ordinary least squares for the model in Equation (6.62):

```
model1 = ols('excesshours ~ C(toastermodel)',
   data=toasters_melt).fit()
anova_toasters = sm.stats.anova_lm(model1, typ=2)
```

After fitting the model, we apply the anova_lm function.

As you can see, we are creating a model that explains the excess hours as a function of the toaster model. The C in front of the variable toastermodel makes it clear to Python that the variable should be treated as categorical. Note also that we are able to specify the type of sum of squares we want to apply as a parameter to anova_lm. Let us look at the results:

We need to tell Python to treat our toastermodel variable as categorical.

```
> print(anova_toasters)


                   sum_sq   df      F        PR(>F)
C(toastermodel)    886.4    2.0  59.35714  1.30656e-10
Residual           201.6   27.0    NaN          NaN
```

This starts looking like the result summary from Table 6.8.

This table still does not show the sum of squares and the totals. We can write a function to help us with that:

```
def anova_summary(aov):
   aov2 = aov.copy()
   aov2['mean_sq'] = aov2[:]['sum_sq']/aov2[:]['df']
   cols = ['sum_sq', 'df', 'mean_sq', 'F', 'PR(>F)']
   aov2.loc['Total'] = [aov2['sum_sq'].sum(),
      aov2['df'].sum(), np.NaN, np.NaN, np.NAN]
   aov2 = aov2[cols]
   return aov2
```

A function to calculate the sum of squares and the totals.

Let us take a look:

```
> anova_summary(anova_toasters)

                  sum_sq    df      mean_sq
C(toastermodel)   886.4     2.0     443.200000
Residual          201.6     27.0    7.466667
Total             1088.0    29.0    NaN


         F            PR(>F)
59.357143   1 306568e-10
         NaN          NaN
         NaN          NaN
```

This is now a good ANOVA summary similar to Table 6.8.

The F statistic and *p*-value are the same as obtained before, but we now have more information about the results of our analysis of variance. However, we do not know which groups are different from each other, we simply know that there are differences.

As mentioned before, check Section 6.7.2.

Let us consider another example that may help put some of the discussions about other tests we have learned into perspective. Usually ANOVA is best employed in the comparison of three or more groups. In the case of two groups we can use a two-sample t-test as we did for our cars dataset in Section 6.6.1. We can, in principle, use ANOVA to make the comparison and simply remember the following relationship for our test statistics in the case of two groups: $F = t^2$.

Let us take a look and note that we are considering that the cars dataset has been loaded as before:

```
> lm_mpg1 = ols('mpg ~ C(am)', data=cars).fit()
> anova_mpg1 = sm.stats.anova_lm(lm_mpg1, typ=2)
> anova_summary(anova_mpg1)


               sum_sq    df     mean_sq            F
C(am)       405.150588   1.0  405.150588   16.860279
Residual    720.896599  30.0   24.029887          NaN
Total      1126.047187  31.0         NaN          NaN


   PR(>F)
 0.000285
      NaN
      NaN
```

ANOVA is better suited to compare three or more groups. For two groups, use a t-test or remember that $F = t^2$.

Using ANOVA to compare the fuel consumption of manual and automatic cars in the dataset from Section 6.6.1.

In this case the F statistic obtained is $F(1, 30) = 16.8602$ with $p < 0.05$. In Section 6.6.1 we obtained a t statistic of -4.1061 and we can verify that $F = t^2$. The result of our ANOVA test indicates that we reject the null hypothesis and so the mpg for automatic cars is different from that of manual ones.

$(-4.1061)^2 = 16.860$.

Let us do one more thing with our cars dataset. We have a variable cyl and so we can get the mean mpg per cyl:

```
> cars.groupby(['cyl'])['mpg'].mean()
cyl
4     26.663636
6     19.742857
8     15.100000
```

We have three levels in the cyl variable. We can use ANOVA to see if there are any differences in the mean fuel consumption per number of cylinders.

We have three groups and using ANOVA to determine if these means are the same or not is now easy to implement:

```
> lm_mpg2 = ols('mpg ~ C(cyl)', data=cars).fit()
> anova_mpg2 = sm.stats.anova_lm(lm_mpg2, typ=2)
> anova_summary(anova_mpg2)


              sum_sq    df     mean_sq
C(cyl)     824.784590   2.0   412.392295
Residual   301.262597  29.0    10.388365
Total     1126.047188  31.0          NaN


        F           PR(>F)
39.697515   4.978919e-09
      NaN            NaN
      NaN            NaN
```

The ANOVA summary for the comparison of the mean fuel consumption per number of cylinders.

The results obtained also indicate that the fuel consumption for cars with different numbers of cylinders is different with $F(2, 19) = 39.6975$, $p < 0.005$. But where is the difference? Well, Tukey's range test may be able to help.

6.7.2 Tukey's Range Test

WE HAVE ANALYSED THE TOASTER data provided by the
Caprica City manufacturer and concluded that at least one
of the mean values is statistically different from the others.
But which one? One common post hoc test that can be
applied is the Tukey's range test, or simply Tukey's test,
which compares the means of each group to every other
group pairwise, i.e. $\mu_i - \mu_j$ and identifies any difference
between two means that is greater than the expected
standard error. In Python we can use the
pairwise_tukeyhsd function in Statsmodels under
statsmodels.stats.multicomp:

Tukey's test can be used to find means that are significantly different from each other.

```
> from statsmodels.stats.multicomp\
   import pairwise_tukeyhsd
> tukey_test = pairwise_tukeyhsd(
   endog=toasters_melt['excesshours'],
   groups=toasters_melt['toastermodel'],
   alpha=0.05)
> print(tukey_test)


Multiple Comparison of Means-Tukey HSD, FWER=0.05
==================================================
 group1   group2  meandiff p-adj   lower    upper
- - - - - - - - - - - - - - - - - - - - - - - - -
centurion eight     10.4   0.001   7.3707  13.4293
centurion five      -2.0   0.2481  -5.0293  1.0293
    eight five     -12.4   0.001  -15.4293 -9.3707
```

We can run a Tukey's range test with the pairwise_tukeyhsd function in Statsmodels.

The p-value for the comparison between the Centurion toaster and Model Five is greater than 0.05 and thus, for a 95% confidence level, we cannot reject the null hypothesis. In other words, there is no statistically significant difference between the means of the Centurion and Five models. The p-values for the comparison between the Centurion toaster and the Model Eight one, on the one hand, and Models Eight and Five on the other hand, are below our significance value. We reject the null hypothesis and can say that there is a statistically significant difference between the means of these groups.

According to the results, the Model Eight toaster has the different mean value.

6.7.3   Repeated Measures ANOVA

AS WE SAW IN SECTION 6.6.5, sometimes we have data that corresponds to a given treatment of the same subject in a repeated manner, for example a measurement that takes into account a before and after situation such as a treatment. We know that these are paired datasets, and in the case of more than two groups, we are interested in looking at the variability effects within subjects as opposed to the between samples approach used in Section 6.7.1 for ANOVA. With that in mind, we want to take a closer look at the within-samples sum of squares, SS_W, and break it further, leaving the sum of squares between samples, SS_B, out of the discussion. The hypotheses are:

We are interested in the variability effects within subjects.

- $H_0 : \mu_1 = \mu_2 = \cdots = \mu_k$, i.e. there is no difference among the treatments

The hypotheses for repeated measures ANOVA.

- H_a: at least one mean is different from the rest

The variation in this case may arise, in part, due to our variables having different means. We want to account for this in our model. Let us call this SS_M, and the variance that is not accounted for is called SS_e, which we treat as an error term. We are now left with the comparison between SS_M and SS_e. When $SS_M > SS_e$, then the variation within subjects is mostly accounted for by our model, leading to a large F statistic that is unlikely for the null hypothesis that the means are all equal.

We want to take into account that the variation may be due by our variables having different means.

For a dataset with n subjects with k treatments, we denote the observation for subject i on treatment j as x_{ij}. The mean for subject i overall treatments is denoted as $x_{i.}$, whereas the mean for treatment j among all subjects is $x_{.j}$. Finally $x_{..}$ is the grand mean for the dataset. The within-subjects sum of squares is:

Some important notation used in repeated measures ANOVA.

$$SS_W = \sum_i^n \sum_j^k (x_{ij} - x_{i.})^2, \qquad (6.63)$$

Within-subjects sum of squares.

and the sum of squares for our model is:

$$SS_M = n \sum_j^k (x_{.j} - x_{..})^2, \qquad (6.64)$$

Sum of squares for our model.

and thus $SS_e = SS_W - SS_M$. The degrees of freedom for our model is $v_M = k - 1$, and $v_e = (k - 1)(n - 1)$. As done in the previous section, the mean squares are $MS_M = SS_M/v_M$ and $MS_e = SS_e/v_e$ and our F statistic is given by $F = MS_M/MS_e$.

In Python, we can use the AnovaRM implementation in the Statsmodels package. We need to specify a melted dataframe containing our data, the dependent variable

We can use the AnovaRM function in Statsmodels.

(depvar), the column that contains the subject identifier (subject), and a list with the within-subject factors. Let us take a look at applying a repeated ANOVA to help of our colleagues at the *USS Cerritos*. Commander T'Ana is looking at the headache treatment study she started and has enlisted the help of 20 volunteers that have been given different drugs: Kabezine, Headezine, Paramoline and Ibuprenine. The overall health score of the volunteers is measured on each of the four drugs.

See Section 6.6.6 for Commander T'Ana's initial pilot study.

The data can be obtained from[22] `https://doi.org/10.6084/m9.figshare.19089896.v1` as a comma-separated value file with the name "starfleetHeadacheTreatment.csv". Let us load the data into a pandas dataframe:

[22] Rogel-Salazar, J. (2022d, Jan). Starfleet Headache Treatment - Example Data for Repeated ANOVA. https://doi.org/10.6084/m9.figshare.19089896.v1

```
> headache = pd.read_csv(
  'starfleetHeadacheTreatment.csv')
> headache.head(3)


  Volunteer  Kabezine  Headezine  Paramoline
0         1      10.0        3.4         1.7
1         2       7.7        3.9         4.3
2         3       7.6        7.6         2.5


Ibuprenine
       5.7
       4.4
       5.9
```

Our data is in a neat table.

As we can see, the data is organised as a neat table that is great for a human to read. However, we know that the

AnovaRM function is expecting a long format table. Let us melt the dataframe taking the Volunteer column as the IDs and the values as the columns in our original dataframe. We will rename the variable name as drug and the value columns as health:

```
> h_melt = pd.melt(headache.reset_index(),
    id_vars=['Volunteer'],
    value_vars=headache.columns,
    var_name='drug', value_name='health')
```

We need to melt our dataframe to use it with AnovaRM.

We can get the tail of the dataframe to see how things look:

```
> h_melt.tail(4)

    Volunteer        drug  health
76         17   Ibuprenine     4.9
77         18   Ibuprenine     4.4
78         19   Ibuprenine     5.3
79         20   Ibuprenine     4.4
```

We now have a long format table.

Let us now feed our melted dataframe to our repeated measures function AnovaRM:

```
> from statsmodels.stats.anova import AnovaRM
> aovrm = AnovaRM(data=h_melt, depvar='health',
    subject='Volunteer', within=['drug']).fit()
```

The AnovaRM function can now be applied.

We can take a look at the results by printing the summary provided by the model instance:

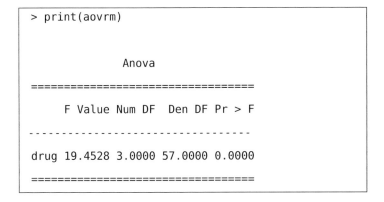

```
> print(aovrm)

            Anova

==================================

    F Value Num DF  Den DF Pr > F

- - - - - - - - - - - - - - - - - - - - - - - - - -

drug 19.4528 3.0000 57.0000 0.0000

==================================
```

With a statistic $F(3,57) = 19.4528$, $p < 0.05$ we can reject the null hypothesis for a 95% confidence level, and conclude that the type of drug used leads to statistically significant differences in overall health measures taken by Commander T'Ana's team.

Surely Commander T'Ana will be happily meowing with the results.

6.7.4   Kruskal-Wallis – Non-parametric One-way ANOVA

BY NOW WE ARE WELL aware that when our data is not normally distributed, we may need to revert to other methods, such as non-parametric tests. This is also true for carrying out an analysis of variance, and one way to evaluate if the medians, m_i, of two or more groups are equal (or not) is the Kruskal-Wallis test. The test is named after William Kruskal and W. Allen Wallis[23]. The test statistic is denoted with the letter H and it can be seen as an extension of the Mann-Whitney U test we discussed in Section 6.6.4, as we estimate the differences in the ranks of the observations.

[23] William H. Kruskal and W. Allen Wallis (1952). Use of ranks in one-criterion variance analysis. *Journal of the American Statistical Association* 47(260), 583–621

As mentioned before, we do not make any assumption about the distribution of the groups except that they have the same shapes. We evaluate the observations in either an ordinal, ratio or interval scale and they are assumed to be independent. As with the Mann-Whitney test, we first need to rank the n observations in the k groups with $n = \sum_i^k n_i$. Our hypotheses are as follows:

- $H_0 : m_1 = m_2 = \cdots = m_k,$

The hypotheses of the Kruskal-Wallis test.

- H_a: at least two of the medians are different.

With R_{ij} being the rank of the j-th observation in the i-th group, and $\overline{R_{i.}}$ being the average rank of the observations in the i-th group, the H test statistic for the Kruskal-Wallis test is given by:

$$H = (n-1) \frac{\sum_{i=1}^{k} n_i \left(\overline{R_{i.}} - \overline{R}\right)^2}{\sum_{i=1}^{k} \sum_{j=1}^{n_i} \left(R_{ij} - \overline{R}\right)^2}, \qquad (6.65)$$

The Kruskal-Wallis test statistic.

where $\overline{R} = (n+1)/2$, i.e. the average of all the R_{ij}. When the data does not have ties, we can express the test statistic as:

$$H = \frac{12}{n(n+1)} \sum_{i=1}^{k} n_i \overline{R_{i.}}^2 - 3(n+1). \qquad (6.66)$$

See Appendix I.

Now that we have our test statistic, to decide on whether we reject the null hypothesis or not, we compare H to a critical cutoff point determined by the chi-square distribution, this is due to the fact that this distribution is a good approximation for H for samples sizes greater than 5. The degrees of freedom for the chi-distribution is $\nu = k - 1$, where k is the number of groups. When the H statistic is greater than the cutoff, we reject the null hypothesis.

See Section 5.5.2 for more information about the chi-squared distribution.

In Python we can use the kruskal function in the stats module of SciPy. We simply need to provide arrays with the data in each of the groups. Let us consider an example. We are following up the learning of Python by new recruits to Starfleet Academy. We saw in Section 6.5.2 that 75% of applicants learn some Python, however they still need to take a course in their first year. New recruits are randomly assigned to one of 3 different methods of learning:

- Instructor-led course with Commander Data in a face-to-face format

- Remote lectures via holographic communicator with Hologram Janeway

- Project-led course following "Data Science and Analytics with Python"[24] and "Advanced Data Science and Analytics with Python"[25]

We are interested to know if the medians of the results are the same or not, indicating that either the method of learning is not important, or it actually makes a difference. Perhaps doing practical work with quality material is better than having Commander Data trying to simplify explanations, or better than just simply having remote lectures without practicals. After having sat the courses, the students are assessed and the results are shown in Table 6.10.

We will use the Kruskal-Wallis test, but first let us capture the data in Python:

We use the kruskal function in SciPy.

[24] Rogel-Salazar, J. (2017). *Data Science and Analytics with Python*. Chapman & Hall/CRC Data Mining and Knowledge Discovery Series. CRC Press
[25] Rogel-Salazar, J. (2020). *Advanced Data Science and Analytics with Python*. Chapman & Hall/CRC Data Mining and Knowledge Discovery Series. CRC Press

Does the method of learning Python make a difference for Starfleet recruits?

Instructor	Holographic Communicator	Project & Book
81.4	75.4	85.1
90.4	100.0	95.5
85.2	83.2	93.8
100.0	80.7	100.0
98.9	78.9	88.2
89.0	78.2	91.7
90.7	84.8	93.2

Table 6.10: Results of the different methods to learn Python for Data Science at Starfleet Academy.

```
instructor = [81.4, 90.4, 85.2, 100.0, 98.9,
    89.0, 90.7]
holographic = [75.4, 100.0, 83.2, 80.7, 78.9,
    78.2, 84.8]
project_book = [85.1, 95.5, 93.8, 100.0, 88.2,
    91.7, 93.2]


df = pd.DataFrame({'instructor': instructor,
    'holographic': holographic,
    'project_book': project_book})
```

We capture the data from Table 6.10 in a pandas dataframe.

Let us look at the median for each method of learning:

```
> df.median()
instructor      90.4
holographic     80.7
project_book    93.2
```

The medians are different, but is the difference statistically significant?

And now we run our statistical test:

```
> from scipy.stats import kruskal
> hstat, p = kruskal(df['instructor'],
  df['holographic'], df['project_book'])
> print('stat = {0:.4f}, p-value= {1:.4f}'.
  format(hstat, p))


stat = 6.7188, p-value= 0.0348
```

Running a Kruskal-Wallis test indicated that the differences are indeed statistically significant.

With an H statistic of 6.7188 and a p-value lower than 0.05, we reject the null hypothesis for a 95% confidence level and conclude that there are differences in the medians for the three different methods of learning.

6.7.5   Two-factor or Two-way ANOVA

WE KNOW HOW TO ASSESS the impact of one factor in a response variable over a number of groups with a one-factor ANOVA. We may also be interested in the impact of two factors on the response variable and get a sense of whether there is an interaction between the two factors in question. In those cases we need to use a two-factor ANOVA.

See Section 6.7.1 for one-factor ANOVA.

When the interactions are important, we need to have multiple measurements for each combination of the levels of the two factors in our analysis. Two-way ANOVA also requires that the samples at each factor level combination are normally distributed, and that the samples have a common variance. We can organise our data in a tabular form such that we have one factor in the columns and another one in the rows as show in Table 6.11.

There are several requirements to run a two-way ANOVA.

Factor R	Factor C				
	Level C_1	Level C_2	$\ldots$	Level C_c	
Level R_1	$x_{R_1C_11}$ $x_{R_1C_12}$ $\vdots$ $x_{R_1C_1n}$	$x_{R_1C_21}$ $x_{R_1C_22}$ $\vdots$ $x_{R_1C_2n}$	$\ldots$ $\ldots$ $\ddots$ $\ldots$	$x_{R_1C_c1}$ $x_{R_1C_v2}$ $\vdots$ $x_{R_1C_cn}$	
	$T_{R_1C_1}$	$T_{R_1C_2}$	$\ldots$	$T_{R_1C_c}$	T_{R_1}
Level R_2	$x_{R_2C_11}$ $x_{R_2C_12}$ $\vdots$ $x_{R_2C_1n}$	$x_{R_2C_21}$ $x_{R_2C_22}$ $\vdots$ $x_{R_2C_2n}$	$\ldots$ $\ldots$ $\ddots$ $\ldots$	$x_{R_2C_c1}$ $x_{R_2C_c2}$ $\vdots$ $x_{R_2C_cn}$	
	$T_{R_2C_1}$	$T_{R_2C_2}$	$\ldots$	$T_{R_2C_c}$	T_{R_2}
	$\ddots$	$\ddots$	$\ddots$	$\ddots$	
Level R_r	$x_{R_rC_11}$ $x_{R_rC_12}$ $\vdots$ $x_{R_rC_1n}$	$x_{R_rC_21}$ $x_{R_rC_22}$ $\vdots$ $x_{R_rC_2n}$	$\ldots$ $\ldots$ $\ddots$ $\ldots$	$x_{R_rC_c2}$ $x_{R_rC_c2}$ $\vdots$ $x_{R_rC_cn}$	
	$T_{R_rC_1}$	$T_{R_rC_2}$	$\ldots$	$T_{R_rC_c}$	T_{R_r}
	T_{C_1}	T_{C_2}	$\ldots$	T_{C_c}	T

Table 6.11: A typical data arrangement for a two-factor ANOVA.

We can denote the number of levels in the column factor as c, and the number of levels in the row factor as r. We have N observations, and the observation in the rck cell of our table is x_{rck}, where $r = R_1, R_2, \ldots, R_r$, $c = C_1, C_2, \ldots, C_c$ and $k = 1, 2, \ldots, n$. With this in mind, we have that $T = \sum_r \sum_c \sum_k x_{rck}$ is the sum of all $N = rcn$ observations. In the same manner we have the following sums:

Important notation used in two-way ANOVA.

$$\sum T_R^2 = T_{R_1}^2 + T_{R_2}^2 + \cdots + T_{R_r}^2, \qquad (6.67)$$

$$\sum T_C^2 = T_{C_1}^2 + T_{C_2}^2 + \cdots + T_{C_c}^2, \qquad (6.68)$$

$$\sum T_{RC}^2 = T_{R_1C_1}^2 + T_{R_1C_2}^2 + \cdots + T_{R_rC_c}^2. \qquad (6.69)$$

As with the one-factor ANOVA, we are interested in different sums of squares, and for the two-factor we have some extra ones. Let us take a look:

$$SS_T = \sum_r \sum_c \sum_k x_{rck}^2 - \frac{T^2}{N}, \qquad (6.70) \qquad \text{Total sum of squares.}$$

$$SS_R = \frac{\sum T_R^2}{nc} - \frac{T^2}{N}, \qquad (6.71) \qquad \text{Sum of squares between rows.}$$

$$SS_C = \frac{\sum T_C^2}{nr} - \frac{T^2}{N}, \qquad (6.72) \qquad \text{Sum of squares between columns.}$$

$$SS_{RC} = \frac{\sum T_{RC}^2}{n} - \frac{T^2}{N} - SS_R - SS_C, \qquad (6.73) \qquad \text{Sum of squares of interactions.}$$

$$SS_E = SS_T - SS_R - SS_C - SS_{RC}, \qquad (6.74) \qquad \text{Residual sum of squares.}$$

As we did in Section 6.7.1, we need to calculate mean squares quantities from the sums above, dividing by the corresponding degrees of freedom. The degrees of freedom follow this relationship: $N - 1 = (r - 1) + (c - 1) + (r - 1)(c - 1) + rc(n - 1)$.

Source of Variation	Sum of Squares	Degrees of Freedom	Mean Square	F Statistic
Between rows	SS_R	$r-1$	MS_R	$\frac{MS_R}{MS_E}$
Between columns	SS_C	$c-1$	MS_C	$\frac{MS_C}{MS_E}$
Interaction	SS_{RC}	$(r-1)(c-1)$	MS_{RC}	$\frac{MS_{RC}}{MS_E}$
Residual	SS_E	$rc(n-1)$	MS_E	
Total	SS_T	$N-1$		

Table 6.12: Table summarising the results of a two-way analysis of variance (two-way ANOVA).

The logic is the same as for one-way ANOVA, and we look at the F distribution to assess our hypothesis. For two-way ANOVA we have the following set of null hypotheses:

Remember that the F statistic is the ratio of the mean squares in question. See Equation (6.55).

- The sample means for the first factor are all equal

- The sample means for the second factor are all equal

The hypotheses of a two-way ANOVA.

- There is no interaction between the two factors

The first and second hypotheses are equivalent to performing a one-way ANOVA for either the row or the column factor alone. We can use a table to summarise the results of a two-factor ANOVA, as shown in Table 6.12.

Sometimes it is useful to look at the degree of association between an effect of a factor or an interaction, and the dependent variable. This can be thought of as a form of correlation between them, and the square of the measure can be considered as the proportion of variance in the

This is effectively the amount of variance that is explainable by the factor in question.

dependent variable that is attributable to each effect. Two widely-used measures for the effect size are the eta-squared, η^2, and omega-squared, ω^2:

$$\eta^2 = \frac{SS_{effect}}{SS_T},$$

(6.75)

$$\omega^2 = \frac{SS_{effect} - \nu_{effect}MS_E}{MS_E + SS_T},$$

(6.76)

where ν_{effect} is the degrees of freedom for the effect.

Let us expand on our study of Python learning among Starfleet Academy. We know that the recruits are assigned to 3 delivery methods of learning as described in Section 6.7.4: instructor, holographic communicator, and project. We are now also encouraging them to revise, and they are assigned 2 methods: mock exams and weekly quizzes. We would like to conduct a two-way ANOVA that compares the mean score for each level of delivery combined with each level of revision.

Our Starfleet recruits are now encouraged to revise using 2 methods. A two-way ANOVA looking at method of delivery and revision combined can be run.

The dataset for this is available at[26] `https://doi.org/10.6084/m9.figshare.19208676.v1` as a comma-separated value file with the name "Python_Study_Scores.csv". Let us read the data into a pandas dataframe:

[26] Rogel-Salazar, J. (2022c, Feb). Python Study Scores. https://doi.org/10.6084/m9.figshare.19208676.v1

```
import pandas as pd
df = pd.read('Python_Study_Scores.csv')
```

Let us look at the mean scores per delivery and revision methods. We can do this easily via a pivot table with pandas:

```
> table = pd.pivot_table(df, values='Score',
   index=['Delivery'], columns=['Revision'],
   aggfunc=np.mean)
> print(table)


Revision      Mock Exam  Weekly Quiz

Delivery

Holographic      90.85        74.89

Instructor       94.31        86.42

Project          96.28        87.33
```

A pivot table can let us summarise the mean scores of delivery v revision.

Let us now run our two-way ANOVA. We do this with the help of a linear model as we did in Section 6.7.1:

```
> formula = 'Score ~ C(Delivery) + C(Revision) +
   C(Delivery):C(Revision)'
> model = ols(formula, df).fit()
> aov_table = sm.stats.anova_lm(model, typ=2)
```

We run our two-way ANOVA with the help of a linear model and the anova_lm method.

Notice that in this case our model takes into account each of the factors and the interaction:

$$\text{Score} = \beta_0 + \beta_d * \text{Delivery} + \beta_r * \text{Revision} +$$
$$\beta_{dr} * \text{Delivery} * \text{Revision}.$$

We can apply the same function we created in Section 6.7.1 to the resulting table from our code above, giving us information about the mean squares:

```
> anova_summary(aov_table)


                              sum_sq      df
C(Delivery)                920.552333    2.0
C(Revision)               1793.066667    1.0
C(Delivery):C(Revision)    192.314333    2.0
Residual                  1046.096000   54.0
Total                     3952.029333   59.0


   mean_sq              F            PR(>F)
460.2761667      23.75968649       3.96E-08
1793.066667      92.55900032       2.64E-13
96.15716667      4.963681154      0.010497559
19.37214815            NaN             NaN
        NaN            NaN             NaN
```

The two-way ANOVA summary for our study of Python learning among Starfleet recruits.

For a 95% confidence level, since the p-values for `Delivery` and `Revision` are both less than 0.05, we can conclude that both factors have a statistically significant effect on the score, rejecting the null hypothesis that the means for each factor are all equal. We can now turn our attention to the interaction effect, with $F(2, 54) = 4.9636$ and $p = 0.010$, indicating that there is a significant interaction between the delivery and revision methods on the score obtained.

We reject the null hypothesis for each of the factors.

But there is a statistically significant interaction between them.

If we are interested in the effect sizes, we can apply the following function to our results table:

```
def effect_sizes(aov):
    aov['eta_sq'] = 'NaN'
```

```
aov['eta_sq'] = aov[:-1]['sum_sq']/
    sum(aov['sum_sq'])
mse = aov['sum_sq'][-1]/aov['df'][-1]
aov['omega_sq'] = 'NaN'
aov['omega_sq'] = (aov[:-1]['sum_sq']-
    (aov[:-1]['df']*mse))/(sum(aov['sum_sq'])+mse)
return aov
```

A function to calculate η^2 and ω^2 for a two-way ANOVA. See Equations (6.75) and (6.76).

Applying this function to the results above, will add the following columns:

	eta_sq	omega_sq
C(Delivery)	0.232932	0.222040
C(Revision)	0.453708	0.446617
C(Delivery):C(Revision)	0.048662	0.038669
Residual	NaN	NaN

6.8   Tests as Linear Models

WE HAVE BEEN DISCUSSING AN entire zoo of statistical tests. It is useful to understand the different assumptions behind them and familiarise ourselves with the names that others use for them so that we can understand the results and interpretations for the given data. A lot of these tests can be expressed in a more familiar way. Take for instance the ANOVA test in Section 6.7 where we appealed to expressing the result in terms of a linear model. It turns out that many of the tests we have described can be expressed in terms of a linear model too.

A lot of the tests we have explored can be expressed as linear models!

6.8.1   Pearson and Spearman Correlations

WE START WITH A LINEAR model such that:

$$y = \beta_0 + \beta_1 x. \qquad (6.77)$$

For the Pearson correlation, the null hypothesis corresponds to having a zero slope in our model, i.e. $H_0 : \beta_1 = 0$. We use Statsmodels instead of `scipy.stats.pearson(x,y)`:

The Pearson correlation corresponds to $H_0 : \beta_1 = 0$ in our linear model.

```
import statsmodels.formula.api as smf


smf.ols('y ~ 1 + x', data)
```

The linear model will give you the slope, not the coefficient r. If you require the correlation coefficient simply scale the data by the standard deviation.

For the Spearman correlation we simply take the rank of the data and so the model is:

$$\mathrm{rank}(y) = \beta_0 + \beta_1 \mathrm{rank}(x). \qquad (6.78)$$

The Spearman correlation requires us to take the rank of the data.

Instead of using `scipy.stats.spearman(x,y)` we can use Statsmodels:

```
smf.ols('y ~ 1 + x', rank(data))
```

6.8.2   *One-sample t- and Wilcoxon Signed Rank Tests*

IN ONE-SAMPLE TESTS, WE are interested in a single number. For a one-sample *t*-test we have:

$$y = \beta_0, \qquad (6.79)$$

and our null hypothesis corresponds to $H_0 : \beta_0 = 0$. Instead of using `scipy.stats.1samp(y)` we can use Statsmodels as follows:

In a one-sample *t*-test we have $H_0 : \beta_0 = 0$.

```
smf.ols('y ~ 1', data)
```

For the Wilcoxon signed rank we simply take the signed rank of the data:

$$\text{signed\_rank}(y) = \beta_0. \qquad (6.80)$$

For the Wilcoxon test, we need to take the rank of the data.

This approximation is better as the number of observations is large, and good enough for $n > 14$. Instead of using `scipy.stats.wilcoxon(y)` we can use Statsmodels:

```
smf.ols('signed_rank(y) ~ 1', data)
```

where we have defined the following function to calculate the signed rank:

```
def signed_rank(df):
    return np.sign(df) * df.abs().rank()
```

A function to calculate signed ranks.

6.8.3 Two-Sample t- and Mann-Whitney Tests

FOR TWO-SAMPLE TESTS, WE are interested to know if a data point belongs to one group (0) or the other (1). We can use a dummy variable x_i as an indicator for the group, and thus the linear model can be expressed as:

$$y = \beta_0 + \beta_1 x_i, \tag{6.81}$$

For the two-sample independent t-test our null hypothesis corresponds to $H_0 : \beta_1 = 0$. Instead of using `scipy.stats.ttest_ind(y1, y2)` we can use Statsmodels:

For the two-sample independent t-test we have that $H_0 : \beta_1 = 0$.

```
smf.ols('y ~ 1 + group', data)
```

where `group` is a dummy variable for each of the two samples.

For the Mann-Whitney test we simply take the signed rank of the data:

For the Mann-Whitney test we need signed ranked data.

$$\text{signed\_rank}(y) = \beta_0 + \beta_1 x_i. \tag{6.82}$$

This approximation is better as the number of observations is large, and good enough for $n > 11$. Instead of using `scipy.stats.mannwhitney(y1, y2)` we can use Statsmodels to fit linear model:

```
smf.ols('y ~ 1 + group', signed_rank(data))
```

6.8.4   *Paired Sample t- and Wilcoxon Matched Pairs Tests*

WHEN WE HAVE PAIRED DATA, we are after a single number
that predicts pairwise differences. Our linear model can
then be written as:

$$y_2 - y_1 = \beta_0, \qquad (6.83)$$

and we can actually simplify this as $y = y_2 - y_1$. This
means that we can express this as a one-sample t test on the
pairwise differences. Our null hypothesis is to $H_0 : \beta_0 = 0$.
Instead of using `scipy.stats.ttest_rel(y1, y2)` we can
use Statsmodels, provided we calculate `diff_y2_y1=y1-y2`:

For a paired sample *t*-test we have $H_0 : \beta_0 = 0$.

```
smf.ols('diff_y2_y ~ 1', data)
```

For the Wilcoxon matched pairs test we simply take the
signed rank of the data:

$$\text{signed\_rank}(y_2 - y_1) = \beta_0. \qquad (6.84)$$

For the Wilcoxon matched pairs test we need singed ranked data.

This approximation is better as the number of observations
is large, and good enough for $n > 14$. Instead of using
`scipy.stats.wilcoxon(y1, y2)` we can use Statsmodels:

```
smf.ols('diff_y2_y ~ 1', signed_rank(data))
```

6.8.5   *One-way ANOVA and Kruskal-Wallis Test*

WE HAVE SEEN THE RELATIONSHIP between ANOVA and
the linear model before, but we can summarise it here as

follows: For one mean for each group we have a model:

$$y = \beta_0 + \beta_1 x_1 + \cdots + \beta_k x_k, \qquad (6.85)$$

We have already explored the relationship of ANOVA with a linear model.

where x_i are group indicators $(0, 1)$ created as dummy variables. The null hypothesis is therefore $H_0 : y = \beta_0$.

Notice that when we have two groups, the test reverts to the equivalent of the independent two-sample t-test, and when there is one group we recover the one-sample t-test. We saw in Section 6.7.1 how we can use Statsmodels instead of `scipy.stats.f_oneway`.

In the case of the Kruskal-Wallis test we need to take the rank of the data:

$$\mathrm{rank}(y) = \beta_0 + \beta_1 x_1 + \cdots + \beta_k x_k. \qquad (6.86)$$

For the Kuskal-Wallis test we need to rank our data.

Et voilà!

7

Delightful Details – Data Visualisation

WHEN LOOKING AT ANSWERING QUESTIONS for research, business decisions or simply to understand and explain things to ourselves, the tools and techniques that we have described in the previous chapters are invaluable. We are able to make sound comparisons and draw conclusions based on evidence. In many occasions, however, simply presenting a table of numbers, or the result of a statistical test and its significance, is not enough. Results are more impactful and call to action when using visual tools to bring the message home.

Simply presenting a table of numbers or the results of a statistical test may not be enough.

We mentioned briefly in Section 1.6 that representing data in tables may work well for some, but there is something to be said about thinking critically about the design choices that help putting across a message that we wish to convey. We are talking about telling a story and we should consider at least the what, who and how for that story to drive meaning. In this chapter we will cover some background on the importance of visual representation and design, particularly

We need to consider the what, who and how for that story to drive meaning.

in the context of presenting statistical quantities. We will then look at how matplotlib helps us with the creation of charts, and cover some best practices when creating data visualisations.

7.1   Presenting Statistical Quantities

PRESENTING STATISTICAL INFORMATION REQUIRES US not only to consider the data and the analysis we have performed (or are performing), but also our target audience. In some cases, the creation of infographics is suitable, but in general, a well-crafted visualisation with visual integrity and excellence is far more powerful. Generally speaking, data can be presented in three ways: Text, tabular or graphical form. The best method is, as always, determined by the data itself, including its format and location. We also need to consider the method of analysis used, and the message we need to convey.

More about visual integrity in Section 7.3.

A table may be more appropriate in situations where all the information requires equal attention or when we want to enable viewers to pick the data of their interest. Similarly, when referring to certain data points in a written paragraph, a table can be of help. In contrast, a graphical representation will enable viewers to have a more general overview of the data. We can use the visual elements described in the previous section to help our viewers understand the results and draw their attention to specific aspects. Let us take a look at each of the methods mentioned above.

A table is appropriate when all information requires equal attention.

A plot can let us get a general overview of the data.

7.1.1 *Textual Presentation*

THIS METHOD OF PRESENTATION IS one that we are all familiar with. It conveys information in writing and where information is presented in sentences, paragraphs, sections, etc. Think of a report or an essay where we are able to provide explanations and interpretations. We need to have clarity in our writing, and this is helped by organising our thoughts into meaningful sentences.

For textual representation, think of a report.

When the statistical information to be conveyed is a few numbers, textual presentation may be suitable. Think for example of summary statistics. However, as the numbers increase, it may be more suitable to use a different kind of presentation, for instance if the message is about trends we may prefer to show a graph.

Use it when there are only a few numbers to be presented.

7.1.2 *Tabular Presentation*

A TABLE IS A SYSTEMATIC summary of statistical information organised into rows and columns. A good table is accompanied by a reference number, a title and a description of the rows and columns included. Tables are most appropriate to use when individual pieces of information are required to be presented.

A distinctive advantage of using tables is that we are able to present both quantitative and qualitative information. We are able to present data that may be difficult to show in a graph, for example by showing figures within a significant

A table lets us present quantitative and qualitative data.

number of decimal places. They also let us present data that
may be expressed in different units or dimensions in a way
that summarises the data. The data in a table must be
organised in a way that lets the viewer draw comparisons
between different components, and therefore balance
between its length and breadth is important. In this way,
anyone is able to understand the data presented.

A table must find balance between
its length and breadth.

Since the data in a table receive the same importance, tables
must be avoided when appealing to the viewer to select
information or when emphasis is required. Using coloured
tables such as heatmaps may support required emphasis,
but one may argue that heatmap tables fall into the category
of graphical presentation.

Avoid using tables if specific data
needs to be emphasised.

7.1.3   Graphical Presentation

THE USE OF GRAPHICS IN statistics is a combination that
should be up there together with great partnerships: R2-D2
and C3-PO, Moulder and Scully, Thelma and Louise, Spock
and Kirk, Batman and Robin, or peanut butter and jelly.
Graphical representation lets us simplify and summarise
complex information through the use of visual elements.
Unlike tables, where individual pieces of information are
presented, graphical representation lets us take a look at the
bigger picture, letting the viewer capture trends, patterns
and relationships in a faster and more concise way.

Many other great couples can be
included here.

No pun intended.

A graphical presentation for our data requires the choice
of visual elements that help us understand the information
encoded in them. In the next chapter we will explore a

variety of graphs from line and bar charts, to scatter plots or histograms. Before we get there, there are a few things that we need to take into account to be able to choose a chart that most appropriately presents the data at hand, and the message we need to convey. Shall we take a look?

We will cover these in more detail in Chapter 8.

7.2   Can You Draw Me a Picture? – Data Visualisation

THEY SAY THAT A PICTURE is worth a thousand words, and if that picture helps make better decisions it may be worth even more. Think, for example, of a recent news article you have read: There would have been one or two key numbers that are suitable to understand the issue in the article, but whenever there is more complex information to capture, our brain is better equipped at understanding patterns, differences and relationships in a visual way. Surely you can do that in words alone, but a visualisation is able to present the key information in a more compact, accessible and faster way. That does not mean that any old picture would do. We all have seen bad visualisations. This is why understanding some ideas behind design and representation comes handy when using pictures to help tell our data stories.

Our brain is better equipped at understanding patterns, differences and relationships visually.

Having some design understanding is of great help.

Data visualisation can be thought of as the representation of data using charts, text, colours, infographics and even animations. Its aim is to display simple, and complex, information to understand relationships, differences and patterns to reveal important details that help transform information into knowledge. It is important to mention that

Data visualisation is the representation of data with charts, text, colours, etc.

data visualisation is not the exclusive realm of designers, or for that matter of data and statistical teams. On the contrary, data visualisation can be used by anyone that requires to tell a story with data, with the aim to generate thoughts, illustrate ideas or discover meaning.

Data visualisation is for everyone!

Let us look at an example. Consider the dataset available at[1] `https://doi.org/10.6084/m9.figshare.19221666.v3` as a comma-separated value file with the name "`jackalope.csv`". Let us load that into a pandas dataframe and look at some descriptive statistics:

[1] Rogel-Salazar, J. (2022b, Feb). Jackalope Dataset. https://doi.org/ 10.6084/m9.figshare.19221666.v3

```
> import pandas as pd
> df = pd.read_csv('jackalope.csv')
> df.shape


(261, 3)
```

We have a dataset with 261 observations and 3 columns.

We can see that we have 3 columns and 261 data observations. We can ask pandas for a description:

```
> df.describe()
                 x              y
count   261.000000     261.000000
mean     14.311111      16.172414
std       6.901846       6.751804
min       1.600000       1.000000
25%       9.150000      12.100000
50%      13.500000      18.100000
75%      19.900000      21.100000
max      28.300000      27.400000
```

Some descriptive statistics for our Jackalope dataset.

We obtain the mean and standard deviation for the dataset
in a matter of seconds. We can even ask for a correlation
matrix:

```
> df.corr()

           x          y

x   1.000000  -0.034559

y  -0.034559   1.000000
```

We seem to have a bit of a
negative correlation between
columns x and y.

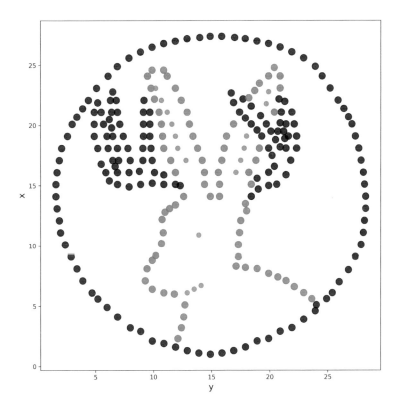

Figure 7.1: A scatter plot for the
jackalope.csv dataset.

It is perhaps not the strongest anticorrelation and we may
want to check if it is statistically significant. However, before
we do any of that, let us look at a scatter plot of the data.
The result is shown in Figure 7.1.

What happened there? Well, although we are able to obtain descriptive statistics and actually run statistical analysis on the data, it turns out that in this case the dataset contains a picture of a cute jackalope. Had we not looked at the data before, we could have started an extensive analysis on a dataset that makes no sense.

Our dataset encodes a picture of a jackalope... not real data to be analysed!

Furthermore, it may be that we are facing datasets whose descriptive statistics are very similar, but whose underlying distributions are very different. This is a point that is best described with the help of the so-called Anscombe's quartet. In 1973 Frank J. Anscombe presented[2] four datasets consisting of eleven points each. They all have identical descriptive statistics, but the distributions are very different. Let us take a look at the dataset, available at[3] `https://doi.org/10.6084/m9.figshare.19221720.v3` as a comma-separated value file with the name "`anscombe.csv`". Let us load the data into a pandas dataframe and take a look:

[2] Anscombe, F. J. (1973). Graphs in statistical analysis. *The American Statistician 27*(1), 17–21

[3] Rogel-Salazar, J. (2022a, Feb). Anscombe's Quartet. https://doi.org/ 10.6084/m9.figshare.19221720.v3

```
> df = pd.read_csv('anscombe.csv')
> df.head(3)

  Dataset   x     y
0       A  10  8.04
1       A   8  6.95
2       A  13  7.58
```

Loading the Anscombe quartet data to pandas.

The data is organised in long form, with each of the four datasets identified by a letter from A to D. Let us group the data and look at the mean and standard deviations:

```
> df.groupby('Dataset').agg({'x': ['mean', 'std'],
  'y': ['mean', 'std']})


                  x                   y
           mean        std       mean        std

  Dataset

  A          9.0   3.316625   7.500909   2.031568

  B          9.0   3.316625   7.500909   2.031657

  C          9.0   3.316625   7.500000   2.030424

  D          9.0   3.316625   7.500909   2.030579
```

The mean and standard deviations of the four groups are the same.

As we can see, the mean and standard deviations are virtually the same. Let us see the correlation:

```
df.groupby('Dataset').corr()


                   x          y
  Dataset

  A       x   1.000000   0.816421

          y   0.816421   1.000000

  B       x   1.000000   0.816237

          y   0.816237   1.000000

  C       x   1.000000   0.816287

          y   0.816287   1.000000

  D       x   1.000000   0.816521

          y   0.816521   1.000000
```

The correlation between the variables in each dataset is also the same.

Once again, the correlation coefficients are effectively indistinguishable. Should we use any of these datasets to perform a regression analysis, we would end up with the same line of best fit. You may think that is great, until you look at the graphic representation of these datasets as shown in Figure 7.2.

However, when we plot the data we see how different the sets are.

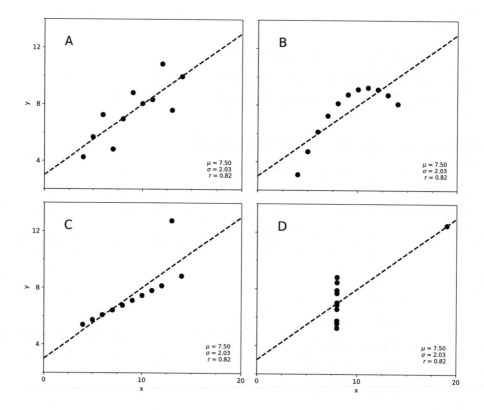

Figure 7.2: Anscombe's quartet. All datasets have the same summary statistics, but they have very different distributions.

Without looking at the data, we could have used a linear model to explain data that is clearly not linear, as shown for example for dataset B; or used a regression for continuous variables for something that may well be categorical, for example dataset D.

It is quite unlikely that when collecting data we end up with a pattern like the jackalope one shown in Figure 7.1. However, I hope you get the idea behind the importance of visualising your data. It helps us in many important things such as:

- Record information: Answer questions, make decisions, contextualise data

  Some great reasons to use visualisation for our data.

- Support reasoning: Develop and assess hypotheses, detect anomalies, find patterns

- Communicate: Present arguments, persuade others, collaborate and find solutions.

Before we are able to run our analyses, and even before we consider what charts are best for our purposes, it is good to take a step back and consider the way our datasets are organised. Not only are we interested in cleaning and curating our data, but we may want to consider if the sets contain information that may be chronological or temporal in nature, spatial or geographical, qualitative or quantitative. It is useful to revise some type of data as this will help choose not just the best visualisation, but also the most appropriate method of analysis.

An important step is to look at how our data is organised.

- Nominal data: Refers to the use of names or labels in the data. For example, robot types: Astromech, Protocol droid, Cylon Centurion, Cylon "toaster", Soong-type synthetic intelligence android-lifeform, etc. A suitable operation for this kind of data is to check for equality using $=$ or $\neq$ operators

  Nominal data use names or labels.

- Ordered data: Refers to the use of natural ordering of the data in question. For example t-shirt sizes: Small, medium, large and extra large. Suitable operators include: $=, \neq, <, >$

- Interval data: This is data that is measured along a scale on which each point is placed at an equal distance from any other point. The location of 0 may be arbitrary. We cannot divide or multiply this data, simply add or subtract it. For example, temperature scale in centigrade, or dates.

- Ratio data: This data has an absolute 0 and, like the interval data above, it uses continuous intervals where a ratio between different data points is available so that we are able to measure proportions. For example, counts and amounts of money in Republic credits, Mexican Pesos, Euros or Pound Sterling.

With this in mind, we can start thinking of creating impactful graphics that support the activities mentioned above and consider the type of data we have at hand. Before we do that, it is useful to consider some aspects of data representation and design. Let us have a look.

7.3   Design and Visual Representation

CREATING A VISUALISATION BASED ON data requires us to think not only of the data available, but also the different visual elements that help us represent the data in a meaningful way. Design principles that help us determine

Ordered data exploits natural ordering in the observations.

Interval data is measured along a scale.

Ratio data lets us measure proportions.

We need to consider the visual elements that we want to include.

what a "good" representation is should be considered and we may learn a thing of two from Edward Tufte, a leading voice in the area of information design and data visualisation. As a matter of fact, the outline of this book follows some of his ideas[4]. We will not do justice to the volume of work from Tufte, but we will draw some general principles that may help us in our quest to find good representations for our data and information.

[4] Tufte, E. (2022). The Work of Edward Tufte and Graphics Press. https://www.edwardtufte.com/tufte/. Accessed: 2022-23-02

Considering that we are interested in using visualisation to help our communication, we can argue that a "good" representation is one that is the most fit for our purpose for maximum benefit. Unfortunately, this means that there is not a single representation that fits all cases, and therefore we need to consider different criteria to help us get there. Tufte talks about "graphical excellence" in terms of usability. In other words, it is the representation of data that provides the user with the greatest number of ideas in the shortest time, using the least amount of ink in the smallest space. Notice that this is different from having a purely decorative image. For a data representation to be of graphical excellence it needs to offer value.

There is not one single "good" representation for our data.

Graphical excellence provides the user with the greatest number of ideas in the shortest time.

Part of that value comes from the fact that the data representation requires "visual integrity". What Tufte talks about in this respect is almost a moral requirement, in the sense that the representation chosen should not distort the underlying data and it should not create a false impression or interpretation. For example, the dimensions used in an image should be dictated by the data itself. Any variations that happen in the representation should relate to the data

Visual integrity implies not distorting the underlying data. It avoids creating a false interpretation or impression.

itself, and not to the creative choices that we may have in the design. For instance, we should not exaggerate a rise or fall in a curve, or use arbitrary starting points in our axes. If we use legends or keys, these should be presented only when necessary and should not be distorted or ambiguous.

Be true to your data!

This brings us to the idea of "maximising the data-ink ratio" which refers to removing superfluous elements from our data representation. Extra elements such as backgrounds, 3D elements or icons may simply distract from the information we are trying to present. Data-ink is defined by Tufte as the ink that is used for the presentation of the data, the data-ink ratio is thus:

We should remove superfluous elements from our visualisations.

$$\text{Data-ink ratio} = \frac{\text{Data-ink}}{\text{Total ink used}}. \qquad (7.1)$$

Tufte's data-ink ratio.

If we remove the data-ink, our graphic loses its content. In contrast, non-data-ink is the ink that can be removed and our representation keeps its integrity. Our goal is to design a representation with the highest possible data-ink ratio.

We also need to mention the idea of "graphical elegance". Tufte considers this not in terms of the subjective beauty of the representation, but instead on the balance between the complexity of the data and the simplicity of the design. This can be thought of as the aim of making complex data accessible. That accessibility may be best assessed by the way our brains are able to more easily perceive visual cues. In 1967 Jacque Bertin published his *Semiologie Graphique*[5], later released in an English translation, where he identified visual variables that can be manipulated to encode

This is the balance between data complexity and design simplicity.

[5] Bertin, J. and M. Barbut (1967). *Sémiologie graphique: Les diagrammes, les réseaux, les cartes.* Gauthier-Villars

information. An interpretation based on these visual variables is shown in Figure 7.3.

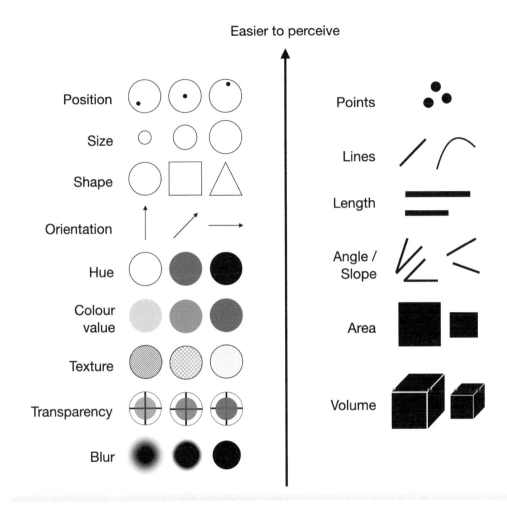

Figure 7.3: Visual variables and their ease of perception.

An important aspect to consider when looking at the visual variables we may want to use is the fact that they are processed by our brain pre-attentively. In other words, they have an impact on us at an immediate level. We can see an example in Figure 7.4, where we are asked to determine how many letters "t" there are in the sequence. By presenting the information in a way that appeals to our pre-attentive perception, we can more easily see that there are 7 letters "t" in panel B. We may be able to describe pre-attentiveness as being "seen" rather than "understood".

Pre-attentive processing is the unconscious cognitive processing of a stimulant prior to attention being engaged.

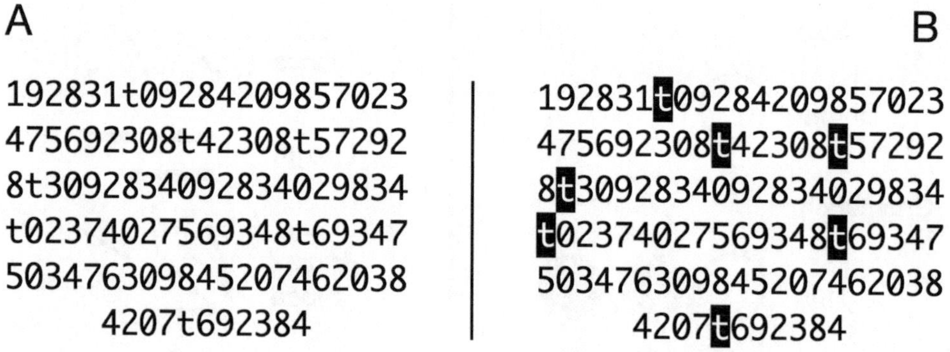

A

192831t09284209857023
475692308t42308t57292
8t3092834092834029834
t02374027569348t69347
50347630984520746 2038
4207t692384

B

192831t09284209857023
475692308t42308t57292
8t3092834092834029834
t02374027569348t69347
50347630984520746 2038
4207t692384

Figure 7.4: How many letters "t" are there in the sequence?

With this in mind, from Figure 7.3, we are able to "see" position more immediately than size, and colour hue more immediately than texture. Similarly, we perceive data points more easily than lines, and we understand differences in length more immediately than differences in area or volume. This is one of the reasons why pie charts, in particular 3D pie charts, are much maligned. We can nonetheless look at comparing areas versus comparing lengths. Take a look at Figure 7.5. We are presented with two circles and are asked to compare the areas. We can tell that one circle is larger than the other one, but it is not immediately obvious by how much. Instead, when we are asked to compare the length

We will cover pie charts in more detail in Section 8.6.

of the bars. We can still tell that one is larger than the other one, but crucially in this case we may be more easily able to tell that the larger bar is about three and a half times longer than the shorter bar.

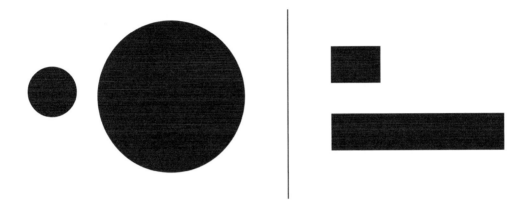

Figure 7.5: Compare the area of the circles v compare the length of the bars.

Combining some of these visual variables in a way that supports graphical excellence can help with communication and usability of our visualisation. Take a look at the pictures shown in Figure 7.6. The use of different shapes immediately helps with distinguishing some points from others. Adding colour differences makes these points jump out of the page.

Graphical excellence in the Tufte sense.

An effectiveness ranking of some of these visual variables is helpfully presented by Jock Mackinlay[6]. The rankings are given in terms of the type of data that is encoded with the visual variables. We present the rankings in Table 7.1 and we can see that position is the highest ranking visual

[6] Mackinlay, J. (1986, Apr). Automating the Design of Graphical Presentations of Relational Information. *ACM Trans. Graph.* 5(2), 110–141

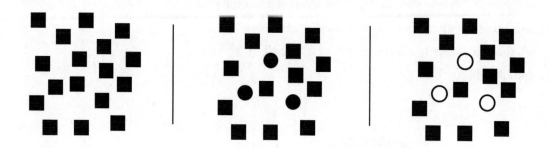

Figure 7.6: Combining visual variables can help our visualisations be more effective.

variable for quantitative, ordinal and nominal data. We can also see that length consistently outranks angle, area and volume. In other words, when presenting data, a viewer may be more easily persuaded to notice a difference in length than a difference in angle or area.

Quantitative	Ordinal	Nominal
Position	Position	Position
Length	Density (Color Value)	Color Hue
Angle	Color Saturation	Texture
Slope	Color Hue	Connection
Area	Texture	Containment
Volume	Connection	Density (Color Value)
Density (Color Value)	Containment	Color Saturation
Color Saturation	Length	Shape
Color Hue	Angle	Length
Texture	Slope	Angle
Connection	Area	Slope
Containment	Volume	Area
Shape	Shape	Volume

Table 7.1: Effectiveness ranking of perceptual tasks for different visual variables.

Another aspect that we have not mentioned before is the textual information that accompanies a visual. The data-ink ratio principle will tell us to minimise superfluous ink. However, in many cases it is preferred, and even unavoidable, to add text to a graphic. Consideration for a suitable typeface is an important area that aids the viewer understand the graphic. We must therefore choose a typeface that makes it easy for a viewer to read short bursts of text such as a heading, bullets or other textual components. Along-side the typeface, we also need to consider the font size, text justification and even colour.

Use a typeface that helps the viewer understand the graphic and consider the font size, colour, or justification.

With a better understanding of the visual variables we can use to encode information, we can turn our attention to the design principles that we can use for our visualisation. Some useful visual design principles that we need to consider include:

Some important visual design principles we need to consider for our data visualisations.

- Balance: How are the visual elements distributed in our visualisation? Are we using a symmetrical or an asymmetrical approach to organising the elements? Is it suitable to organise elements in a radial manner? Are the elements evenly distributed?

- Proximity: How close are the elements that need to be consumed together? Are the elements that are close to each other related?

- Alignment: Are the visual elements suitably aligned vertically, horizontally or diagonally? Are the more important visual elements at the top?

- Emphasis: Are there any visual elements that need to attract more attention? Can we use proximity to bring together or isolate important elements that need to be emphasised? Is there a hierarchical order that we can exploit?

- Contrast: Are there any differences that need to be highlighted?

- Unity: While there are various visual elements in any visualisation, does it feel like they all work together to drive our message? Is there a unifying, harmonious theme, for example by using repetition without becoming monotonous? Are there similar colours, shapes or textures?

As many of us know, design is not a set of ready-made formulae that render perfect results. In many cases, what seems to be a simple and elegant data visualisation may have taken several iterations to be completed so as to distill the complexity into an effective visual. Be prepared to sketch multiple times including with pen and paper. The results will pay off.

Be prepared to have several iterations when preparing data visualisations.

7.4   Plotting and Visualising: Matplotlib

IF WE WANT TO APPLY the principles above in practice, we need to find a way to help us create the graphical elements that are required to bring our data to life via a chart. There are a great number of excellent data visualisation tools, and they all have their advantages and disadvantages. Given that we have been using Python for our discussions in the implementation of statistical analysis, it makes sense to use some of the modules that are available in Python.

We will cover some of these tools in Chapter 8.

There are some really good modules that support very nice visuals such as Seaborn, or interactivity such as Bokeh. The standard library used for plotting in Python is called matplotlib[7] and if you are familiar with MATLAB there is an API called pyplot that uses similar syntax.

Matplotlib supports the object orientation used in Python, and offers a comprehensive set of tools to create static, interactive and animated visualisations. As usual, the first step is to load the module:

```
import numpy as np
import matplotlib.pyplot as plt
```

[7] Hunter, J. D. (2007). Matplotlib: A 2D graphics environment. *Computing in Science & Engineering* 9(3), 90–95

In a Jupyter notebook you can use the magic command %pylab inline to load NumPy and matplotlib.

7.4.1 Keep It Simple: Plotting Functions

IMAGINE YOU REQUIRE TO GRAPH a simple function such as $y = \sin(x)$, and we are interested in creating a graph between $-\pi \leq x \leq \pi$. The first thing we require is to get the necessary data to create the plot. We can generate it with Python by creating an equally spaced vector to hold the values for x, and use that as an input to calculate y. An easy way to create the vector is to use NumPy and its linspace(a,b,n) which creates an n-array between the values a and b.

We want to create a plot of $y = \sin(x)$ for $-\pi \leq x \leq \pi$.

```
> x = linspace(-np.pi ,np.pi, 100)
> y = np.sin(x)
```

We use linspace to create our data.

Finally the plot of the points can be obtained as follows:

```
fig, ax = plt.subplots(figsize=(10, 8))
plt.plot(x, y)
plt.show()
```

We are creating a couple of objects to hold the figure and axes with the subplots method. As you can see, we can specify the size of the figure with a tuple. The show command displays all open figures. Although the command above creates the plot as required, there may be other information that we may want to include such as a suitable different line style or labels and a title.

The result is shown in Figure 7.7, but we have not finished yet.

7.4.2 Line Styles and Colours

BY DEFAULT, THE LINE PLOTS created with matplotlib use solid lines with a colour palette that starts with a pale blue color. If we wanted to specify a blue, solid line we could use the following command:

```
plot(x,y,'b-')
```

This commands creates a line plot with a blue, solid line.

The third argument is a string whose first character specifies the colour, and the second the line style. The options for colours and styles are shown in Table 7.2. We can also indicate the thickness of the line to be used in the plot with the linewidth argument. For example, to create a black, solid line of width 3 we issue the following command:

We can also use the abbreviation lw.

```
plt.plot(x, y, 'k-', linewidth=3)
```

Colours		Styles	
b	blue	o	circle
c	cyan	- .	dash dot
g	green	- -	dashed
k	black	:	dotted
m	magenta	+	plus
r	red	.	point
w	white	-	solid
y	yellow	*	star
		x	x mark

Table 7.2: Colours and line styles that can be used by matplotlib.

7.4.3   Titles and Labels

IT IS USUALLY A VERY good practice to add information that tells the viewer what is being plotted as well as include a descriptive title to the figure. In matplotlib we can add labels and a title with the following methods: xlabel, ylabel and title. For our sinusoidal plot from Section 7.4.1 we want to label the axes x and y and include a title that reads: "Plot of $\sin(x)$". We can do this with the following commands:

Remember, however, the data-ink ratio mentioned in Section 7.3

```
plt.xlabel(r'$x$', fontsize=14)
plt.ylabel(r'$y$', fontsize=14)
plt.title(r'Plot of $\sin(x)$',
    fontsize=16)
```

Adding a title and axes labels.

Please note that we are able to use LaTeX style commands in the annotations, and with the help of fontsize we can dictate the size of the font for each annotation.

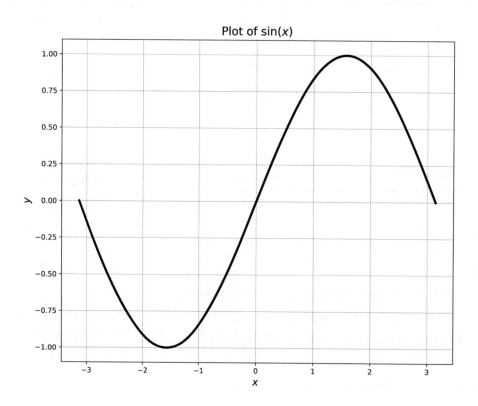

Figure 7.7: Plot of the function $y = \sin(x)$ generated with matplotlib.

7.4.4   Grids

IN SOME CASES THE ADDITION of grids may be helpful to guide the eye of our viewers to some particular values in the plot. We can add a grid in a similar way to the creation of the plot itself:

```
plt.grid(color='gray', ls = '--', lw=0.5)
```

This command adds a grid to our plot.

In this case we have a grey dotted line of width 0.5. The end result of all the commands above can be seen in Figure 7.7.

7.5 *Multiple Plots*

SOME GRAPHICS MAY REQUIRE US to show multiple plots in the same figure. All we need to do is tell matplotlib to use the same axes. Let us create a figure that shows not only $\sin(x)$ but also $\cos(x)$. We replace the code above with the following:

We can add other plots using the same axes.

```
plt.plot(x, y, 'k-', linewidth=3,
    label=r'$\sin(x)$')
plt.plot(x, np.cos(x), 'k--', lw=2,
    label=r'$\cos(x)$')
```

Here we are plotting $\sin(x)$ and $\cos(x)$ in the same chart.

You can see that we have added a new parameter to our commands: label. This helps us add a label to each line so that we can include a legend:

```
plt.legend()
```

We can add a legend to distinguish the plots using the label parameter attached to each series

This will create a text box that provides a list of line–styles, as they appeared in the plot command, followed by the label provided. The end result can be seen in Figure 7.8.

7.6 *Subplots*

WE HAVE SEEN HOW TO plot two line charts in the same axes. This is useful when a comparison between the plots needs to be highlighted. In other cases we may want to create separate figures for each plot. In this case we can exploit the fact that we are using subplots to generate our figure. The

We can use the subplots command to plot our data in separate figures.

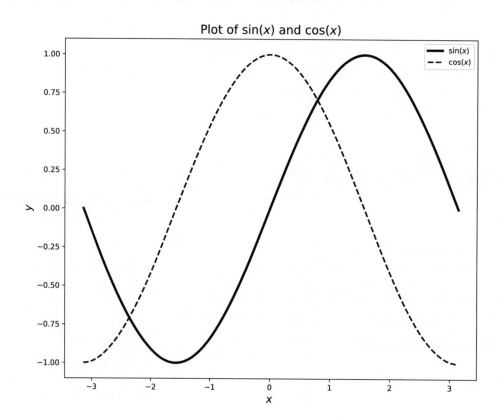

Figure 7.8: Plot of the functions $\sin(x)$ and $\cos(x)$ generated with matplotlib.

arrangement can be achieved with the subplot(m,n), where m and n define the plot array. For example, take a look at the following code:

```
fig, axs = plt.subplots(2, 2, figsize=(10, 8))
axs[0, 0].plot(x, y, 'k-')
axs[0, 1].plot(x, np.cos(x), 'k-')
axs[1, 0].plot(x, x, 'k-')
axs[1, 1].plot(x, x**2, 'k-')
```

We are creating a 2×2 array of plots. We select the axis with the following notation: $[m, n]$.

Apart from specifying the size of the overall figure, the first command contains the following syntax: `subplot(2,2)`. This specifies that the window should be split into a 2×2 array. The object axs is now an array of axes, and we can refer to each one of them with relevant array notation. We can see that we have plotted the $\sin(x)$ and $\cos(x)$ functions in the first two axes, and then we added plots for x and x^2 to the other two.

We could request a figure with m rows and n columns with `subplot(m,n)`.

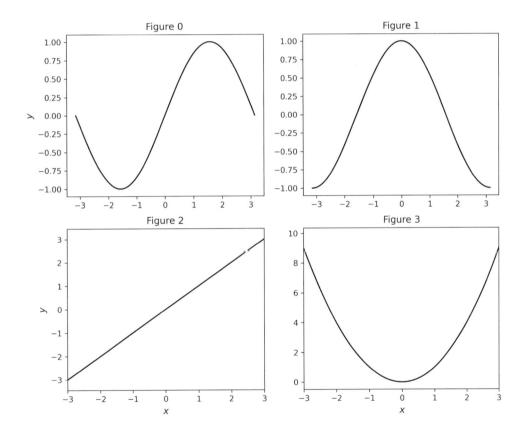

Figure 7.9: Subplots can also be created with matplotlib. Each subplot can be given its own labels, grids, titles, etc.

Each of the axes in the figure has its own title, labels, legend, etc. We can add labels to the x axes for the bottom row of plots, and to the y axes of the first column of plots:

```
axs[1, 0].set_xlabel('$x$', fontsize=12)
axs[1, 1].set_xlabel('$x$', fontsize=12)
axs[0, 0].set_ylabel('$y$', fontsize=12)
axs[1, 0].set_ylabel('$y$', fontsize=12)
```

Each subplot has its own title, labels, legend, etc.

In this example we are using the object-oriented syntax for matplotlib and hence the difference in some commands used in the previous section.

We can modify the range of the axes with the help of set_xlim() and set_ylim(). Here we will change the x limits for the bottom row of axes:

We can specify the axes limits with set_xlim() and set_ylim().

```
axs[1, 0].set_xlim(-3, 3)
axs[1, 1].set_xlim(-3, 3)
```

We can flatten the axs object to run a loop over it. In this case we will add a title counting the number of axes:

```
for i, ax in enumerate(axs.flat):
    ax.set_title('Figure {0}'.format(i))
```

We can set a title for each plot programmatically.

The end result can be seen in Figure 7.9.

7.7   Plotting Surfaces

WE CAN ALSO USE MATPLOTLIB to create graphs in three dimensions. We refer to these graphs as surfaces and they are defined by a function $z = f(x, y)$. We need to specify the fact that we need to plot this in a 3d projection as follows:

```
fig = plt.figure(figsize=(10,8))

ax = plt.axes(projection='3d')
```

We need to specify that we want to plot a surface by specifying a 3D projection.

We also require to consider the range of values for the x and y variables. In this case we are going to use an interval $[-5, 5]$ for both of them. We will use this information to create a grid that contains each of the pairs given by the x and y values. Let us consider a spacing of 0.25 between points; we can therefore calculate x and y as:

```
X = np.arange(-3, 3, 0.25)

Y = np.arange(-3, 3, 0.25)
```

We first specify the range for each of the axes.

and our grid can be calculated with the NumPy command meshgrid:

```
X, Y = np.meshgrid(X, Y)
```

We can then create a mesh to plot our surface.

We can check that the new arrays generated are two-dimensional:

```
> X.shape, Y.shape

((24, 24), (24, 24))
```

We are now able to evaluate our surface. Let us look at the following function:

$$f(x, y) = \exp\left(-x^2 - y^2\right). \tag{7.2}$$

Let us plot a Gaussian function in 3D.

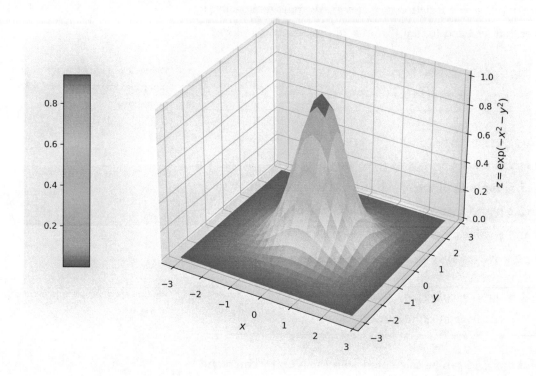

This is a Gaussian function in 3D. In Python we can calculate this as follows:

```
Z = np.exp(-X**2-Y**2)
```

We create our surface as follows:

```
from matplotlib import cm
surf = ax.plot_surface(X, Y, Z, cmap=cm.jet,
    linewidth=0, antialiased=False)
ax.set_zlim(0, 1.01)
```

Figure 7.10: A surface plot obtained with the plot_surface command. Please note that this requires the generation of a grid with the command meshgrid.

We create our surface with plot_surface and provide the arrays X, Y, Z.

Notice that we are importing the cm module which contains colour maps that provide us with colour palettes for our graphs. In Table 7.3 we have the names of the colour maps available in matplotlib.

Let us now add a colour bar to aid with reading the values plotted and include some labels. The result can be seen in Figure 7.10.

```
fig.colorbar(surf, shrink=0.5, aspect=7,
   location='left')
ax.set_xlabel(r'$x$', fontsize=12)
ax.set_ylabel(r'$y$', fontsize=12)
ax.set_zlabel(r'$z=\exp(-x^2-y^2)$', fontsize=12)
plt.show()
```

We finally add a colour bar and some labels.

Sequential	Sequential 2	Diverging	Qualitative	Miscellaneous	Cyclic
Greys	binary	PiYG	Pastel1	flag	twilight
Purples	gist_yarg	PRGn	Pastel2	prism	twilight_shifted
Blues	gist_gray	BrBG	Paired	ocean	hsv
Greens	gray	PuOr	Accent	gist_earth	
Uranges	bone	RdGy	Dark2	terrain	
Reds	pink	RdBu	Set1	gist_stern	
YlOrBr	spring	RoYlBu	Set2	gnuplot	
YOrRd	summer	RaYlGn	Set3	gnuplot2	
OrRd	autumn	Spectral	tab10	CMRmap	
PuRd	winter	coolwarm	tab20	cubehelix	
RdPu	cool	bwr	tab20b	brg	
BuPu	Wistia	seismic	tab20c	gist_rainbow	
GnBu	hot			rainbow	
PuBu	afmhot			jet	
Y GnBu	gist_heat			turoo	
PuBuGn	copper			nipy_spectral	
BuGn				gist_ncar	

Table 7.3: Names of colormaps available in matplotlib.

7.8   Data Visualisation – Best Practices

WITH THE KNOWLEDGE WE NOW have regarding design, visual variables, perception and even matplotlib, we are in a better position to consider more specific points about widely used charts and when they are best suited. We close this chapter with some best practices that will make our work more impactful.

Some best practices that will make our work more impactful.

Visual cues are all around us, and visual communication permeates every aspect of our lives. With so much information presented to us, we may end up becoming blind to the messages encoded in graphics, rendering them ineffective and even forgettable. It is our aim to make decisions that make our data visualisation simple and effective carriers of information. The following areas can help set the scene for this:

Our aim is to communicate effectively with the aim of graphics.

- **If content is King, context is Queen**: Assuming that you have identified a suitable source of reliable data, and it is ready to be used for analysis, you can embark on extracting useful information from it. Your content is ready and without it there is no message. However, it is also important to take into account the overall background of that information, setting the arena for it to become knowledge and drive action. Context is therefore Queen: An equal companion to content

Context provides the audience with tools that make the content more understandable.

- **Message clarity for the appropriate audience**: We have mentioned that data visualisation communicates. If so, what is the message that you need to convey and what is the goal of the visualisation? That clarification can be sharpened by considering who the intended audience for the visualisation is. One thing that I find useful is to think about what the viewer is trying to achieve when presented with the graphic, and take into account the questions they may care about. It is sometimes useful to direct the query to them in the first place. In that way you are more likely to create a visualisation that addresses their needs

Consider the questions a viewer may care about. That will make your visual more meaningful.

- **Choose a suitable visual**: This is easier said than done, but in order to be effective in communicating with a visual, we need to make sure that we are selecting a display that is appropriate for the type of data we need to present. We also need to consider if the audience may be familiar with the graphics we use, particularly if we use complex visualisations. We also need to ensure that the graphical representations we create have integrity in the sense discussed in Section 7.3. It is important that from the first moment the viewer looks at the visual they get an accurate portrayal of the data. Consider what it is that you are showing:

  Select a visual representation appropriate for the type of data to be presented.

  - Comparison: Use bar charts, column charts, line charts, tables or heat maps

  - Relationship: Use a scatter plot or a bubble chart

  - Composition and structure: Use stacked bars or pie charts

    Pie charts only if there are a small number of components.

  - Distribution: Use histograms, box plots, scatter plots or area charts

- **Simplicity is best**: This is a case where the cliché of "less is more" is definitely true. A simple graphic is much more effective than one that has a lot of clutter. Make sure that you include scales and labels on axes. However, you may not need labels in every single data point or every bar in a chart. Are you using a colour palette that is effective in communicating your message and are they accessible to a wide range of viewers? Include only the necessary data and if appropriate add a succinct title

  Just because you can add some visual elements, it does not mean you should. Keep your visuals simple!

- **Iterate and sketch**: A good, effective visualisation may require you to consider different designs, and you should be prepared to take an iterative approach to the task. Sketching your ideas may help bring better, more polished designs that communicate better.

  Do not be afraid to go back to the literal drawing board and iterate.

8

Dazzling Data Designs – Creating Charts

R2-D2 AND C3-PO, SPOCK AND KIRK, Eddie and Patsy,
Tom and Jerry... I am sure you can think of many other
famous couples, and in Chapter 7 we added to the list the
amazing pairing of statistical analysis and data visualisation.
They go so well with one another that it is almost
impossible to think of any statistical analysis that does not
rely on the use of graphics to explore, explain and exhort. In
many cases, we are so used to certain charts, that we need
no further instruction on how to read the information in
them. Nonetheless, when we are trying to paint a picture
with our data, it is useful to remind ourselves of what kind
of data we are able to present with each of them, but also
consider which chart may aid our data story better.

We included Spock and Kirk,
Batman and Robin, and peanut
butter and jelly, among others.

Look at Section 7.8 for some best
practices.

8.1 *What Is the Right Visualisaton for Me?*

DAZZLING DATA DESIGNS CAN BE created more easily when
we consider the general aim of some of the charts we know

Question	Aim	Data Types	Chart
How is the data distributed?	Distribution	1 Continuous	Histogram, Box plot, Violin plot
How often does each value appear?	Comparison	1 Categorical	Bar chart, Pie chart
How do the parts relate to the whole?	Composition	1 Categorical	Bar chart, Stacked bar chart
Is there a trend or pattern?	Trend	1 Continuous & 1 Ordinal	Line chart, Area chart
Is there a correlation between variables?	Relationship	2 Continuous	Scatterplot, Bubble chart
How often do certain values occur?	Comparison	2 Categorical	Heatmap
Are the distributions similar in each grouping?	Distribution & Comparison	1 Continuous & 1 Categorical	Small multiples of 1 continuous with a categorical encoding (e.g. colour)

Table 8.1: Given the question of interest, and the type of data provided, this table provides guidance on the most appropriate chart to use.

and love. In a simplified manner, we can think of several aims for our visualisations. In Table 8.1 we show some of the questions and aims that we may have for our graphics, while taking into account the type of data needed for each. The following are typical use cases:

1. **Distribution**: We are interested to use charts that show us how items are distributed to different parts. Some charts that are useful for this are line charts, histograms and scatter plots.

   For distribution, use line charts, histograms or scatter plots.

2. **Relationship**: A typical use of statistics is to show the relationship between variables. Scatter plots or bubble charts are great choices for this.

   For a relationship, use scatter plots or bubble charts.

3. **Trend**: Sometimes we need to indicate the direction or

   For a trend, use line or bar charts.

tendency of our data over a period of time or over an ordered progression. Line charts or bar charts as well as area charts can help.

4. **Comparison**: We can use visualisations to compare 2 or more variables. Items can be compared with the use if bar charts, heatmaps, pie charts. If we need to compare different partitions of our dataset we can use small multiples.

Small multiples is a series of similar charts that use the same scale and axes. This lets us compare them easily.

5. **Composition**: Sometimes we are interested to find out how the whole is composed of different parts. A typical example of this is a pie chart. Area charts and stacked bar charts are also good for this aim.

For composition, use stacked bars or pie charts.

Following these general guidelines will help you create your dazzling data designs that will inform, persuade and delight. They will help you choose the most appropriate visualisation to use, and save you a lot of time. For example, if you have data that changes over time, a line chart is a good solution. If you have more than one variable over the same period of time, you can present multiple lines in the same graphic. In the case where you need to emphasise how the values rise and fall you may want to experiment using an area chart.

Use the guidelines above to help you select a good chart for your purposes.

For comparisons, a bar chart works really well in the vast majority of cases. Not only is it a chart that needs no explanation, but also uses length as the visual encoding for the comparison, making it really easy for your viewer to understand. If the comparison is over groups of data you can use grouped or stacked bar charts.

Remember the design principles covered in Section 7.3.

To show parts of a whole or talk about proportions, consider using bar charts, stacked bar charts or even pie or donut charts. Remember that areas and angles are more difficult to discern than length, and if you have many parts to show, a pie chart may get too busy.

Bear in mind that areas and angles are more difficult to discern than length.

If what you want to show is a distribution, a histogram or a box plot may be the best choice. Scatter plots let us present a large number of values and display the trend. If you have three variables to encode, a bubble chart lets us encode the third variable in the size of the marker. We will cover each of these choices in more detail later on in this chapter. Before we do that, let us talk about available Python tools that can help us in our task

The tools we wil cover are: matplotlib, pandas, Seaborn, Bokeh and Plotly.

8.2   Data Visualisation and Python

THE NEXT THING TO CONSIDER for creating our data visualisation master pieces is what tools we have at our disposal. There are several options and since this is a book based on Python, we will mention a couple of tools you may want to explore. In the previous chapter we have already talked about matplotlib as the standard module for data visualisation. There are other options and we will briefly introduce them here. We will start with the visualisation capabilities of pandas, making this a really well-rounded module for end-to-end data analysis. We will also introduce a couple of widely-used libraries: Seaborn, Bokeh and Plotly. Later in the chapter we will address the creation of the charts mentioned above using these tools.

See Section 7.4 for more information about matplotlib.

8.2.1   *Data Visualisation with Pandas*

WE KNOW THAT PANDAS IS an excellent companion to manage data structures and data analysis. In Section ?? we covered how pandas can help us make our data analysis much simpler by using series and dataframes. In turn, these objects let us carry out data exploration with the use of various methods. One important method that is part of these objects is the `plot`, which is a wrapper on the plot methods from matplotlib's pyplot. In other words, we can apply this method directly to series or dataframes to create visualisations for the information contained in the objects.

Pandas dataframes have a `plot` method that lets us create data visualisations based on the data in the dataframe.

This means that we can employ similar syntax to that of matplotlib, but apply it directly to the objects. Consider creating the following dataframe based on some random data generated with NumPy. We name the columns in our dataframe A and B and use the `cumsum` method to find the cumulative sum over each column:

Running this in your machine may result in a different outcome.

```
import numpy as np
import pandas as pd


timeSeries = np.random.randn(1000, 2)
df = pd.DataFrame(timeSeries, columns=['A', 'B'])
cm = df.cumsum()
```

Remember that the data may be different in your computer because we are using random numbers.

We can now apply our knowledge of pandas to describe the data and look at some potentially useful information. In this case, we are interested in creating a line plot to visualise the cumulative sum for each column. We can easily do this as follows:

```
import matplotlib.pyplot as plt
cm.plot(style={'A': 'k-', 'B': 'k:'},
title='Time Series Cumulative Sum')
```

We are using the plot method for our dataframe.

Note that we are using the plot method for the pandas dataframe, and we are passing arguments to determine the style of each line. We also add a title to the plot. The styling follows the same syntax discussed in 7.4.2. The result can be seen in Figure 8.1.

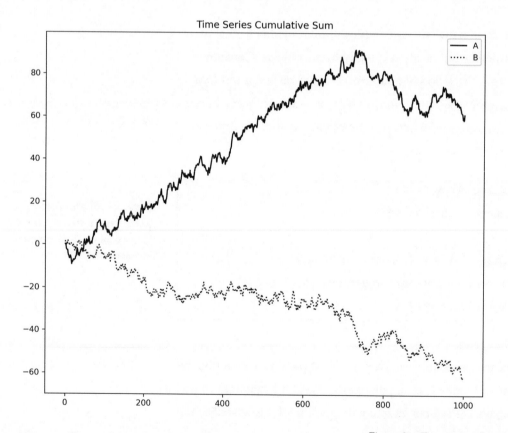

Figure 8.1: Time series plot created with pandas.

As you can see, it is very straightforward to create a line plot. The same philosophy can be used for other charts, and all we need to do is to specify the kind of chart we are interested in with the `kind` parameter, including:

- Bar plots: `'bar'` or `'barh'`

- Histograms: `'hist'`

- Boxplots: `'box'`

We can apply the `kind` parameter to create all these plots with pandas.

- Area plots: `'area'`

- Scatter plots: `'scatter'`

- Pie charts: `'pie'`

We will look at each of these separately in the following pages.

8.2.2   Seaborn

CREATING PLOTS WITH MATPLOTLIB, OR pandas for that matter, seems to be enough, so why use other libraries? The answer to that may become clear when you try to create visualisations that are more than a pair of axes and a few lines or bars. Things can get a very complex, very quickly. Michael Waskom introduced seaborn[1] as a way to simplify some of those complexities via a high-level interface to matplotlib, with close integration to pandas data structures.

[1] Waskom, M. L. (2021). Seaborn: Statistical data visualization. *Journal of Open Source Software 6*(60), 3021

Seaborn understands statistical analysis and this makes it easier to create visualisations that need to communicate statistical results from scratch. Furthermore, the library automatically maps data values to visual attributes such as style, colour and size. It also adds informative labels such as axis names and legends. To use Seaborn all you need to do is install the library, and import it as follows:

Seaborn understands statistical analysis.

```
import seaborn as sns
```

You may find that the standard alias or abbreviation for the library is sns. It is said that the alias was proposed by Waskom as a tribute to the fictional character Samuel Norman Seaborn from the TV show The West Wing, played by Rob Lowe for four seasons.

Great to see I am not alone in giving a nod to favourite fictional characters!

In Seaborn we can specify the dataframe where our data is stored, and operate on the entire object. We can use the columns in the dataset to provide encodings for different attributes such as colour, hue, size, etc. We can re-create the plot from the previous section as follows:

```
sns.set_theme(style='whitegrid')
sns.lineplot(data=cm, palette='dark',
   linewidth=2.5).\
   set(title='Time Series Cumulative Sum')
```

Creating a line plot with Seaborn.

Note that we are specifying a theme for our plot and Seaborn gives us some beautiful styles for our plots. Here we are using one that automatically adds grids for our axes. The line plots are created with the lineplot function and we specify the data to be plotted with the data parameter; you can see that we are also adding a palette to be used and the line width for our graph. Finally, we use the set method to include a title. The end result can be seen in Figure 8.2.

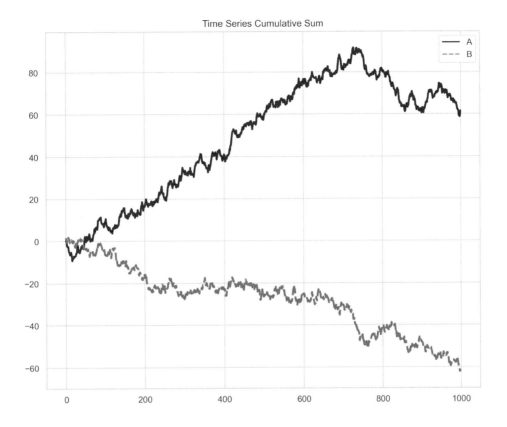

Figure 8.2: Time series plot created with Bokeh.

8.2.3   Bokeh

SOMETIMES IT IS USEFUL TO provide our viewers not only with a chart, but also enable them to interact with it. One tool that lets us do that is Bokeh. Bokeh[2] is a powerful and versatile library with concise syntax to create interactive graphics over large or streaming datasets. The name of the library is taken from the term *bokeh* used in photography, in turn derived from the Japanese word 暈け/ ボ ケ meaning "blur". It refers to the aesthetic quality of the blur produced in images with parts that are out-of-focus.

[2] Bokeh Development Team (2018). Bokeh: Python library for interactive visualization. https://bokeh.pydata.org/en/latest/

The rendering in Bokeh is done directly in HTML and JavaScript. This means that we can extend our creations by adding custom JavaScript. After installing Bokeh in your machine you can call import the following:

Bokeh can be extended with custom JavaScript commands.

```
from bokeh.plotting import figure
from bokeh.io import show, output_notebook
```

The code above assumes we are working on a Jupyter notebook. That is why we are importing the output_notebook function. If you are working on a script, you will probably be better sending the output to a file and you will instead need to import the following:

```
from bokeh.io import output_file
output_file('myfilename.html')
```

We are sending the output to an HTML file.

Note that in the code above we are sending the output to an HTML file with the name myfilename.html.

For us to reproduce the cumulative sum plot from Section 8.2.1 we are adding a column to our cm dataframe to serve as the values for the x-axis:

```
cm['idx'] = cm.index
```

We are adding a column to our dataframe so that we can reproduce our chart with Bokeh.

We are doing this so that we can use the dataframe as a source of data for Bokeh. This will become clearer when we start creating our chart.

The following code creates a Bokeh figure with a given title. We then add different elements to our chart, in this case two lines with data coming from our cm dataframe:

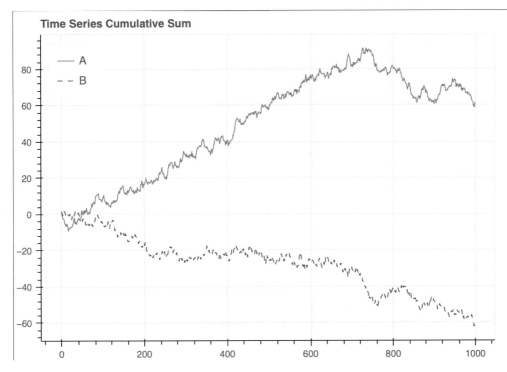

Figure 8.3: Time series plot created with seaborn.

```
p = figure(title = 'Time Series Cumulative Sum')
p.line(x='idx', y='A', source=cm,
    legend_label='A')
p.line(x='idx', y='B', source=cm,
    legend_label='B', line_color='red',
    line_dash='dashed')
p.legend.location = 'top_left'
```

Note that we are adding elements to the p object that holds our Bokeh figure.

We are passing the names of the columns inside the dataframe to the parameters for x and y, indicating the dataframe in the source parameter. In the third code line we are changing the colour and line style. Finally, we indicate to Bokeh where to place the legend with the information

428   J. ROGEL-SALAZAR

given to legend_label for each of the lines. Figure 8.3
shows the chart created. In your notebook or HTML page
you will see a menu that lets you interact with the chart by
panning and zooming and even a way to export your chart.

Bokeh offers interactivity, enjoy it!

8.2.4   Plotly

ANOTHER GREAT TOOL TO CREATE interactive plots is
Plotly[3]. The API is provided by Plotly, a company
headquartered in Quebec, Canada, and offers a number of
open-source and enterprise products. Their JavaScript
library called Plotly.js is offered as open-source and it
powers Plotly.py for Python. They also support other
programming languages such as R, MATLAB, Julia, etc.

[3] Plotly Technologies Inc (2015).
Collaborative data science.
https://plot.ly

We will assume that you are using a Jupyter notebook
to create your Plotly charts. We will be using the Plotly
Express module, which provides functions that let us create
entire figures in a simple way. Plotly Express is part of the
full Plotly library, and is a good starting point to use Plotly.

We will be using the Plotly
Express module.

After installing Plotly you can import Plotly Express as
follows:

```
import plotly.express as px
```

We will be using the original dataframe for our cumulative
sum. We can re-create the chart from Section 8.2 as follows:

```
fig = px.line(cm)
fig.show()
```

The code to re-create our chart in
Plotly is very simple.

The result will be an interactive chart similar to the one shown in Figure 8.4. In your Jupyter notebook you will also find some controls to interact with the plot, letting you pan, zoom, autoscale and export the chart.

Plotly also supports interactivity.

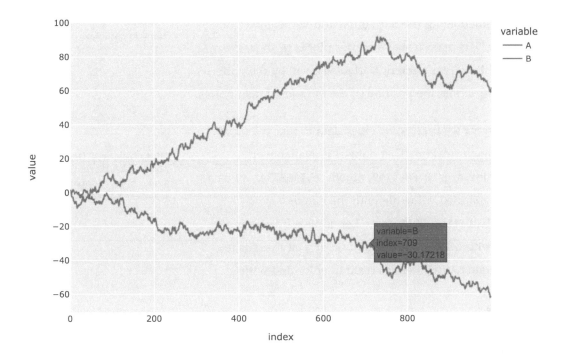

Figure 8.4: Time series plot created with Plotly.

Note that Plotly has automatically added a legend and placed it outside the plot area. It also added labels to the axes and has rendered the plot in a nice looking theme. You can also see that hovering on top of the line gives us information about that part of the plot.

Plotly has automatically added labels, legends, etc. Fantastic!

8.3   Scatter Plot

A SCATTER PLOT DISPLAYS THE values of two different variables as individual points. The data for each point is represented along the horizontal and vertical axes of our chart. The main use of a scatter plot is to show the relationship of two numeric variables given by the pattern that emerges from the position of the individual data points.

A scatter plot uses markers to represent values for two different numeric variables.

In Section 6.4 we used some cities data to take a look at measuring correlation. That dataset is available at[4] `https://doi.org/10.6084/m9.figshare.14657391.v1` as a comma-separated value file with the name "GLA_World_Cities_2016.csv". Let us start by creating a simple scatter plot of the population of a city versus its approximate radius. Let us create the plot first with matplotlib:

[4] Rogel-Salazar, J. (2021a, May). GLA World Cities 2016. https://doi.org/ 10.6084/m9.figshare.14657391.v1

```
fig, ax = plt.subplots(figsize=(10,8))
ax.scatter(x=gla_cities['Population'],
  y=gla_cities['Approx city radius km'], s=50)
ax.set_xlabel('Population')
ax.set_ylabel('Approx city radius km')
ax.set_title('Population v City Radius
  (matplotlib)')
```

Creating a scatter plot with matplotlib.

The result can be seen in Figure 8.5. The position of each dot on the horizontal and vertical axes indicates the value of each of the two variables in question. We can use the plot to visually assess the relationship between the variables.

We are using the attribute s as the size of the dots in the scatterplot.

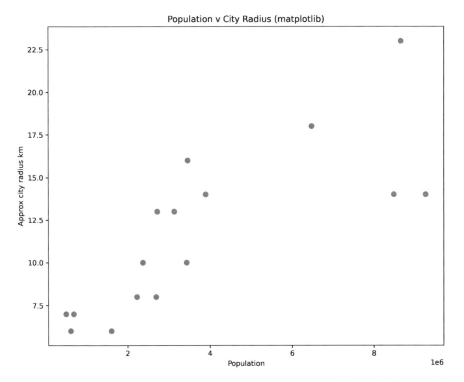

We may want to encode other information in the scatterplot, for example, capture the classification for the size of the city, i.e. Mega, Large, Medium or Small. We can map the categories into a colour map and use this to present the information as the colour of the dot in the scatter plot:

Figure 8.5: Scatterplot of city population versus its approximate radius size. The plot was created with matplotlib.

```
c_map = {'Mega': 'r', 'Large': 'b', 'Medium':
   'g', 'Small': 'black'}
colours = gla cities['City Size'].map(c_map)
```

We want to encode the size of the city in the colour of our markers.

We are colouring Mega with red, Large with blue, Medium with green and Small with black.

432   J. ROGEL-SALAZAR

Let us now create the plot with this new information using pandas with the help of the scatter method. In this case we are using the mapping above as the value passed to the c attribute, which manages the colour of the marker. The result can be seen in Figure 8.6.

We are printing the plots in black and white, but you shall be able to see them in full colour in your computer.

```
gla_cities.plot.scatter(
    x='Population', y='Approx city radius km',
    title="Population v City Radius (pandas)",
    s=50, c=colours)
```

A scatter plot created with pandas.

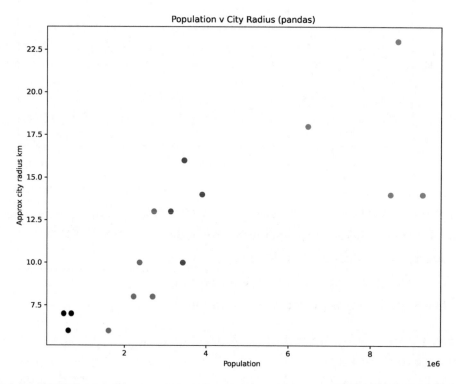

In the example above we have not added a legend to clarify what each colour means. This is not a good thing as we want our plot to communicate effectively. We can write

Figure 8.6: Scatterplot of city population versus its approximate radius size, the colour is given by the city size category in the dataset. The plot was created with pandas.

some code to create the legend or we can use other visualisation tools that simplify the work for us. Let us take a look at embedding the category of the city in the colour of the marker, and furthermore embed yet another property in the size of the marker. This is sometimes referred to as a **bubble chart**. We will use Seaborn to create the plot. In this case we need to use the `scatterplot` method.

In a bubble chart we can encode another property in the size of the markers.

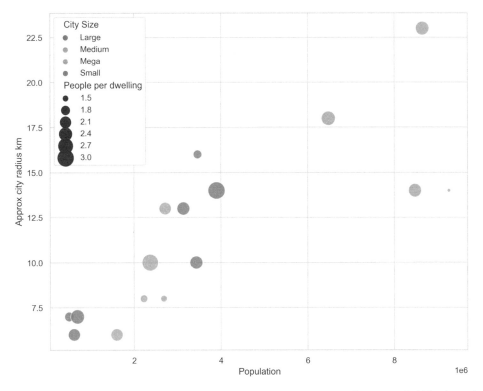

Figure 8.7: Bubble chart of city population versus its approximate radius size. The colour is given by the city size category in the dataset, and the marker size by the people per dwelling. The plot was created with Seaborn.

```
sns.scatterplot(data=gla_cities,
    x='Population', y='Approx city radius km',
    hue='City Size', alpha = 0.8,
    size='People per dwelling', sizes=(20, 500))
```

Here, the colour of the markers is managed by the hue property, and we are using the column City Size for this purpose. In case the markers overlap, we are using a transparency of 0.8 given by the alpha parameter. Finally, the size of the bubbles is given by the People per dwelling column in the dataset and we pass a tuple that manages the minimum and maximum sizes for the bubbles. The end result can be seen in Figure 8.7. Please note that the legends are automatically generated for us.

The syntax in Seaborn makes it easy to create complex plots.

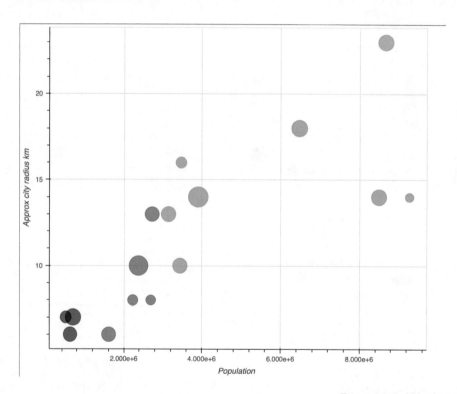

Figure 8.8: Bubble chart of city population versus its approximate radius size. The colour is given by the city size category in the dataset, and the marker size by the people per dwelling. The plot was created with Bokeh.

In Bokeh the scatter plot can be reproduced as follows: To make the code a bit more readable, we first create some arrays with the information to be used in the plot:

```
x = gla_cities['Population']
y = gla_cities['Approx city radius km']
s = gla_cities['People per dwelling']
```

We can now pass these objects to the scatter method. Note that we are passing the array called s as the size of the markers, and using the colours mapping created for the pandas example. The result can be seen in Figure 8.8.

Bokeh offers a lot of flexibility, but it may take more code to get there.

```
p = figure(width=750, height=500)
p.xaxis.axis_label = 'Population'
p.yaxis.axis_label = 'Approx city radius km'
p.scatter(x=x, y=y, size=10*s, color=colours,
    alpha=0.6)
show(p)
```

The solution above looks good, but it still leaves us with some work to do with the legends and the colour mapping. A great solution to this is the plotting backend provided by Pandas Bokeh[5], providing support for pandas dataframes. Let us first import the library:

[5] P. Hlobil (2021). Pandas Bokeh. https://github.com/PatrikHlobil/Pandas-Bokeh

```
import pandas_bokeh
pandas_bokeh.output_notebook()
```

We now create a new column to hold the sizes of the markers based on the People per dwelling column:

An alternative is to use Pandas Bokeh, which supports pandas dataframes.

```
gla_cities['bsize']=10*\
    gla_cities['People per dwelling']
```

We can now use the `plot_bokeh` method for the pandas dataframe to create our scatter plot.

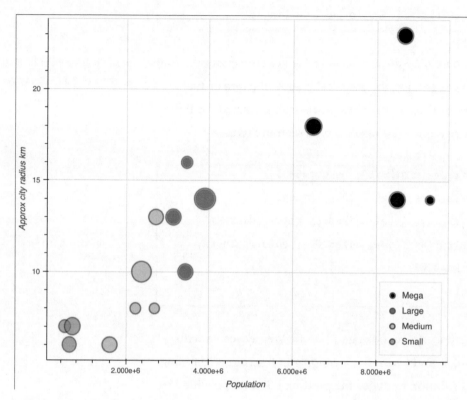

Figure 8.9: Bubble chart of city population versus its approximate radius size, the colour is given by the city size category in the dataset, and the marker size by the people per dwelling . The plot was created with Bokeh using the Pandas Bokeh backend.

```
p_scatter = gla_cities.plot_bokeh.scatter(
  x='Population',
  y='Approx city radius km',
  category='City Size',
  size='bsize', alpha=0.6,
  legend = "bottom_right")
```

As you can see we have the best of both worlds, a simple way of creating a scatter plot and the interactivity provided by Bokeh.

Finally, let us create the scatter plot with the help of Plotly.
In this case we call the scatter method of Plotly Express.
The result is shown in Figure 8.10.

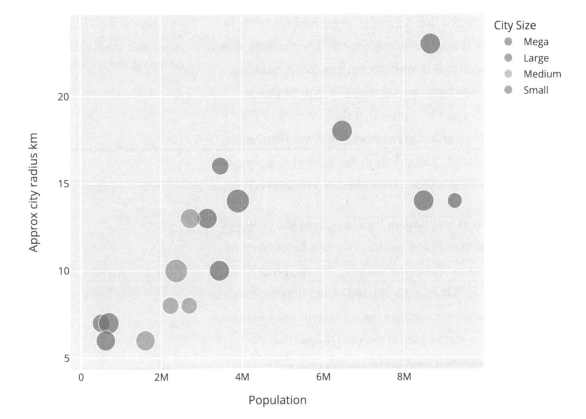

```
fig = px.scatter(gla_cities, x='Population',
    y='Approx city radius km',
    color='City Size',
    size='People per dwelling')


fig.show()
```

Figure 8.10: Bubble chart of city population versus its approximate radius size. The colour is given by the city size category in the dataset, and the marker size by the people per dwelling. The plot was created with Plotly.

8.1   Line Chart

A LINE CHART IS EXACTLY what it sounds like: It is a plot
that uses connected line segments, organised from left to
right, to show changes in a given value. The variable shown
in the horizontal axis is continuous, providing meaning
to the connection between segments. A typical case is
time. It is important to ensure that the intervals of the
continuous variable in the horizontal axis are regular or
equally distributed. The values in the vertical axis represent
a metric of interest across the continuous progression.

A line chart displays a series of
data points that are connected by
lines.

Since a line chart emphasises the changes in the values of
the variable shown in the vertical axis as a function of the
variable shown in the horizontal one, this can be used to
find patterns in that change. A good example is the result of
a regression analysis, where a line of best fit can be shown
together with a scatter plot of the data in question.

A line chart is good to show trend
and/or relationship.

The examples discussed in Section 8.2 when talking about
the different visualisation packages used in this chapter are
all line charts. We will therefore avoid repetition and simply
encourage you to refer to that section to see how to create
line charts. In summary we have the following commands
for creating line plots with the libraries we are exploring in
this book:

See Section 8.2 for examples of
how to create line charts.

- Matplotlib: Use the `plot` method of `pyplot`

- Pandas: Use the `plot` method of the `DataFrame` object

- Seaborn: Use the `lineplot` method of `seaborn`

- Bokeh: Use the `line` method of the `figure` object

- Plotly: Use the `line` method of `plotly.express`

However, we will show a nice feature of Seaborn to plot regression lines out of the box. For this matter we will use the "`jackalope.csv`" dataset from Section 7.2. We will be using the `jointplot` method that lets us combine different plots in a simple manner. We need to provide the `kind` of plot to draw; the options include:

The `jointplot` method in Seaborn lets us combine different statistical plots.

- `'scatter'` for a scatter plot

- `'kde'` for a kernel density estimate

- `'hist'` for a histogram

These are some of the plots we can combine with `jointplot`.

- `'hex` for a hexbin plot

- `'reg'` for a regression line

- `'resid'` for a residuals plot

As mentioned above, we are interested in creating a regression line given the observation. We first read the data into a pandas dataframe and then create the plot:

```
df = pd.read_csv('jackalope.csv')
sns.jointplot(x='x', y='y"', data=df,
   kind='reg', color='black');
```

We are creating a scatter plot with Seaborn and we are requesting a regression line to be added.

Note that we are plotting the values of x and y in the dataset contained in the dataframe `df` and request a regression plot with the `kind='reg'` parameter. The result

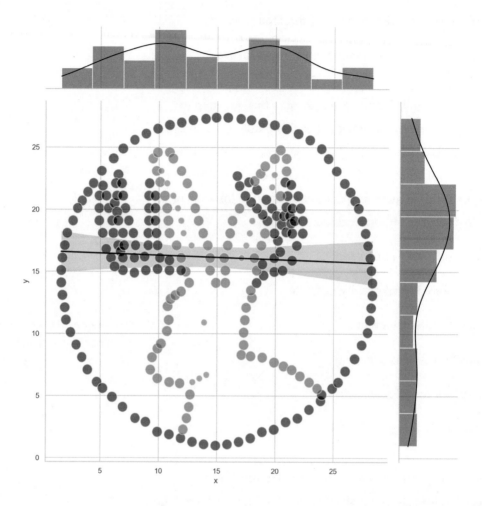

contains a scatter plot plus marginal histograms and a regression line including a confidence interval. The result is in Figure 8.11.

Figure 8.11: A scatter plot for the jackalope.csv dataset including a regression line and marginal histograms created with the jointplot method of Seaborn.

8.5   Bar Chart

IN MANY SITUATIONS IT IS necessary to compare values for different categories. As we know from the discussion

A bar chart shows numeric values for levels of a categorical feature as bars.

on perception and visual representation in Section 7.3, we
are better at distinguishing differences in length than other
encodings. In a bar chart the comparison between different
categories uses the length of each bar, and this can be done
either horizontally or vertically.

Let us continue working with the data from the
"GLA_World_Cities_2016.csv" file. We are interested in
comparing the total population of the cities contained in the
data by country. We first create a dataframe with the
information grouped by country:

We will create a bar chart of
population by country. First we
will group our data.

```
pop = gla_cities.groupby('Country')[[
    'Population']].sum()
```

We can now use this dataframe, indexed by country, to
create a bar chart with matplotlib as follows:

```
ax.bar(x=pop.index, height=pop['Population'],
    color='gray', edgecolor='k')
ax.set_xlabel('Country')
ax.set_ylabel('Population (for the Cities in
    the dataset)')
```

Creating a bar chart with
matplotlib can easily be done.

The result can be seen in Figure 8.12. Note that we are using
the index of the grouped dataframe for the horizontal axis,
whereas the height is given by the population column of the
grouped dataframe. We also specify the colour and the edge
line for all the bars.

Let us re-create the same plot but this time using the
methods of the pandas dataframe itself:

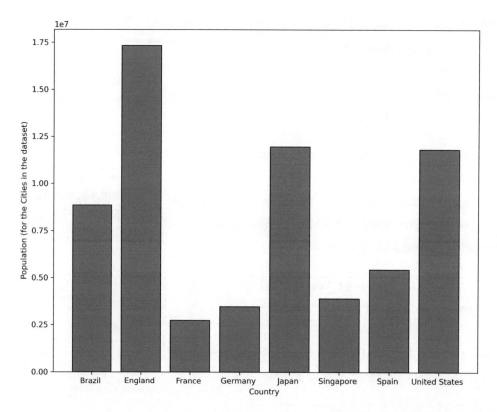

Figure 8.12: A bar chart for the total population per country for the cities contained in our dataset. The plot was created with matplotlib.

```
pop.plot(y='Population', kind='barh',
    rot=45, color='gray', edgecolor='k')
ax.set_xlabel('Country')
ax.set_ylabel('Population (for the Cities in
    the dataset)')
```

With the help of the plot method of the dataframe we create a horizontal bar chart (kind='barh'), and we specify that the labels are rotated by 45 degrees.

We can create a (vertical) bar chart with kind='bar'.

Sometimes it is important to represent multiple types of data in a single bar, breaking down a given category (shown in one of the axes) into different parts. In these situations

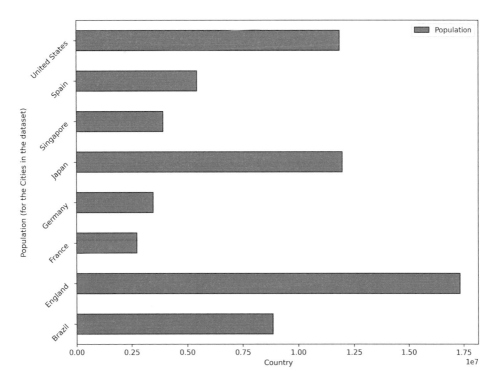

Figure 8.13: A horizontal bar chart for the total population per country for the cities contained in our dataset. The plot was created with pandas.

we can use a stacked bar chart where each bar is segmented into the components of the subcategory shown in the graph.

For example, we may want to look at the population per country in the cities contained in the dataset as above, but we are interested in looking at how each of the city size categories contribute to each population. We can do this with the help of groupby in pandas:

```
popcitysize = gla_cities.groupby(['Country',
    'City Size'])[['Population']].sum().unstack()
```

Pandas can help us unstack our grouped dataframe.

In the code above, we are asking pandas to unstack the dataframe, so that we can use the full dataframe to create our stacked bar chart as follows:

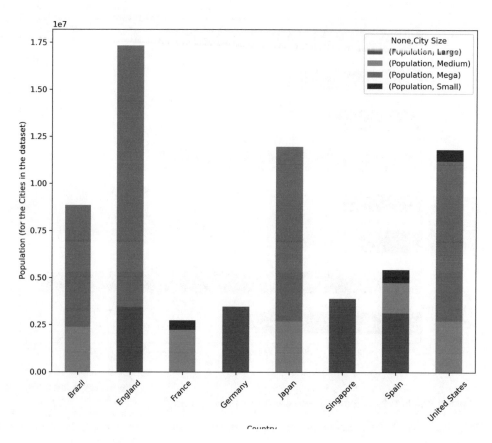

Figure 8.14: A stacked bar chart for the total population per country for the cities contained in our dataset categorised by city size. The plot was created with pandas.

```
popcitysize.plot(kind='bar', stacked=True,
   rot=45, ax=ax)
ax.set_xlabel('Country')
ax.set_ylabel('Population (for the Cities in
   the dataset)')
```

In this case we use the property stacked=True to create a stacked bar chart. The result of the code above is shown in Figure 8.14. We can create a column chart with stacked=False where the bars will be shown side by side. This can be useful for comparisons within each category.

Creating a stacked bar chart with pandas.

Let us create a column chart with Seaborn:

```
sns.barplot(data=gla_cities, x='Population',
   y='Country', hue='City Size',
   ci=None, estimator=sum)
```

A bar chart with Seaborn.

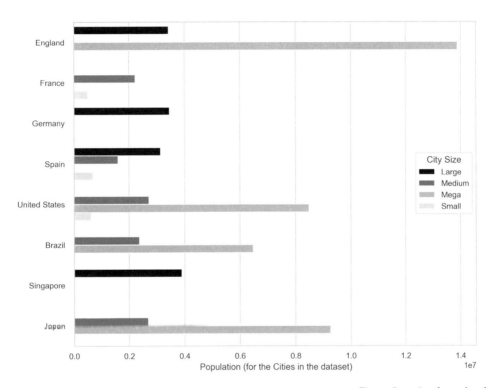

Figure 8.15: A column bar for the total population per country for the cities contained in our dataset categorised by city size. The plot was created with Seaborn.

Since Seaborn is geared towards statistical plotting it creates by default a plot for the mean of the values. We can change the default and instead in get a total. This is why we use the estimator=sum parameter. We are removing the confidence interval with ci=None. Note that we are not required to use pandas to group the data first. Finally, we can orient the plot by placing the categorical variable in either the x or y parameter. The result can be seen in Figure 8.15

We do not need to group the data first when using Seaborn.

It is also possible to flatten the grouped dataframe and use
it to create our plot. Let us do that and use Pandas Bokeh to
create our chart.

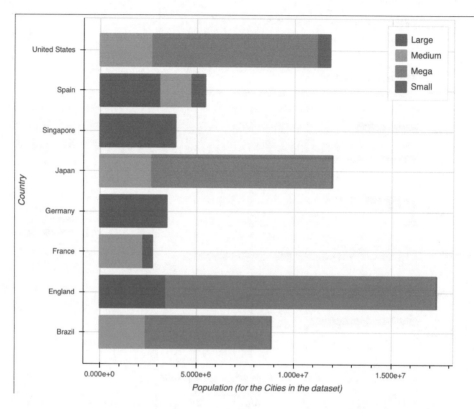

Figure 8.16: A stacked bar chart
for the total population per
country for the cities contained
in our dataset categorised by city
size. The plot was created with
Pandas Bokeh.

```
popf = pd.DataFrame(popcitysize.to_records())
popf.columns = ['Country','Large', 'Medium',
   'Mega', 'Small']


p_stacked_hbar = popf.plot_bokeh(
   x='Country', stacked=True, kind='barh',
xlabel='Population (for the Cities in
   the dataset)')
```

A horizontal bar chart created
with Pandas Bokeh.

Finally, let us create a stacked bar chart using Plotly using the popf dataframe created above. The result is shown in Figure 8.17.

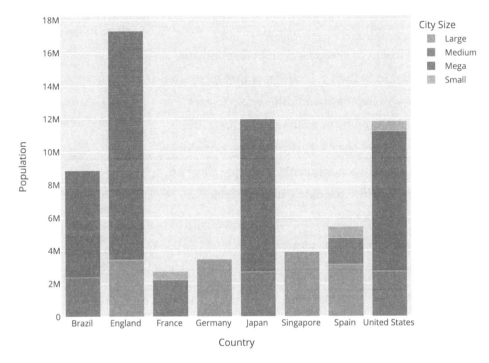

```
fig = px.bar(popf, x='Country',
  y=['Large', 'Medium', 'Mega', 'Small'],
fig.show()
```

Figure 8.17: A stacked bar chart for the total population per country for the cities contained in our dataset categorised by city size. The plot was created with Plotly.

8.6   Pie Chart

AN ALTERNATIVE TO A BAR chart to show comparison between values is the pie chart. A pie chart is a circular chart that reflects the proportion of different data groups or categories. Instead of showing the actual value (as in the

The slices of pie chart show the relative size of the data.

bar chart), a pie chart shows the percentage contribution as a part of the whole. Since this is a circular chart, there are no horizontal or vertical axes, and instead we show the proportion with the help of an angle.

As you may recall from our discussion on perception and visual representation in Section 7.3, we know that it is easier to visualise differences in length and differences in area. This is one of the reasons why sometimes bar charts are preferred to the use of pie charts, particularly on occasions where the distinction between segments in the pie chart are close to each other. Consider the data shown in Table 8.2.

Consider using a bar chart when thinking of pies, your viewers will thank you.

Category	Value
A	10
B	11
C	12
D	13
E	11
F	12
G	14

Table 8.2: A table of values to create a pie chart and compare to a bar chart.

Let us put the data above in a pandas dataframe.

```
cat = list('ABCDEFG')
val = [10, 11, 12, 13, 11, 12, 14]
df = pd.DataFrame('category': cat, 'value': val)
```

We now calculate a percentage of the total for each entry:

To create our pie chart, we need to calculate a percentage of the total.

```
df['pct']=df['value']/df['value'].sum()
```

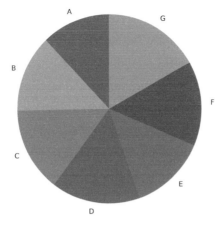

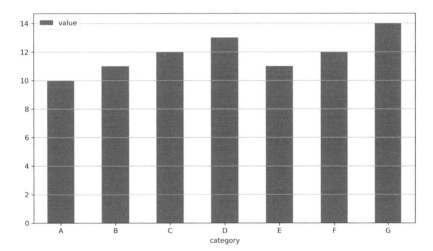

Figure 8.18: Top: A pie chart of the information shown in Table 8.2. The segments are very similar in size and it is difficult to distinguish them. Bottom: A bar chart of the same data.

Let us create a pie chart with this information:

```
plt.pie(df['pct'], labels=df['category'],
    startangle=90)
plt.axis('equal')
```

We are using the pie method in matplotlib to plot the percentage column calculated before and labelling the segments with the corresponding category. The `startangle` parameter determines where we start drawing the pie. The result can be seen in the top part of Figure 8.18.

The segments are so similar in size that it is difficult to distinguish which may be larger or even which are actually the same. We may have to add legends to support our viewers, but this implies altering the data-ink ratio of our chart. If the segments shown are more obviously different in size from each other, a pie chart is great. However, as we have seen in the example above, we may be asking for extra cognitive power from our viewers. This gets much worse as we add more and more segments to the pie, making it impossible to read. These are some of the reasons why there are some detractors to the use of pie charts.

If the segments are similar in size, it may be difficult to draw a comparison.

See Section 7.3 about the data-ink ratio.

Instead, let's see what happens when we create a bar chart with the same data as shown at the bottom of Figure 8.18. First, we may be able to use the actual values rather than a percentage. Second, the length of the bars can be easily compared with each other, and it is immediately obvious to see which one is the longest.

We can distinguish things better with a bar chart, and we can use the actual values in the data.

A compromise between the compactness of a pie chart, and the readability of a bar chart is a donut chart. It is a pie chart with its centre cut out. This is a simple change, but it helps avoid confusion with the area or angle perception issues of the pie chart. Let us create a donut chart of the data in Table 8.2 with pandas:

Appropriately, a donut chart is a pie chart with the centre cut out.

```
df.set_index('category').plot.pie(y='pct',
    wedgeprops=dict(width=0.3),
    autopct="%1.0f%%", legend=False)
```

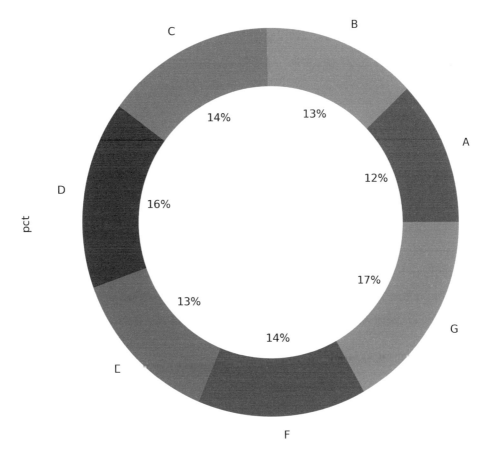

Figure 8.19: A donut chart of the data from Table 8.2 created with pandas.

We are able to take the centre our with the wedgeprops property where the width indicates the width of the segments in the donut. In this case we are also adding labels for the percentage value of each segment and indicate the format to be used. Finally, we take out the legend as it is not necessary. The plot can be seen in Figure 8.19.

With Pandas Bokeh we can recreate the pie chart as follows:

```
p_pie = df.plot_bokeh.pie(
    x='category', y='pct' )
```

A pie chart with Pandas Bokeh.

Whereas in Plotly we can draw the same graph with:

```
fig = px.pie(df, values='value',
    names='category', hole=0.7)
fig.show()
```

And with Plotly.

Since the plots obtained with Bokeh and Plotly are very similar to the one obtained with matplotlib we are not showing them here. Please note that Seaborn relies on matplotlib to create pie charts so we are also skipping that. All in all, pie charts are recommended to be used only in cases where there is no confusion, and in general you are better off using a bar chart. One thing you should definitely avoid is to use 3D pie charts or exploding pies, even if for comedic effects!

The only 3D pies you should have (it at all) are edible ones.

8.7   Histogram

WE HAVE BEEN TALKING EXTENSIVELY about the distribution of data and how important it is when thinking about statistical tests. In Chapter 5 we cover a few of the most important probability distributions and in their shape is a distinctive feature for each of them. When thinking of data points, we often need to consider how they are distributed and one way to represent this distribution is through a histogram.

A histogram shows frequency distribution.

A histogram is similar to a bar chart in the sense that we use rectangular shapes to construct our representation. In a histogram we use the length of the rectangle to represent the frequency of an observation, or a set of observations, in an interval. The base of each rectangle represents the class interval or bin. Note that the shape of the histogram depends on the number of class intervals or bins we use. The rectangles in a histogram are presented right next to each other. Throughout Chapter 5 we used histograms to show the shape of various probability distributions.

Note that in a bar chart the width of the bar has no special meaning. In a histogram it does!

Let us start by looking at how to build a histogram with matplotlib. We are going to be using the cars dataset we encountered in Chapter 4 and available[6] at `https://doi.org/10.6084/m9.figshare.3122005.v1`. We will create a histogram of the miles per gallon variable:

[6] Rogel-Salazar, J. (2016, Mar). Motor Trend Car Road Tests. https://doi.org/10.6084/m9.figshare.3122005.v1

```
plt.hist(cars['mpg'], bins=15, color='gray')
plt.xlabel('MPG')
plt.ylabel('Frequency')
```

A histogram with matplotlib.

We are using `hist` to create the histogram and we provide the number of bins with the `bins` parameter; here we have 15 bins. The histogram generated by the code above can be seen in Figure 8.20. You can try changing this number and see what happens to your histogram. The default is 10.

Try changing the number of bins in the code above.

We may want to look at the distribution of our variable cut by a different feature. For instance, we may need to look at the histogram for automatic and manual transmission given by the variable am:

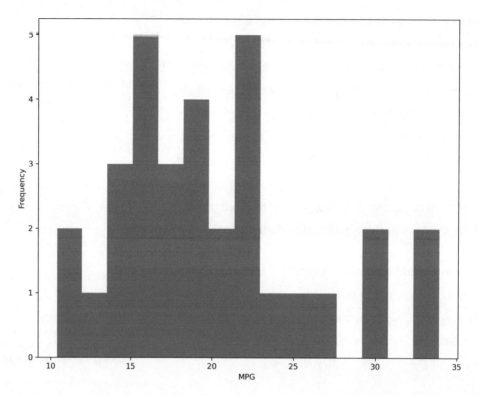

Figure 8.20: A histogram of the miles per gallon variable in the cars dataset. The chart is created with matplotlib.

```
aut=cars[cars['am']==0][['mpg']]

man=cars[cars['am']==1][['mpg']]
```

We can use these dataframes to create our histograms. We are going to be using the hist method of the pandas dataframes:

```
aut.hist(alpha=0.8, label='Automatic',
   color='black')
man.hist(alpha=0.8, label='Manual', color='gray')
plt.legend()
```

A histogram with pandas.

We are using the default bins (i.e. 10) and we are also adding a suitable legend to our plot so that we can

distinguish the automatic from the manual data. The plot is
shown in Figure 8.21.

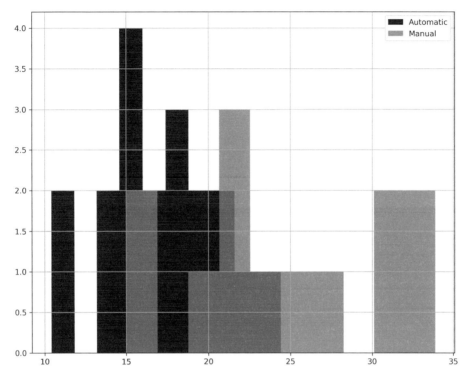

Figure 8.21: Histogram of the
miles per gallon as a function of
the type of transmission. The chart
is created with pandas.

Seaborn can make the task a bit easier with `histplot` as we
can pass the `hue` parameter to separate the automatic and
manual histograms. Let us take a look:

```
sns.histplot(data=cars, x='mpg', hue='am',
   bins=15, kde=True)
plt.ylabel('Frequency')
plt.xlabel('Miles per Gallon')
plt.legend(title='Transmission',
   loc='upper right',
   labels=['Automatic', 'Manual'])
```

Seaborn has a `histplot` function
that creates beautiful histograms.

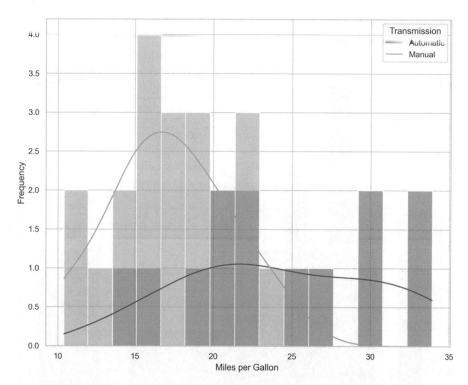

Figure 8.22: Histogram of the miles per gallon as a function of the type of transmission. The chart is created with Seaborn.

The result is shown in Figure 8.22. Notice that we are also requesting Seaborn to plot a kernel density estimate (KDE) with kde=True. This is a representation of the data using a continuous probability density curve. We are also improving the look of the legend a bit to make it more readable.

We can combine the individual series obtained before into a single dataframe and use it to create our plot:

```
df=pd.concat([aut, man], axis=1)
df.columns=['Automatic', 'Manual']
```

We will use this new dataframe to create our histogram with Pandas Bokeh.

Let us use the dataframe df above to plot our histogram using Pandas Bokeh. The plot can be seen in Figure 8.23.

```
df.plot_bokeh.hist(bins=10,
    ylabel='Freq', xlabel='Miles Per Gallon',
    line_color="black")
```

A histogram with Pandas Bokeh.

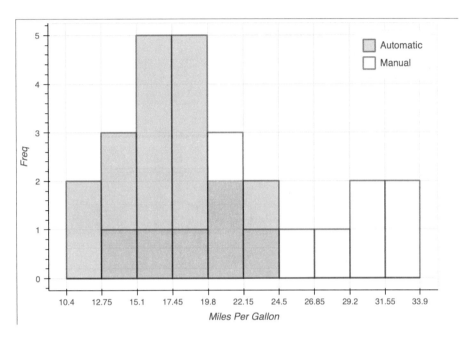

Figure 8.23: Histogram of the miles per gallon as a function of the type of transmission. The chart is created with Pandas Bokeh.

Finally, let us create the histogram with Plotly as follows:

```
fig = px.histogram(cars, x='mpg', color='am',
    nbins=16)
fig.update_layout(barmode='overlay')
fig.update_traces(opacity=0.75)
fig.show()
```

A histogram with Plotly.

The result is in Figure 8.24. Before we close this section, let us see the pairplot method in Seaborn. It shows pairwise relationships in a dataset. In this way we can look at the

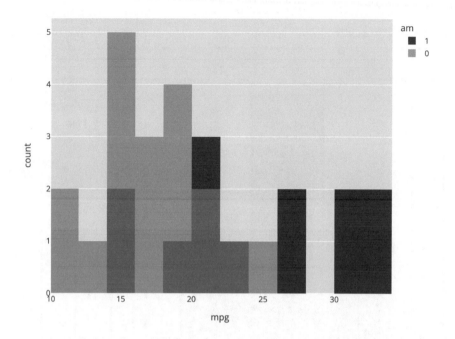

Figure 8.24: Histogram of the miles per gallon as a function of the type of transmission. The chart is created with Plotly.

distribution of a variable in the diagonal of the grid chart, and scatter plots of the pairwise relations in the off-diagonal. Let us create one to see the relationship of the miles per gallon and the horse power per transmission:

```
mycars = cars[['mpg','hp','am']]
sns.pairplot(mycars, diag_kind='kde',
  kind='scatter', hue='am')
```

Seaborn's `pairplot` lets us plot multiple pairwise bivariate distributions.

The pairplot created is shown in Figure 8.25. Notice that we can choose to show a histogram in the diagonal by changing `diag_kind` to `'hist'` and we could obtain regression lines by changing `kind` to `'reg'`. Try that for yourself!

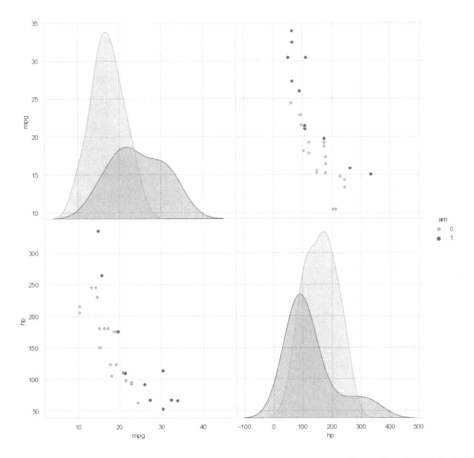

Figure 8.25: Pairplot of the cars dataset showing the relationship between miles per gallon and horse power per transmission type.

8.8   Box Plot

WE HAVE SEEN HOW THE distribution of a variable can be seen with the help of a histogram, but that is not the only way to visualise this information. An alternative way is the use of a box plot, sometimes referred to as a whisker plot.

See Section 8.7.

Take a look at the box plot diagram shown in Figure 8.26. A box plot represents the quartiles of the data, the maximum and minimum values and even outliers by showing them

See Section 4.4.2 for more information on quartiles.

past the whiskers of the boxplot. The body of the box plot is
given by the first and third quartiles (Q_1 and Q_3 in the
diagram), the line inside the box represents the median of
the data and the whiskers show the maximum and
minimum values.

Let us take a look at creating a box plot for the miles per
gallon variable in our cars dataset.

```
plt.boxplot(cars['mpg'])
plt.set_xlabel('MPG')
```

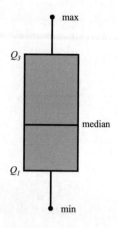

Figure 8.26: Anatomy of a boxplot.

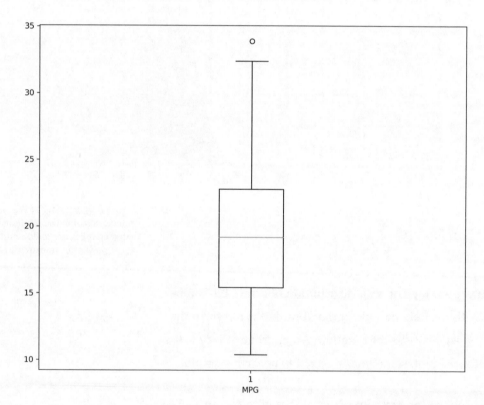

The box plot is shown in Figure 8.27. Notice how the box
plot summarises the data in a neat single graphic.

Figure 8.27: Box plot of the miles
variable in the cars dataset. The
chart is created with matplotlib.

In Section 6.6.1 we use the cars data as an example of the comparison of the mean of two groups. In that case we wanted to know if the difference in the mean value of the miles per gallon variable as a function of the transmission was statistically significant. We can depict that information with the help of a box plot. Let us use pandas to create the plot shown in Figure 8.28.

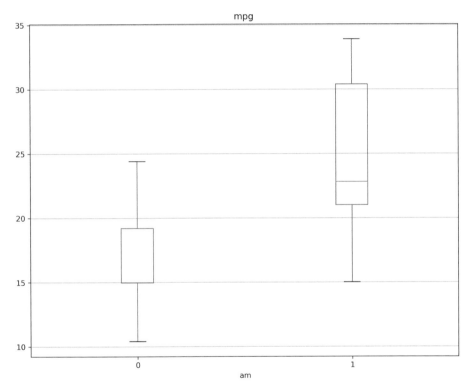

Figure 8.28: Box plot of the miles per gallon as a function of the type of transmission. The chart is created with pandas.

A box plot with pandas.

```
cars[['mpg','am']].boxplot(column='mpg',
   by ='am')
plt.grid(axis='x')
```

Notice that the width of the box does not have meaning, but it is possible to use other representations. For example, in the case of the so-called violin plot, instead of using a rectangle for the body of the graphic, we use approximate density distribution curves. Let us use Seaborn to see the different things we can do to represent the same data:

We can use other representations apart from a box. Be mindful that the chart may be more difficult to interpret.

```
sns.boxplot(x='am', y='mpg',
    data=cars)
```

A box plot with Seaborn.

The code above will generate the chart showing in the left panel of Figure 8.29.

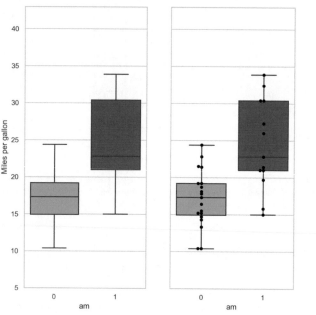

Sometimes it is useful to superimpose the data points that make up the box plot, and we can do this in Seaborn by combining the code above with a swarm plot as follows:

Figure 8.29: Left: Box plots of the miles per gallon as a function of the type of transmission. Middle: Same information but including a swarm plot. Right: Same information represented by violin plots. Graphics created with Seaborn.

```
sns.swarmplot(x='am', y='mpg', data=cars
```

A swarm plot includes the data points in our box plot.

The result is the chart shown in the middle panel of Figure 8.29. Finally, we can create the violin plot shown in the right panel of Figure 8.29 as follows:

```
sns.violinplot(x='am', y='mpg', data=cars)
```

Seaborn lets us create violin plots too.

You may notice that in the violin plot, right in the middle of each density curve, there is a small box plot, showing a little box with the first and third quartiles and a central dot to show the median. Violin plots are sometimes difficult to read, so I would encourage you to use them sparingly.

There is a small box plot inside the violin plot!

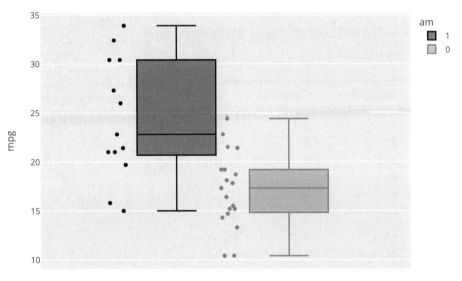

Figure 8.30: Box plot of the miles per gallon as a function of the type of transmission. The chart is created with Plotly.

Finally, let us re-create the box plot chart with the help of Plotly as shown in Figure 8.30.

```
fig = px.box(cars, y='mpg', color='am',
    points='all')
fig.show()
```

A box plot with Plotly.

Notice that we are using the `points='all'` parameter to show the data observations alongside the box plots. This is similar to the swarm plot created with Seaborn.

8.9   Area Chart

AN AREA CHART IS A special form of a line graph. We can think of it as a combination of a line and a bar chart to show how the values of a variable change over the progression of a second (continuous) variable. The fact that the area below the line is filled with a solid colour lets us demonstrate how various data series rise and fall.

An area chart combines a line chart and bar chart to show progression.

Star date	Enterprise	Cerritos	Discovery
47457.1	22	9	2
47457.2	21	6	3
47457.3	15	9	5
47457.4	18	5	7
47457.5	13	7	7
47457.6	25	5	2
47457.7	13	6	1
47457.8	21	4	9
47457.9	11	8	4
47458.0	13	5	5

Table 8.3: First encounters by notable Starfleet ships.

Consider the data in Table 8.3 showing the number of recent first encounters made by notable Starfleet ships. We assume

For any fellow StarTrek fans, the data is totally made up.

STATISTICS AND DATA VISUALISATION WITH PYTHON   465

that we have created a pandas dataframe called df with this
data ready to plot some area charts. In matplotlib we can
use the stackplot method, see Figure 8.31.

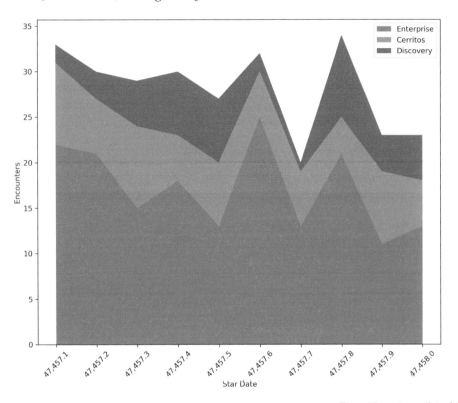

Figure 8.31: Area plot of the
data from Table 8.3 created using
matplotlib.

```
plt.stackplot(df['stardate'], df['enterprise'],
    df['cerritos'], df['discovery'],
    labels=['Enterprise', 'Cerritos', 'Discovery'])
plt.legend()
plt.xticks(rotation=45)
xlabels=[f'{label:,}' for label in df['stardate']]
plt.xticks(df['stardate'].values, xlabels)
plt.xlabel('Star Date')
plt.ylabel('Encounters')
```

An area chart lets us express how
different components relate to
the whole over time, enabling a
comparison too. Here is code to
create one with matplotlib.

The values in the area chart are stacked, in other words, the count of the second series starts at the end of the first series, not at zero. Let us create an unstacked area chart with pandas and the `area` method of the dataframe. See Figure 8.32.

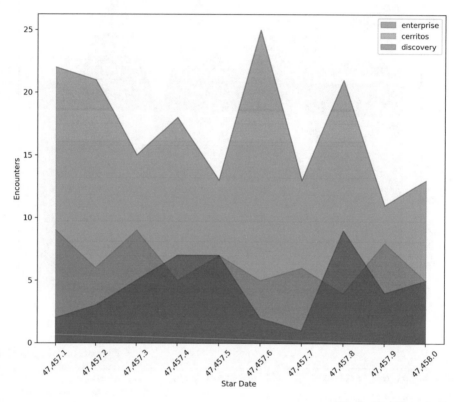

Figure 8.32: Unstacked area plot of the data from Table 8.3 created with pandas.

```
idxdf = df.set_index('stardate')
idxdf.plot.area(rot=45,
    stacked=False)
xlabels = [f'{label:,}' for label in idxdf.index]
plt.xticks(idxdf.index, xlabels)
plt.xlabel('Star Date')
plt.ylabel('Encounters'))
```

An area chart with pandas.

The area chart can be reproduced in Pandas Bokeh with the area method. The result of the code below is shown in Figure 8.33:

```
p=df.plot_bokeh.area(x='stardate',
    stacked=True,
    ylabel='Encounters',
    xlabel='Star Date')
```

An area chart with Pandas Bokeh.

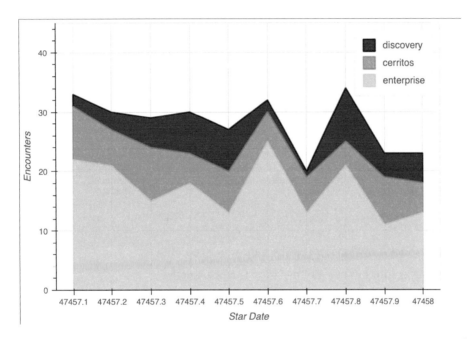

Figure 8.33: Area plot of the data from Table 8.3 created using Pandas Bokeh.

Finally, let us use Plotly to create the same graph, shown in Figure 8.34. We employ the area method as follows:

```
fig = px.area(df, x='stardate',
    y=['enterprise', 'cerritos', 'discovery'])
fig.show()
```

An area chart with Plotly.

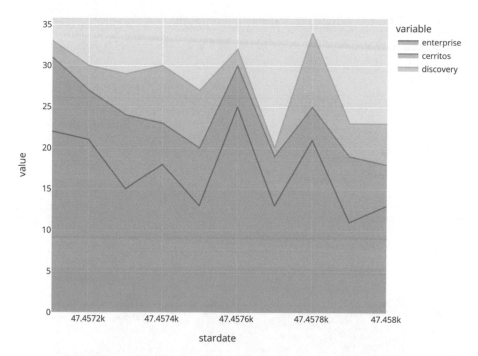

Figure 8.34: Area plot of the data from Table 8.3 created using Plotly.

8.10   Heatmap

A HEATMAP IS A CHART that depicts the values in a variable of interest using colours in a scale that ranges from smaller to higher values. As we discussed in Section 7.3, presenting information in a way that appeals to our pre-attentive perception makes it easier to pick out patterns. If we are interested in grabbing the attention of our viewers by highlighting important values, we make sure that the colours used in our heatmap do the work for us.

A heatmap represents data in a way that values are depicted by colour.

Let us prepare a small summary of the number of cars per transmission and number of cylinders:

```
wrd = {0: 'Manual', 1:'Automatic'}
cars['transmission'] = cars['am'].map(wrd)


carcount = cars.groupby(['transmission', 'cyl']) \
   .count().rename(columns = 'Car': 'cars') \
   .filter(['transmission', 'cyl', 'cars']) \
   .reset_index()
```

We first group our data to create a table to show the count of cars per transmission and number of cylinders.

A pivot table lets us summarise our information:

```
> carheatmap = carcount.pivot(index = 'cyl',
   columns = 'transmission')
> carheatmap = carheatmap['cars'].copy()
> print(carheatmap)


transmission    Automatic    Manual
        cyl
         4          8          3
         6          3          4
         8          2         12
```

A pivot table lets us read the count table in a straightforward way.

We can now create our heatmap with matplotlib as follows:

```
import matplotlib as mp
color_map = mp.cm.get_cmap('binary')
plt.pcolor(carheatmap, cmap = color_map)
xt=np.arange(0.5, len(carheatmap.columns), 1)
yt=np.arange(0.5, len(carheatmap.index), 1)
plt.xticks(xt, carheatmap.columns)
plt.yticks(yt, carheatmap.index)
plt.colorbar()
```

The pivot table can be used to create our heatmap with matplotlib.

The heatmap created with the code above is shown in Figure 8.35.

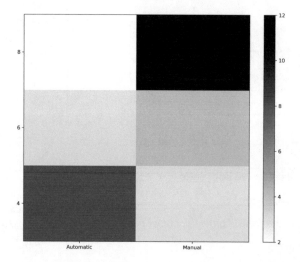

Figure 8.35: Heatmap of the number of cars by transmission type and number of cylinders. Plot created using matplotlib.

In pandas we can modify the styling of the dataframe to show the table cells with the appropriate gradient.

transmission	Automatic	Manual
cyl		
4	8	3
6	3	4
8	2	12

Figure 8.36: Heatmap of the number of cars by transmission type and number of cylinders in a pandas dataframe.

```
carheatmap.style.background_gradient(
    cmap ='binary', axis=None)\
    .set_properties(**{'font-size': '20px'})
```

In pandas we can modify the style to create a heatmap directly in our dataframe.

Notice that we are using the parameter axis=None to apply the same gradient to the entire table. We are also changing the font size of the cells so that they are easily read. The result is shown in Figure 8.36.

Let us see how Seaborn has us covered to create the same heatmap. See Figure 8.37.

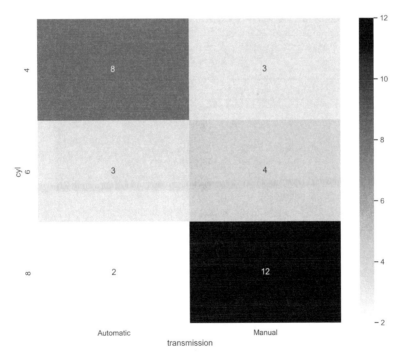

Figure 8.37: Heatmap of the number of cars by transmission type and number of cylinders created with Seaborn.

```
sns.heatmap(carheatmap,
    cmap='binary', annot=True,)
```

As you can see, Seaborn provides a much easier way to create the heatmap compared to matplotlib. With Plotly we also have a simple way to create the heatmap:

```
fig = px.imshow(carheatmap,
   text_auto=True)
fig.show()
```

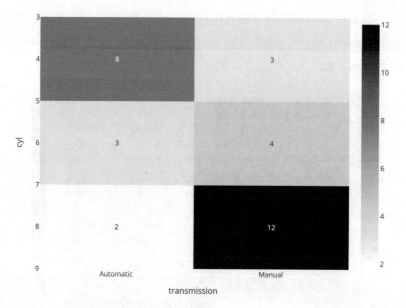

Figure 8.38: Heatmap of the number of cars by transmission type and number of cylinders created with Plotly.

The result of the code above is shown in Figure 8.38.

With Pandas Bokeh there is no heatmap API, but we can use the native Bokeh instructions to create it. We will be working with the carcount dataframe:

```
from bokeh.palettes import Greys
transm=list(carcount['transmission'].unique())
```

```
colors=list(Greys[5])

colors.reverse()

mapper = LinearColorMapper(palette=colors,

    low=carcount.cars.min(),

    high=carcount.cars.max())

TOOLS = 'hover,save,pan,box_zoom,reset,wheel_zoom'
```

At the time of writing, Pandas Bokeh does not support heatmaps. We can use Bokeh directly instead.

In the code above we have created a few objects that will help us create our heatmap. First we are using a black-and-white colour palette given by Greys, and reversing the order of the colours to match the look of our other heatmaps. We need to map the range of values in the dataset to the palette and that is the aim of mapper. Finally, the TOOLS string lets Bokeh know what tools to show when rendering the chart.

Let us now create the heatmap. This requires a bit more code than in the previous examples. First we create a figure object with the range of the horizontal axis to cover the transmission types. We also let Bokeh know what tools to show and their location. The tooltips object lets us specify what information will be shown when users hover on the squares that form our heatmap grid. Here we show the transmission type and the number of cars.

Creating a heatmap with Bokeh requires a bit more code than with other modules.

```
p = figure(title="Number of cars" ,

    x_range=transm,

    tools=TOOLS, toolbar_location='below',

    tooltips=[('transmission', '@transmission'),

    ('Num. Cars', '@cars')])
```

First we create a figure object to hold our chart.

We are now ready to attach the rectangles that will form our heatmap. We do this with the rect method, where we specify the information that goes in each of the axes as well as the height and width of the rectangular area. We also specify the colour of the rectangles and the lines.

```
p.rect(x='transmission', y='cyl', width=1,
    height=2, source=carcount,
    fill_color={'field': 'cars',
    'transform': mapper},
    line_color='gray')
```

We use rectangles to create the areas in our heatmap.

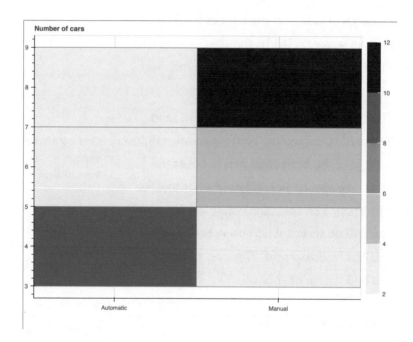

Figure 8.39: Heatmap of the number of cars by transmission type and number of cylinders created with Bokeh.

Finally, we add a colour bar that will help users determine what the colours mean and how they relate to each other. Here is where we use our mapper object and determine the ticks to show as well as the format. We add the bar to the layout and show our finished heatmap. The result is the heatmap shown in Figure 8.39.

```
color_bar = ColorBar(color_mapper=mapper, ticker=
    BasicTicker(desired_num_ticks=len(colors)),
    formatter=PrintfTickFormatter(format="%d"))
p.add_layout(color_bar, 'right')
show(p)
```

A colour bar will let our viewers gauge the value depicted by each rectangle.

A

Variance: Population v Sample

LET US START WITH THE population variance where we take the sum of the square differences from the mean and divide by the size of the population, n:

$$\sigma^2 = \frac{1}{n} \sum_{i=1}^{n} (x_i - \mu)^2 . \qquad (\text{A.1})$$

For a sample, we are interested in estimating the population variance. We can start from the definition above:

$$\sigma_b^2 = \frac{1}{n} \sum_{i=1}^{n} (x_i - \bar{X})^2 . \qquad (\text{A.2})$$

This is a biased estimate. To correct for this we need to consider that we are only taking samples.

In this case, the random variable x_i deviates from the sample mean $\bar{X}$ with variance σ_b^2. In turn, the sample mean $\bar{X}$ also deviates from μ with variance $\frac{\sigma^2}{n}$. This can easily be seen by considering that the sample mean, $\bar{X}$, is calculated every time using different values from one sample to the next. In other words, it is a random variable with mean μ and variance $\frac{\sigma^2}{n}$.

We are interested in estimating an unbiased value of σ^2, i.e. s^2, the sample variance. We have therefore a random variable x_i that deviates from μ with a two-part variance: $s^2 = \sigma_b^2 + \frac{s^2}{n}$. This relationship can be expressed as:

$$s^2 = \frac{n}{n-1}\sigma_b^2, \tag{A.3}$$

which tells us what our unbiased estimator should be. Replacing this information in (A.2) we have that:

$$s^2 = \frac{1}{n-1}\sum_{i=1}^{n}(x_i - \bar{X})^2, \tag{A.4}$$

which is the expression for the population variance given in Equation (4.21).

B

Sum of First n Integers

WE ARE INTERESTED IN CALCULATING the sum of the first n integers $S_n = 1 + 2 + \cdots + n$. Let us arrange the sum as follows:

$$S_n = 1 + 2 + 3 + \cdots + n \tag{B.1}$$

$$S_n = n + (n-1) + (n-2) + \cdots + 1 \tag{B.2}$$

We can calculate $2S_n$ by grouping the two expressions above:

$$2S_n = n + 1 + (2 + n - 1) + (3 + n - 2) + \cdots$$
$$+ (n+1) \tag{B.3}$$
$$= (n+1) + (n+1) + (n+1) + \cdots$$
$$+ (n+1) \tag{B.4}$$

The factor $n + 1$ is repeated n times and therefore we can write that

$$2S_n = n(n+1). \tag{B.5}$$

Therefore we have that:

$$S_n = \sum_{k=1}^{n} k = \frac{n(n+1)}{2}. \qquad \text{(B.6)}$$

C

Sum of Squares of the First n Integers

LET US START WITH THE following binomial expansion:

$$(k-1)^3 = k^3 - 3k^2 + 3k - 1. \qquad \text{(C.1)}$$

We can rearrange the terms as follows:

$$k^3 - (k-1)^3 = 3k^2 - 3k + 1. \qquad \text{(C.2)}$$

Let us now sum both sides:

$$\sum_{k=1}^{n}(k^3 - (k-1)^3) = 3\sum_{k=1}^{n}k^2 - 3\sum_{k=1}^{n}k + \sum_{k=1}^{n}1 \qquad \text{(C.3)}$$

It is useful at this point to consider the definition of a telescoping sum. This refers to a finite sum where pairs of consecutive terms cancel each other, leaving only the initial and final terms. For example, if a_k is a sequence of numbers, then:

$$\sum_{k=1}^{n}(a_k - a_{k-1}) = a_n - a_0. \qquad \text{(C.4)}$$

The sum on the left-hand side of Equation (C.3) telescopes and is equal to n^3. We have therefore the following:

$$n^3 = 3\sum_{k=1}^{n} k^2 - 3\frac{n(n+1)}{2} + n \qquad \text{(C.5)}$$

$$3\sum_{k=1}^{n} k^2 = n^3 + 3\frac{n(n+1)}{2} - n \qquad \text{(C.6)}$$

$$\sum_{k=1}^{n} k^2 = \frac{n^3}{3} + \frac{n(n+1)}{2} - \frac{n}{3} \qquad \text{(C.7)}$$

$$\sum_{k=1}^{n} k^2 = \frac{n(n+1)(2n+1)}{6}. \qquad \text{(C.8)}$$

D

The Binomial Coefficient

LET US MOTIVATE THE DISCUSSION of the binomial coefficient by thinking of sequences. We can consider making an ordered list of distinct elements of length k from n elements. For the first element in our sequence there are n ways to pick it. Once the first element is chosen, there are $n - 1$ ways to pick the second, and $n - 2$ to pick the third. This will continue until we get to the k-th element: There are $n - k + 1$ ways to pick it. The number of sequences that can be constructed is therefore given by:

$$n(n-1)(n-2)\ldots(n-k+1) = \frac{n!}{(n-k)!} = P(n,k), \quad \text{(D.1)}$$

where $P(n,k)$ is called a permutation of k elements from n.

The permutation above is an ordered sequence. If instead we are interested in unordered arrangements, we are looking for a combination $C(n,k)$. For each sequence, we want to identify the $k!$ permutations of its elements as being the same sequence, this means that the combinations are given by

$$C(n,k) = \frac{n!}{(n-k)!k!} = \binom{n}{k}. \qquad \text{(D.2)}$$

D.1 Some Useful Properties of the Binomial Coefficient

WE ARE GOING TO START by deriving a useful expression for the $C(n-1, k-1)$:

$$C(n-1, k-1) = \binom{n-1}{k-1}, \qquad \text{(D.3)}$$

$$= \frac{(n-1)!}{((n-1)-(k-1))!(k-1)!}, \qquad \text{(D.4)}$$

$$= \frac{(n-1)!}{(n-k)!(k-1)!}. \qquad \text{(D.5)}$$

For the next useful property, let us recall that $x! = x(x-1)!$. This lets us express the binomial coefficient as:

$$\binom{n}{k} = \frac{n(n-1)!}{(n-k)!k(k-1)!}, \qquad \text{(D.6)}$$

$$= \frac{n}{k}\frac{(n-1)!}{(n-k)(k-1)!}, \qquad \text{(D.7)}$$

$$= \frac{n}{k}\binom{n-1}{k-1} \qquad \text{(D.8)}$$

E

The Hypergeometric Distribution

E.1 The Hypergeometric vs Binomial Distribution

LET US START WITH THE hypergeometric distribution:

$$f(k, N, K, n) = \frac{\binom{K}{k}\binom{N-K}{n-k}}{\binom{N}{n}}, \qquad \text{(E.1)}$$

and let us keep the ratio $K/N = p$ fixed. We want to show that:

$$\lim_{N \to \infty} f(k, N, K, n) = \binom{n}{k} p^k (1-p)^{n-k}. \qquad \text{(E.2)}$$

Let us express Equation (E.1) in terms of factorials:

$$\frac{\binom{K}{k}\binom{N-K}{n-k}}{\binom{N}{n}} = \frac{K!}{k!(K-k)!} \cdot \frac{(N-K)!}{(n-k)!(N-n-(K-k))!} \cdot$$

$$\frac{n!(N-n)!}{N!} \qquad \text{(E.3)}$$

We now rearrange some of the terms so that we can recover the binomial coefficient $\binom{n}{k}$:

$$
\frac{\binom{K}{k}\binom{N-K}{n-k}}{\binom{N}{n}} = \frac{n!}{k!(n-k)!} \cdot \frac{K!}{(K-k)!} \cdot \frac{(N-K)!}{(N-n-(K-k))!}
$$
$$
\frac{(N-n)!}{N!}, \tag{E.4}
$$

$$
= \binom{n}{k} \cdot \frac{K!/(K-k)!}{N!/(N-k)!} \cdot
$$
$$
\frac{(N-K)!(N-n)!}{(N-k)!(N-K-(n-k))!)} \tag{E.5}
$$

$$
= \binom{n}{k} \cdot \frac{K!/(K-k)!}{N!/(N-k)!} \cdot
$$
$$
\frac{(N-K)!/(N-K-(n-k))!}{(N-n+(n-k))!/(N-n)!} \tag{E.6}
$$

$$
= \binom{n}{k} \cdot \prod_{i=1}^{k} \frac{(K-k+i)}{(N-k+i)} \cdot
$$
$$
\prod_{j=1}^{n-k} \frac{(N-K-(n-k)+j)}{(N-n+j)} \tag{E.7}
$$

Taking the limit for large N and fixed K/N, n and k, we have:

$$
\lim_{N\to\infty} \frac{K-k+i}{N-k+i} = \lim_{N\to\infty} \frac{K}{N} = p, \tag{E.8}
$$

and similarly:

$$
\lim_{N\to\infty} \frac{N-K-(n-k)+j}{N-n+j} = \lim_{N\to\infty} \frac{N-K}{N} = 1-p. \tag{E.9}
$$

Hence:

$$
\lim_{N\to\infty} f(k, N, K, n) = \binom{n}{k} p^k (1-p)^{n-k} \tag{E.10}
$$

F

The Poisson Distribution

F.1 Derivation of the Poisson Distribution

IN SECTION 5.3.5 WE OBTAINED the following differential equation to find the probability of getting n successes in the time interval t:

$$\frac{dP(n,t)}{dt} + lP(n,t) = lP(n-1,t). \qquad \text{(F.1)}$$

The equation above can be solved by finding an integrating factor, $v(t)$, such that we can get a total derivative for the left-hand side when multiplying by $v(t)$, i.e.:

$$v(t)\left[\frac{dP(n,t)}{dt} + lP(n,t)\right] = \frac{d}{dt}\left[v(t)P(n,t)\right]. \qquad \text{(F.2)}$$

The integrating factor for the equation above is:

$$v(t) = \exp\left[\int l \, dt\right] = e^{lt}, \qquad \text{(F.3)}$$

and thus we have that:

$$\frac{d}{dt}\left[e^{lt}P(n,t)\right] = e^{lt}lP(n-1,t). \tag{F.4}$$

Using Equation (F.4) we have that for $n = 1$:

$$\frac{d}{dt}\left[e^{lt}P(1,t)\right] = e^{lt}lP(0,t) = le^{lt}e^{-lt} = l \tag{F.5}$$

where we have used Equation (5.62). We can now integrate both sides of the result above:

$$e^{lt}P(1,t) = \int l\,dt = lt + C_1 \tag{F.6}$$

Since the probability of finding an event at $t = 0$ is 0, we have that $C_1 = 0$. This result can be generalised to n by induction giving us the following expression for the Poisson probability:

$$P(n,t) = \frac{(lt)^n}{n!}e^{-lt}. \tag{F.7}$$

F.2   The Poisson Distribution as a Limit of the Binomial Distribution

IN SECTION 5.3.5 WE MENTIONED that the Poisson distribution can be obtained as a limit of the binomial distribution. As we divide the time interval into more subintervals, the binomial distribution starts behaving more and more like the Poisson distribution. This is the case for a large number of trials i.e. $n \to \infty$, and we fix the mean rate $\mu = np$. Equivalently, we can make the probability p be very small, i.e. $p \to 0$.

Let us start with the binomial distribution, and we express the probability $p = \mu/n$:

$$P(X) \;=\; \lim_{n\to\infty} \binom{n}{k} \left(\frac{\mu}{n}\right)^{k} \left(1 - \frac{\mu}{n}\right)^{n-k}, \qquad \text{(F.8)}$$

$$=\; \lim_{n\to\infty} \frac{n!}{k!(n-k)!} \left(\frac{\mu}{n}\right)^{k} \left(1 - \frac{\mu}{n}\right)^{n-k}, \qquad \text{(F.9)}$$

$$=\; \lim_{n\to\infty} \frac{n!}{(n-k)!n^{k}} \left(\frac{\mu^{k}}{k!}\right) \left(1 - \frac{\mu}{n}\right)^{n}.$$

$$\left(1 - \frac{\mu}{n}\right)^{-k}. \qquad \text{(F.10)}$$

Let us look at the ratio $n!/(n-k!)$: For the case where integer n is greater than the k. This can be expressed as the successive product of n with $(n-i)$ down to $(n-(k-1))$:

$$\frac{n!}{(n-k)} = n(n-1)(n-2)\cdots(n-k+1), \qquad k < n, \quad \text{(F.11)}$$

In the limit $n \to \infty$ the expression above is a polynomial whose leading term is n^{k} and thus:

$$\lim_{n\to\infty} \frac{n(n-1)(n-2)\cdots(n-k+1)}{n^{k}} = 1. \qquad \text{(F.12)}$$

Our expression for the probability mass function is therefore written as:

$$P(X) = \left(\frac{\mu^{k}}{k!}\right) \lim_{n\to\infty}\left(1 - \frac{\mu}{n}\right)^{n} \lim_{n\to\infty}\left(1 - \frac{\mu}{n}\right)^{-k}. \qquad \text{(F.13)}$$

We can use the following identities to simplify the expression above:

$$\lim_{n \to \infty} \left(1 - \frac{x}{n}\right)^{-n} = e^{-x}, \qquad \text{(F.14)}$$

$$\lim_{n \to \infty} \left(1 - \frac{x}{n}\right)^{-k} = 1, \qquad \text{(F.15)}$$

and therefore the probability mass function is given by

$$P(X) = \frac{\mu^k}{k!} e^{-\mu}, \qquad \text{(F.16)}$$

which is the expression for the probability mass function of the Poisson distribution.

G

The Normal Distribution

G.1 *Integrating the PDF of the Normal Distribution*

IN SECTION 5.4.1 WE MENTIONED that we can find the proportionality constant C in Equation (5.74) for the probability distribution function of the normal distribution. Given that the area under the curve must be one, we have that:

$$f(x) = C \int_{-\infty}^{\infty} \exp\left[-\frac{k}{2}(x-\mu)^2\right] dx = 1. \qquad \text{(G.1)}$$

Sadly, the integral above does not have a representation in terms of elementary functions. However, there are some things we can do to evaluate it. We can follow the steps of Poisson himself.

Before we do that, let us make a couple of changes to the expression above. First let us define the variable:

$$u = \sqrt{\frac{k}{2}}(x-\mu), \text{ and so } du = \sqrt{\frac{k}{2}}dx.$$

In this way, we can express Equation (G.1) as:

$$f(x) = C\sqrt{\frac{2}{k}}\int_{-\infty}^{\infty} e^{-u^2}\,du = 1. \qquad (G.2)$$

Let us concentrate on the integral in expression (G.2):

$$J = \int_{-\infty}^{\infty} e^{-u^2}\,du. \qquad (G.3)$$

Instead of tackling the integral as above, we are going to look at squaring it and transform the problem into a double integral:

$$\begin{aligned}
J^2 &= \left(\int_{-\infty}^{\infty} e^{-x_1^2}\,dx_1\right)\left(\int_{-\infty}^{\infty} e^{-y_1^2}\,dy_1\right), \\
&= \int_{-\infty}^{\infty}\int_{-\infty}^{\infty} e^{-(x_1^2+y_1^2)}\,dx_1\,dy_1. \qquad (G.4)
\end{aligned}$$

We can express the double integral in polar coordinates such that

$$J = \int_0^{2\pi}\int_0^{\infty} re^{-r^2}\,dr\,d\theta. \qquad (G.5)$$

The radial part of the integral can be done by letting $u = r^2$, and thus $du = 2rdr$. Applying this to Equation (G.5):

$$\begin{aligned}
J^2 &= \frac{1}{2}\int_0^{2\pi}\int_0^{\infty} e^{-u}\,du\,d\theta, \\
&= -\frac{1}{2}e^{-r^2}\Big|_0^{\infty}\int_0^{2\pi} d\theta, \\
&= -\frac{1}{2}(1)\int_0^{2\pi} d\theta.
\end{aligned}$$

The angular part is readily solved as follows:

$$J^2 = \frac{1}{2} \int_0^{2\pi} d\theta,$$

$$= \frac{1}{2} \theta \Big|_0^{2\pi},$$

$$= \pi,$$

and therefore $J = \sqrt{\pi}$.

Substituting back into Equation (G.1), we have that:

$$C\sqrt{\frac{2}{k}} \sqrt{\pi} = 1,$$

$$C = \sqrt{\frac{k}{2\pi}}. \qquad\qquad (G.6)$$

and recall that $k = 1/\sigma^2$ as shown in Equation (5.80).

G.2   Maximum and Inflection Points of the Normal Distribution

WE ARE NOW INTERESTED IN finding the maximum value of the probability distribution function of the normal distribution, as well as its inflection points. For the maximum we have need to calculate $df(x) = 0$:

$$df(x) = -\frac{1}{\sigma^3 \sqrt{2\pi}} (x - \mu) \exp\left[\left(\frac{x-\mu}{\sigma}\right)^2\right] = 0 \qquad (G.7)$$

The expression above is only equal to zero when $x - \mu = 0$ and hence $x = \mu$. This tells us that the Gaussian function has its maximum at the mean value μ.

Let us now look at the inflection points. In this case, we need to solve for $d^2 f(x) = 0$:

$$d^2 f(x) = -\frac{1}{\sigma^3 \sqrt{2\pi}} \left(\frac{(x - \mu)^2}{\sigma^2} - 1 \right) e^{-\frac{1}{2}\left(\frac{x-\mu}{\sigma}\right)^2} = 0. \quad \text{(G.8)}$$

The expression above is equal to zero when:

$$\left(\frac{x - \mu}{\sigma} \right)^2 = 1. \quad \text{(G.9)}$$

Solving for x we have that the inflection points of the Gaussian distribution are at $x = \mu \pm \sigma$. This means that they lie one standard deviation above and below the mean.

H

Skewness and Kurtosis

EXPRESSIONS FOR THE SAMPLE SKEWNESS and kurtosis in terms of their mean (μ_1), variance (μ_2), skewness (γ_1) and kurtosis (γ_2)[1]. With n being the sample size, for the skewness, we have that:

Pearson, E. S. (1931, 05). I. Note on tests for normality. *Biometrika* 22(3-4), 423–424

$$\mu_1(g_1) = 0,$$

$$\mu_2(g_1) = \frac{6(n-2)}{(n+1)(n+3)},$$

$$\gamma_1(g_1) = \frac{\mu_3(g_1)}{\mu_2(g_1)^{3/2}} = 0,$$

$$\gamma_2(g_1) = \frac{\mu_4(g_1)}{\mu_2(g_1)^2} - 3,$$

$$= \frac{36(n-7)(n^2+2n-5)}{(n-2)(n+5)(n+7)(n+9)}.$$

For the kurtosis:

$$\mu_1(g_2) = \frac{6}{n+1},$$

$$\mu_2(g_2) = \frac{24n(n-2)(n-1)}{(n+1)^2(n+3)(n+5)},$$

$$\gamma_1(g_2) = \frac{6(n^2-5n+2)}{(n+7)(n+9)}\sqrt{\frac{(n+3)(n+5)}{n(n-2)(n-3)}},$$

$$\gamma_2(g_2) = \frac{36(15n^6 - 36n^5 - 628n^4 + 982n^3 + 5777n^2 - 6402n + 900)}{n(n-3)(n-2)(n+7)(n+9)(n+11)(n+13)}.$$

I

Kruskal-Wallis Test – No Ties

LET US START WITH THE following expression for the H statistic:

$$H = (n-1) \frac{\sum_{i=1}^{k} n_i \left(\overline{R_{i\cdot}} - \overline{R}\right)^2}{\sum_{i=1}^{k} \sum_{j=1}^{n_i} \left(R_{ij} - \overline{R}\right)^2}. \qquad (\text{I.1})$$

Let us concentrate on the denominator and expand it:

$$\sum_{i=1}^{k} \sum_{j=1}^{n_i} \left(R_{ij} - \overline{R}\right)^2 = \sum_{i=1}^{k} \sum_{j=1}^{n_i} R_{ij}^2 - 2R_{ij}\overline{R} + \overline{R}^2. \qquad (\text{I.2})$$

Let us recall that $\overline{R} = (n+1)/2$, and we can rewrite as a sum as follows $\sum_{i=1}^{k} \sum_{j=1}^{n_i} R_{ij}/N$. We can use these expressions to write the following:

$$\frac{n(n+1)}{2} = \sum_{i=1}^{k} \sum_{j=1}^{n_i} R_{ij}. \qquad (\text{I.3})$$

We can use the expression above to recast Equation (I.2) in terms of a double sum:

$$\sum_{i=1}^{k} \sum_{j=1}^{n_i} R_{ij}^2 - \sum_{i=1}^{k} \sum_{j=1}^{n_i} 2R_{ij}\overline{R} + \sum_{i=1}^{k} \sum_{j=1}^{n_i} \overline{R}^2. \qquad (\text{I.4})$$

With the assumption that there are no ties in the ranked observations, the first term of Equation (I.4) is the sum of squared ranks, i.e. $1^2 + 2^2 + \cdots + n^2$ and thus can be expressed as:

$$\frac{n(n+1)(2n+1)}{6}. \qquad (I.5)$$

The second term of Equation (I.4) can be written as:

$$2\overline{R}\frac{n(n+1)}{2} = \frac{n(n+1)^2}{2}. \qquad (I.6)$$

Finally, the third term of Equation (I.4) shows that $\overline{R}^2$ appears n times and thus we can express it as:

$$n\overline{R}^2 = \frac{n(n+2)^2}{4}. \qquad (I.7)$$

We can therefore express the denominator as follows:

$$\frac{n(n+1)(2n+1)}{6} - \frac{n(n+1)^2}{2} + \frac{n(n+1)^2}{4},$$

$$\frac{[2n(n+1)(2n+1)] - [6n(n+1)^2] + [3n(n+1)^2]}{12},$$

$$\frac{(n+1)[2n(2n+1) - 6n(n+1) + 3n(n+1)]}{12},$$

$$\frac{(n+1)(n^2-n)}{12} = \frac{(n+1)n(n-1)}{12}. \qquad (I.8)$$

Let us now look at the numerator and do the same sort of expansion:

$$\sum_{i=1}^{k} n_i(\overline{R_{i\cdot}} - \overline{R})^2 = \sum_{i=1}^{k} n_i\left(\overline{R_{i\cdot}}^2 - 2\overline{R_{i\cdot}}\,\overline{R} + \overline{R}^2\right),$$

$$\sum_{i=1}^{k} n_i \overline{R_{i\cdot}}^2 - n_i 2\overline{R_{i\cdot}} \, \overline{R} + n_i \overline{R}^2,$$

$$\sum_{i=1}^{k} n_i \overline{R_{i\cdot}}^2 - \sum_{i=1}^{k} n_i 2\overline{R_{i\cdot}} \, \overline{R} + \sum_{i=1}^{k} n_i \overline{R}^2. \tag{I.9}$$

Let us look at the second term of Equation (I.9). We know that the $\overline{R_{i\cdot}} = \sum_{j=1}^{n_i} R_{ij}/n_i$, and thus:

$$\sum_{i=1}^{k} n_i 2\overline{R_{i\cdot}} \, \overline{R} = (n+1) \sum_{i=1}^{k} \sum_{j=1}^{n_i} R_{ij}. \tag{I.10}$$

The double sum above is the sum of ranks such that $1 + 2 + \cdots + n$ and that is equal to $n(n+1)/2$ when there are no ties. The second term thus is equal to $n(n+1)^2/2$.

For the last term of Equation (I.9) we have that:

$$\sum_{i=1}^{k} n_i \overline{R}^2 = \frac{(n+1)^2}{4} \sum_{i=1}^{k} n_i = \frac{n(n+1)^2}{4}. \tag{I.11}$$

Let us now plug back Equations (I.8), (I.9) and (I.10) as well as (I.11) into our original Expression (I.1):

$$H = \frac{12(n-1)}{n(n+1)(n-1)} \left(\sum_{i=1}^{k} n_i \overline{R_{i\cdot}}^2 - \frac{n(n+1)^2}{2} + \frac{n(n+1)^2}{4} \right),$$

$$= \frac{12}{n(n+1)} \sum_{i=1}^{k} n_i \overline{R_{i\cdot}}^2 - \frac{12}{n(n+1)} \frac{n(n+1)^2}{4},$$

$$= \frac{12}{n(n+1)} \sum_{i=1}^{k} n_i \overline{R_{i\cdot}}^2 - 3(n+1). \tag{I.12}$$

Bibliography

Abramowitz, M. and I. Stegun (1965). *Handbook of Mathematical Functions: With Formulas, Graphs, and Mathematical Tables*. Applied Mathematics Series. Dover Publications.

Anaconda (2016, November). Anaconda Software Distribution. Computer Software. V. 2-2.4.0. `https://www.anaconda.com`.

Anscombe, F. J. (1973). Graphs in statistical analysis. *The American Statistician 27*(1), 17–21.

Arfken, G., H. Weber, and F. Harris (2011). *Mathematical Methods for Physicists: A Comprehensive Guide*. Elsevier Science.

Bayes, T. (1763). An essay towards solving a problem in the doctrine of chances. *Philosophical Transactions 53*, 370–418.

Berkowitz, B. D. (2018). *Playfair: The True Story of the British Secret Agent Who Changed How We See the World*. George Mason University Press.

Bernoulli, J., J. Bernoulli, and E. D. Sylla (2006). *The Art of*

Conjecturing, Together with Letter to a Friend on Sets in Court Tennis. Johns Hopkins University Press.

Bertin, J. and M. Barbut (1967). *Sémiologie graphique: Les diagrammes, les réseaux, les cartes*. Gauthier-Villars.

Bokeh Development Team (2018).   Bokeh: Python library for interactive visualization. https://bokeh.pydata.org/en/latest/.

Bostridge, M. (2015). *Florence Nightingale: The Woman and Her Legend*. Penguin Books Limited.

Bowley, A. L. (1928). The Standard Deviation of the Correlation Coefficient. *Journal of the American Statistical Association 23*(161), 31–34.

Bradley, M. *Charles Dupin (1784 - 1873) and His Influence on France*. Cambria Press.

Brown, M. B. and A. B. Forsythe (1974). Robust tests for the equality of variances. *Journal of the American Statistical Association 69*(346), 364–367.

Buckmaster, D. (1974). The Incan Quipu and the Jacobsen hypothesis. *Journal of Accounting Research 12*(1), 178–181.

Busby, M. (2020).   Cambridge college to remove window commemorating eugenicist. www.theguardian.com/education /2020/jun/27/cambridge-gonville-caius-college - eugenicist-window-ronald-fisher. Accessed: 2021-02-14.

D'Agostino, R. and E. S. Pearson (1973). Tests for Departure from Normality. Empirical Results for the Distributions of b_2 and $\sqrt{b_1}$. *Biometrika 60*(3), 613–622.

D'Agostino, R. B. (1971, 08). An omnibus test of normality for moderate and large size samples. *Biometrika 58*(2), 341–348.

D'Agostino, R. B. (1970, 12). Transformation to normality of the null distribution of g_1. *Biometrika 57*(3), 679–681.

de Heinzelin, J. (1962, Jun). Ishango. *Scientific American* (206:6), 105–116.

Díaz Díaz, R. (2006). Apuntes sobre la aritmética maya. *Educere 10*(35), 621–627.

Fisher, R. (1963). *Statistical Methods for Research Workers*. Biological monographs and manuals. Hafner Publishing Company.

Franks, B. (2020). *97 Things About Ethics Everyone in Data Science Should Know*. O'Reilly Media.

Gartner (2017). Gartner Says within Five Years, Organizations Will Be Valued on Their Information Portfolios. www.gartner.com/en/newsroom/press-releases/2017-02-08-gartner-says-within-five-years-organizations-will-be-valued-on-their-information-portfolios. Accessed: 2021-01-04.

Gauss, C. F. (1823). *Theoria combinationis observationum erroribus minimis obnoxiae*. Number V. 2 in Commentationes Societatis Regiae Scientiarum Gottingensis recentiores: Classis Mathemat. H. Dieterich.

Good, I. J. (1986). Some statistical applications of Poisson's work. *Statistical Science 1*, 157–170.

Hand, D. J. (2020). *Dark Data: Why What You Don't Know Matters*. Princeton University Press.

Hassig, R. (2013). El tributo en la economía prehispánica. *Arqueología Mexicana 21*(124), 32–39.

Heath, T. L. (2017). *Euclid's Elements (The Thirteen Books)*. Digireads.com Publishing.

Heffelfinger, T. and G. Flom (2004). Abacus: Mystery of the Bead. http://totton.idirect.com. Accessed: 2021-02-03.

Henderson, H. V. and P. F. Velleman (1981). Building multiple regression models interactively. *Biometrics 37*(2), 391–411.

Howard, L. (1960). Robust tests for equality of variances. In I. Olkin and H. Hotelling (Eds.), *Contributions to Probability and Statistics: Essays in Honor of Harold Hotelling*, pp. 278–292. Stanford University Press.

Hunter, J. D. (2007). Matplotlib: A 2D graphics environment. *Computing in Science & Engineering 9*(3), 90–95.

Ioannidis, Y. (2003). The history of histograms (abridged). www.vldb.org/conf/2003/papers/S02P01.pdf. Accessed: 2021-02-14.

Jones, E., T. Oliphant, P. Peterson, et al. (2001–). SciPy: Open source scientific tools for Python. http://www.scipy.org/.

Kolmogorov, A. (1933). Sulla determinazione empirica di una legge di distribuzione. *Inst. Ital. Attuari, Giorn. 4*, 83–91.

Laplace, P. S. and A. Dale (2012). *Pierre-Simon Laplace Philosophical Essay on Probabilities: Translated from the Fifth French Edition of 1825 with Notes by the Translator*. Sources in the History of Mathematics and Physical Sciences. Springer New York.

Lichtheim, M. (2019). *Ancient Egyptian Literature*. University of California Press.

Loupart, F. (2017). Data is giving rise to a new economy. *The Economist* - www.economist.com/briefing/2017/05/06/data-is-giving-rise-to-a-new-economy. Accessed: 2021-01-02.

Mackinlay, J. (1986, Apr). Automating the Design of Graphical Presentations of Relational Information. *ACM Trans. Graph.* 5(2), 110–141.

Mann, H. B. and D. R. Whitney (1947, Mar). On a test of whether one of two random variables is stochastically larger than the other. *Ann. Math. Statist.* 18(1), 50–60.

McCann, L. I. (2015). Introducing students to single photon detection with a reverse-biased LED in avalanche mode. In E. B. M. Eblen-Zayas and J. Kozminski (Eds.), *BFY Proceedings*. American Association of Physics Teachers.

McKinney, W. (2012). *Python for Data Analysis: Data Wrangling with Pandas, NumPy, and IPython*. O'Reilly Media.

McKinsey & Co. (2014). Using customer analytics to boost corporate performance.

Melissinos, A. C. and J. Napolitano (2003). *Experiments in Modern Physics*. Gulf Professional Publishing.

P. Hlobil (2021). Pandas Bokeh. https://github.com/PatrikHlobil/Pandas-Bokeh.

PA Media (2020). UCL renames three facilities that honoured prominent eugenicists. www.theguardian.com/education/

2020/jun/19/ucl-renames-three-facilities -that-honoured-prominent-eugenicists. Accessed: 2021-02-14.

Pearson, E. S. (1931, 05). I. Note on tests for normality. *Biometrika* 22(3-4), 423–424.

Pearson, K. (1920). Notes on the history of correlation. *Biometrika* 13(1), 25–45.

Pearson, K. (1968). *Tables of the Incomplete Beta-Function: With a New Introduction*. Cambridge University Press.

Pletser, V. (2012). Does the Ishango Bone Indicate Knowledge of the Base 12? An Interpretation of a Prehistoric Discovery, the First Mathematical Tool of Humankind. *arXiv math.HO 1204.1019*.

Plotly Technologies Inc (2015). Collaborative data science. https://plot.ly.

R. A. Fisher (1918). The correlation between relatives on the supposition of mendelian inheritance. *Philos. Trans. R. Soc. Edinb. 52*, 399–433.

Richterich, A. (2018). *The Big Data Agenda: Data Ethics and Critical Data Studies*. Critical, Digital and Social Media Studies. University of Westminster Press.

Rogel-Salazar, J. (2014). *Essential MATLAB and Octave*. CRC Press.

Rogel-Salazar, J. (2016, Mar). Motor Trend Car Road Tests. https://doi.org/ 10.6084/m9.figshare.3122005.v1.

Rogel-Salazar, J. (2020). *Advanced Data Science and Analytics with Python*. Chapman & Hall/CRC Data Mining and Knowledge Discovery Series. CRC Press.

Rogel-Salazar, J. (2021a, May). GLA World Cities 2016. https://doi.org/ 10.6084/m9.figshare.14657391.v1.

Rogel-Salazar, J. (2021b, Dec). Normal and Skewed Example Data. https://doi.org/ 10.6084/m9.figshare.17306285.v1.

Rogel-Salazar, J. (2022a, Feb). Anscombe's Quartet. https://doi.org/ 10.6084/m9.figshare.19221720.v3.

Rogel-Salazar, J. (2022b, Feb). Jackalope Dataset. https://doi.org/ 10.6084/m9.figshare.19221666.v3.

Rogel-Salazar, J. (2022c, Feb). Python Study Scores. https://doi.org/ 10.6084/m9.figshare.19208676.v1.

Rogel-Salazar, J. (2022d, Jan). Starfleet Headache Treatment - Example Data for Repeated ANOVA. https://doi.org/ 10.6084/m9.figshare.19089896.v1.

Rogel-Salazar, J. (2017). *Data Science and Analytics with Python*. Chapman & Hall/CRC Data Mining and Knowledge Discovery Series. CRC Press.

Rothamsted Research (2020). Statement on R. A. Fisher. www.rothamsted.ac.uk/news/statement-r-fisher. Accessed: 2021-02-14.

Samueli, J.-J. (2010). Legendre et la méthode des moindres carrés. Bibnum journals.openedition.org/bibnum/580. Accessed: 2021-02-14.

Satterthwaite, F. E. (1946). An approximate distribution of
  estimates of variance components. *Biometrics Bulletin* 2(6),
  110–114.

Scheinerman, E. A. (2012). *Mathematics: A Discrete
  Introduction.* Cengage Learning.

Scientific Computing Tools for Python (2013). NumPy.
  `http://www.numpy.org`.

Seaborn, J. B. (2013). *Hypergeometric Functions and Their
  Applications.* Texts in Applied Mathematics. Springer New
  York.

Shapiro, S. S. and Wilk, M. B. (1965, 12). An analysis
  of variance test for normality (complete samples)†.
  Biometrika 52(3-4), 591–611.

Short, J. E. and S. Todd (2017).   What's your
  data worth?   MIT Sloan Management Review,
  sloanreview.mit.edu/article/whats-your-data-worth/.
  Accessed: 2021-01-08.

SINTEF (2013).   Big Data, for better or worse:
  90% of world's data generated over last two
  years.   www.sciencedaily.com/releases/2013/
  05/130522085217.htm. Accessed: 2021-01-01.

Smirnov, N. V. (1939). Estimate of deviation between
  empirical distribution functions in two independent
  samples. *Bulletin Moscow University* 2(2), 3–16.

Stahl, S. (2006). The evolution of the normal distribution.
  Mathematics Magazine 79(2), 96.

Statista (2020).   The 100 largest companies in the world by market capitalization in 2020. www.statista.com/statistics/263264/top-companies-in-the-world-by-market-capitalization. Accessed: 2021-01-03.

Strang, G. (2006). *Linear Algebra and Its Applications*. Thomson, Brooks/Cole.

Student (1908). The probable error of a mean. *Biometrika 6*(1), 1–25.

The Event Horizon Telescope Collaboration (2019). First M87 Event Horizon Telescope Results. I. The Shadow of the Supermassive Black Hole. *ApJL 875*(L1), 1–17.

Three Dragons, David Lock Associates, Traderisks, Opinion Research Services, and J. Coles (2016). Lessons from Higher Density Development. Report to the GLA.

Tufte, E. (2022). The Work of Edward Tufte and Graphics Press. https://www.edwardtufte.com/tufte/. Accessed: 2022-23-02.

Tukey, J. W. (1977). *Exploratory Data Analysis*. Number v. 2 in Addison-Wesley Series in Behavioral Science. Addison-Wesley Publishing Company.

van der Zande, J. (2010). Statistik and history in the German enlightenment. *Journal of the History of Ideas 71*(3), 411–432.

Vinten-Johansen, P., H. Brody, N. Paneth, S. Rachman, M. Rip, and D. Zuck (2003). *Cholera, Chloroform, and the Science of Medicine: A Life of John Snow*. Oxford University Press.

Waskom, M. L. (2021). Seaborn: Statistical data visualization. *Journal of Open Source Software 6*(60), 3021.

Wasserstein, R. L. and N. A. Lazar (2016). The ASA statement on p-values: Context, process, and purpose. *The American Statistician 70*(2), 129–133.

Welch, B. L. (1947, 01). The generalization of 'Student's' problem when several different population variances are involved. *Biometrika 34*(1-2), 28–35.

Wilcoxon, F. (1945). Individual comparisons by ranking methods. *Biometrics Bulletin 1*(6), 80–83.

William H. Kruskal and W. Allen Wallis (1952). Use of ranks in one-criterion variance analysis. *Journal of the American Statistical Association 47*(260), 583–621.

Index

For Product Safety Concerns and Information please contact our
EU representative GPSR@taylorandfrancis.com Taylor & Francis
Verlag GmbH, Kaufingerstraße 24, 80331 München, Germany